W9-CZZ-288

3 0301 00026362 0

From

The Follett Book Company

1929.

AN OUTLINE OF THE
HISTORY OF CHRISTIAN LITERATURE

THE MACMILLAN COMPANY
NEW YORK · BOSTON · CHICAGO · DALLAS
ATLANTA · SAN FRANCISCO

MACMILLAN & CO., LIMITED
LONDON · BOMBAY · CALCUTTA
MELBOURNE

THE MACMILLAN CO. OF CANADA, LTD.
TORONTO

AN OUTLINE OF THE

History of
Christian Literature

BY

GEORGE LEOPOLD HURST, B.D.

New York
THE MACMILLAN COMPANY
1926

All Rights Reserved

LIBRARY
College of St. Francis
JOLIET, ILL.

Copyright, 1926,
By THE MACMILLAN COMPANY.

Set up and electrotyped.
Published March, 1926.

Printed in the United States of America by
THE FERRIS PRINTING COMPANY, NEW YORK.

809
H 958

PREFACE

This Outline has been prepared to meet the need of English speaking Protestants who seek guidance along an hitherto untrodden path.

The educated reader who is interested in literature and its history has at present no easily accessible work that tells the story of Christian literature, and a few laymen have at their command the material for tracing that story from the beginning. In this book I have tried to tell it for them in the simplest and most direct way.

In consequence of this popular purpose the references to authorities have been restricted to books that should be found in every well furnished Public Library, and all technical and critical discussions have been rigidly excluded.

Each part of the Outline might have been crowded with detail until every chapter became a book. The enumeration and adequate discussion of any one period of Christian literature would be the labour of a lifetime. But by the aid of this Introduction the non-theological reader will be able to gain a general view of the inexhaustible subject.

I hope that the young student of theology will also find the Outline useful. There are numberless histories of Christian dogma, theology, organisation, etc., but hitherto there has been no history of the Church's literature. The student is obliged to seek through many disjointed references that which he may wish to consider as a whole.

v

67011

PREFACE

A chair of Christian literature should be associated with every Divinity School in order that the future preachers and teachers of the Church might learn where to find the unfailing springs which have poured forth inspiration and instruction in every Christian age.

GEORGE L. HURST.

St. Andrew's Manse,
Buckingham,
Quebec.

CONTENTS

PART I

THE RECORDS OF THE FAITH

PART II

THE DEFENCE OF THE FAITH

PART III

THE SCHOOLS OF THE FAITH
(A. D. 150-300)

CONTENTS

PART IV

THE DEFINITION OF THE FAITH
(A. D. 300-800)

PART V

THE MEDIÆVAL AGE
(A. D. 800-1300)

PART VI

THE REFORMATION PERIOD
(A. D. 1300-1600)

CONTENTS

PART VII
THE MODERN PERIOD
(A. D. 1600-1800)

PART I
THE RECORDS OF THE FAITH

An Outline of the History of Christian Literature

CHAPTER I

THE ORIGINS

Christianity is a literary religion. Before the first Christian century was half completed the followers of Jesus Christ had begun to write in the interests of their faith, and, from that time until the present, Christian literature has continued to grow. Today it is a literature as great and as rich as any, and is one of the most remarkable achievements of the Church. It has become naturalised in almost every Western nation, it has laid under tribute almost every European tongue, and many of its makers have been master-craftsmen of the literary art.

This immense section of the world's literature is too large and too varied for adequate description in this book, which only tries to outline the subject and to give a truthful impression of its growth and character.

The study of Christian literature must begin with the *New Testament*, a collection of writings set apart by common consent as the primary Christian classics. This collection contains many of the forms in which the literary spirit of the Faith has clothed its messages. Here are gracious legends, authentic history, brief memorabilia, carefully arranged biographies, romances of devout speculation, hymns, meditations, prophecies, letters of sorts, and massive treatises on theology and on practical religion.

1

The twenty-seven books of the canonical *New Testament* comprise four biographies of Jesus, a book of Church history, twenty-one letters, and an apocalypse. Their order is logical rather than chronological, for some of the letters were in circulation years before the biographies attained their present forms.

The New Testament is the product of development; its first five books are composite works which retain many traces of the earlier writings that underlie them. Among the most important of these primitive sources was a *Collection of the Sayings of Jesus*. Fragments of this document are scattered in groups of Sayings over the first three Gospels, in which the same utterances are found in different forms, or in different sequences (cp. Matt. v.1-12 with Luke vi.20-26; and Matt. vi.21 with Luke xii.34). Such variants are common; they show that the present groups of Sayings are not first hand reports of continuous discourses, but are the accumulated spoil of many addresses, and were arranged by other hands before the Synoptic writers used them.

Many of the Sayings are perfect specimens of literary grace. Some have the picturesque character of parables; others are sermonic; others again are cast in the poetic forms of the "Wisdom" literature of the Old Testament. There is much variety and beauty in these "Wisdom" forms, which range from the simple three-lined strophe to the elaborate strophe of twelve lines.

Matt. vii.7 is an excellent illustration of the former:

> Ask, and it shall be given you;
> Seek, and ye shall find;
> Knock, and it shall be opened unto you.

Matt. vi.19-21 is a fine specimen of the longer forms:

> Lay not up for yourselves treasures upon the earth,
> Where moth and rust doth consume,
> And where thieves break through and steal:
> But lay up for yourselves treasures in heaven,

> Where neither moth nor rust doth consume,
> And where thieves do not break through nor steal:
> For where thy treasure is, there will thy heart be also.

These Sayings, now scattered over the Synoptic narratives, originally formed the contents of a carefully arranged book, which was in circulation before the year 50; its use by the Evangelists partly explains why the *First* and *Third Gospels* have so much material in common.

Another of the now lost documents that preceded the present New Testament, was a *Book of Testimonies*,[1] containing passages collected from the Old Testament to prove that Jesus was the Christ. Like the *Book of Sayings*, this *Book of Testimonies* took shape during a series of years. It was enlarged, arranged, and adjusted to the needs of the times, until its contents assumed a definite literary character. It was "classified into sections with titles, brief explanations, and frequent insertions of questions and comments" by its editors. When its original purpose of convincing the Jews had been served, it became a handbook of Christian doctrine, and as such it can be traced for several centuries.

Evidences of its use by the writers of the New Testament appear in the composite character of many Old Testament quotations; in the ascription of quotations to the wrong authors; and in the forced interpretations given to some passages (cf. Mark i.2, 3; Matt. xxvii.9; Matt. ii.15, 23).

All the indications point to MATTHEW the publican as the original compiler of the Testimonies, and the generous use made of the document by the author of the *First Gospel*, gave "his work the right to be called the *Gospel according to Matthew.*"[2]

These two primitive books were soon followed by connected descriptions of the Master's career. Many such memoirs were written (cp. Luke i.1, 2), but all are lost, save one written by JOHN MARK under the direction of

---

[1] Rendel Harris, *Testimonies* (1916) Part I.
[2] F. C. Burkitt, *The Gospel History and its Transmission*, p. 126.

Peter. This became the nucleus of the *Second Gospel*, and also the foundation of the other two Synoptic biographies of Jesus.

JOHN MARK also wrote the story of the Jerusalem Church, which now underlies the first twelve chapters of the *Book of the Acts*. He is sometimes credited with the authorship of certain Acts of Peter, of Stephen, and of Philip. He seems to have been one of the most active of the early Christian writers.

Among this "epi-Christian literature,"—to use DeQuincey's phrase—were the *Acts of John the Baptist*, by some of his disciples, in which the Synoptic evangelists found useful material (Mark i.2-8; Matt. iii.1-17; Luke i.5-25) and which, later on, moved the author of the Fourth Gospel to insist upon the inferiority of the great forerunner's work (John i.6-8, 13-27, etc).

All these primitive writings were in the vernacular. Jesus had used the Aramaic dialect of the common people and had sternly rebuked those who, by adhering to the Scriptural Hebrew, took away 'the key of knowledge' from the multitude (Luke xi.52). Traces of Aramaic exist in the frequent use of the words "immediately" and "straightway" (Mark i.10, 12, 18, 20, 21, 28, etc.) and in the needless use of the word "began" (Mark v.17-20, etc.). Both the *Book of the Sayings of the Lord*, and the *Book of Testimonies*, were probably in Aramaic, but the Gospels were written in the ordinary Greek of the wider world into which Christianity quickly made its way.

Thus far priceless material had been gathered. The literary impulse was not long delayed. The spirit of poetry touched the Christian faith, and the Church became "a nest of singing birds." PAUL found a baptismal hymn ready to his hand:

> Awake, thou that sleepest,
> And arise from the dead,
> And Christ shall shine upon thee. (Eph. v.14.)

He could also use a funeral hymn:

> It is sown in corruption;
> It is raised in incorruption:
> It is sown in dishonour;
> It is raised in glory:
> It is sown in weakness;
> It is raised in power:
> It is sown a natural body;
> It is raised a spiritual body.   (1 Cor. xv.42-44.)

Even the Creed could be sung:

> He who was manifested in the flesh,
> Justified in the spirit,
> Seen of angels,
>
> Preached among the nations,
> Believed on in the world,
> Received up into glory.   (1 Timothy iii.16.)

The conversion of SAUL of Tarsus added to the makers of Christian literature a writer whose fresh and forceful genius produced some of the most valuable and honoured books in the Canon. Although his letters follow the customary type by beginning with a formal salutation and ending with a gracious benediction, they are marvellously varied in style, in contents and in character. His intense feeling controlled by his immediate purpose gave each letter an individual quality and colour.

The *Epistle to Philemon* is a personal letter to an old friend. Romans xvi.1-20, is a note of introduction carried by the deaconess Phoebe to the Church at Ephesus. *Galatians* attempted to save the Churches of Antioch, Iconium, Lystra and Derbe, from surrendering their spiritual liberty; it bears obvious marks of the apostle's anger and anxiety. *Romans* is a most masterly piece of theological argument addressed to a Church that the writer had neither founded nor visited. *Ephesians* and *Colossians* are encyclicals. The *Epistles to the Corinthians* are luminous moral treatises, of which the present form is the result of compressing into two, the four original letters written by PAUL to his converts in Corinth.

These four letters (2 Cor. vi.14, vii.1; 1 Cor.; 2 Cor. x.1-xiii.10; 2 Cor. i.1-vi.1-13; with vii.2-ix.) belong to one of the most critical periods of the apostle's career; they vividly reflect the problems as well as the passions that agitated the Church, and are invaluable records of the writer's moral and literary temper. Among other points of literary interest they contain examples of his practice of quoting from the letters to which his own were replies, *e.g.*:

Now '*concerning things sacrificed to idols: We know that we all have knowledge.*' Knowledge puffeth up but love buildeth up. If any man thinketh that he knoweth anything, he knoweth not yet as he ought to know; but if any man loveth God, the same is known of Him. Concerning therefore '*the eating of things sacrificed to idols, we know that no idol is anything in the world, and that there is no God but one.*' For though there be that are called gods, whether in heaven or on earth; as there are gods many, and lords many; yet '*to us*

There is one God, the Father,
Of Whom are all things,
And we unto Him;
And one Lord, Jesus Christ,
Through whom are all things,
And we through him.

Howbeit in all men there is not that knowledge:' (1 Cor. viii.1-7.) [3]

These *Epistles to Corinth* also contain some of the finest and most familiar literary passages in the writings of the Apostle, such as "The Eulogy of Charity" (1 Cor. xiii), and

---

[3] The extracts from the letter sent to Paul by the Corinthians are here put in italics.

"The Assurance of Immortality" (1 Cor. xv. 50-58).
Others of his Letters, like those *To the Thessalonians* and
that *To the Church at Philippi*, are rich in revelations of a
great personality, strong, gentle, affectionate, masterful,
magnetic, always under the constraint of a majestic faith.

CHAPTER II

HEBREW CHRISTIANITY

The burning of Rome in 64 led the Imperial authorities to make a ferocious attack upon the Church in the metropolis, an attack that prompted PETER to write an Epistle, *1 Peter*, to warn and prepare the Hebrew-Christians of the Provinces. This is a beautiful and gracious letter, full of practical counsel, marked by an early and simple theology, and is a real treasure house of moral and spiritual teaching.

But something even more terrible than persecution drew near. In 66 the signs of the times pointed to the overthrow of Jerusalem, and under the shadow of this impending doom many were ready to welcome the literature of apocalypse, as a shaded lantern for travellers in peril.

A *Small Apocalypse*, Mark xiii.7-8, 18-20, 24-27, written by an unknown Jew, was used by the author of a little Christian broadsheet to add weight to his own warnings to the Church, Mark xiii.5 -6, 9-13, 21-23, 28-29. This *Small Apocalypse*, as enlarged by its Christian editor, should be compared with the so-called *Greater Interpolation* in the *Third Gospel*, Luke ix.51-xviii.1-14, where the prophecies of the rejection of Israel are represented as part of the ordinary teaching of Jesus.

During these anxious days, JOHN MARK gathered his various material together and wrote the *Second Gospel*, 68. The plan is quite simple; after a brief Introduction, i.1-13, there is a narrative of the work of Jesus in Galilee, i.14-ix.50, then follows a record of His ministry in Judea, x-xiii, and finally comes the tragic story of the Passion, Death, and Resurrection, xiv-xvi.1-8.

8

Some of the exhortations and visions subsequently gathered into *The Apocalypse* belong to this time. So also do the Hymns of rejoicing which grace the opening chapter of the *Third Gospel*. These Hymns reflect the emotions of the Christian refugees who fled to Pella from the horrors of the fall of Jerusalem in 70. Luke i.46-55, is a Hymn of four strophes framed on Old Testament models; there are some striking parallels to it in the *Psalms of Solomon*. Luke i.68-75, a Hymn in three strophes, reflects the rising hope of approaching relief.

The growing need for guidance in worship gave rise to other forms of literature, of which the earliest extant specimen is found chapters vii.-xv. of *The Teaching of the Apostles*, a work also known as *The Didache*. These chapters originally formed a separate book, entitled *The Teaching of the Lord by the Twelve Apostles to the Nations* which contained a compendium of Christian teaching as given to the Gentiles; it preserves "an idyllic picture of primitive guileless Christianity," the earliest existing non-canonical representation of the primitive Christian community. SYMEON of Jerusalem is credited with its authorship, about the year 65.

The free simplicity of the Church of that day appears in such passages as these:

> if thou art able to bear the whole yoke of the Lord, thou shalt be perfect; but if thou art not able, what thou art able, that do (Chap. vi.).
> baptise into the name of the Father, and of the Son. and of the Holy Spirit, in running water. But if thou hast not running water; baptise in other water, and if thou canst not in cold, then in warm. But if thou hast neither, pour water upon the head thrice, into the name of the Father and Son and Holy Spirit (Chap. vii.).

The latest Hebrew-Christian writing in the New Testament is the *Epistle of James,* a homily written in fluent Greek at the beginning of the second century, 100-120. The fact that Jesus and His work receive the barest notice suggests that the address was prepared for Jewish readers to whom definite Christian doctrine would have been distasteful.

The Epistle contains a variety of practical observations and moral exhortations, many of which are written in the style of the "Wisdom" literature.

> Let the brother of low degree glory in his high estate:
> And the rich, in that he is made low:
> Because as the flower of the grass he shall pass away.
> For the sun ariseth with the scorching wind, and withereth the
> the grass;
> And the flower thereof falleth, and the grace of the fashion of it
> perisheth:
> So also shall the rich man fade away in his goings.
> (Chap. i.9-11.)

The third chapter has been extracted from the work of some Alexandrian writer, as the three disjointed passages, iv.11-12; iv.13-17; v.1-6, have been borrowed from a Jewish Apocalypse. A "considerable number of otherwise unrecorded sayings of Jesus" add much to the interest and value of this late non-apostolic work.

CHAPTER III

GENTILE CHRISTIANITY

Hebrew Christianity was ruined when Jerusalem was overthrown in 70 by the armies of the Roman general Titus; but the Hebraic spirit was not killed, it needed reinterpretation and fresh expression. Both came from PHILO, B.C. 20-A.D. 50, the illustrious Jew of Alexandria, who revived the glory of the first school of his city, not however as a poet, like Apollonius Rhodius or Theocritus, but as the defender of the Old Testament against the inroads of Hellenism. His writings exercised a strong and lasting influence on Christian literature; the *Epistle of Barnabas*, the *Epistle to the Hebrews*, and the *Fourth Gospel*, bear traces of it.

The *Epistle of Barnabas*, written between 70 and 79, is not the work of the comrade of PAUL, but of a strongly anti-Judaistic writer of Alexandria, whose object was to show that Christianity displaces Judaism. In his opinion, ceremonial Judaism was of semi-heathen origin; but the inward, spiritual Judaism which was perfected or superseded by Christianity was inspired of God.

This writer often makes foolish and trifling use of allegories (chapters 6-11), but he has command of eloquent imagery and lofty idealism to emphasise the message of his letter—"Let us become spiritual, a perfect temple unto God."

The anonymous *Epistle to the Hebrews* elaborates the theme of Barnabas in almost classical language, and with a grace of style that makes it "the first piece of Christian literature in the technical sense of the word." With great skill

11

it maintains the argument that Christianity supersedes Judaism, supplanting its sacrifices, its priesthood, and its covenant (x.1-10). Many passages of this Epistle take rank with the finest specimens of religious eloquence; *e.g.* the "Eulogium of the Hebrew Martyrs" (xi.32-40), and the "Vision of the Race of Life" (xii.1-2).

Philo's influence on Christian writing is seen at its best in this Epistle which was most probably written for the benefit of the Alexandrian Church, 80-90.

The plea put forward by these works, viz., that Christianity was altogether emancipated from the Law, was not accepted without challenge. Judaic traditions were strong in many sections of the Church, and were bound to find utterance. One of the earliest of the books written to maintain those traditions was *The Teaching of the Apostles,* often called the *Didache,* a composite work that reached its present form by a process of addition. The first six chapters consist of a Jewish tract entitled *The Two Ways,* written about 50, to contrast the way of light and the way of darkness. This tract was used by a Christian writer as an introduction to his own work *The Teaching of the Lord by the Twelve Apostles to the Nations,* written about 65. Finally a third writer, 72-80, completed the work in its present form, by adding chapter sixteen.

The Genealogies of the First and Third Gospels belong to the same school. *The Genealogy* in Matthew i.1-17 and the Birth Stories in Matthew i.18-21; ii.1-18, 19-23, were probably once part of a Hebrew-Christian document. The Genealogy given in Luke iii.23-38, was, on the other hand, part of an Aramaic or of a Palestinian-Greek document.

The *First Gospel* as a completed whole is an invaluable document of the renaissance of the Hebrew Christianity of this period. It is free from the crudities of the now lost *Gospel according to the Hebrews,* but preserves a deep reverence for the Old Testament, although it insists upon the distinctive character of Christianity, and its need for a separately organised Church. In fact it is in this Gospel that the Church speaks for the first time in Christian literature with confidence and power (xviii.15-18).

Originally intended to be a manual of the Faith for the use of teachers, this Gospel makes generous quotations from the *Book of Testimonies*, gives copious passages from the Sayings and offers various devices to assist memory, perhaps in imitation of the famous Rabbi Akiba ben Joseph, 50-135.

The *Apocalypse* or *Book of the Revelation*, 95-106, although a product of the school of Asia Minor, also reflects the spirit of Hebrew Christianity especially in its desire for Divine vengeance. Some of the material in it was taken from Jewish sources (*e.g.* vii.1-8; xi.1-13; xii.) and some was borrowed from earlier apocalyptic writings (*e.g.* vii.9-17; xiv.6-12; xviii.; xx.).

Apocalyptic literature is the "literature of picture and symbol whose use and value lie wholly in their vivid presentation . . . . of that which no picture or symbol can adequately represent." The New Testament *Apocalypse* is the greatest of all the Christian apocalypses, and it is also one of the most vexing problems of the early literature of the Faith. The range of vision, the magnificent imagery, the depth of feeling and splendour of assurance that characterise it make it supreme in its class. Some of the finest examples of Christian writing are found in this work of unknown authorship (cf. vii.13-17; xviii.2-19; xix.11-16; xxi.1-4).

The troubled stream of Hebrew Christianity runs to earth after this, leaving only a few signs of its existence in out-of-the-way places.

An otherwise unknown ARISTO of Pella left a now lost *Dialogue* between a Hebrew Christian, Jason, and an Alexandrian Jew, Papiscus, c. 130-170. This Dialogue condemned the tendency to make the Faith increasingly Hellenistic; and, as Origen says, showed that the prophecies concerning the Christ are applicable to Jesus.

An *Apocalypse of Peter* shared for a time a popularity equal to that enjoyed by the canonical Apocalypse and kept its place in the popular mind until the vaster vision of DANTE displaced it. It contained a prophecy given by Jesus to His disciples concerning the coming of false prophets; a vision of Paradise seen by Peter; and an account of the Inferno, in which the lost souls were tormented by punishments suggested by their sins. It can scarcely be later than 150, and may be even earlier.

CHAPTER IV

THE NEW UNIVERSALISM

The Hebrew renaissance, inspired by PHILO, met with strong and ultimately successful opposition from the frankly Hellenistic spirit which sympathised with Western culture and welcomed the best influences of Orientalism. This new universalism is first represented in Christian literature by the quite simply Hellenic *Epistle of* Clement of Rome, fl. 75-96, sent to the Church of Corinth.

The writer desired to restore harmony to the divided Church. His letter is therefore, in the main, an appeal for submission to authority in the spirit of meekness. It is now a most valuable picture of Church conditions at the end of the first century.

Two noble treatises by LUKE, the beloved physician, belong to this time, and breathe the same spirit of freedom from Jewish traditions. Both the *Third Gospel* and the *Acts of the Apostles* were written for one Theophilus of whom nothing is known.

The Gospel, 80-90, is historical in method but religious in purpose; the carefully collected and arranged material is consistently interpreted in the interests of universalism.

LUKE is the historical Evangelist; his purpose is to write the Life of Jesus, not merely to give an account of His public ministry, and he seeks to give a more comprehensive, more complete, and more strictly chronological story than either *Mark* or *Matthew* had done. He is deeply indebted to the Book of Sayings and to the Gospel of Mark; more than three-fourths of his work is derived from them. But he uses other sources, which neither of these possessed (*e.g.* v. 1-

15

11; vii.11-17, 36-50; viii.1-4; most of the Greater interpolation (ix. 51-xviii. 1-14), xxiii. 39-43; xxiv. 13-35.
His universalism appears in many passages (*e.g.* iv.25-27;
vi.24-26; vii.4-5; xix.1-9) and in such incomparable parables as those of the "Two Debtors," the "Good Samaritan," the "Lost Piece of Silver," the "Lost Sheep," the
"Prodigal Son," "Dives and Lazarus," the "Phrarisee and
the Publican," etc.

Many of the characteristic notes of the *Third Gospel* reappear in the book of the *Acts of the Apostles,* a remarkable
record of the growth of Christianity from Jerusalem,
through Syria, Cilicia, Asia Minor, Macedonia, and Greece,
to Rome. This history is made up from hearsay traditions,
from earlier Acts written by JOHN MARK, from LUKE'S own
Journal (cf. xvi. 10-17; xx.5-15; xxi.1-18; xxvii.1;
xxviii.1-6) and from information supplied by persons and
churches concerned.

LUKE was a gifted historian whose work is a "well-
ordered and artistically arranged composition," which falls
into four nearly equal parts (i-vii; viii-xiv; xv-xxi.26; xxi.
27-xxviii.). He probably wrote to prove the innocent
character of Christianity and thus save the faithful from
persecution during the dark years of the reign of Domitian,
81-96.

These first literary ventures of the new universalism were
soon surpassed by the writings of a Christian group in Asia
Minor. The seven Churches, to which a quasi-Hebraic
idealist addressed the Letters that now form a secondary Introduction to the *Apocalypse* (ii. 1-iii. 21), were for a time
the intellectual headquarters of Christendom. A brilliant
company gathered there. Among others were JOHN THE SON
OF ZEBEDEE, ANDREW and PHILIP of the apostolic college,
ARISTION, JOHN THE ELDER, POLYCARP, PAPIAS of Hierapolis, and MELITO of Sardis. Several members of the
group were accomplished literary men, and never perhaps

has Christianity been more prolific of literature than during the second century, in Asia.

The *Fourth Gospel,* the work of an unknown author or authors, was the supreme achievement of this school. It is the result of a definite attempt to reconcile Christian belief with the current culture of Asia Minor, during the lifetime of the third generation of believers. At the moment of its composition it was the most philosophic interpretation of the person and ministry of Jesus hitherto attempted. It presupposes the writings of PAUL; it carries PAUL'S teaching to its logical conclusions. It is the Gospel of the Incarnation.

There are many differences between the *Fourth Gospel* and the *Synoptics;* differences of standpoint, of material and of the order of events; but the *Fourth Gospel* is unique in its use of great allegories of Christian experience (iii.1-13; iv.7-26; ix.1-34; xi.1-44) and in the speeches that it puts into the mouth of Jesus (*e.g.* v.19-47; vi.32-57; viii.34-40; x.1-18; xiv.12-31; xv.1-27; xvi.1-16).

The *First Epistle of John,* a letter similar in style and spirit to the Gospel, unites a strong appeal for fellowship in the Church, with an equally strong denunciation of Docetism, the earliest known Christian heresy concerning which JEROME, in after years, said: "The blood of Christ was still fresh in Judaea when His body was said to be a phantom."

The defence of orthodoxy and the growth of ecclesiasticism go together, and in the Catholic or Pastoral Epistles there are valuable reflections of the ecclesiastical situation as it was at the beginning of the second century. Although these Letters contain passages from the hand of PAUL (cf. 2 Tim. i.15-18; iv.9-22; Titus i.1-6,10-13; ii-iii.7), they cannot be ascribed to him as a whole. They are the work of writers who used extracts from his writings in order to continue his service among the developing Western Churches.

The "faithful sayings" referred to in these Epistles, probably were parts of a creed which was used in the catechism.

The chronological order of the letters is *2 Timothy; Titus; 1 Timothy.*

All the writings of the New Testament were at first without any divisions of chapters, verses, or words. .The troubles arising from such a lack were probably less when books were few and precious than they would be now, when books are numberless, and readers are accustomed to indexes and concordances. But the need of making references led AMMONIUS of Alexandria, in the third century, to divide the Gospels into sections, "regulated by the substance of the narratives contained in them."

Then EUTHALIUS, fl. 450, also of Alexandria, devised a system of divisions for all the books of the New Testament, except the Apocalypse. He next led the Greek Church to adopt a uniform plan for the public Lessons. This did not include the Gospels or the Apocalypse; but it arranged fifty-seven Lessons from the other books, thus making special provision for Christmas, Epiphany, Good Friday and Easter. He also perfected the prevailing systems of dividing the text into lines or verses.

EUTHALIUS therefore deserves mention as one of the pioneers in that formal and scientific study of the New Testament, of which perhaps REV. CANON SIR J. C. HAWKINS is the best modern exponent.

CHAPTER V

DOMESTIC LITERATURE

Here it will be convenient and not seriously out of place to review other early Christian literature that was omitted from the "canon" of the New Testament. "The manifold variety of life and thought in early Christianity" are not fully realised if the books "which had their home in the unfamiliar and secluded places of its life" are neglected. "From the point of view of the historian of literature no line can be drawn between canonical and uncanonical books; all alike sprang from the Christian life of their age to serve the religious needs of the community, and it was only the call of a grave necessity in the Church's controversy with error that led to a distinct separation being made."[1]

This literature which concerned the domestic life of the Church may be divided into Romances; Homilies; Records; Letters.

i. ROMANCES.

The first, and in some respects the most important of the Romances, is *The Shepherd*, written by the pious but somewhat stupid prophet HERMAS, fl. 150, a brother of Pius, bishop of Rome.

HERMAS pictures himself as an elderly married man, with a termagant wife and some ill-brought up children. His book consists of Five Visions, Ten Similitudes, and Twelve Commandments. It is an allegory; the first of the type of which JOHN BUNYAN'S *Pilgrim's Progress* is the most popular representative. It was written to declare that the Church was corrupt and deeply marked by worldliness; that a time

[1] A. F. Findlay, *Byways in Early Christian Literature*, pp. 3-5.

of distress was coming when the evils would be purged away; that repentance was possible before that time began; and that HERMAS was the divinely ordained preacher of that repentance.

The Shepherd is an orthodox work which was sometimes quoted as 'Scripture' and sometimes publicly read in the churches. It has been called "a good but dull novel," but it is a veritable mine of information concerning the Church in Rome and the growing institutionalism of the Faith.

A more common type of romance is found in the *Prote-vangelium* (Earliest Gospel) *of James*. This is a composite product of ecclesiastical circles; some parts of it belong to the second century, but it did not attain its final form until the fifth century.

The stories of the *Protevangelium* deal with the birth of Mary, the mother of Jesus; the birth of Jesus and the accompanying wonders; the subsequent experiences of Joseph; the visit of the Magi, etc. These stories are told with much grace of language and imagery. The description of Anna's lament for her childlessness is very beautiful.

> Woe is me! what am I like?
>   I am not like the birds of heaven,
>   For even the birds of heaven are fruitful before Thee,
>   O Lord.
> Woe is me! what am I like?
>   I am not like the beasts of the earth,
>   For even the beasts of the earth are fruitful before Thee,
>   O Lord.
> Woe is me! what am I like?
>   I am not like this earth,
>   For even this earth bears its fruits in due season and
>   blesses Thee, O Lord.[2]

The book had an immense vogue, in some places it was more popular than the Gospels themselves.

Another reflection of the popular Christianity of the age is preserved in the *Acts of Peter, John, Andrew, Thomas,*

---

[2] *Ibid.*, p. 152.

and *Paul*, c. 150-160; the work of an Ephesian writer whom tradition calls LEUCIUS CHARINUS. These Acts preserve many precious legends of the apostles' last days, interspersed with doctrines that the Church strenuously denounced and resisted. Pope Leo I ordered that "they should be utterly swept away and burned" but they were too much to the popular liking to be destroyed and kept their hold upon many communities for centuries. The famous Quo Vadis legend derives from the *Acts of Peter* (chap. 35).

Perhaps the most popular of all such romances is the *Acts of Paul and Thecla*, 160-170, which still captures the reader's interest as adventure follows upon the heels of adventure while the maiden Thecla pursues the Apostle with fervent devotion until his martyrdom separates them for ever. This "highly romantic work of the imagination" is graced with many touches of real poetry; *e.g.* Thecla is "tied to the window like a spider" as she listens to Paul preaching outside; when she is waiting to be burned she looks for the Apostle "as a lamb in the wilderness looks for the shepherd."

This Romance was written to give the appearance of apostolic authority to the changes that were taking place in the teaching and the institutions of the Church. It harmonised with the popular religious taste and reflected the prevailing moral standards.

The early Christian Romances appear in full dress in the so-called *Clementines,* a collection of stories that describe the life of Clement of Rome as if he himself were their author. Many critical battles have been fought over these works which consist of three principal parts: i. The Homilies; ii. The Recognitions; iii. The Epitome. Other pieces, sometimes associated with these are an *Epistle to James;* the *Martyrdom of St. Clement;* the *Epistle of St. Peter to St. James of Jerusalem,* and the *Testimony.*

With the exception of the twenty Homilies and the Recognitions the work has little value. It may be regarded as a series of short novels written to ascribe the honour of ecclesiastical supremacy to James and Jerusalem. In some passages the arch-enemy Simon Magus serves as a thinly disguised representation of the apostle Paul, whose teaching, that Christians are free from the Jewish Law, is repeatedly opposed.

In their original form the *Clementine Romances* probably date from about 161, in their present form they belong to the period 200-220.

ii. HOMILIES.

It is an easy step from the Clementines to *The Preaching of Peter,* 100-125; an early rival of the canonical *Acts of the Apostles,* and by some critics regarded as the foundation of the Homilies.

The Homilies were written addresses, prepared to be read during the Church services; sometimes the author read his own work, as was the case with the so-called *Second Epistle of Clement.* This work is a sermon on Isaiah, chapter 54, prepared by an unknown preacher, either of Rome or of Corinth, 135-140.

It is a rare homiletical relic of the age; natural, simple, and appropriate in style; somewhat marred by repetition, but of admirable spirit. Its theme is the duty of a moral life in gratitude for the gift of salvation.

The wrongly titled *Second Epistle of Peter,* 140-160, takes its true place among the Homilies. It is the work of one under the influence of Alexandria who prepared it as a warning against false prophets and gnostic heretics.

iii. RECORDS.

A few fragmentary Records can be traced during these early days. Among these are some precious but tantalising relics of the writings of PAPIAS of Hierapolis, 65-155. As a "hearer of John and an associate of Polycarp," his testimony concerning the evangelic tradition is of the highest value. His chief work is a series of *Expositions of the Sayings of the Lord,* in five books. In the preface of this work he says:

> I shall not hesitate to set down for you along with my interpretations, by way of confirming their truth, all that I carefully learned from the elders and carefully remembered. For I did not take pleasure, as so many do, in those who talk a great deal, but in those who teach the truth; nor in those who relate alien commandments, but in those who record such as were given by the Lord to the Faith and are derived from the truth itself.[3]

These Sayings of the Lord which PAPIAS interpreted, were The Testimonies which entered so largely into the composition of the Gospels.

Other fragments of his writings relate that "Matthew composed the Sayings in Hebrew, and every one interpreted them as he could"; that "Mark having become the interpreter of Peter wrote accurately everything that he remembered of the things that were either said or done by Christ"; they also contain some extravagant apocryphal reports of the work and words of Jesus.

Among other Records are the important fragments of the *Gospel of Peter,* 110-130; an apocryphal work, of which an account of the Passion and Resurrection of Jesus alone remains. This account is much longer than the corresponding sections of the Gospels, and it differs from them in many details.

The fragments begin with the hand-washing of Pilate:

> But of the Jews none washed his hands, neither Herod nor any of His judges; and since they did not choose to wash them, Pilate rose up. And then Herod the king commandeth the Lord to be taken, saying

---

[3] Eusebius, *Ecclesiastical History,* III., 39.

unto them, 'Whatsoever things I command you to do to Him, do ye.'

The story of the Crucifixion contains interesting additions to the Gospel narratives. Thus after the words of the penitent thief, it adds:

> And they had indignation against him and commanded that his legs should not be broken, that he might die in torment.
>
> Now many went about with lamps, supposing that it was night. . . .And the Lord cried aloud, saying, My Power, Power, thou hast forsaken me. . . .

"The most striking characteristic of the fragment is found in the description of the resurrection. . . ."

> Now in the night in which the Lord's Day was dawning, while the soldiers were keeping guard, two by two in a watch, there was a great voice in heaven, and they saw the heavens opened and two men descending from thence with much light and drawing near to the tomb. And the stone which had been set at the door rolled away of itself and made way in part, and the tomb was opened and both young men entered. The soldiers, therefore, when they saw this, awakened the centurion and the elders. . . .again they see coming forth from the tomb three men, two of them supporting the other, and a cross following them . . . .And they heard a voice from the heavens saying, Hast Thou preached to them that sleep? and a response was heard from the cross, Yea.

As an illustration of the unsettled character of the Christian story, and of the demand for fresh restatements of the great events the *Gospel of Peter* is a valuable addition to the earlier records.

iv. LETTERS.

Letters form an important branch of this early literature. All the genuine writings of CLEMENT of Rome, IGNATIUS and POLYCARP are in the form of Letters, "modelled more or less after the pattern of the canonical Epistles. . . . . but called forth by pressing temporary needs. In no case is any literary motive prominent."

Much of the literature already noticed might be classified as Letters, although other titles are given to it; but the priceless writings of IGNATIUS of Antioch, c.70-125, who surnamed himself 'Theophorus'—'God-borne'—are Epistles pure and simple.

These Letters exist in two collections, in different languages, and with differences of contents which present to critical study one of the most difficult problems in early Christian history. Both the longer and the shorter versions contain seven Epistles; viz., to the Ephesians; to the Magnesians; to the Trallians; to the Romans; to the Philadelphians; to the Smyrnaeans; and to Polycarp.

They are truly heroic declarations of the glory of martyrdom, and are full of zeal for the power of the episcopate, as well as of hatred of heresy and schism.

I do indeed desire to suffer, but I know not if I be worthy to do so.

I hope as a prisoner in Christ Jesus to salute you, if indeed it be the will of God that I be thought worthy of attaining unto the end.

Suffer me to become food for the wild beasts, through whose instrumentality it will be granted me to attain to God. I am the wheat of God, and let me be ground by the teeth of the wild beasts, that I may be found the pure bread of Christ.

we should look upon the bishop even as we would upon the Lord Himself.

LIBRARY
College of St. Francis
JOLIET, ILL.

67011

I exhort you to study to do all things with a divine
harmony, while your bishop presides in the place of
God. . . . be ye united with your bishop, and those that
preside over you, as a type and evidence of your immortality.

without the bishop ye should do nothing.

Stop your ears . . . . when any one speaks to you
at variance with Jesus Christ . . . .

if any one preach the Jewish law unto you, listen
not to him.

The earnest evangelical passion of IGNATIUS floods the
whole series of these letters; approval and exhortation are
prevailing notes in this martyr's exultant fervour.

POLYCARP of Smyrna, 70-155, the recipient of one of
the Ignatian Epistles, is the author of an *Epistle to the
Philippians,* 112, which lacks the fire and spiritual passion
of his friend's work, but which is a useful aid to the study
of the second century Church. POLYCARP is a notable figure
in the literary history of Christianity; he was a disciple of
JOHN the apostle and numbered among his pupils IRENAEUS,
and MELITO of Sardis.

The "inspired industry" of DIONYSIUS of Corinth, fl.
170, produced some pastoral Letters which acquired so much
authority that even heretics circulated modified versions of
them.   Only a few fragments of these Pastorals remain.
The relic of the *Letter to the Roman Church* contains the
earliest testimony that Peter like Paul, suffered martyrdom
in Italy, and at the same time.

PART II
THE DEFENCE OF THE FAITH

CHAPTER VI

THE APOLOGIES

The Faith, having gained prominence and power by the help of its early literature, was obliged to take up the attitude of self defence against various opponents.

Judaism was the first antagonist; Hebrew Christianity was an enemy almost as bitter as Judaism proper; the popular pagan religion waged ceaseless warfare against the new teaching; and the civil power, with all the forces at its command, offered a long and relentless opposition.

Christian literature was therefore turned into a weapon of defence. During the second century the work of writing Apologies or Defences absorbed the attention of Christian men of letters, who gave their best gifts to the task. "All Christian literature is in a sense an Apologia;" but these early Apologists wrote special treatises to deny the slanders and to disarm the hatred which provoked the unjust persecution of a religion that was blameless, peaceable and loyal to the State.

The Apologies are valuable aids to an understanding of the "objections urged against Christianity by contemporaries." As specimens of Christian literature, they serve to reveal the mind of the Church in the second century, and to show the range of learning over which that mind was accustomed to move.

Many of the Apologists were deeply in debt to Athens for their culture; they were philosophers of the Faith, and with them the language of Christianity becomes literary, if not classical.

The earliest of the Apologies was the work of QUAD-
RATUS, whom tradition describes as bishop of Athens in
126, and as "famous for his prophetic gifts." He submitted
An Address on behalf of the Christians, to the Emperor
Hadrian on the occasion of a royal visit to Athens in 125
or 126.

All but a few fragments are lost; but from the remaining
relics it appears that the Address laid stress upon the public
character of the work of Christ, and also claimed that some
whom Christ had healed, "have lived to our own times."

A Letter to Diognetus, written by one who veiled his
identity under the *nom-de-plume* of "a disciple," is "the
most striking Christian pamphlet of early times." The
original Letter consisted of the present chapters 1-10; the
chapters 11-12 were added later, perhaps by PANTAENUS of
Alexandria. The date of the work is about 150.

This is a philosopher's Apology; exquisitely graceful and
concisely arranged, and "conveys the impression of high literary power." It answers three questions, viz., On what
God do Christians rely and how do they worship Him?
What is the "charity" which they have one for another?
What is this new race or profession that has invaded society?

The substance of the answers to these questions appears
in the following passage:

> In one word, Christians are to the world what the
> soul is to the body. The soul is dispersed through all
> the limbs of the body: so the Christians are dispersed
> through all the cities of the world. The soul dwells
> within the body, yet is not part thereof: so the Chris-
> tians dwell in the world, and yet they are no part of
> it. . . . The flesh hates the soul and makes war upon
> it, though the soul injures it not, but only hinders it
> from indulging its lusts: so the world hates the Chris-

tians, though they injure it not, but only set themselves against its pleasures. The soul loves the flesh that hates it: so do Christians love those that hate them. . . . God has assigned them a certain place, to fill, and it is not lawful for them to refuse to fill it.

The "disciple" who wrote to Diognetus has been identified by some critics with ARISTIDES, who wrote an effective Apology in his own name, and presented it either to the Emperor Hadrian or, according to the Syriac version, to Antoninus Pius. The original has perished, but three versions of it remain; the Armenian, the Syriac, and the Greek.

Among the adventures of this Apology was the remarkable use made of it in an old romance, *The History of Barlaam and Joasaph* (or *Josaphat*) where it appears as "a defence of Christianity delivered by Barlaam before the Indian ruler Abenner and his son Joasaph."[1]

"The language and thought of the writer are simple and straight-forward; in fact he is more of a child than a philosopher, ... but this simplicity of treatment, so far from being a weakness, often adds greatly to the natural impressiveness of the subject, and gives the work a place by the side of the best Christian writings of his age."[2]

An *Address to the Greeks,* by the 'Assyrian' TATIAN, 110-172, was only one of the infinite number of works ascribed to him by JEROME. It is written with an indifference to style which was part of TATIAN'S protest against the Greeks. Yet he had literary gifts; he could command a noble rhetoric; he had the gift of appeal; he could draw word-portraits with rare skill, like that of the actor:

I have often seen a man . . . . giving himself excessive airs of daintiness and indulging in all sorts of

---

[1] For the romance cf. F. Max Muller, *Chips from a German Workshop,* new ed. (1895), Vol. IV., pp. 444-457.

[2] Rendel Harris, *Cambridge Texts and Studies* (1891), I., 1.

effeminacy; sometimes darting his eyes about; sometimes throwing his hands hither and thither, and rav-
ing with his face smeared with mud; . . . . a solitary
accuser of all the gods, an epitome of superstition, a
vituperator of heroic deeds, an actor of murders, a
chronicler of adultery, a store house of madness, ...
and yet such a man is praised by all (Chap. xxii.).

The Address consists of a preface and two main divisions.
The first division gives a sketch of the Christian teaching;
the second division proves that Christianity is older than the
heathen faiths. As an exposure of the worst side of the Greek
cults TATIAN'S book has permanent value; as a description
of the contrast between the sanity of the new Faith and the
immoral unreason of the old it was an effective Apology.

TATIAN followed strange ascetic courses after the death
of his master, JUSTIN MARTYR, 114-168, one of the bright
lights of the age. JUSTIN took the position that "whatever
is rightly said among all men belongs to us Christians",
and therefore retained his philosopher's cloak. He opened
the way for a fresh interpretation of Christianity by teaching that revelation satisfies reason and crowns philosophy.

Two Apologies, and a *Dialogue with Trypho the Jew,*
came from his pen; in all likelihood he also wrote an *Address
to the Greeks.* The *First Apology,* 150-155, was addressed
to Antoninus Pius on behalf of "those of all nations who
are unjustly hated and wantonly abused." It is well considered, and is argued with dignity and confidence. JUSTIN
describes Christians as "the best friends that a ruler could
desire." They are those

who believe in a God whose eye no crime can escape,
no falsehood deceive; . . . . who look for an eternal
judgment, not only on their deeds, but even on their
thoughts!

Their moral conversion proves the reality of their faith in Christ:

> We who once delighted in adultery, now are become chaste; once given to magic, now are consecrated to the one good God; once loving wealth above all things, now hold all our goods in common, and share them with the poor; once full of hatred and slaughter, now live together in peace, and pray for our enemies, and strive to convert our persecutors.

The *Second Apology*, written soon after the first, is a less important work as a defence of Christianity; but its vivid pictures of the perils of persecution 'for the Name' add much valuable material to the history of the period.

JUSTIN'S dialogue with Trypho, an Ephesian Jew, was held about 148 but the report of it was written after 155. Friendliness between Jews and Christians "was probably exceptional and in any case the *Dialogue* makes it clear how incapable the representatives of the two related faiths were of coming to any understanding."[3] Trypho was a cultured Jew, with an open, tolerant mind, and the easy courtesy of the literary class. He wondered how Christians could profess to serve God, and yet disregard His Law; and how they could believe in a human Saviour. JUSTIN answers him by denying that the Law is permanently binding; he then undertakes to prove the divinity of Christ; finally, he declares that the true Israel consists of those who believe in the new revelation of grace.

"The whole Dialogue . . . . is a perfect storehouse of early Christian interpretation of Scripture." It shows that while the Old Testament held a place of high esteem, there was another measure of truth for the Church, and all forms of faith were tried by that new standard.

JUSTIN'S philosophic temper was characteristic of the

[3] A. F. Findlay, *Byways of Early Christian Literature*, p. 103.

Apologists of the time. Under its moderating influence
MILTIADES, the sophist of the Churches, wrote a now lost
Apology addressed to the Rulers of this World. The rulers
to whom this learned plea for toleration was offered were
probably Marcus Aurelius and Verus.

The brilliant and versatile MELITO, "the philosopher,"
bishop of Sardis, d. 177, joined the ranks of the literary
apologists in 170, by offering to the Emperor, probably
Caracalla, a *Personal Plea,* containing a skilful, courteous,
modest and well-informed argument for the Faith. In this
address he claimed that idols are not gods:

> For, if a man call fire God, it is not God, because it
> is fire; and, if a man call water God, it is not God,
> because it is water; . . . . and, if he so call those pieces
> of wood which we burn, or those stones which we
> break, how can these things be gods?

Thence he passed to the origin of idols, and finally to a
plea that the Emperor might believe the true God.

> For, according as thou hast acknowledged Him here,
> will He acknowledge thee there; and, if thou account
> Him here superfluous, He will not account thee one of
> those who have known Him and confessed Him.

Two years later, 172, MELITO addressed Marcus Aurelius,
in a strongly social or political *Apology,* of which only a
few fragments exist. He is credited with many other works.
The *Treatise on the Incarnation* was a definite contribution
to the development of theology, and gained for its author a
reputation as one of the greater lights of Christian Asia.

The Key ascribed to MELITO, which has been called one
of the most curious writings of the ancient Church bearing on the subject of the allegorical interpretation of Scripture, and which "consists of a catalogue of many hundreds
of birds, beasts, plants, and minerals, that were symbolical

of Christian virtues, doctrines, and personages,"[4] is now known to be a work of the Middle Ages.

Another Christian philosopher, ATHENAGORAS by name, also appealed to Marcus Aurelius. His work, entitled *The Embassy*, 176-177, carefully describes and indignantly repudiates the three charges of atheism, cannibalism, and lust, which were commonly urged against Christians in connection with their midnight Eucharists. ATHENAGORAS pleads for an impartial trial that would lead to a just verdict; he then makes a vigorous assault on the demon-inspired idolatries and wickednesses of paganism.

To the Emperor, for whom his book was intended, he says:

> May you, by considering yourselves, be able to discover the heavenly kingdom also! For as all things are subservient to you, father and son, who have received the kingdom from above (for 'the king's soul is in the hand of God,' saith the prophetic Spirit), so to the one God and the Logos proceeding from Him, the Son. apprehended by us as inseparable from Him, all things are in like manner subjected.

ATHENAGORAS is decidedly superior to most of the Apologists. "Elegant, free from superfluity of language, forcible in style, he rises occasionally into great power of description, and his reasoning is remarkable for clearness and cogency."

Towards the end of *The Embassy*, ATHENAGORAS says, "let the argument upon the Resurrection stand over." He fulfilled the promise implied by these words by writing a *Treatise on the Resurrection*.

The name of CLAUDIUS APOLINARIUS (or Apolinaris) fl. 160-180, is associated with various Apologies: *Against the Greeks; On Truth; Against the Jews; Against the Montanists;* but little of them is left. His *Apology to Mar-*

---

[4] W. E. H. Lecky, *Rationalism in Europe,* Vol. I., p. 264, note 1.

cus *Aurelius,* 172, is represented by three fragments only. He is, however, memorable in literary history as the preserver of the earliest known version of the story of the Thundering Legion.

THEOPHILUS of Antioch, 115-183, is described as "one of the precursors of that group of writers who, from Irenaeus to Cyprian, not only break the obscurity which rests on the earliest history of the Christian Church, but alike in the east and in the west, carry it to the front in literary eminence, and distance all their heathen contemporaries".[5]

He wrote an *Apology to Autolycus,* in order to convince him that Christianity was true and of divine authority, and at the same time to show that paganism was false and foolish. Like ATHENAGORAS he indignantly denies the horrible calumnies made against the Christian fellowship and worship; but unlike many of the Apologists he draws his arguments mainly from the Old Testament, making but few references to any of the writings of the New Testament. The three parts of the Apology were written at different times; the last part soon after the death of Marcus Aurelius, *i.e.* 180.

---

[5] W. Sanday, *Studia Biblica,* p. 90.

CHAPTER VII
THE MARTYROLOGIES

The literature of Apology not only served to expose the injustice of persecution, but also to quicken an intellectual interest in the philosophy of Christianity.

The practical interest of the Church was, however, diverted into other than philosophical channels, by the increasing violence of hostility. Written defences might arm the minds of believers, but they failed to sheath the sword of the persecutor. When persecution became the settled policy of Rome, Christian literature became an exultant record of the fidelity of the confessors, and a monument to their spiritual conquest over cruelty and death.

The New Testament contains the germs of martyrology.

Antipas my witness, my faithful one, who was killed among you, where Satan dwelleth.

I saw underneath the altar the souls of them that had been slain for the word of God, and for the testimony which they held.

I saw the woman drunken with the blood of the saints, and with the blood of the witnesses of Jesus.

And I saw . . . . the souls of them that had been beheaded for the testimony of Jesus, and for the word of God (Rev. ii.13; vi.9; xvii.6; xx.4).

The earliest authentic Martyrology, after these brief notices in the New Testament, is contained in a *Letter to the Church of Philomelium,* 155, which gives an account of the trial and death of POLYCARP, as reported by an eye-witness from Smyrna. The whole narrative is vitally graphic, and is a most valuable human document.

> When he came near, the proconsul asked him whether he was Polycarp: who, confessing that he was, he persuaded him to deny the faith, saying, 'Reverence thy old age'; with many other things of the like nature, as their custom is: concluding thus, 'Swear by Caesar's fortune. Repent, and say, take away the wicked.' Then Polycarp, looking with a stern countenance upon the whole multitude of wicked Gentiles that was gathered together in the lists, and shaking his hand at them, looked up to heaven, and groaning, said, 'Take away the wicked.' But the proconsul insisting and saying 'Swear, and I will set thee at liberty; reproach Christ;' Polycarp replied, 'Eighty and six years have I now served Christ, and He has never done me the least wrong; how then can I blaspheme my King and my Saviour?'

IRENAEUS, 120 or 130-202, was most probably the author of a *Letter from the Churches of Lyon and Vienne* to the Churches of Asia and Phrygia, telling them of the persecution in Gaul in 177. This glowing and pathetic story well deserves the eulogium of Renan: "The enthusiasm, the mystic tone of the style, the spirit and sweetness and good sense which mark the whole recital inaugurate a new rhetoric, and make this piece the pearl of the Christian literature of the second century".[6]

The heroine of the story is the little slave, of whom the author says:

> the blessed Blandina, last of all, after having like a noble mother encouraged her children, and sent them on before her victorious to the King, trod the same path of conflict which her children had trod, hasten-

---

[6] *Marcus Aurelius*, chap. xx.

ing on to them with joy and exultation at her departure, not as one thrown to the wild beasts, but as one invited to a marriage supper.

The persecution which raged at Lyon in 177, was followed in 180 by an equally savage attack upon the Christians of Numidia. *The Acts of the Scillitan Martyrs* mentions twelve of the sufferers by name. This martyrology is one of the earliest documents of the North African Church, and is the earliest specimen of Christian Latin, 202.

It is an excellent example of *Acts* of Martyrs. It has all the appearance of a legal document. It gives the date of the trial; the names of the accused; and the name of the proconsul—Saturininus, who tried them. The trial was short.

> Speratus said, The Empire of this world I know not; but rather I serve that God Whom no man hath seen nor with these eyes can see.
>
> Cittinus said, We have none other to fear save only our Lord God Who is in heaven.
>
> Donata said, Honour to Caesar as Caesar but fear to God.
>
> Vestia said, I am a Christian.
>
> Secunda said, What I am, that I wish to be. . . .
>
> And so they all together were crowned with martyrdom.

The *Passion of Perpetua and Felicitas*, who suffered with others at Carthage in 202, was written as a new model of those "ancient illustrations of faith, which both testify to God's grace and tend to man's edification," and as such it is invaluable. It was probably prepared by TERTULLIAN, who wove into it Perpetua's story, "as she left it, described by her own hand and with her own mind" (chap. i-iii); and Saturus's account of his vision of God (chap. iv-x).

Christian literature contains no finer first-hand description of mystical experience, nor any more intensely human document than this. Tender, pathetic, rich in the spirit of devotion, a brilliant reflection of the procedure of persecution, and saturated with religious enthusiasm, it appeals to both the imagination and the heart. The portraits are alive: Perpetua, a young mother, twenty-two years of age, the central figure of the company; her father seeking to turn her from the faith; Felicitas glad to recover from childbirth in prison so that she might fight with the wild beasts; Saturus and the rest; are all drawn with exquisite fidelity. The details of the imprisonment, of the repeated struggles in the Arena, of the evidences of the confessors' courage, modesty and endurance make this Passion a most precious literary heritage.

The *Acts of Thascius Caecilius Cyprian,* who was beheaded in 258, give the clearest information as to the spirit and the forms of Roman persecution. The original official documents are closely followed, but they are lit up with vivid descriptions of the persons involved.

Another account of Cyprian's Passion was written, in the history of the sufferer's life, by PONTIUS, one of his disciples.

The noble army of martyrs inspired other literature beside that which recorded their Passions. The dignity of martyrdom became the theme of glowing panegyrics, in which the most laudatory epithets were applied to those who suffered. The thirst for martyrdom was inflamed; the commemoration of the days of the martyr's deaths was encouraged; the merits and powers of confessors were extolled. Such praises rapidly became extravagant, until at length they trembled on the verge of blasphemy.

TERTULLIAN, 150-220, probably began his literary career by writing *To the Martyrs,* 197, in which his strong views on self-denial and separation from the world formed the starting-point of an enthusiastic glorification of the state of the condemned. They are reminded that they are "called to the military service of the living God," and that they are "Christian athletes" whose training ground is the prison.

In 208, he wrote *Flight in Persecution,* a somewhat "wild and fanatical" work, describing persecution as "that fan which even now cleanses the Lord's threshing floor," flight from which is derogatory to the honour of God.

The persecution of 211, moved him to write on the advantages of martyrdom. He called this work *Scorpions,* because the opponents of martyrdom, like scorpions that strike, sting, and kill, must be crushed. Martyrdom, he declares, is according to the will and command of God, it discloses the Divine generosity, it is a believer's final defence of his faith.

In an address *To Scapula,* the proconsul who authorised the persecution of 211, TERTULLIAN made a grave and sober appeal for justice. Scapula should consider the exemplary behaviour of Christians; he should recall the ills that have befallen persecutors; he should "remember to be humane."

> Spare thyself, Scapula, if thou wilt not spare us. Spare Carthage, if thou wilt not spare thyself. Spare thy Province, which the mere mention of thine intention has subjected to the threats and extortions of soldiers and of private foes.

ORIGEN, 185-254, also, whose father had suffered for the faith in 208, sent an *Exhortation to Martyrdom* to Ambrosius and Theoctetus, prisoners during the persecution of 235-237. The book is an expression of the writer's true feeling. He encourages the condemned to look beyond the present to their reward, and to the profit that there is in the blood of the saints.

By the time of CYPRIAN, 200-258, this type of Christian literature had become fixed. The letters of CYPRIAN to various martyrs and confessors express the popular feeling of the Church towards those about to suffer; his treatise, the *Exhortation to Martyrdom*, addressed to Fortunatus, 252 or 257, represents the official mind. It consists of a number of biblical passages, arranged to sustain the bishop's arguments against idolatry, and to support the faith of the imprisoned. It urges and teaches that martyrdom:

> is a baptism greater in grace, more lofty in power, more precious in honour—a baptism wherein angels baptise —a baptism in which God and His Christ exult—a baptism after which no one sins any more—a baptism which completes the increase of our faith—a baptism which, as we withdraw from the world, immediately associates us with God. In the baptism of water is received the remission of sins, in the baptism of blood the crown of virtues.

ARNOBIUS, fl. 284-305, the rhetorician of Sicca, sought to destroy the ground on which persecution was commonly justified by refuting the charge that public misfortunes were inflicted by the gods because of Christian impieties. His work *Against the Heathen*, 303, is a tremendous denunciation of the whole social fabric of his day. It is written in a tedious and rather confused style; it shows ignorance of the Old Testament, and only an imperfect knowledge of the New; but the sincerity of the author's faith is revealed by his condemnation of heathen immorality and his criticisms of pagan worship.

This work is divided into seven books of unequal length. The first two are devoted to the defence of Christianity, the remainder to the exposure of paganism. As a writer, ARNOBIUS stands among those whose style is that of a declining age.

The brilliant pupil of ARNOBIUS, LUCIUS CAELIUS LACTANTIUS, 260-340, marked the end of the age of persecution by writing a vigorous polemic entitled *The Deaths of the Persecutors,* 314. His Latin was of such purity as to win for him the title of the Christian Cicero. The book contains a collection of historical facts which tend to show that all the emperors who persecuted the Christians died miserably. It is a work of very considerable learning to which the reader may turn for many details not easily found elsewhere.

The book covers the history of persecution from Nero to Diocletian; its publication indicated that the Church was relieved of all fear of danger and felt confident of the favour of the Emperor. The nature of the work may be gathered from the fourth chapter:

> This long peace, however, was afterwards interrupted. Decius appeared in the world, an accursed wild beast to afflict the Church—and who but a bad man would persecute religion? It seems as if he had been raised to sovereign eminence, at once to rage against God, and at once to fall; for, having undertaken an expedition against the Carpi, ... he was suddenly surrounded by the barbarians, and slain, together with great part of his army; nor could he be honoured with the rites of sepulture, but, stripped and naked, he lay to be devoured by wild beasts and birds—a fit end for the enemy of God.

CHAPTER VIII

THE REFUTATION OF HERESY

Other enemies than popular hatred and civil persecution harassed the growing Church with frequent and violent assaults, against which the makers of Christian literature were obliged to set up fresh defences. The most formidable of these foes was heresy in its almost numberless forms. Against it the Church raised the general defence that the true doctrine was that which the whole body of believers accepted; heresy was the local or partial belief of some small section, misguided as to the true interpretation of the Faith.

The earliest heresy which left its traces on the literature was Docetism; the view that the body of Jesus was a phantom. The *First Epistle of John* was the first of many refutations of this error. JUSTIN MARTYR denounced it in his Letters, so also did POLYCARP and IRENAEUS in theirs. SERAPION of Antioch, fl. 199-211, forbade the use of the *Gospel of Peter* because it was tainted with this heresy.

This decision was the product of SERAPION'S second thoughts. His first hasty perusal of the Gospel discovered nothing heretical in it; he therefore gave instructions that it should be read in the Church at Rhosus. Later developments however convinced him that this approval was ill-advised; he re-read the work, and then wrote a pastoral Letter recalling his sanction.

A much more formidable foe soon appeared in the form of the widespread heresy of Gnosticism. This heresy included a wide variety of religious views, all of which sprang from the desire for mystic or supernatural knowledge. It arose in many places under the inspiration of various leaders, whose "highly speculative systems . . . . sought to explain the origin of evil, the nature of the Divine being, and the interaction of the spiritual and the material." Gnosticism formulated mysterious rites, through which redemption could be attained; it inspired a mystical experience of approach to the Divine; and it separated its own devotees, as men on a higher plane, from the common crowd of religious worshippers.

Gnosticism exerted a deep and enduring influence upon Christian literature. More than any other cause, it obliged the Church to realise the need of having a canon of the New Testament; "It secured for the Old Testament its permanent place as a sacred book . . . . In the *Letter of Ptolemaeus to Flora* (preserved by EPIPHANIUS),[1] we find the earliest attempt at biblical criticism. The Commentaries of HERACLEON laid the foundations of exegesis . . . . and among the other contributions may be reckoned the Christian Hymn. Gnostic literature abounded in hymns . . . . and these were taken over in not a few cases and adapted to the service of the Church."[2]

The *First Epistle of John* led the attack against the speculations of Gnosticism, by denouncing the distinction between Jesus and Christ which was one of the characteristics of the teaching of Cerinthus (ii.22-23; v.1). The *Pastoral Epistles*, as well as the so-called *Second Epistle of Peter* show hostility to the growing menace (I Tim. i.4; II iv.2-4; Titus i.16; iii.9).

The first writing expressly designed to counteract the Gnostic teaching was that of AGRIPPA CASTOR, fl. 135, a most distinguished author in his day. His work was a refutation of the teaching of BASILIDES, and, in the opinion of EUSEBIUS, "ably exposes the fallacy of his heresy."[3]

---

[1] Epiphanius, *Heresies*, xxxiii. 3-7.
[2] Cf. E. F. Scott, *Ency. of Religion and Ethics*, Vol. VI., pp. 240-241.
[3] *Ecclesiastical History*, IV., 7.

JUSTIN MARTYR wrote a now lost *Syntagma*, to refute the heresy. It is however, in the *Clementine Homilies*, that the first existing serious attack appears. These Homilies used a fanciful and fictitious series of personal encounters between the Apostle Peter and Simon Magus, as a framework in which to develop the orthodox doctrines of God, sin, and salvation in opposition to the arch-heretic's speculations.

The classical Christian refutation of Gnostic heresies is the work of IRENAEUS, 140-200, whose intellectual perceptions are very sure. Deeply stirred by the conversion of a friend to the sect of the Valentinians, he planned a comprehensive work to expose their errors. The work grew under his hands until it became an almost encyclopaedic treatise, the *Refutation and Overthrow of Falsely Called Knowledge*, 182-187, usually quoted as *Against Heresies*. The Refutation not only deals with the Valentinian form of Gnosticism, but also exposes the errors of "all heresies."

In the first book IRENAEUS describes the teachings of the twelve sects; in the second he advances the Christian arguments against them; the third and fourth books give a scholarly statement of Christian doctrine, which is restated in more simple form in book five.

As a memorial of the opinions and practices of the Church of the age, it is a most valuable record; as a Christian criticism of Gnosticism, it is merciless and complete. The style is hard, and the matter tedious to a modern reader, but the work is an immense help to the historian. It "stereotyped the genius of orthodoxy and founded the polemic method of the Church."

The literary history of this rich mine of argument and of information, is a history of mischance. Much of the original Greek has perished, although the whole survives in Latin translations; but it has been damaged by the ravages of time and patched by quotations from later writers and by editors eager to repair the losses.

IRENAEUS followed this larger work with a Letter to his friend Florinus, warning him against the errors of this heresy. He called it *Monarchy or the Supreme Rule:* its thesis was that God is not the author of evil. He also preserves an epigram on "the terrible Marcus," a Gnostic of the school of Valentinus, who aggravated the errors of his heresy by magical rites and moral iniquity. The epigram is ascribed to "the saintly elder"; this was probably POTHINUS, bishop of Lyons before IRENAEUS.

> Marcus thou maker of idols, inspector of portents,
> Skill'd in consulting the stars and deep in the deep arts of magic,
> Ever by tricks such as these confirming the doctrines of error
> Furnishing signs unto those involved by thee in deception,
> Wonders of power that is utterly severed from God and apostate,
> Which Satan thy true father enables thee still to accomplish
> By means of Azazel that fallen and yet mighty angel
> Thus making thee the precursor of his own impious actions.

This is the earliest known specimen of critical poetry in Christian literature.

HIPPOLYTUS of Portus, 170-236, a great controversialist, unquestionably the most learned member of the Roman Church of his day, and one of the "earliest anti-popes known to history," composed the *Philosophumena,* or *Refutation of of all the Heresies,* directed in the main against the Ophite sect of the Gnostics.

This "small book against thirty-two heresies . . . . written in a clear dignified style" was the second anti-heretical book which HIPPOLYTUS had written. The first composed about twenty years before contains many extracts from otherwise unknown Gnostic writings.

EPIPHANIUS of Salamis, c. 315-402, another strenuous champion of orthodoxy, made an Exposition of the true faith to counteract Arianism in Pamphylia, and another, the *Ancoratus,* in 374, for the benefit of the Christians in

Egypt. His great anti-heretical work the *Panarion* c. 376, not only attacks Gnosticism but also many other unorthodox forms of Christianity. The name, *Panarion,* implies that EPIPHANIUS designed it to be a religious medicine chest containing a number of various antidotes to the "poisonous bite of the heretical serpent." At the end he gives a glorifying description of the Church universal, its faith, its manners and its ordinances.

An interesting pen portrait of the arch-heretic ARIUS is given in chapter 69:

> He was in stature very tall, downcast in visage, with manners like a wily serpent, captivating to every guileless heart by that same crafty bearing. Always dressed in short cloak and scanty tunic, he was pleasant of address, ever persuading souls and cajoling them.

What little is known of the treatise of PHILASTER of Brescia, fl. 370-390, shows that the number of so-called heresies could be multiplied almost indefinitely. PHILASTER enumerated one hundred and fifty-six; among them he reckoned denial of the plurality of the heavens; the view that the giants of Genesis vi. were the children of angels; the belief that the age of the world was not accurately known; the idea that there is an infinite number of worlds; the practice of using heathen names for the days of the week; and carelessness in reckoning chronology.

Together with Docetism and Gnosticism, a third heresy, Marcionism, called forth Christian defensive writings. MARCION, fl. 150, "the Pontic mouse who nibbled away the Gospels," was one "of the most noted and most permanently influential of the heretics of the second century." He planned to reform Christianity by a return to the pure Word, which he defined in two works; the *Evangelicum,* and the

Apostolicon. The *Evangelicum* was an abridged edition of
the Third Gospel; the *Apostolicon* contained ten of the
Epistles of the New Testament, arranged as follows: Galatians; 1 and 2 Corinthians; Romans i-xiv.; 1 and 2 Thessalonians; Ephesians renamed Laodiceans; Colossians; Philippians; and Philemon.

MARCION interpreted the antitheses—Law and Gospel—
Sin and Grace—Faith and Works—as the contrasted hall-
marks of two opposed religions; the religion of Jehovah of
the Old Testament, and the religion of the God and Father
of Jesus Christ, of the New. "He denied that the Old Testament proceeds from the same God as does the New."

From this standpoint, he inferred that the world was
created by the inferior deity, that the body of Jesus was not
material, that asceticism was essential to holiness, and that
marriage was inconsistent with true Christianity. These were
the views maintained and defended in a large work entitled
Antitheses.

Marcionism grew apace, and Christian literature necessarily
gave heed to its errors.   JUSTIN MARTYR denounced it,
MAXIMUS, fl. 180, wrote a book *On Matter*, which both
ORIGEN and METHODIUS used to confute the Marcionites.
IRENAEUS in his *Refutation*, protested against its dismem-
berment of St. Paul's Epistles. HIPPOLYTUS, EPIPHANIUS,
and the Armenian ESNIK, fl. 450, all controverted it.

But the vehement wrath of orthodoxy was vented without restraint against both heretic and heresy, in the treatise
Against Marcion, 208, by TERTULLIAN, 155-222; a work
full of interest, but marked by a polemical savagery rarely
surpassed. The tone in which it is written may be judged
by the description of MARCION, who is said to be

> fouler than any Scythian, more roving than the wagon-
> life of a Sarmatian, more inhuman than the Massa-

gatae, more audacious than an Amazon, darker than the cloud, colder than winter, more brittle than ice, more deceitful than the Ister, more craggy than Caucasus.

A similar fury of speech characterises TERTULLIAN'S criticism of MARCION'S *Antitheses*. The practices and personalities, as well as the doctrines of the heretics received the roughest handling from this stalwart African defender of the faith, who did not spare the dualism, the subjective and arbitrary treatment of Scripture, or the spiritualism of this error.

There is a dialogue "on the right faith in God," entitled *Against the Marcionists*, by an unknown author, who gave the name Adamantius to the orthodox disputant. It is not a work of the first rank, part of it is taken from the work of MAXIMUS *On Matter*, the argument is not always to the point, and the style is dull and unattractive, but it was used as an authority by greater writers, and doubtless served a useful purpose in its day.

The unknown author of *Commentaries on Thirteen Epistles of St. Paul*, commonly quoted as AMBROSIASTER, speaks of the Marcionites in the latter half of the fourth century, as "on the verge of extinction."

The literary defenders of the Faith were called into fresh action by the heresy of Montanism. About 156, Montanus, of the Phrygian Church, took up the cry of a more ascetic morality in the interest of an ecstatic emotionalism, which he claimed to be the result of the action of the Spirit of God by Whom he was inspired as the Old Testament prophets had been inspired. Speaking as the mouth piece of the Divine he would say:

I have come not as an angel or ambassador but God the Father.

He extolled celibacy, denounced second marriages as adulterous, preached the virtues of fasting, of vegetarianism, and of abstinence from wine; and toured the Province in the company of two women, who exhibited the effects of spiritual ecstasy.

APOLLONIUS of Ephesus, fl. 150-190, undertook to arrest the schism by criticising the teachers as well as the teaching. His *Refutation* was severe enough in personal condemnations:

> Who is this new teacher?. . . This is he that taught the dissolutions of marriage, he that inspired laws of fasting . . . . who established exactors of money, and under the name of offerings, devised the artifice to procure presents . . . . Does it not appear to you that the Scripture forbids any prophet to receive gifts and money? When therefore I see a prophetess receiving both gold and silver and precious garments, how can I fail to reject her?
>
> Tell me does a prophet dye? Does a prophet paint? Does a prophet delight in ornament? Does a prophet play with tablets and dice? Does he take usury?

This *Refutation* roused TERTULLIAN to attack the movement. In a now lost work *On Ecstasy,* he protested against the questionable character of its advocates; its misuse of the truth; and its frivolity and mercenary greed.

Letters in the same critical strain were written by CLAUDIUS APOLINARIUS of Antioch, during the years 160-180. SERAPION of Antioch, like many other teachers in later years, made good use of these Letters to confirm the faith of waverers.

The waverers were many. VICTOR, Bishop of Rome, 189-198, definitely favoured the movement. TERTULLIAN, also, driven by the "envy and abuse of the Roman clergy," finally embraced the new prophecy, which he had once condemned.

But the issue was never in doubt; Montanus was formally condemned in 172; and the arguments of ASTERIUS URBANUS, fl. 232, the writings of MILTIADES, of CAIUS of Rome, 200-220, and the fixation of the New Testament Canon, all served to discredit the unregulated emotionalism of the heretics. By the time of AUGUSTINE, Montanism had disappeared.

PART III
THE SCHOOLS OF THE FAITH
(A.D. 150-300)

CHAPTER IX

THE SCHOOL OF CARTHAGE

The Christian thinkers connected with the Churches of Asia Minor formed the first group to which the name of a school can be given. Their chief literary works have already been noticed; their last outstanding representative was IRENAEUS, the disciple of POLYCARP, who had been one of the disciples of the apostle John.

During the two centuries that elapsed between the work of TERTULLIAN and the work of CASSIAN, the literary history of Christianity is the history of various schools of thought, each of which made its own contribution to the statement and the discussion of the Faith. "Minds trained in different intellectual surroundings, and swayed by different religious and ethical preconceptions naturally interpreted the facts of Christian experience and the tradition in various ways."[1]

The School of Carthage was a school of rigorous morality and practical religion. It regarded the Gospel as calling for a discipline of life that separated the Church from the world by an almost uncompromising aloofness. In literature the School has the special distinction of being the means whereby the Latin language, with all its riches of thought and style, was brought into the service of Christianity.

Until the middle of the second century, Greek was the language of the Church; but with the publication of the Apology entitled *Octavius*, 180-190, which was written by the converted Roman lawyer, MARCUS MINUCIUS FELIX, the new Faith began to make use of Latin.

---

[1] A. F. Findlay, *By-Ways in Early Christian Literature*, Preface, p. v.

The Apology takes the form of a dialogue between Octavius, a Christian, and Caecilius, a pagan, who, however, at last declares himself overcome by the arguments of his opponent. MINUCIUS thus describes the occasion of the discussion:

> when in the early morning we were going along the shore towards the sea, that breathing the air might gently refresh our lungs, and that the yielding sand might sink down under our easy footsteps; Caecilius, observing an image of Serapis, raised his hand to his mouth, as is the custom of the superstitious common people, and pressed a kiss on it with his lips.

But a greater than MARCUS MINUCIUS FELIX was needed to recast the substance of Christian teaching in the mould of the Latin mind. That was a task that called for a vigorous, creative personality, and such a personality was found in QUINTUS SEPTIMUS FLOREUS TERTULLIAN, born a pagan in Carthage, but converted to Christianity, 192. He became a member of the "ill-fated Church of North Africa, with its stern enthusiasm, its austere discipline, and its intensely practical religion." He was "sufficiently master of the Greek language to be able to write treatises in it," nevertheless he became the actual creator of a Christian Latinity; he was the most prolific of all the Latin writers, the most original and personal.

TERTULLIAN lives in his books; brilliant, rhetorical, one-sided, full of paradoxes, ever speaking from his heart, "always sick with the fevers of impatience." He wrote his strong convictions under the impulse of fiery passion, and his messages burned themselves into the memory and speech of the Church.

> You cannot surely forbid the Truth to reach your ears by the secret pathway of a noiseless book.

In the case of the gods . . . . the sacredness is great in proportion to the tribute they yield . . . . Majesty is made a source of gain. Religion goes about the taverns begging.

Whenever the soul comes to itself . . . . it speaks of God . . . . noble testimony of the soul, naturally Christian.

Unless I am utterly mistaken, there is nothing so old as the Truth.

If the Tiber rises as high as the city walls, if the Nile does not send its waters up over the fields, if the heavens give no rain, if there is an earthquake, if there is a famine or pestilence, straightway the cry is 'The Christians to the lion.'

We conquer in dying; we go forth victorious at the very time we are subdued.

The oftener we are mown down, the more in number we grow; the blood of Christians is the seed.

All the known writings of TERTULLIAN are argumentative; they are weapons of war, designed for attack or defence. It is impossible to arrange them in the order of their production; they fall within the period, 195-218, but only two of them are approximately dated, and even the general division of them into orthodox and montanistic must be made without certainty.

Eight works belong, in all probability, to TERTULLIAN'S orthodox years, 195-202. These are the *Letter to the Martyrs*, 197, the *Treatises on Repentance; Prayer; Baptism,* and *Patience,* 197-199, the two *Letters to his Wife,* and the *Prescription of Heretics,* 199.

After he became a Montnaist in 202, he seems to have written thirteen books. Five editions of a work *Against Marcion* were issued between 200 and 207, the third edition being published in "the thirteenth year of Severus."

Then came the *Soldier's Crown, Chastity,* and *Flight in Persecution,* 202-203. *Scorpions,* the *Veiling of Virgins, Monogamy,* and *Modesty* followed, 203-204. After these *The Body of Christ,* and the *Resurrection of the Flesh,* were written some time before 207.

It is almost impossible to date his other works, some of which are of the highest value. They include *The Soul, Against Praxeas, Fasting, Against Valentinus, To Scapula, Shows, Idolatry,* the *Dress of Women,* the *Apology, To the Nations, The Witness of the Soul, The Cloak, Against Hermogenes,* and *Against the Jews.*

The titles of these works are on the whole clear indications of their contents. Their paramount interests reappear in many forms, but especially in connection with the social life of the age, the pagan religion, and the character, behaviour, and worship of the Christians.

The *Prescription of Heretics,* his imperishable work, marks an important step in ecclesiastical development by advocating a standard of faith whereby all Christian professors should be tried. TERTULLIAN states this rule of faith, claims that it was taught by Christ, and urges:

> So long as its form exists in its proper order, you may seek and discuss as much as you please, and give full rein to your curiosity, in whatever seems to you to hang in doubt, or to be shrouded in obscurity . . . . although it is better for you to remain in ignorance, lest you should come to know what you ought not, because you have acquired the knowledge of what you ought to know. 'Thy faith,' He says, 'hath saved thee' not your skill in the Scriptures.

THASCIUS CAECILIUS CYPRIANUS—CYPRIAN—200-258, carried the Carthaginian school a step farther towards its full development. A confessed disciple of TERTULLIAN whose works he read daily, he cultivated a purer style by following classical and post-classical models. His "diction is free and pleasing, and flows in a trànquil and clear, almost transparent stream. His language is enlivened and exalted by the warmth of his feelings. Quite frequently the page is colored by images and allegories chosen with taste and finished with skilful attention to the smallest detail".

CYPRIAN poured out his heart in an *Epistle to Donatus,* for whom he unveiled the world as he had known it in his pre-Christian days:

> consider yourself transported to one of the loftiest peaks of some inaccessible mountain, thence gaze on the appearances of things lying below you. . . . Consider the roads blocked up by robbers, the seas beset with pirates, wars scattered all over the earth . . . .
>
> And now, if you turn your eyes to the cities you will behold a concourse more fraught with sadness than any solitude. The gladitorial games are prepared. . . . Living men . . . . fight with beasts, not for their crime, but for their madness. . . . In the theatres also you will behold what may well cause you grief and shame . . . . the Forum echoes with the madness of strife. . . .

A treatise on *The Vanity of Idols,* showing that the idols are not God, is largely a compilation from the *Octavius* of MINUCIUS FELIX, and the *Apology* of TERTULLIAN. In 248 CYPRIAN wrote *Testimonies against the Jews* for the instruction of his son Quirinius.

After his elevation to the bishopric of Carthage, he turned a fresh page in the literature of Latin Christianity, by writing the earliest Latin-Christian Letters. In these most valuable works he discusses morals, discipline, organisation, and doctrine, with the view of consolidating the episcopal system, and in order to deal both faithfully and leniently with those who had lapsed during persecution. CYPRIAN claimed and represented the authority of the organised Church; his *Epistles* are therefore "a primary source of authoritative information concerning the life and discipline" of the Church of his day.

The outstanding questions of his age were the questions of the readmission of the "lapsed" to the peace of the Church. *i.e.* to the Eucharist, and of the standing of bishops in relation to their dioceses and to Rome. CYPRIAN resisted the policy of Novatus of Carthage and Novatian of Rome, who both favoured strict measures towards the "lapsed". He opposed the arrogance of Stephen of Rome toward the bishops of the Provinces. His *Exhortation to Martyrdom,* 257, addressed to Fortunatus of Lucca, consists of a collection of Scripture passages likely to confirm the faithful under the stress of persecution. It was commended by his own example in 258 when he suffered death as "a standard bearer of the sect and an enemy of the gods."

In COMMODIAN of Gaza in Syria, fl. 250, Latin Christian poetry had its first exponent. His poems reflect the unrest of the age of the Gothic invasions of the third century, and in more than one instance refer to the events with which CYPRIAN had to deal.

From a literary point of view the work of COMMODIAN is worthless. Hallam speaks of it as "a philological curiosity"; it suffered from the change in Latin "which gradually resulted in the formation of the Romance languages." The two poems bore the titles, *Instructions for Christian discipline against the Gods of the Nations,* and *The Apologetic Song against Jews and Heathen.* The Instructions contains eighty acrostic poems, the last of them when read from below upward yields the description, "Commodian one of Christ's poor." The Apologetic Song had for its theme, the coming of Anti-Christ, the end of the world, the Resurrection, and Christian duty in view of the approaching doom.

To this North African school also belongs ARNOBIUS—

Afer—of Sicca, f1. 280-305, a spiritual disciple of TERTUL-
LIAN and CYPRIAN. His *Disputations against the Heathen*,
303, portrays many features of the current mythology as
few other writings have done. It is a work of wide knowledge, and on the whole of clear style although occasionally
the meaning is obscure. "As a storehouse of old Latinity,
and of allusions to points of antiquity—to heathen mythology and ceremonial, to law, education and amusements—
his work is of the greatest interest and importance."

CHAPTER X

THE SCHOOL OF ALEXANDRIA

Side by side with the rigorous and austere School of Carthage, the philosophical and speculative School of Alexandria grew to exert deeper and more widespread influence on Christian literature.

As early as 186 a Christian Academy existed in Alexandria under the direction of PANTAENUS, of whose works only two meagre morsels remain. He was followed in 190, by TITUS FLAVIUS CLEMENS—CLEMENT—150-216, one of the greater lights of the Church.

Although the interest of CLEMENT lay with philosophy rather than with literature, he was an "epoch-making figure in the history of the growth of early Christian literature." His wide learning, like that of his contemporaries, was uncritical and dependent upon extracts and compilations. He was credulous and curious but at the same time versatile, liberal-minded, and optimistic.

Five of CLEMENT'S works have been preserved. The three major books contain the growing structure of his theology; these are the *Exhortation to the Greeks;* the *Instructor;* and the *Miscellanies.* The two lesser works are entitled *Who is the Rich Man who is saved?*, and the *Outlines, i.e.* outlines of expositions of Scripture.

The "three principal extant works form a connected series. The first is an exhortation to the heathen to embrace Christianity, based on an exposition of the comparative character of heathenism and Christianity; the second offers a system of training for the new convert, with a view to the regulation of his conduct as a Christian; the third is an introduction to Christian philosophy."[1]

CLEMENT sought to express the Christian faith in the terms of philosophy, to replace the decadent gnosticism, and to give Christianity possession of the mind of the world. This purpose is constantly before him in the Exhortation or Address, which was written prior to 189.

> do not suppose the song of salvation to be new, as a vessel or a house is new. For 'before the morning star it was' and 'in the beginning was the Word.' Error seems old but truth seems a new thing.

> Why I beseech you, fill up life with idolatrous images, by feigning the winds, or the air, or fire, or earth, or stones, or stocks, or steel, or this universe, to be gods . . . ? It is the Lord of the spirits, the Lord of the fire, the Maker of the universe, Him who lighted up the sun, that I long for.

> Whom shall I take as a helper in my enquiry? We do not, if you have no objection, wholly disown Plato. How, then, is God to be searched out, O Plato? 'For both to find the Father and Maker of this universe is a work of difficulty; and having found Him, to declare Him fully, is impossible.' Why so? By Himself, I beseech you! 'For He can by no means be expressed.' Well done, Plato! Thou hast touched on the truth.

The *Instructor*, or *Pedagogus*, 190, is a manual of manners in which the whole round of personal life is discussed with an intimacy that leaves nothing to be desired. It "often assumes a facetious tinge and occasionally runs over into broad humour." The first book describes the Tutor, who is the Word Himself, the children whom He trains, and His method of instruction. The second book contains general instructions as to daily life in eating, drinking, furniture,

---

[1] *Dictionary of Christian Biography.* Vol. I., p. 561.

sleep, etc.; and the third after an inquiry into the nature of true beauty, goes on to condemn extravagance in dress, etc., both in men and women.

At the end of this work Clement added a *Hymn to Christ the Saviour*, "that for sheer beauty, for gladness and purity of feeling is unmatched in early Christian literature."

> Bridle of colts untamed, over our wills presiding;
> Wing of unwandering birds, our flight securely guiding.
> Rudder of youth unbending, firm against adverse shock;
> Shepherd, with wisdom tending lambs of the royal flock:
> Thy simple children bring in one, that they may sing
> In solemn lays their hymns of praise
> With guileless lips to Christ their King.

The Miscellanies, or Stromata, 202, literally patchwork coverlet, was originally called *Tapestries of Scientific Commentaries according to the True Philosophy*. In this work CLEMENT poured out the contents of his memory and his notebooks, with little regard to order. It is an uncatalogued collection of literary treasures, with "a gay epitome of Greek literature in every sentence," to which more than a hundred authors lent quotations.

CLEMENT had a definite purpose before him when he wrote this apparently unmethodical book. He sought to claim for Christianity the power of satisfying all the demands of life. All knowledge can be unified in the mind of the true gnostic, *i.e.* in the mind of the Christian thinker.

> Let these notes of ours . . . . be of varied character—and as the name implies, patched together—passing constantly from one thing to another, and in a series of discussions hinting at one thing and demonstrating another. 'For those who dig for gold,' says Heraclitus, 'dig much earth and find little gold.' But those who are of the truly golden race, in mining for what is allied to them, will find the much in little. . . . . As, they say, when a certain slave once asked

at the oracle what he should do to please his master, the Pythian priestess replied, 'You will find if you seek.'

The little work *Who is the Rich Man that is Saved?*, 204, is a homily on Mark x.17-31. It teaches that the spirit in which wealth is possessed and used must be a spirit of detachment and unselfishness.

The work of CLEMENT was of epoch-making importance in Hellenizing Christianity; after him philosophy became integral to the discussion of the Faith. He opened the mind of the Church to all that had been well said by the thinkers of all ages. His most characteristic saying is perhaps contained in the words:

> The way of truth is therefore one. But into it, as into a perennial river, streams flow from all sides.

ORIGEN, 185-254, who succeeded CLEMENT as head of the School, was the greatest intellect of the Eastern Church, "the most distinguished and most influential of all the theologians of the ancient Church," and the first theologian to write a full systematic treatise of Christian doctrine. He stood alone in his day as a master of Hebrew. His Expositions of Scripture and his statements of doctrine furnished points for long continued controversies. Whole classes of his writings perished as a result of the edict of Justinian, 543, of the judgment of the Fifth General Council, 553, and of the Gelasian Decretal of books to be received and not to be received.

"ORIGEN'S writings . . . . were, it is said, measured by thousands, and yet, as he argued, they were all one, one in purpose and in spirit . . . . multitude really lies in contradiction and inconsistency. A few books which are charged with errors are many. Many books which are alike inspired by the truth are one."

"This claim which ORIGEN makes to an essential unity—

a unity of purpose and spirit—in all his works is fully justified by their character. Commentaries, homilies, essays, tracts, letters, are alike animated by the same free and lofty strivings, toward a due sense of the Divine Majesty, and the same profound devotion to the teaching of Scripture."[2]

The *Principles of Things,* 230 is the earliest specimen of a dogmatic work in the Christian literature; it is also ORIGEN'S most speculative book. In it he surveyed all the ground of the later creeds in the hope of being able to form a philosophy of faith. The four books into which it is divided, deal with God and creation: creation and providence: man and redemption: the Bible. "The intellectual value of the work may best be characterised by one fact. A single sentence taken from it was quoted by BUTLER as containing the germ of his Analogy."

His Expositions cover the whole Bible; the *Commentary on John,* the first fruits of his labours at Alexandria, marks an epoch in Christian literature and theological thought. Amid much that is faulty from the modern standpoint it contains fine thoughts and subtle criticisms; it "grapples with great difficulties: it unfolds great ideas."

ORIGEN'S Bible work was crowned by his *Hexapla,* which contained in fifty volumes six critical versions of the Old Testament. The *Tetrapla,* was a later work which ORIGEN formed by extracting the third, fourth, fifth and sixth columns from the *Hexapla.*

From these vast labours of scholarship ORIGEN turned to write *Eight Books against Celsus,* 248, in which he gave to ante-Nicene Christianity its greatest Apology. Celsus, a cultured heathen, had published in 178, *A True Discourse,* laughing, raging and scoffing at the Faith, in imitation of his satirical friend Lucian of Samosata. The Discourse was soon forgotten, but fifty years later, Ambrose, ORIGEN'S

---

[2] B. F. Westcott, *History of Religious Thought in the West,* pp. 211, 212.

patron, met with a copy and urged the theologian to answer it. After some hesitation, he "threw himself heart and soul into the controversy," and in no other of his works has he shown greater learning. Notwithstanding digression, excessive detail, and occasional confusion of thought, *Against Celsus* is an invaluable landmark in Christian literature. ORIGEN quoted the entire work of Celsus, piece by piece, and answered each piece in turn.

> This Jew of Celsus still accuses the disciples of Jesus of having invented these statements, saying to them: 'Even although guilty of falsehood, ye have not been able to give a colour of credibility to your inventions.' In answer to which we have to say, that there was an easy method of concealing these occurrences—that, namely, of not recording them at all . . . . Celsus, indeed, did not see that it was an inconsistency for the same persons both to be deceived regarding Jesus, believing Him to be God . . . . and to invent fictions about Him, knowing manifestly that these statements were false.

The School of Alexandria had already welcomed the allegorical method of interpreting Scripture, but the genius of ORIGEN gave it a wider vogue. He explained the method in the *Principles* (Bk. IV., chap. i.). "As man is said to consist of body, soul and spirit, so also does Sacred Scripture. The body is the historical sense, the soul is the moral or religious sense, the spirit is the figurative, typical, mystical sense." From the standpoint of this theory, interpretation is the work of "transforming the sensible Gospel into a spiritual one." Allegorism was responsible for innumerable extravagances in Christian literature, until in the work of EMMANUEL SWEDENBORG, 1688-1772, it found final advocacy.

ORIGEN left Alexandria in disgrace, 231, under the displeasure of his bishop. None such as he stood ready to assume his place, and ere long the famous school came to an end. Heraclas held the headship for a short time. He was followed by DIONYSIUS, who remained in office until 247, when he became bishop.

DIONYSIUS wrote many books, but little remains of them beyond their titles. Fragments of a work *On Nature,* and of *Two Books on the Promises,* are in existence. His Letter to the anti-pope Novatian, is a noble and memorable document.

THEOGNOSTUS succeeded him; and after him came PRIE-RIUS, fl. 280-300; of their writings only a few sentences have survived.

The influence of the scholarship and speculative theology of ORIGEN was maintained by his disciples. ALEXANDER of Jerusalem, d. 250, founded the theological library at Jerusalem. GREGORY THAUMATURGUS, 210-270, and ATHENODORUS, his brother, were outspoken in his praises. On the other hand, critics were not wanting. METHODIUS of Olympus, 260-312, traversed his teaching in two now lost works: the *Resurrection,* and *Created Things.* His only extant work is *The Banquet,* a Platonic symposium on chastity, carried on by ten virgins. Their feelings, at length, find expression in "a genuine lyric, a hymn of praise to Christ the Bridegroom," which is sung by one of the virgins, while the others respond in the chorus:

> I keep myself pure for Thee, O Bridegroom,
> And holding a lighted torch I go to meet Thee.

CHAPTER XI

THE SCHOOL OF EDESSA

The School of Edessa represents the Syrian Christians, who include all those Christians whose liturgical services and ordinary conversation were in the Syriac language. The classical Syriac was spoken at Edessa and was in use far and wide for literary purposes.

The literature of Syriac Christianity consists in the main of homilies in prose and verse, hymns, expositions, commentaries, liturgies, and legends. The Greek that was used at first was ere long translated into Syriac, which thus became cultured and literary. This mingling of the two languages left its mark on the work known as the *Pilgrimage of Silvia (Etheria)*, which belongs to the end of the fourth century. A bishop is represented as preaching in Greek, a presbyter meanwhile rendering the sermon into Syriac.

The origins of Syriac Christianity are faintly outlined in a fourth century discourse, *The Doctrine of Addai*, compiled from two or three sources. Its account of the teaching of Addai, during 125-150, probably summarises the creed of the early Syrian Church. The same discourse appears elsewhere as a Homily. There is also an account of the labours of Palut, whose ordination by Serapion of Antioch in 197, connected the Syrian with the Greek Church.

The so-called heretic BARDAISAN or BARDESANES, 155-222, was a really original thinker, who brought a thorough knowledge of heathen religion to the discussion of Christianity. He is credited with being the author of 'many' works; among them being *Dialogues against the Marcion-*

ites; the *Apology,* in which he resisted the persuasion to deny that he was a Christian; and a *Dialogue on Fate.*

This Dialogue is either the same work as *The Book of the Laws of Countries,* or else a copious extract from it. *The Book of the Laws of Countries* is the only surviving representative of Bardesanist literature. It takes the form of a discussion on the mysteries of Providence; BARDAISAN contributes to the discussion a connected speech equal to one-third of the whole, as well as many short statements. The theme under consideration is that wealth and poverty, sickness and health, death, and all things not within our own control are a work of destiny; but that the soul possesses free will.

CLEMENT of Alexandria quotes from it as a writing of the "Eastern School":

> Destiny is a conjunction of many contrary powers, which are invisible and non-apparent, directing the motion of the stars and acting through them . . . . From the strife and conflict of these powers the Lord delivers us, and grants us peace from the battle-array of the powers and the angels. . . . Until baptism, destiny is therefore true, but afterwards the astrologers are no longer found to speak truth.

The son of BARDAISAN, HARMONIUS, fl. 150, who wrote in both Greek and Syriac, put his views into *A Book of One Hundred and Fifty Hymns,* prepared to be sung at the Feasts of the martyrs. The Hymns were the first adaptation of Syriac to metre and to musical accompaniment. Their success was widespread and long continued. They were in popular use until the poems of EPHREM SYRUS, about a century later, supplanted them.

The most striking and original piece of Syriac literature is the *Acts of Judas Thomas,* really a religious novel, although most of it is composed of prayers, sermons, and

eulogies of virginity and poverty. It belongs to the early part
of the third century.

Embedded in the Acts is a short gnostic epic poem, The
Hymn of the Soul, "and we may indulge the pleasing fancy
that it was the work of BARDAISAN himself or of his son
HARMONIUS."[1] It relates the adventures of the soul that
goes down to Egypt to find the pearl of great price in order
that it may come to its own in the kingdom of the Father.

i

While I was yet but a little child in the house of my Father,
Brought up in luxury, well content with the life of the palace,
Far from the East, our home, my Parents sent me to travel,
And from the royal Hoard they prepared me a load for the
    journey,
Precious it was yet light, that alone I carried the burden.

iii

For they decreed, and wrote on my heart that I should not forget it:
'If thou go down and bring from Egypt the Pearl, the unique one,
Guarded there in the Sea that envelops the loud-hissing Serpent,
Thou shalt be clothed again with thy Robe and the Tunic of
    scarlet,
And with thy Brother, the Prince, thou shalt inherit the Kingdom.'

xiii

Then I seized the Pearl and homewards started to journey,
Leaving the unclean garb I had worn in Egypt behind me;
Straight for the East I set my course, to the light of the home-land,
And on the way in front I found the Letter that roused me—
Once it awakened me, now it became a Light to my pathway.

xx

Clad in the Robe I betook me up to the Gate of the Palace,
Bowing my head to the glorious Sign of my Father that sent it;
I had performed His behest and He had fulfilled what He promised,
So in the Satraps' Court I joined the throng of the Chieftains—
He with favor received me and near Him I dwell in the Kingdom.[2]

The earliest historical narrative belonging to the School
of Edessa, is the *Martyrology of Shamona and Guria*, who
suffered in 297. It is not a contemporary record, and it ap-

---

[1] F. C. Burkitt, *Early Eastern Christianity*, p. 216.
[2] *Ibid.*, pp. 218-223.

pears at greater length and with more detail in a later work by THEOPHILUS, *The Martyrology of Habib the Deacon*, whose death took place during the first quarter of the fourth century.

APHRAATES, d 350, the Persian sage, was responsible for the earliest authentic piece of Syriac Christian literature of which the date is known. His twenty *Homilies* give a continuous exposition of the Syriac creed, in the form of acrostics, of which the initial letters make up the alphabet. The first ten belong to the year 337, the rest were delivered on special occasions at various later dates.

APHRAATES used a simple style, enriched with generous quotations from Scripture; but he was given to much digression and repetition and sometimes he misses the point of his quotation. Nevertheless his writings exercised a widespread influence. The Syrian Church used its own creed instead of that of Nicæa, and as the *Discourse on Penitents* shows, this tended to restrict the membership of the Church to baptised celibates only.

The Edessene School found its best representative and most influential writer in EPHRAIM the Syrian, commonly called EPHREM SYRUS, 308-379, who left his home in Nisibis when it surrendered to Persia in 363, and "came to Edessa, that so splendid a sun might not be hidden in a chamber underground."

As a ward and pupil of the distinguished JAMES of Nisibis, 280-338, he was early acquainted with literature and his interest in it never ceased. He became a somewhat diffuse writer of vast fertility, the master of an elegant style, with a measure of true poetic inspiration. His skill lay in his command of metre; he usually wrote in lines of seven syllables. He was fully aware of his powers and popularity:

> When I was a child . . . . I saw as in a dream that which has become a reality. From my tongue there

sprang a vine-twig, which grew and reached to heaven: it brought forth fruit without end, and leaves without number. It spread, it grew, it lengthened, it expanded itself, it went round about, it stretched abroad till it reached the whole creation. All beings gathered of it, and there was no lack: yea, the more they plucked, so much the more its clusters multiplied. Those clusters were sermons, those leaves were hymns, and God was the giver. To Him be glory for His grace . . . .

SOZOMEN the historian supports this testimony when he says that EPHREM wrote three hundred times ten thousand lines.

As a poet, his name is given to fifty-six *Hymns against Heretics*, intended to refute the teaching of Marcion, Bardaisan and Mani; eighty-five *Against Sceptics*, eighty-five *Funeral Hymns*, seventy-six *On Repentance*, as well as to many others written for festival occasions.

The *Nisibene Hymns*, 350-361, serve the purposes of the historian, as they are associated with the Persian invasion. The first twenty-one describe the siege of Nisibis in 350, and carry on the story of the strife until the fall of the city, 363. The Hymns 26-34 deal with schisms and strifes in Edessa and Haran, during the years 360-370. The remaining Hymns, 35-77, treat of religious subjects—the overthrow of Death and Satan; the Resurrection of the body: the consolations of religion in view of Death and the grave.

EPHREM wrote Commentaries on all the books of the Bible, more than a thousand Homilies, a *Treatise on False Doctrine*, and some Tracts on the ascetic life. As an interpreter of Scripture he held a middle course between literalism and allegorism; he maintained that there is first the literal interpretation, and secondly the spiritual one; he therefore habitually gives both. Thus on Isaiah xxv. 7 he says,

"Though the prophet is speaking of Sennacherib he has a covert reference to Satan."

Among his disciples who were also Syriac writers, ISAAC THE ELDER, deserves remembrance. He is the author of a work on the three Persons of the Trinity, "a book of very dark disputation and involved discourse." It is entitled *A Book of the Faith of the Holy Trinity and of the Incarnation of the Lord.*

The Syriac *Doctrine of the Apostles,* generally called the *Edessene Canons,* 350, a form of Church Order, is a genuine reflection of the ecclesiastical conditions of the age; but the so-called *Apostolical Constitutions,* 375, although written in Syriac is really a Greek work.

A fourth great name belonging to this School is that of RABBULA, bishop of Edessa, 412-435, whose energy and zeal earned for him the title of "the common master of Syria, Armenia, Persia, nay of the whole world." His Canons or *Commands and Admonitions to Priests and to Sons of the Covenant Living in the Country,* registers the breakdown of the sacerdotalism of APHRAATES. A fragment of a dogmatic sermon shows his hostility to Nestorianism, as does also a Letter to Cyril in which RABBULA denounces THEODORE of Mopsuestia as the author of the heresy. He translated a book by CLEMENT entitled *The Right Path* as a further aid to the cause of orthodoxy.

RABBULA'S chief literary distinction, however, is that he displaced the *Diatessarion* of TATIAN from its place of honour in Syriac Christianity, by preparing a version of the Gospels in the vernacular. This version was known as *The Separate Gospels* and, in its revised form, is known as *The Peshitta.*

Some six hundred and forty Letters are ascribed to his pen, and it is known that he wrote a number of liturgical Hymns addressed to the Mother of God; to Saints and

Martyrs; and extolling Repentance, the Cross, the Resurrection, the Foot-Washing, the Eucharist, etc.

RABBULA was succeeded in the headship of the School by IBAS, bishop of Edessa, 435-457, whose theological views were in stout opposition to those of his master. He was a translator rather than an original writer, and to his zeal in spreading the works of Nestorian writers is largely due the permanent hold which that heresy kept upon the Christianity of those regions.

ISAAC of Antioch, d. 460, called "the Great," and "the Elder," has left material that is most useful as a help to an understanding of the sectaries of the time. His many works in Syriac have been praised as among the best in that language. He was the author of some descriptive Poems and of at least one hundred and four metrical Discourses, which deal for the most part with the life of ascetics.

Two doctrinal Discourses deal with the subjects of the Person of Christ and the Incarnation. The former makes striking use of the figure that Ezekiel saw in his vision of the chariot (Ezekiel chap. i.) :

> From the appearance of his middle upward,
>   He was like unto fire devouring;
> From the appearance of his middle downward,
>   He was like the Bow in the clouds.
> For Messias it was who was shown
>   In the chariot mystically
> His Godhead and His Manhood
>   Appeared in the likenesses:
> Two aspects, one Person: two Natures, one Saviour.
> In the chariot His likeness and His mystery,
>   In His Gospel His sureness and His truth;
> His shadow in the chariot—His body behold in the Gospel!

JACOB of Sarug, 452-521, of whom the Syriac liturgies speak as "the most eloquent mouth and pillar of the Church," is reported to have employed seventy writers in making copies of his works. He was the author of a Liturgy, an *Order of Baptism,* an *Order of Confirmation,* and a number of Epistles. His poetical works include seven hundred and sixty Homiletic poems, some Hymns and Psalms. "In wealth of words and ease of expression he ranks next to Ephraim."

JOHN of Ephesus or of Asia, 505-590, deserves to be mentioned as the first Syrian Church historian, although he stands apart from the Catholic tradition as a Monophysite. His *History of the Church* "originally consisted of three parts of which the third only is known to be extant." In this third part he claims to have begun the story in "the times of Julius Caesar"; the record ends about the year 585.

PHILOXENUS, 460-525, also a Monophysite, was responsible for the *Philoxenian Syriac Version;* a rendering that is extremely literal. He was the writer of many books, and of many Letters. *The Incarnation of the Word of God,* and *The Trinity and the Incarnation,* maintained that the divine and the human elements were separate in the nature of Christ, in whom, PHILOXENUS asserted, there was but one nature and one will.

CHAPTER XII

THE SCHOOL OF CAPPADOCIA

When ORIGEN left Alexandria in 231, he settled at Caesarea in Cappadocia, where he established a school. There he won over to Christianity, THEODORUS, who is known to history as GREGORY THE WONDER-WORKER (Thaumaturgus), 210-270. GREGORY is not one of the great lights of Christian literature, but he has left a *Panegyric on Origen,* which gives a vivid picture of the great scholar and of his methods of teaching.

> In true Socratic fashion he sometimes overthrew us by argument, if he saw us restive and starting out of the course. . . . The process was at first disagreeable to us, and painful; but he so purified us . . . . and prepared us for the reception of the words of truth . . . . by probing us and questioning us, and offering problems for our solution . . . . there was no subject forbidden to us; nothing hidden or inaccessible. We were allowed to become acquainted with every doctrine, barbarian or Greek, or things spiritual or civil, divine or human. . . .

GREGORY'S *Metaphrase of Ecclesiastes* was useful in its day. It is a "singularly modest and sensible commentary" that may still be read "for its sound ethical wisdom." He also wrote an *Outline of the Faith,* and a *Canonical Letter.*

GREGORY THE ILLUMINATOR, 257-332, the "Sun" of Armenia, was most probably a disciple of this school; but his career is enveloped in mystery.

The fervent GREGORY of Nazianzen, 329-389, was a really representative Cappadocian. His friendship with BASIL was a vital influence in his life; but the teaching of ORIGEN had an even stronger power over his mind. He and BASIL made a collection of extracts from the writings of ORIGEN, to which they gave the name of the *Philocalia;* GREGORY also shared in the work of compiling the famous Rules which BASIL drew up for the regulation of monasteries.

Julian, "the apostate," had been a fellow student with GREGORY at Athens; but this fact did not prevent the theologian issuing two Invectives against the emperor's anti-Christian policy, 365. In one of his Orations he thus mockingly describes the visit of Julian to Eleusis:

> as my fine fellow proceeded in the rites, the frightful things assailed him, unearthly noises as they say, and unpleasant odours, and fiery apparitions, and other fables and nonsense of the sort. Being terror-struck at the novelty, ... he flies for help to the Cross, his old remedy, and makes the sign thereof against his terrors and makes an ally of him whom he persecuted. And what follows is yet more horrible.
>
> The seal prevailed: the demons are worsted: the terrors are allayed. And then, what follows? The wickedness revives: he takes courage again: the attempt is repeated, the same terrors return: again the sign of the Cross, and the vanishing demons: the neophyte in despair (Oration iv.).

After the accession of Theodosius, 379, GREGORY delivered his *Words of a Theologian,* or *Five Orations on the Trinity.* These Orations were defences of the Nicene creed against the Eunomian and Macedonian heresies. They are the finest expositions of Trinitarian doctrine produced by the Eastern Church. His other forty Orations are either eulogies of saints, or Sermons. These still retain part of the charm that originally held their hearers enthralled. The modernness of GREGORY'S thought may be seen in his words on the doctrine of the Holy Spirit.

> You see lights breaking upon us gradually; and the order of Theology, which it is better for us to keep, neither proclaiming things too suddenly, nor yet keeping them hidden to the end. For the former course would be unscientific, the latter atheistical. . . . I will add another point . . . . Our Saviour had some things which He said could not be borne at that time by His disciples. . . . And again He said that all things should be taught us by the Spirit when he should come to dwell amongst us. Of these things one, I take it, was the Deity of the Spirit himself, made clear later on, when such knowledge should be seasonable and capable of being received after our Saviour's restoration, when it would no longer be received with incredulity because of its marvellous character (Oration xxxi.).

In an *Apologetic for Himself,* 362, he defended his refusal of ordination, and discussed the duties and difficulties of the true pastor.

GREGORY'S Poems afford an "example of composition according with the literary taste of the latter part of the fourth century," but they are monotonous and without unity. They "illustrate the final failure of metrical Christian poetry in Greek." Their thirty thousand lines contain epigrams, elegies, and, most interesting of all, the poem entitled *His own Life.*

BASIL, 329-379, surnamed "the Great," who became the most famous of the Cappadocians, won an outstanding place in the literary history of Christianity. "In purity and perspicuity he surpasses most of the heathen as well as the Christian writers of his age."

He wrote *Against Eunomius,* 363; *On Baptism; On True Virginity; Renunciation of worldly Goods; The Ascetical Life; Faith, The Judgment of God; Monastic Institutions; Reproofs to delinquent Monks and Nuns* (a very early penitential) ; and a book on *Monastic Constitutions.*

The monastic life fascinated him; he tells the story of his own conversion to it, in one of his three hundred and sixty-five Letters.

> First of all, I was minded to make some mending of my ways, long perverted as they were by my intimacy with wicked men. Then I read the Gospel and I saw there that a great means of reaching perfection was the selling of one's goods, the sharing of them with the poor, the giving up of all care for this life, the refusal to allow the soul to be turned by any sympathy to the things of earth. And I prayed that I might find some one of the brethren who had chosen this way of life. . . . And many did I find . . . . I admired their continence in living, and their endurance in toil; I was amazed at their persistency in prayer, and at their triumphing over sleep . . . . in hunger, in thirst, in cold, in nakedness, they never yielded to the body. . . . And I prayed that I too, as far as in me lay, might imitate them (Epistle ccxxiii.).

His work on *The Holy Spirit,* 375, kept its reputation as a great exposition for many centuries: but the most celebrated of all his works is the series of nine Homilies on the six days of Creation as described in Genesis. This series is called *The Hexaemeron;* it is marked by a lucidity that made it clear to all, by a thoroughness that the wisest can admire, and by a wealth of allegory that made it very popular.

BASIL'S widest and most enduring influence, however,

sprang from his book on *Morals*, and his famous monastic Rules. The Liturgy ascribed to him is still used in the Eastern Church; but in its present form it is the growth of centuries.

GREGORY of Nyssa, 335-396, BASIL'S younger brother, turned to literature rather than to a public career, because of physical weakness and a retiring disposition, and he soon surpassed his teachers in the range of his intellectual interests and in constructive mental ability. He became the real successor of ORIGEN; a truly "Platonic Christian," who, like ORIGEN, tried to build a speculative philosophy on a Christian foundation.

He wielded a prolific pen, facile with clever comparisons and glittering rhetoric, but much given to exaggeration, digression, and prolixity. Notwithstanding these drawbacks in style, his writings were unsurpassed as clear and acute statements of doctrine.

In his interpretation of Scripture he was wholly given to allegorism; even his fundamental ideas were often fanciful, *e.g.* in his treatise on the *Creation of Man*, he proceeds on the theory that, before God, humanity is treated as an individual man; and in the *Superscriptions of the Psalms*, he maintains that the five books of the Psalter are five steps to moral perfectness.

His doctrinal works gave weighty answers to the opponents of the catholic creed; they now form one of the chief sources of knowledege of the heresies which they condemn. They included *Against Eunomius; To Ablavius against the Tritheists; On Faith against the Arians; Ten Syllogisms against the Manichaeans;* and *The Anti-heretic*, a work in opposition to the Apollinarians. GREGORY contradicted heathen superstitions in a book on *Fate*, and sought to enlighten educated non-Christians by giving them the *Larger Catechetical Oration*. In the preface to this Oration he says with broad-minded wisdom:

> . . . . the same method of teaching will not be suitable in the case of all who come to hear the word, but as the forms of religion vary, so also the instruction must be adapted to meet them. . . . For he who follows the Jewish religion starts from one set of preconceptions, and he who is born and bred in Hellenism starts from another. . . . You will not apply the same remedy to the polytheism of the Greek as you apply to the Jew's disbelief in the Only-begotten God, nor will you in the case of those who have gone astray among heresies use the same arguments in each case to overthrow their erroneous fancies . . . .

In an *Oration on the Deity of the Son and the Holy Spirit*, GREGORY gives a very lively picture of the stir caused by the Arian controversy.

> Why! to-day there are men, like those Athenians, who 'spend their time in nothing else but either to tell or to hear some new thing' . . . . You know quite well to whom I refer. With such the whole city is full; its smaller gates, forums, squares, thoroughfares; the clothiers, the money-lenders, the victuallers. Ask about pence, and he will discuss the Generate and the Ingenerate. Enquire the price of bread, he answers: Greater is the Father, and the Son is subject. Say that a bath will suit you, and he defines that the Son is made out of nothing.

AMPHILOCHUS of Iconium, fl. 374-394, belonged to the School of Cappadocia by right of his religious and critical orthodoxy, as well as by his close connection with GREGORY of Nazianzen. His *Letter to Seleucus*, giving the youth directions for the conduct of his studies and his life, is a poem characterised by graphic and effective descriptions. The three hundred and thirty-three lines of which it is composed are considered by the poet to be an appeal for love to the Trinity.

The "Melodist" ROMANOS, fl. 491-525, who carried the Greek accentual hymn to its perfection, may be remembered here. He received credit for writing a thousand Hymns of the type known as *contakia,* an invention of his own. These stately Hymns are not brief, simple songs, but magnificent narrative poems, rich in feeling, stately in expression, frequently marked with dramatic power. ROMANOS was "the greatest poet of the Byzantine age and perhaps the greatest ecclesiastical poet of any age."[1]

---

[1] H. O. Taylor, *The Classical Heritage of the Middle Ages,* pp. 260-262.

CHAPTER XIII

THE SCHOOL OF ANTIOCH

A theological School was organised at Antioch and taught by the presbyter Malchion, during the episcopate of PAUL of Samosata, 260-272. PAUL was a brilliant, but a morally disagreeable man; a favourite and courtier of Queen Zenobia. He represented the high-water mark of theological speculation in his day, but his views brought him into disrepute and the neglect of his writings has resulted in their practical destruction.

The "Celebrated Chronographer," JULIUS AFRICANUS, 175-242, whom some regard as among the most learned of early Christian writers, was a forerunner of the school and an early representative of the scientific spirit that ruled its interpretation of Scripture. The School of Alexandria may be regarded as the headquarters of the allegorists; the School of Antioch made historical exposition the cardinal point of its teaching.

JULIUS AFRICANUS was essentially a historical critic. In a *Letter to Origen concerning the Apocryphal Book of Susannah,* he offers several proofs that the work is 'spurious.' This Letter is the only complete work of his now extant; but parts of a *Letter to Aristides* exist, and there are a few fragments of his 'accurately laboured' *Chronology.* Both these works are evidences of his interest in the historical setting of the Christian faith and in the historical interpretation of the New Testament records.

The School of Antioch emerges into the light of dependable tradition under the headship of LUCIAN, 240-312, a rare scholar after ORIGEN'S own heart. He was a native of

Samosata; he studied at Edessa, and going thence to Antioch, he there became head of the School.

His chief work in literature was the revision of the Syrian Text of the New Testament; in conjunction with his colleague DOROTHEUS, he prepared a revised edition of the *Septuagint*, which became so popular as to receive the name of the *Vulgate*—a name now universally given to the Latin version by JEROME.

Under his influence the School of Antioch became the nursery of the Arian doctrine; "many of the Arians and Semi-Arians were his pupils, and did not consciously deviate from his teaching." He fostered the historical temper; followed the inductive method, and reverenced Aristotle. Among his well known disciples were Eusebius of Nicomedia, Menophantis of Ephesus, Theognis of Nicaea, Maris of Chalcedon, Leontius of Antioch, Athanasius of Anazarbus, Asterius the sophist, and Arius the arch-heretic. These appealed to him as an authority in doctrine, calling themselves Collucianists.

The great period of the School began when DIODORUS of Tarsus, 330-394, became its leader. If not the founder, he was "the chief promoter of the rational school of Scriptural interpretation of which his disciples, CHRYSOSTOM and THEODORE and THEODORET were such distinguished representatives."

DIODORUS was equally vigorous as an antagonist of Arianism as he was of the heathenism that Julian attempted to re-establish. His writings roused the Emperor to upbraid him as "the great Nazarene" who had "deserted the philosophy of Athens for the boorish theology of fishermen."

Most of his writings were works of controversy, against Jews, pagans or heretics; the others were expositions of doctrine and Scripture. They have all perished; his Arian opponents burned sixty of his books, and time and neglect have destroyed the rest, with the exception of a few fragments.

JOHN of Antioch, 345-407, surnamed CHRYSOSTOM, is not only the most illustrious member of the School of Antioch, but also the most famous of the Greek fathers, the greatest of the old Greek preachers, and perhaps the most popular orator of the Eastern Church. He is the outstanding figure in the first of the four great controversies that disturbed the relations between the Churches of Antioch and Alexandria during the fifth century.

His life has been divided into five epochs[2] "(a) His life as a layman at Antioch till his baptism and admission as a reader, A. D. 347-370; (b) his ascetic and monastic life, A. D. 370-381; (c) his career as deacon, presbyter and preacher at Antioch, A. D. 381-398; (d) his episcopate at Constantinople, A. D. 398-404; (e) exile, A. D. 404-407."

CHRYSOSTOM won his reputation as a preacher when he delivered *Twenty-one Sermons on the Statues*, 387, after the mob had destroyed some statues of the Emperor and expected drastic punishment.   These Sermons make one of the most remarkable series of discourses of which the history of preaching has any record.   They are models of the purest cast.   "Neither Cicero nor Demosthenes ever produced greater, or more elevated, or more lasting effects on their hearers than St. Chrysostom . . . ."

His Homilies, which number over six hundred, reveal the "art of engaging the passions in the service of virtue, and of exposing the folly as well as the turpitude of vice, almost with the truth and spirit of a dramatic representation." Thus in *Homily xiii.*:

> What a day did we see last Wednesday. . . .   This was the day when that fearful tribunal was set in the city, and shook the hearts of all, and made the day seem no better than the night . . . .

_____
[2] *Dictionary of Christian Biography.*   Vol. I., p. 518.

These things then beholding, I cast in my mind 'That Dread Tribunal'; and I said within myself, 'If now, when men are the judges, neither mother, nor sister, nor father, nor any other person, though guiltless of the deeds which have been perpetrated, can avail to rescue the criminals, who will stand by us when we are judged at the Dread Tribunal of Christ? Who will dare to raise his voice? Who will be able to rescue those who shall be led away to such unspeakable punishments?'

In a work entitled *The Priesthood,* written to excuse his avoidance of the bishopric in 370, he pictured his life as a monk in the desert, with all its advantages above the anxious life of an overseer of the Church. This book is reckoned among the ablest, the most instructive, and the most eloquent of all his writings. He wrote *Against the Opponents of the Monastic Life,* 374; a short treatise entitled *A Comparison of the King and the Monk,* 374; and also *Two Letters to a Young Widow;* in all of which he extolled the life of the desert. During his years of exile he published the stoical treatise, *No One Is Injured except by Himself;* and an Apology, *To Those Who Are Scandalised by Adversity.*

The *Expositions of Scripture,* for which he is most celebrated, and which covered the whole of the Bible, are not all extant. Those which do remain exhibit all the characteristic qualities of the Antiochene method of interpretation; the sound historical temper, the grammatical criticism, and the healthy common sense, which served as a necessary antidote to excessive allegorism.

THEODORE of Mopsuestia, 350-428, although a less popular figure than Chrysostom, was a more independent thinker and a more important theologian. He applied the historical method of Biblical interpretation more thoroughly than any member of the School, but his style was prosaic and monotonous.

As the real founder of the Nestorian heresy, his work is best considered in connection with that teaching. His book on *The Person of Christ against Apollinarius of Laodicœa*, like his criticisms of the title of "the mother of God," applied to Mary, was sober, thoughtful, and essentially ethical. He crossed swords with AUGUSTINE in a work called *The Teaching that Men Sin by Nature and Not by Consent*.

His brother POLYCHRONIUS of Apamea, d. 430, is known only by fragments of Expositions, which show how well he followed the traditions of the School. An *Exposition of Ezekiel* is the only one of his works that exists in anything like completeness. His style is clear and concise, contrasting favourably with the loose and complex manner of THEODORE. "His maner of exposition is scholarly and serious, breathing at the same time an air of deep piety."

It remains to recall the name of THEODORET, 386-458, whose theological sympathies were also with the school of his native city. Surrounded by gnostics, sympathetic towards Nestorians, and unwilling to subscribe to the creed of Nicæa; he was bound to justify his own views. He wrote a *Refutation of Cyril's Twelve Anathemata of Nestorius*, 430; three Dialogues, against CYRIL'S teaching, under the title *Eranistes*, 446,—a "work of remarkable interest and of permanent value for theological students," and an Apology for Christianity; which consisted of ten addresses on Providence. These addresses show THEODORET'S "literary power in its highest form, as regards the careful selection of thoughts, the nobility of his language, the elegance and purity of his style, and the force and sequence of his arguments."

In praise of primitive Christianity, and in opposition to "Hellenism" he wrote *On Curing the Influence of the Greeks*, 438, the last and most perfect of the Graeco-Christian Apologies. His greatest controversial work is that entitled *The Epitome of False-fabled Heresies*, 451; this covers an immense variety of anti-Catholic doctrines and is therefore still valuable to the student of dogma. In the last of its five books, THEODORET enumerates the chief articles of the Christian faith and of the moral law, as the best defence against heresy.

PART IV
THE DEFINITION OF THE FAITH
(A. D. 300-800)

CHAPTER XIV

THE MAKING OF THE CREED

Among the pupils of LUCIAN of Antioch, was a clever and influential presbyter, ARIUS, 256-336, whose ministry in Alexandria was first disturbed by his support of Meletius of Lycopolis in an attack on the prevailing views about episcopacy; and next, and much more seriously, by his attempt to simplify the doctrine of the person of Christ.

ALEXANDER, bishop of Alexandria, entered into this doctrinal dispute, but laid himself open to the charge of being a Sabellian, by some of the passages contained in a charge to his clergy, 318, on the subject of the Unity of the Godhead. Thus began the heresy of Arianism with which the Church was convulsed for nearly a century.

ARIUS put his opinions into writing in a Letter to EUSEBIUS of Nicomedia, in the course of which he declares:

. . . . we say, and believe, and have taught, and do teach, that the Son is not begotten, nor in any way part of the Unbegotten; and that He does not derive His subsistence from any matter; but that by His own will and counsel He has subsisted before time, and before ages as perfect God, only-begotten and unchangeable.

And that He existed not, before He was begotten, or created, or purposed, or established. For He was not unbegotten.

These statements were modified in a Letter to ALEX-
ANDER:

> We acknowledge One God, . . . who begat an
> Only-begotten Son before eternal times, . . . and begat
> Him, not in semblance, but in truth; and that He made
> him to subsist at His own will, unalterable and un-
> changeable; perfect creature of God, but not as one of
> the creatures; offspring but not as one of things be-
> gotten.

This, as ATHANASIUS afterwards said, "is a part of what
ARIUS and his fellows vomited from their heretical hearts."

The only other writing of his in existence consists of
fragments of *Thalia* (a good feast), a semi-poetical miscellany that became immensely popular, so that the streets and
wharves rang with snatches of it. PHILOSTORGIUS, the
Arian historian, says that "Arius wrote songs for the sea
and for the mill and for the road, and then set them to suitable music," but these have perished. The relics of the
Thalia, exist as disjointed quotations, such as:

> The Unbegun made the Son a beginning of things
> originated;
> And advanced Him as a Son to Himself by adoption.

> He has nothing proper to God in proper subsistence.
> For He is not equal, no, nor one in essence with Him.

> Foreign from the Son in essence is the Father,
> For He is without beginning.

> At God's will the Son is what and whatsoever He is.
> And when and since He was, from that time He has
> subsisted from God.

This was the fuel of the controversial fire that raged
throughout the Church. The heresy was a clerics' heresy, a

diluted hellenism tempered by Scripture. It was condemned by the Council of Alexandria, 321, and ARIUS was deposed; his writings were publicly burned, and even to possess them was made a capital offence.

Feeling ran high; the Church was divided; Constantine therefore, for political reasons, and in the interest of the unity and peace of the empire, convened the first ecumenical Council to meet at Nicæa in 325. The Council gave rise to much literature which is dominated by the name of ATHANASIUS.

ATHANASIUS, 295-373, had already published an Apology entitled *Against the Nations,* 318, and a Treatise, *The Incarnation of the Word,* 318, before he attended his Bishop ALEXANDER to the Council. Thenceforward until his death, the literary history of the definition of the Creed is the history of his writings. He was an author by necessity rather than by choice; he wrote with the simple directness of a man of action; but his work has a studied finish, which, with its verve, keenness, and occasional glints of humour, places it among the most readable of the writings of the Greek Fathers.

The Incarnation of the Word ranks as one of the most brilliant pamphlets of early Christian times. It covers the whole subject from the creation of man to the promise of the second advent of Christ, with well reasoned and persuasive argument.

> For as, when the likeness painted on a panel has been effaced by stains from without, he whose likeness it is must needs come once more to enable the portrait to be renewed on the same wood . . . . in the same way also the most holy Son of the Father, being the Image of the Father came to our region to renew man once made in His likeness.

The list of the writings of ATHANASIUS is a long one.

His first anti-Arian work was an *Encyclical* on the *Deposition of Arius,* this was followed by an *Exposition of the Faith,* 328, which ends with the passage:

> The Father, possessing His existence from Himself, begat the Son, as we said, and did not create Him, as a river from a well and as a branch from a root, and as brightness from a light, things which nature knows to be indivisible; through whom to the Father be glory and power and greatness before all ages, and unto all the ages of the ages. Amen.

Each year of his episcopal office, 328-335, was the occasion of a *Festal Letter* written at Easter to his clergy. Midway through the "golden decade" of his career, 346-356, he produced a *Defence against the Arians,* "the most authentic source of the history of the Church in the first half of the fourth century." This *Defence* was written to counteract the efforts of the semi-Arian or Eusebian party; it contains a number of documents of prime importance for the years 327-347. Before his third exile, 356, he sent forth a *Defence of the Nicene Formula,* with a *Letter to Eusebius* as an Appendix.

During exile ATHANASIUS was in close touch with the monks of the Nitrian desert, and under their influence he wrote the fantastic but noble *Life of Anthony,* one of the founders of Christian monachism.

In a strong *Apology to Constantius,* 357, ATHANASIUS next defended himself against four serious charges; viz., that he had poisoned the mind of Constans against the Emperor; that he had written to the "tyrant" Magnentius; that he had celebrated the Easter festival of 355 in a new unconsecrated Church; that he had disobeyed an imperial order to go to Italy. His *Defence of his Flight,* 357, was an answer to the charges of Leontius of Antioch and George of Laodicaea, who attributed his escape to cowardice, because forsooth when I was sought by them I did not surrender myself into their hands.

His third exile, 356-360, gave him leisure also for the production of four solid *Orations against the Arians.* Hitherto the controversy had been largely a personal and a political one; the doctrinal issue now began to be emphasised, and the various parties sought to define their views. In the four Orations, ATHANASIUS tried to focus these definitions and to score a doctrinal victory by discrediting his critics. "They gather up all the threads of controversy against Arianism proper, refute its appeal to Scripture, and leave on record for all time the issues of the great doctrinal contest of the fourth century."[1]

In *The Councils of Ariminum and Seleucia,* 359, commonly referred to as *The Synods,* he held out the olive branch of peace to his old conservative enemies. The three parts of this work form a "worthy conclusion of the anti-Arian writings which are the legacy and the record of the most stirring and eventful period of the noble life of (the) great bishop."[2]

The victory of orthodoxy at the Council of Nicæa, 325, brought about inevitable reactions. Two pupils of ARIUS, Valens of Nursia, 300-373, who led the Arians of the West, and Ursacius of Singidunum from the East, were bitter opponents of ATHANASIUS. Theognis of Nicæa, made a desperate effort on behalf of ARIUS at the Council of Tyre, 335, and EUSEBIUS of Nicomedia, 260-342, did his utmost to render the decision of Nicæa null and void.

EUSEBIUS gathered around himself a company of those who were bent on the overthrow of ATHANASIUS. ASTERIUS of Petra stood forth as the spokesman of early Arianism, thereby moving MARCELLUS of Ancyra, who had supported ATHANASIUS at the Council, to write a reply which brought about his own deposition by the Synod of Constantinople, 336.

---

[1] *Select Writings of Athanasius,* ed. by Archibald Robertson, p. 303.
[2] *Ibid.* p. 450.

EUSEBIUS of Caesarea justified the decision of the Synod in a work, *Against Marcellus Bishop of Ancyra,* 336. This is a simple exposition of the views which had been condemned. It claims that the teaching of MARCELLUS was based upon malice, mistaken readings of Scripture, and hopelessly bad exegesis. It reduces his doctrine to this: he "confesses neither beginning nor end of the Son of God in accordance with piety."

In a later work, *The Theology of the Church, a Refutation of Marcellus,* EUSEBIUS set himself definitely to controvert the teaching which his earlier book had exposed. His vehement hatred of Arianism had led MARCELLUS into the heresy of Sabellius, and EUSEBIUS charges this against him again and again.

The attack was justified by the subsequent action of MARCELLUS when he joined his pupil PHOTINUS, whose book entitled *Against All Heresies,* was so offensive to the Arians as to lead them to depose him in 351.

ACACIUS was both a writer and a patron of literature; he succeeded his teacher EUSEBIUS of Caesarea as bishop of that city in 340, and, two years later, became the leader of the Semi-Arians on the death of EUSEBIUS of Nicomedia.

Unfortunately his *Life of Eusebius the Historian,* has perished; fragments of a *Reply to Marcellus of Ancyra,* exist in the work of EPIPHANUS on Heresies; but neither his *Commentary on Ecclesiastes,* nor his other writings remain.

CYRIL of Jerusalem, 315-386, is an outstanding representative of the rise and growth of Semi-Arianism. He keeps his place in literary history because of the eighteen *Catechetical Lectures* delivered while he was still a catechist, 347. These are the earliest existing examples of anything in the shape of a formal system of theology. They are valuable as historical documents because of their testimony to the canon of Scripture, to the prevailing views on the main articles of the Creed, and because they reflect the ritual usages of the fourth century.

CYRIL'S lectures to the baptised are also extant; they bear the title of the five *Mystagogical Lectures.*

It is only just to him to remember that at the Council of Constantinople he declared his agreement with the Nicene Creed, and his acceptance of its test word, Homoousion. His works "do not rank at all high . . . and few would care to read them for their own sake; nor has CYRIL any claim to a place among the masters of Christian thought, whose writings form the permanent riches of the church."

The traditions of Christian literature outside the immediate interests of the doctrinal issue were maintained by LUCIUS CAELIUS LACTANTIUS of Firmium (Firmum), 260-340. He was one of the most learned men of his age, a rhetorician not a theologian, the master of an exquisite Latin style, on account of which he was called the Christian Cicero. In his youth he gained fame by a metrical *Symposium,* composed of a hundred riddles. After his conversion he wrote a "most beautiful" treatise entitled *The Wrath of God,* to refute the teaching of the Epicureans and the Stoics by showing that anger is as possible to God as pity. His great work *The Divine Institutes,* 305-310, is at once an Apology, a manual of theology, and an introduction to the Christian religion, intended to complete or to supersede the less elaborate treatises of MINUCIUS FELIX, TERTULLIAN, and CYPRIAN.

This fine work is in two main divisions, of which the first makes an exposure of false religion in the three treatises: *False Religion; The Origin of Error;* and *False Wisdom.* The second part of the book contains an exposition of true religion in four treatises: *True Wisdom and Religion; Justice; The True Cultus;* and *The Blessed Life.*

All the wisdom of man consists in this alone, the knowledge and worship of God: this is our tenet, this

our opinion. Therefore with all the power of my voice
I testify, I proclaim, I declare: Here, here is that which
all philosophers have sought throughout their whole
life; and yet, they have not been able to investigate, to
grasp, and to attain to it, because they either retained
a religion which was corrupt, or took it away altogether.

LACTANTIUS also wrote *The Workmanship of God*, 304,
a treatise of the human body which "may challenge comparison with Cicero's *De Natura Deorum* in point of style,
and is far superior to it in depth and originality." He compressed the substance of his *Divine Institutes* into single book
which he called *The Epitome*, 315. In a historical apology
entitled *The Manner in which the Persecutors died*, 314, he
gave examples of the calamities that had befallen the Imperial
enemies of the Faith (page 42).

"Among the papyri discovered at Oxyrhynchus during
the last few years was found a fragment on which was written part of a Christian hymn, music as well as words, which
was judged to date from about the year 300. The following
is the translation:

> Of the light of the dawn let nought be silent,
> Nor let the bright stars be wanting in praise.
> Let all the fountains of the rivers lift up their song
> To the Father and Son and to the Holy Spirit.
> So let all powers on earth cry aloud, cry aloud Amen, Amen.
> Might and honour, glory and praise to God,
> Only Giver of all that is good.   Amen, Amen."

Among other names to be recalled from those stormy times
is that of NONNUS of Panopolis, a city of the Egyptian The-
baid. In his pre-Christian days he had written a poem entitled the *Dionysiaca*, describing the birth, conquests and
apotheosis of Dionysius. The poem may have been intended
as "an allegory of the march of civilization across the ancient world" or merely as a description of "the gradual estab-

lishment of the cultivation of the vine and the power of the Wine-God."

His *Paraphrase of the Fourth Gospel,* faithfully reproduces the whole text, with poetical expansions to vivify the scenes or to interpret the emotions of the actors. The florid style and exuberant fancy of NONNUS made his work influential with later writers even down to the sixteenth century.

The chief of all the Greek Christian poets was SYNESIUS of Cyrene, 373-414, who, although not a great poet, "attempted with success a style of poetry of which . . . . hardly any previous examples" exist. He has spiritual fervour and exaltation, his odes are rich in rapture, with the note of ecstasy that belongs to neo-Platonism rather than to Christianity.

SYNESIUS was a genuine bookman:

> I have lessened my estates, and many of my slaves have bought their freedom from me, I have no money in women's ornaments or in coin, but I have many more books to leave than I inherited.

The manifold interests of his life are interestingly pictured in the one hundred and fifty-six Letters which remain from his correspondence; but his Christian Hymns are the most important of his works.

> For what are strength and beauty,
> And what are gold and fame,
> And what are kingly honours,
> Compared with thoughts of God.
> Let others drive the chariot,
> Let others bend the bow,
> Let others heap up riches,
> And hug the joy of gold.
> Be mine to lead unnoticed
> A life remote from care,
> Unknown indeed to others,
> But not unknown to God.

CHAPTER XV

THE DISCUSSION OF THE CREED

The definition of the Creed at Nicæa produced a series of 'heresies', each with its own literature. Viewed from the standpoint of the history of doctrine, these heresies were theological discussions that led to definiteness of thought and carefulness of statement. During their lifetime they were symptoms of an unrest that the Nicene settlement had failed to banish; they indicated that the Faith may be a variety in unity, that a catholic creed need not restrain liberty of thought. As a matter of fact "the eighteen or more creeds, which Arianism and semi-Arianism produced between the first and the second Oecumenical Councils (325-381), are leaves without blossoms and branches without fruit." [1]

AETIUS, carrying the views of Arius to their logical issue, affirmed that the Son is *unlike* the Father. His chequered career of adventure brought him at length to the study of philosophy, and with him "the strife between Aristotelianism and Platonism among theologians seems to have begun."

Several of his theological Letters are known. EPIPHANIUS records and refutes forty-seven of the three hundred heretical propositions which AETIUS laid down.

His renowned pupil and secretary EUNOMIUS, 330-393, became the most powerful champion of his doctrines. He defined and arranged the teaching of AETIUS, to which he added the weight of a moral earnestness, a pure life, and a singularly fine character.

As a writer he was more copious than elegant, but his works gained a great reputation among his followers, and

---

[1] *Dictionary of Christian Biography*, Vol. I., p. 156.

in spite of their obscurity of style and weakness of argument were much dreaded by the orthodox party. His *Defence*, 363, which has been recovered from BASIL'S celebrated and elaborate *Refutation* of it, is his most famous work; it was intended to refute the Nicene doctrine of the Trinity. He outlined his doctrine in *The Exposition of the Faith*, 383, which he submitted to Theodosius. BASIL'S attack upon him in the *Refutation* provoked him to prepare *A Defence of my Defence*, of the value of which he seems to have been very doubtful. All that remains of this exists in the passages which are quoted by GREGORY of Nyssa, who, according to PHO-TIUS, "treated the wretched thing with the contumely it deserved."

The writings of EUNOMIUS are illustrations of the matter-of-fact literalism of a purely intellectual theology, which would be called rationalism to-day. As the result of various Imperial edicts most of them have been destroyed. GREGORY of Nyssa preserves the scanty relics in his refutation entitled *Against Eunomius*, in which he blackens his opponent's character as much as possible.

A somewhat less rationalistic literalism appeared in *Two Dialogues*, written by MACEDONIUS, one of the leaders of the semi-Arian party.

HILARY of Poitiers, d. 368, championed the orthodox cause against the Arians in Gaul, and against the semi-Arians in Phrygia. His earliest work was an appeal to Constantius, 355, for the protection of the orthodox against Arian perse-cution. It sounds the note of liberty of conscience.

> God has taught men the knowledge of Himself; He has not exacted it. By His wonderful and heavenly operations, He wins authority for His precepts, and re-jects a will that only confesses Him perforce. If force of that sort were employed to promote true religion, the teaching of a bishop would go out to meet it and

say: 'He does not need service under stress of necessity: He does not want worship under compulsion . . .
A man must seek God in singleness of heart; get to
know Him in worship; love Him in charity; revere
Him with fear, and hold fast to Him by uprightness
of purpose.

A second *Appeal* to the Emperor, 360, was a protestation
of innocence of the charges for which he had suffered exile.
HILARY laments the controversies concerning the Faith:

It is a thing equally deplorable and dangerous that
there are as many creeds as opinions among men, as
many doctrines as inclinations, and as many sources
of blasphemy as there are faults among us, because we
make creeds arbitrarily and explain them arbitrarily.

These appeals failed of their purpose. HILARY therefore
changed his tone, and in a Letter to the bishops of Gaul,
Against Constantius, 360, expressed both anger and scorn.

HILARY'S great work is *The Trinity*, 350, otherwise
known as *Against the Arians*, or, *On the Faith*. This is the
first important contribution, in Latin, to the discussion of
the doctrine of the Godhead. It begins with a consideration
of natural religion as the preparation for revelation; thence
it proceeds to expound the baptismal formula, the union of
the two natures in Christ, the unity of His person, and the
prophetic forecasts of these truths. The various heresies of
the day are refuted; "Their quarrel is our faith." The unity
of the Godhead is then upheld, and, finally, there is a careful
discussion of the texts to which the Arians appealed.

In this important book, at once bold and charitable, there
is a longer, more methodical, and more consecutive anti-
Arian argument than even Athanasius himself had found
time to write.

From his place of exile HILARY sent to the bishops of Gaul

an eirenicon *The Synods of the Catholic Faith against Arians and Those Who Agree with the Prevaricators among the Arians*, 358. This work is also known as *The Faith of the Easterns, The Synods of the Greeks*, or simply as *An Epistle*. His book *Against Auxentius*, 365, led to his own dismissal from Milan. During his exile he wrote a letter to his daughter Abra respecting marriage and enclosed a Morning and an Evening Hymn. Like his *Book of Hymns* the latter is lost, but the Morning Hymn, "Lucis largitor splendide," is one of the choice treasures of Latin Hymnody.

FOEGADIUS of Agen, 315-393, a less important man than HILARY wrote as a Catholic *Against the Arians*. A few other orthodox treatises, *The Orthodox Faith against the Arians*, and *A Book of the Faith*, numbered among the Orations of GREGORY Nazianzen, also belong to FOEGADIUS.

A second discussion of the Creed is associated with the name of APOLLINARIUS (or APOLLINARIS), d. 390, a notable man of letters, whose writing was so extensively plagiarised that LEONTIUS of Byzantium, 485-543, issued a protest against the practice: *Against Those Who Offer Us Certain Works of Apollinarius Having Falsely Inscribed Them with the Names of Holy Fathers*. He gave credit to APOLLINARIUS for *The Partial Faith*, a work usually attributed to GREGORY THAUMATURGUS; for *The Incarnation of the Son of God*, often ascribed to the pseudo-Athanasius; and also for the *Union of the Body and the Divinity of Christ*, commonly accredited to the pseudo-JULIUS of Rome.

Some most difficult questions of Christian pseudepigraphy are therefore connected with the name of APOLLINARIUS. His fame does not rest on these questionable writings however, but on his views of the person of Christ. Accepting the division of human nature into body, soul, and spirit, he attributed a human body and soul to Christ, but claimed that the Logos took the place of the human spirit. This doctrine opened "the long line of Christological controversies, which resulted in the Chalcedonian symbol."

Only fragments remain of the works of APOLLINARIUS of which the names are known, and these fragments only exist in the writings of those who undertook to refute him. He is more favourably known as the collaborator with his father in the effort to rewrite the Scriptures in classical forms when Julian forbade Christians to study Greek literature, 362.

THEODORE of Mopsuestia, 350-428, must be held responsible for the beginning of the third important discussion of the Creed. His protest against calling the mother of Jesus, 'the mother of God,' started NESTORIUS, d. 451, on his career of controversy. "In THEODORE'S writings, indeed, can be traced all the principles of Nestorianism, of which he is the real founder." This heresy was a product of the principles of the School of Antioch, in opposition to Apollinarianism.

NESTORIUS was a disciple of THEODORE, and celebrated for his eloquence and austerity. His writing began with an orthodox statement in *The Merchandise of Heraclides of Damascus*—his own story and apology. Other works of his, *Theopaschites*, and his autobiography entitled *The Tragedy, or Letters to Cosmos*, are now lost; so also is his *Incarnation of the Lord*, in which he commented upon sixty-two passages of Scripture, giving them interpretations favourable to his teaching.

The outstanding and relentless antagonist of NESTORIUS was CYRIL of Alexandria, 376-444, "a character not only unamiable, but singularly deficient in the graces of the Christian life." He represented in his own vehement and self-assertive way the School of Alexandria in its opposition to the School of Antioch.

His friend and mentor ISIDORE of Pelusium, d. 440, was a candid critic:

> Sympathy does not see distinctly; but antipathy does not see at all. If then you would be clear of both sorts of blearness of vision, do not indulge in violent negations, but submit any charges made against you to a just judgment . . . . Many of those who were assembled at Ephesus speak satirically of you as a man bent on pursuing his private animosities, not as one who has at heart the cause of Jesus Christ.

Contests with the Novatians, the Jews, and JOHN CHRYSOSTOM, prepared CYRIL for the main controversy of his life—the long struggle with NESTORIUS. Although his style lacks elegance and eloquence, and is often tedious and sometimes obscured, CYRIL takes high rank as a dogmatic theologian; his precise and rigid definitions of orthodoxy are perfect reflections of his firm convictions.

In 429 he dealt with Nestorianism in his *Easter Letter;* in a longer Letter addressed to all who within his jurisdiction were "practising the solitary life," he defended the title "Mother of God" as meaning "Mother of the manhood of Him who being in the form of God assumed the form of a servant" and suffered the death of the Cross. He wrote three *Letters to Nestorius;* the second of which acquired high authority as a symbolic treatise; the third contained twelve anathemas to which NESTORIUS was invited to subscribe and thus escape condemnation.

> seeing that thou hast given offence to the universal Church, and hast cast the leaven of a novel and strange heresy among the people . . . . (for copies of thy sermons have been circulated everywhere), what satisfactory account can any longer be given of our silence, or how are we not bound to remember Christ's words. 'Think not that I am come to send peace on the

earth' . . . . For when the Faith is being tampered
with, perish reverence for parents, as a thing unseason-
able and pregnant with mischief, and let the law of
natural affection to children and brethren be set aside,
and let religious men count death better than life, that,
as it is written, they may obtain a better resurrection.

He wrote an *Apology for the twelve Anathemas;* and a
work *Against Nestorius,* 430, in which "he comments on
passages in NESTORIUS'S Sermons, and by all forms of argument and illustration sets forth the question really at stake:
Had the Divine Son Himself become incarnate, or had He
closely allied Himself to a man?" He drew up against his
own opponents *Twelve Anathematisms,* of the justice of
which he later issued a Defence. His *Thesaurus* is a work on
the Trinity, written with remarkable lucidity in the form
of a dialogue. In *The Right Way,* he made an elaborate
survey of former heresies for the information of the Emperor
Theodosius. He disclaimed any sympathy with Apollinarianism in *A Reply to the Easterns.* Besides these works he
wrote many expositions, apologetic works and mystical
treatises, *e.g. Worshipping in Spirit and in Truth.*

The *Liturgy of St. Mark,* in its present form, may have
come from CYRIL'S hand; the invocation of the Spirit is
looked upon by some as certainly being his:

the very Paraclete, the Spirit of Truth, the Holy, the
Lord, the Life-giving; Who spake in the Law and by
the Prophets and the Apostles . . . One in His nature,
Manifold in His Energies, Fountain of Divine graces;
Consubstantial with Thee, Proceeding from Thee,
Fellow-sharer in the throne of Thy Kingdom, and of
Thine Only-begotten Son, our Lord and God and
Saviour Jesus Christ.

The Coptic Church was the scene of the activity of
EUTYCHES, 380-456, whose championship of orthodoxy

against NESTORIUS, aroused suspicion of his own views. The charges against him were serious enough to engage the attention of the 'Robber' synod of Ephesus, 449, and he was acquitted. "The Christian world was rent in pieces" until, in 451, the Council of Chalcedon declared against him after the *Tome of* LEO the Great, Bishop of Rome, had been read.

> Having read your letter, dearly beloved Brother, at the tardiness of which we were surprised, and having had the proceedings of the Episcopal Synod explained to us, we now understand the scandal which had arisen among you touching the orthodox faith. What before was obscure is now manifest. And Eutyches, who bore the honoured title of Presbyter, is shown to be exceedingly foolish and ignorant . . . . For what can be more iniquitous than to be wise toward impiety, and to refuse to yield to those who are wiser and more learned than himself? But men fall into this folly, when, on being prevented by some obscurity from becoming acquainted with the truth, they have recourse, not to the writings of the Prophets, not to the Epistles of the Apostles, not to the authority of the Gospels, but to themselves, and thus become teachers of error because they have not been disciples of the truth.

This *Tome,* belongs to the year 449, but was not read at the 'Robber' synod. After being read and adopted at Chalcedon, it gained an authority almost equal to a Creed; some readers looked upon it as a miraculous work, corrected by the apostle Peter himself. It is in two parts: one part is a dogmatic Epistle to Flavian; "a masterly, profound and clear analysis of the orthodox doctrine of the two natures in one person"; the other part is an Address to the Council of Ephesus.

LEO'S literary activity was constant and varied; he persuaded CASSIAN to write on *The Incarnation*, 429; his own *Letters to Turribus of Astorgia*, 441, brought about the condemnation of the Spanish Priscillianists; his Sermons gave him the rank of the first great preacher of the Roman Church. Ninety-six Sermons exist; they are marked by a rather ambitious style—brilliant, antithetical and full of memorable phrases.

> These are the men through whom the light of Christ's Gospel shone on thee, O Rome, and through whom thou, who wast the teacher of error, was made the disciple of Truth. These are thy holy Fathers and true shepherds, who gave thee claims to be numbered among the heavenly kingdoms, and built thee under much better and happier auspices than they by whose zeal the first foundations of thy walls were laid; and of whom the one that gave thee thy name defiled thee with his brother's blood . . . (Sermon lxxxii. Feast of St. Peter and St. Paul).

The decision of Chalcedon, which steered a middle course between the heresies of NESTORIUS and of EUTYCHES, under the direction of LEO'S *Tome*, displeased many whose objections soon threw both Church and Empire into confusion. TIMOTHY AELURUS (the cat), 400-477, became the accepted leader of the Monophysites, who insisted upon the one nature of Christ. He described his own undiluted orthodoxy in a *Refutation of the view sustained at Chalcedon*.

The bitter strife engendered by this form of ultra-loyalty to the Nicene symbol was practical rather than literary, but it led to the publication of the EMPEROR ZENO'S *Henoticon*, 482. This document was a plea for the general acceptance of the decisions of the three Councils, Nicæa, Constantinople I, and Ephesus.

> The Emperor Caesar Zeno, pious, victorious, triumphant, supreme, ever-worshipful Augustus, to the most

reverend bishops and clergy, and to the monks and laity throughout Alexandria, Egypt, Libya and Pentapolis.

Being assured that the origin and constitution, the might and invisible defence of our sovereignty is the only right and true faith, which, through divine inspiration, the three hundred and eighteen holy Fathers assembled at Nicaea set forth, and the hundred and fifty holy Fathers who, in like manner met at Constantinople, confirmed; we night and day employ every means of prayer, of zealous pains, and of laws, that the holy Catholic and Apostolic Church in every place may be multiplied, the incorruptible and immortal mother of our sceptre.

The declaration of faith following this preamble, was acceptable to neither party; it divided the Monophysites into two camps, and opened a breach between Rome and Constantinople that remained unhealed for thirty-five years.

JOHN MAXENTIUS, fl. 520, Metropolitan of the Province of Scythia, represented the monks of his Province in an effort to state the faith in such a way as to exclude both the Nestorian and the Eutychian heresies. He drew up in their name an explanation of their faith, *On Professing Christ;* but this did not prove to be acceptable in Rome whither it was taken. Later he wrote a striking *Reply to the Letter of Hormisdas,* a *Profession of Faith,* and a brief *Reason for the Uniting of the Word of God to Peculiar Flesh.*

The Emperor Heraclius attempted to heal the schism; his chief helper was SERGIUS of Constantinople, fl. 610-638, whose *Ecthesis (Exposition) of the Faith* he published as his own in 638. This document concealed rather than removed the differences in the Church; it gave rise to the heresy of Monothelism, and was withdrawn by Constans II, ten years later.

HONORIUS of Rome, addressed two Letters to SERGIUS in favour of peace, but his views were condemned.

The chief champion of orthodoxy in this contention was SOPHRONIUS of Jerusalem, 560-638, an unwearied opponent of the Monothelites, whose *Synodical Epistles to Sergius and Honorius* were prolix and elaborate professions of faith which resisted any compromise with the heretics. His work on the *Mystery of the Incarnation* served the same purpose.

Modern Greek liturgical books attribute to him "The Candlelight Hymn," which BASIL has preserved and JOHN KEBLE translated:

> Hail! gladdening Light, of His pure glory poured
>   Who is th' immortal Father, heavenly, blest,
> Holiest of Holies—Jesus Christ our Lord!
>   Now we are come to the sun's hour of rest,
>   The lights of evening round us shine,
> We hymn the Father, Son, and Holy Spirit divine,
>   Worthiest art Thou at all times to be sung
>   With undefiled tongue,
>   Son of our God, Giver of Life, alone!
> Therefore, in all the world, Thy glories, Lord, they own.

This "honey-tongued champion of the truth," also wrote the *Typicon* in the interests of orthodoxy, and a *Life of St. Mary of Egypt;* as well as tediously long lives of St. Cyrus and St. John, in favour of monasticism. He won a literary reputation apart from his fame as a controversial theologian by his many Homilies, and especially by a collection of sacred Hymns. These are "long narratives, on the Annunciation, the Nativity, the visit of the Magi, the Baptism, the Triumphal Entry, the Last Supper, the Cross. the Ascension; on St. Paul, St. John, St. Stephen, and certain saints. The most interesting is on the Holy Places, giving an insight into the appearance of Jerusalem and the spots held sacred in his day."

MAXIMUS THE CONFESSOR, 580-662, also opposed the *Henoticon* in the interests of orthodoxy, but PYRRHUS, d. 655, a Monothelite patriarch of Constantinople, 638-641, carried on a lively debate with him in favour of the *Ecthesis*, 645. The Record of this discussion is the most elaborate exposition which exists of the Monothelite teaching and its tendencies. PYRRHUS was won over by the debate, and was received into communion at Rome, but later on he returned to his heretical opinions.

MAXIMUS, favourably known by this discussion, is still better known by his *Scholia on the pseudo-Dionysian books,* for the Scholia brought the great mystic to the general attention of the Church.

CHAPTER XVI

THE LIFE OF FAITH

The theological controversies concerning the two natures of Christ served to emphasise the view expressed in many early writings that man has both a higher and a lower nature —the life of the spirit and the life of the flesh. Religion was constantly explained as an effort to overcome the lower man in order that the higher man might be absolutely free from all degrading control. These views were basic to monasticism, which its advocates ever regarded as the true life of faith.

The literature of the monastic life is one of the wealthiest sections of Christian literature. It offers to the student of psychology records of first-rate importance; it enables the student of religion to penetrate into some of the most out-of-the-way regions of his subject.

Paul of Thebes is called "the founder of the monastic life," by JEROME. He had many imitators as a solitary hermit, until PACHOMIUS, 285-346, instituted a form of community life; thus creating the first religious Order for which he prepared the first monastic Rule.

This *Rule of Pachomius* was commonly believed to have been divinely inspired, and to have been written by an angel on a brass tablet. By its provisions three monks shared one cell, all the company took their meals in common, all wore their white goat-skins day and night, and prayer was enjoined twelve times in the day, twelve times in the evening, and twelve times at night.

With the growth of the movement other Rules were soon

prepared. The *Rule of St. Anthony* relinquished the purely solitary life; the *Rule of Shenoudi* added the vow of obedience to the discipline of PACHOMIUS; the heretical EUSTATHIUS of Sebaste, 300-377, in his *Constitution of Ascetics* strengthened the demand for obedience in connection with that "self-righteous and heretical form of asceticism," of which he was the founder in Armenia.

These Rules are known indefinitely and at second hand; we reach the first extant authentic Rule with BASIL of Caesarea, "the first regulator-general of monasticism," who modified the extreme asceticism of PACHOMIUS, abolished the anchorite form of monasticism, brought the monks nearer to the cities, and made manual labour an integral part of the day's duty. The famous *Rule of St. Basil,* consists of two parts: the *Greater Monastic Rule,* a series of fifty-five regulations; and the *Lesser Monastic Rule,* which comprises three hundred and thirteen ordinances in the form of question and answer. His theory of the life of faith appears in the question:

> God has made us, like the members of our body, to need one another's help. For what discipline of humility, of pity, or of patience can there be if there be no one to whom these duties are to be practised? Whose feet wilt thou wash—whom wilt thou serve—how canst thou be last of all—if thou art alone?

This more generous idea of community life was still further broadened by TYRANNIUS RUFINUS, 342-410, at first the friend but ultimately the enemy of JEROME. His free Latin translation of the *Rule of Basil* condensed the material without bringing order into its confusion; but it added the provision for "double" houses, *i.e.,* the association of nunneries with monasteries.

The first organiser of the ascetics of Nitria was Ammon, d. 345. He was followed by Macarius Junior, or the Alexandrine, d. 395, who instituted the first community in that part of the Nile valley which bears his name. Another Macarius, the Great, or the Egyptian, 300-390; and Paphnutius, an outstanding figure at Nicaea, accepted the freer coenobitic ideal. So also did SERAPION of Thumis, fl. 350, surnamed Scholasticus, who wrote "an admirable book" *Against the Manichaeans,* a work on *The Titles of the Psalms,* and some Letters. One of his Letters addressed to the hermits of the desert extols, in most extravagant terms, the life which they had chosen to lead.

ARSENIUS, 354-449, left the court of Theodosius the Great, where he had been tutor to Arcadius and Honorius, the Emperor's sons, and fled to Egypt in 394, in order "to cleanse his soul." His fame rests upon his self-sacrificing life rather than upon his book *The Exhortation to Monks,* in which the results of his deep religious experience are given. It bids the monks "keep guard all round":

> Seek God and He will appear to you: hold Him fast, and He will abide with you.
>
> Whenever a man has fallen into sin, if he will but say heartily, 'Lord God, I have sinned, forgive me!' the soul-wasting power of melancholy will cease.

A fresh development began when BENEDICT of Nursia, 480-543, the founder of the famous monastery at Monte Cassino in 529, issued the one literary work of his life, the *Monastic Rule.* This was a complete code of monastic duty in seventy-three chapters; it organised the earlier disciplines, and furnished a standard to the whole Church of the West. "It breathes a spirit of mildness and consideration, while by the sanction for the first time given to study, it opened the way for those literary pursuits which afterwards developed themselves so largely within convent walls."

CHRODEGANG of Metz, 705-706, adapted BENEDICT'S Rule to suit communities of secular clergy, living the canonical life. This *Rule for Canonicals* exists in two forms: the original form in thirty-four chapters, intended for the clergy under the jurisdiction of its editor; and a longer form of eighty-six chapters, for the use of canonical clergy in general. Under the provisions of this Rule the cathedral clergy were to live under a common roof, occupy a common dormitory, and submit to the authority of a special officer.

CHRODEGANG was skilled in Latin, "which was fast becoming the language of educated men in all parts of Europe," as well as in his own tongue. He "exercised an influence almost unique at that time both in church and state"; his promotion of the literary interests of the northern monasteries is a lasting honour to his name.

Apart from the main stream of monasticism, which, in the West, followed the course marked out by BENEDICT, there were smaller separate movements. The monastic discipline of Ireland, left permanent impressions upon the mind of COLUMBAN, 543-615, who journeyed to France, with twelve companions in 585, and in due course established his celebrated monastery at Luxeuil and soon afterwards a second establishment at Fontaines. His Rule, somewhat lacking in definite directions for the details of daily living, was regarded as being needlessly strict in its demand for absolute obedience, for constant hard work, and for daily self-denial.

Another similar representative of the religious life was ABRAHAM of Cascar, often called the Great, fl. 502, who from his cave near Nisbis, spread monastic discipline among the Nestorians. He wrote Letters, *Expositions of Scripture,* a *Commentary on the Logic of Aristotle,* and he drew up a Rule for the government of the monks.

It was inevitable that Monasticism should reap a rich harvest of Biography from the romantic lives and miraculous pieties of its representatives. The fertile seed from this harvest grew into those *Legends of the Saints* which some centuries later gave Europe its popular literature.

Of such biographies the *Life of St. Anthony* by ATHANASIUS is the classical type. Its eulogy of the supernatural experiences and unworldly virtues of its hero made him the ideal monk for centuries. It gives a vivid and valuable reflection of the psychology of the primitive religious solitaries.

> Once someone knocked at the door of my cell, and going forth I saw one who seemed of great size and tall. Then when I enquired 'Who art thou?' he said, 'I am Satan.' Then when I said 'Why art thou here?' he answered, 'Why do the monks and all other Christians blame me undeservedly? Why do they curse me hourly?' Then I answered, 'Wherefore dost thou trouble them?' He said, 'I am not he who troubles them, but they trouble themselves, for I am become weak. . . . . I have no longer a place, a weapon, a city. The Christians are spread everywhere, and even the desert is filled with monks.' . . . . Then I marvelled at the grace of the Lord, and said to him: . . . . 'the coming of Christ hath made thee weak, and He hath cast thee down and stripped thee.' But he having heard the Saviour's name, and not being able to bear the burning from it, vanished.

ISIDORE of Pelusium, fl. 395, deeply affected by the exile of ATHANASIUS among the "holy solitaries," became a coenobite at Tabenna. His Letters contain much of the material of monastic history and biography. He castigates the inhospitality, the gluttony, the pugnacity, and the idleness of the monks, whose "disorderliness" led them to the cities and to the public shows, "as if all that the angelic life required were a cloak, a staff, and a beard."

In JEROME, 346-420, whose full name is EUSEBIUS

HIERONYMUS, monasticism had one of its most enthusiastic advocates, and one of its most illustrious literary representatives. For five years he lived as a hermit in the wilderness of Chalcis, in northern Syria, and later settled in Bethlehem, 386, where he lived for thirty-four years until his death. His love of literature is reflected in the story of his conversion:

> Many years ago, when, for the Kingdom of Heaven's sake, I had cut myself off from home, parents, sisters, relatives and—harder still—from the dainty food to which I had been accustomed, ... I still could not bring myself to forego the library that I had formed for myself at Rome with great care and toil. . . . . I would fast only that I might afterwards read Cicero. After many nights spent in vigil, after floods of tears called from my inmost heart, after the recollection of my past sins, I would once more take up Plautus . . . . about the middle of Lent a deep-seated fever fell upon my weakened body. . . . . Suddenly I was caught up in the spirit and dragged before the judgment seat of the Judge. . . . . Asked who and what I was, I replied 'I am a Christian.' But He who presided said, 'Thou liest, thou art a follower of Cicero, not of Christ.' For 'where thy treasure is, there will thy heart be also.' Instantly I became dumb, and amid the strokes of the lash . . . . I began to cry and bewail myself, saying, 'Have mercy upon me, O Lord.' . . .
>
> Under the stress of that awful moment . . . . I made oath and called upon His name saying: 'Lord, if ever again I read such, I have denied Thee' . . . . Thenceforth I read the books of God with a zeal greater than I had previously given to the books of men (Epistle xxii.).

JEROME began his literary career, by helping RUFINUS

in his translations; he then passed on to the role of apologist against LUCIFER of Calaris, 379; against HELVIDIUS, 383, and against JOVINIAN the gnostic, 392.   He wrote in his own defence, and in defence of the orthodoxy of ORIGEN against JOHN of Jerusalem, 398.

His interest in monasticism shows clearly in his *Life of Paul the Eremite of Thebes,* in the *Life of Malchius the Captive,* and in the *Life of Hilarion,* a Palestinian leader of monachism, 290-371.   His enthusiasm for the monastic life led him to criticise the clergy with an unsparing pen.

There are others . . . . who seek the presbyterate and the diaconate simply that they may be able to see women with less restraint.   Such men think of nothing but their dress; they use perfumes freely—and see that there are no creases in their leather shoes.   Their curling hair shows traces of the tongs; their fingers glisten with rings; they walk on tip-toe across a damp road, not to splash their feet.   When you see men acting in this way think of them rather as bridegrooms than as clergymen.

JEROME is the best of the Christian letter writers.   His epistles are full of life and movement; crowds of his contemporaries pass across the pages; appreciations, criticisms and denunciations are scattered with a lavish hand.   "The letters that passed between ST. JEROME and ST. AUGUSTINE may well be read for the noble passage of controversy they exhibit between the two great men; the letter of ST. JEROME to Sunnia and Fretela for its biblical criticism; to Evangelus for remarks on ecclesiastical orders."   The vitality of his Epistles appears in such passages as this:

Had the scenes of the Passion and of the Resurrection been elsewhere than in a populous city with court and garrison, with prostitutes, play-actors and buffoons, and with the medley of persons usually found

in such centres; or had the crowds which thronged it
been composed of monks; then a city would be a de-
sirable abode for those who have embraced the monastic life (*Epistle* lviii.).

For a just judgment of JEROME'S writings, generous
allowance must be made for his rough, irritable and coarse
temperament, which brought together in strange contrast a
lofty ideal of saintliness, and a reckless violence of temper. But when all deductions are made, JEROME appears in
his works as one of the most valuable writers of his age
and certainly the most learned; the chief link between the
religion and culture of the East and West. For several subsequent centuries he was the master of Christian prose.

He was an assiduous user of other men's labours; he translated and continued *The Chronicles of Eusebius* from 330
to 380; he continued the same author's *Ecclesiastical History* under the title *Illustrious Men,* or a *Catalogue of Ecclesiastical Writers,* 392; and he based the work on *The Sites and
Names of Hebrew Places,* 390, on the same writer's *Onomas-
ticon.* He used a work of PHILO'S for his own book on
The Interpretation of Hebrew Names, 390; as he also laid
under tribute various writings of Jewish Rabbis for his
work entitled *Questions of Hebrew in Genesis.*

His most enduring monument is the revised Latin New
Testament, universally known as *The Vulgate,* 381-385;
the revised Old Testament came later, 392-404. In his
Preface to The Four Evangelists, 383, he thus addresses Pope
Damasus:

> You urge me to revise the old Latin version and, as
> it were, to sit in judgment on the copies of the Scrip-
> tures which are now scattered throughout the whole
> world; and inasmuch as they differ from one another,
> you would have me decide which of them agree with

the Greek original. The labour is one of love, but at the same time both perilous and presumptuous; for, in judging others, I must be content to be judged by all; and how can I dare to change the language of the world in its hoary old age, and carry it back to the early days of its infancy?

The literature of Monasticism was enriched by RABBULA'S *Admonitions for Monks*, 325, a work of great interest for the study of monachism in the Eastern Church. PALLADIUS, 367-420, gathered together seventy brief biographies of Egyptian monks in his famous *Lausiac History*, 420, which "like all writings concerning the Egyptian monks, was, to the confusion of later students . . . . at times called *Paradise*" [1] (cp. *History of the Monks* by RUFINUS; *Words of the Elders* by PALLADIUS; *The Spiritual Meadow* by MOSCHUS).

This work is named after Lausus to whom it is dedicated; its character may be estimated from the following extract:

> The first time that I set foot in the city of the Alexandrians . . . . I met in the city a wonderful man, distinguished in every respect, both as regards character and knowledge, Isidore the priest, hospitaller of the Church of Alexandria . . . . When I met him he was an old man seventy years of age, who lived another fifteen years, and then died in peace. Up to the very end of his life he wore no linen except a head band, never had a bath, nor partook of meat . . . . He was so benevolent and peaceable that even his enemies, the unbelievers, themselves reverenced his shadow because of his exceeding kindliness . . . . I often knew him to weep at table, and when I asked the cause of his tears I heard him say: 'I shrink from partaking of irrational food, being myself rational and

---

[1] H. B. Workman. *The Review of the Churches*, Jan., 1924, p. 89.

destined to live in a paradise of delight owing to the power given us by Christ.'[2]

The industrious RUFINUS, 345-410, in an ambitious *History of the Monks,* described the whole monastic movement as it appeared in 394, to travellers down the Nile from Lycapolis to Alexandria. In spite of its importance, this History is surpassed in interest by the famous *Pilgrimage of Etheria—Silvia*—sometimes called *The Pilgrimage to the Holy Places.*

The *Biography of Martin of Tours,* 316-400, by SULPICIUS SEVERUS, 355-420, expresses the monastic mind more truly than most works of its kind, and, thanks to its author, it left a wonderful impression of the saint's career. It is rich in edifying anecdote.

> . . . . at a certain period, when he had nothing except his arms and his simple military dress, in the middle of winter . . . . he happened to meet, at the gate of the city of Amiens, a poor man destitute of clothing . . . . Taking therefore the sword with which he was girt, he divides his cloak unto two equal parts, and gave one part to the poor man, while he again clothed himself with the remainder. Upon this some of the by-standers laughed, because he was now an unsightly object, and stood as but partly dressed . . . .
>
> In the following night, when Martin had resigned himself to sleep, he had a vision of Christ arrayed in that part of his cloak with which he had clothed the poor man. He contemplated the Lord with the greatest attention, and was told to own as his the robe which he had given. Ere long he heard Jesus saying with a clear voice to the multitude of angels standing round: 'Martin, who is still but a catechumen, clothed me with this robe.'

[2] *The Lausiac History of Palladius* (1918), trans. by W. K. Lowther Clarke.

SULPICIUS SEVERUS, "who has never been discredited as a writer or as a Christian," was at home among such themes, as his series of *Dialogues concerning the Monks of the East,* and his *Sacred History,* show.

PETRONIUS of Bologna, fl. 400, is reputed to be the author of *The Lives of the Fathers,* a record of the lives of Egyptian anchorites, which became to many dwellers in the desert the rule and mirror of their profession, but some uncertainty attaches to this work which may have been confused with one of the compositions or translations of RUFINUS.

The historian THEODORET of Cyrrhus, 393-458, was attracted to this form of literature by seven years of monastic life; he wrote a *Religious History,* which consists of the life-stories of thirty celebrated hermits and ascetics, whose extraordinary penances and extravagant miracles are recorded with undoubting faith. Thus he describes the austerities practiced for more than forty years by two well-born ladies Marana and Cyra. They lived in a small stone enclosure, open to heat and cold, rain and snow; long hoods covered the upper part of their bodies, hiding their faces, breasts, and hands, and chains of iron hung round their necks, waists and wrists. During their pilgrimage to Jerusalem, they neither ate once on the journey thither nor on their return, only breaking their fast in the Holy City.

CYRIL of Scythopolis, fl. 555, who became an ascetic at sixteen years of age, wrote in simple style the lives of John the Silentiary, Euthymius, Sabas, Theodosius the Archimandrite, Cyriacus the Anchoret, and Theognius the Ascetic of Cyprus. His works have been largely interpolated by METAPHRASTES, the tenth century legendist of Constantinople.

The *Spiritual Meadow* of JOHN MOSCHUS, 555-620, is a collection of anecdotes and sayings gathered by the author in the various monasteries he had visited. There are better and brighter reflections of the social conditions of the age in the *Life of St. John the Merciful,* by LEONTIUS of Neapolis in Cyprus, fl. 582-602, whose work abounds in vivid descriptions.

The joys of the ascetic life are extolled by EUCHERIUS of Lyons, d. 449. After some experience in high civic official life EUCHERIUS retired from the world, remaining in retreat until called to the see of Lyons, 434. He addressed to HILARY of Arles a *Letter, or Little Book, in praise of the Desert,* 428, which reflects the delight he had received from reading some of the Collations of CASSIAN. EUCHERIUS recalls the biblical records of works in the wilderness— the giving of the Law, the manna, the experiences of Moses, Elijah, John the Baptist, and Jesus. "O great praise of the wilderness, that Satain who conquered in heaven should have been conquered in the Desert."

The miraculous element in the life of the monk gave it one of its chief charms, the holy man rose in popular esteem in proportion to his power to work wonders. GREGORY of Tours, 538-594, makes this aspect of monastic life the subject of several of his works, concerning which he gave instructions to his successors:

> Although these books of mine are written in a somewhat unpolished style, I nevertheless adjure all the priests of the Lord, who after my unworthy self shall be pastors of the church of Tours, I adjure them by the coming of our Lord Jesus Christ, and by the day of judgment, a day of terror to all the wicked, as they hope to escape confusion and damnation at that dread day, that they shall never suffer these books of mine to be destroyed or to be copied with selections and omissions; but these my books shall remain with my successors, complete and unaltered as I have bequeathed them (*History of the Franks,* X., 31).

His first work was a record of the *Miracles of St. Martin*

(of Tours) in four books, the composition of which was spread over four years, 575-578. About the year 585 he wrote the *Miracles of St. Julian,* and a work on the *Glory of the Martyrs.* These records were followed by the *Glory of the Confessors,* 588, and by the *Lives of the Fathers,* 594. In the last book GREGORY gives biographical accounts of twenty monks of Gaul. The seven other records are included under the general title of *Seven Books of Miracles* which GREGORY specifies among his writings.

An excellent picture of the general character of Syrian monasticism as it existed from the middle of the fourth century until the end of the ninth century is given by THOMAS of Marga in his *Book of Governors,* 840. This is really the history of the great Nestorian monastery of Beth Abhe in Mesopotamia. It "occupies a unique position in Syriac literature, and it fully deserves the veneration with which it has been and is still regarded by all classes of Nestorians to whom it is known."[3] It is full of interesting narratives of saintly men told in a naïve and candid spirit.

A *rationale* of monasticism grew out of the practice by an inevitable process of thought. AMBROSE of Milan, 340-397, an "entirely masculine and authoritative personality," in whom the Church first stepped forward to champion the cause of justice and humanity against the legalised tyranny of the civil power, although not a monk himself, was among the first to explain the "higher life" and its way of perfection.

AMBROSE preached in praise of virginity as soon as he was raised to the bishopric; he afterwards digested these Sermons into three books *On Virgins* addressed to his sister Marcellina. Among his expository writings are books on *Flight from the World,* and on *Jacob and the Blessed Life.* Other works that deal more directly with the same theme are *Virginity,*

---

[3] E. W. Budge, *The Book of Governors* (1893), Intro.

an *Exhortation to Virginity,* the *Lapse of a Consecrated Virgin,* and the three books to Marcellina.

"The strong commendations of virginity which are to be found throughout his works, but especially in several small treatises on this subject, are based, not on a theory of self denial, but rather on one of detachment from the cares of the world and the troubles inseparable from matrimony and parentage. According to him, marriage is the more painful state, as well as the less favourable to spiritual devotion."[4]

> it is certain that in the higher kinds of Christian devotion these two things are the most excellent, the Clerical function and the Monastic rule. The first is trained to be obliging and courteous in its behaviour, the second is accustomed to abstinence and endurance; the one lives as on a theatre, the other in secret; the one is seen, the other hidden (Epistle 1xiii.71).

AMBROSE was a prolific author. He wrote a work entitled *The Faith,* 378-380, to explain the orthodox belief to the Emperor Gratian. Other outstanding books are *The Holy Spirit,* 381; *the Sacraments,* 382; *the Incarnation of the Lord in the Sacrament; Penitence,* 384; *the Office of the Ministry,* 387; beside many Expositions of Scripture, a few Orations, and a large number of Letters. Gibbon says that his writing is "without the spirit of Tertullian, the copious eloquence of Lactantius, the lively wit of Jerome or the grave energy of Augustine." Jerome's 'lively wit' compared him to a crow decked out in alien feathers.

His Sermons are manly and practical but disappointing; like his Commentaries they are overshadowed by his Hymns, concerning which he says in his *Sermon againt Auxentius:*

> Moreover they assert that the people have been beguiled by the strains of my hymns. I deny not this either. It is a lofty strain, than which nothing is more

---
[4] *Dictionary of Christian Biography,* Vol. I., p. 98.

powerful. For what can be more powerful than the confession of the Trinity which is daily celebrated by the mouth of the whole people.

This may refer to the "Te Deum" of which with AUGUSTINE he may possibly have been the author. He was certainly the father of Christian song and chant, "the writer of noble Latin hymns, the inventor of the Ambrosian musical ritual and that system of antiphonal chanting on which and on the Gregorian modes, the plain song of the Anglican Church is founded." Next to the "Te Deum" perhaps the "Veni Redemptor gentium" is best known:

> Come thou redeemer of the earth
> And manifest thy virgin birth
> Let every age adoring fall;
> Such birth befits the God of all.

JOHN CASSIAN of Nola, 360-435, compiled and arranged the data of Western monasticism. He carried over the rules of Eastern monastic life and established them in the communities of the West. His *Institutes of the Renunciants,* was written about 420. The first four of its twelve books described the monastic rule, the remaining eight books dealt with the moral difficulties that beset the Renunciants, as the coenobites of Egypt were then called. Because of this ethical section the work is sometimes referred to as *The Remedies of the Chief Vices.* The better known *Collations* or *Conferences of the Fathers* is an account of the experiences which CASSIAN had enjoyed during his journeyings among the Egyptian hermits. It is a "mirror of monastics"; "the theory or philosophy of primitive Christian Monachism finds its fullest expression" in it.

CASSIAN also wrote, at the suggestion of LEO, *The Incarnation of Christ,* 429, in opposition to Nestorianism.

Other writers contributed to the explanation of the prin-

ciples underlying the development of monasticism. CHRY-
SOSTOM defended the movement in his work on *Monachism,*
365. CAESARIUS of Arles, 469-542, the author of a gracious
book on *Grace and Free Will,* drew up *Rules for Monks,*
and *Rules for Virgins.* His Sermons reveal the simplicity of
his mind, and the kindliness of his spirit.

> The care of our soul, my dear brothers, strongly
> resembles the cultivation of the soil: as in the ground,
> we pluck up some things in order to sow others which
> shall be good, so should it be for our soul; what is
> evil should be rooted up, what is good should be
> planted; let pride be taken away, and humility take
> its place; let avarice be rejected, and mercy cultivated
> (Advice to the faithful that they read the Divine writ-
> ings).

SALVIAN of Marseilles, 400-490, who wrote a great work
on the *Guidance of God,* extolled the life of separation from
the world. NILUS ABBAS, 365, 430, wrote *The Excellence
of the Monks.* "His epistles are very curious and interesting
reading, detailing the assaults made on him by demons, and
replying to the various queries of every kind, doctrinal, disciplinary, and even political with which he was assailed by
his admirers." "There is no more copious source for illustrations of the life and times of the close of the fourth century than this correspondence."

CHAPTER XVII

AUGUSTINE

Monastic retreat often failed to bring the higher religious experiences within reach of those who had forsaken the world in order to attain them. The outward habit of separation had been emphasised at the expense of the cultivation of the inward spirit to which alone those experiences are possible. A change of emphasis in Christian thinking was urgently needed and was brought about by the labours of AURELIUS AUGUSTINE of Hippo, 354-430, "the father of mediaeval Christianity."

AUGUSTINE was a remarkably representative man. He united a passion for doctrinal orthodoxy with a deep devotion to the monastic ideal, and in him also the two chief cultures of the world met and mingled. Born in Africa and educated in Rome, his training was essentially of the West, but his spiritual philosophy was of the East. Early in life he became a Manichean, after a few years he was converted to neo-Platonism, and ultimately to the Christian faith. His teaching however derived its essential characteristics from his own profound religious experiences.

AUGUSTINE was ever a writer, and after his conversion he was constantly immersed in literary labours. From his first retreat at Cassisiacum he sent out a criticism of the New Academy. As a candidate for Christian baptism he wrote *The Blessed Life*, 386, the record of a discussion on the Stoic philosophy in relation to the ideal of life, and of the Academic scepticism in relation to the search for truth. He next attempted to offer a philosophy of evil in a work on

The Order of the World. His *Soliloquies* are informal meditations on self-knowledge and the acknowledgement of God.

> Now I love Thee only, I follow Thee only, I seek Thee only, I am prepared to serve Thee only, because Thou only dost justly rule, I desire to be of Thy law. Command, I pray, and impose whatever Thou wilt; but cleanse and open my ears, with which I may hear Thy voices. Cleanse and open my eyes, with which I may see Thy signal. Cast out insanity from me that I may know Thee (Chap. i.5).

Although in the three works entitled *The Soul and its Origin*, the *Soul and its Immortality*, 387, and the *Greatness of the Soul*, 388, there are traces of neo-Platonism, yet the orthodoxy of AUGUSTINE was sound. He proved this in *The True Religion*, 390, as well as in a later work on *Heresies*, 430, in which he attacked eighty-eight heterodox sects.

Soon after he became a presbyter, 391, he addressed a work on *The Utility of Believing* to his intimate friend Honoratus of Carthage, for the purpose of inducing him to abandon his Manichaean views.

> Let there be some one . . . . who for the first time sees and perceives the changes of day and night, and the constant order of the heavenly bodies, and changes of the years divided into four parts, the leaves falling and returning to the trees, the infinite power of seeds, the beauty of the light, the varieties of colours, sounds, scents and tastes; he is stupified and overwhelmed with miracles, but we despise all these things, not because of the ease of understanding them, for what is more obscure than the causes of these? but surely because of our constantly perceiving them.

The subject of a later controversy was already before his

mind in 395 when he completed a book on *Free Will*, in which his friend Evodius acts the part of the questioner.

After his mother's death, he prepared his spiritual autobiography, the immortal *Confessions*, 397. This is the first autobiography in all literature, as it is also the first classical record of Christian experience written since the New Testament. The framework of the book is the story of AUGUSTINE'S life and doings down to the time of his mother's death; round this frame-work the author weaves one of the most illuminating expositions of the soul's communion with God ever given to the world. Some passages have become almost as familiar as household words:

> In the agitation of my spirit I retired into the garden belonging to the house, knowing how evil I was, but ignorant of the good Thou hadst in store for me. Alypius followed me, and we sat remote from the house, and with vehement indignation I rebuked my sinful spirit because it would not give itself up to God. I found I wanted a will . . . . When deep meditation had collected all my misery into the view of my heart, a great storm arose producing a large shower of tears . . . . I rose up hastily from Alypius . . . . I prostrated myself under a fig-tree, and with tears bursting out, I spake to this effect: 'How long, Lord, wilt Thou be angry? for ever? Remember not my old iniquities' . . . . Thus I spake, and wept in the bitterness of my soul, and I heard a voice as from a neighbouring house of one repeating frequently, 'take up and read, take up and read' . . . . I returned hastily to the place where Alypius was sitting; for there I had placed the book of St. Paul's Epistles. I seized it, opened, and read what first struck my eyes; 'not in rioting and drunkenness, not in chambering and wantonness, not in strife and envying; but put ye on the Lord Jesus

Christ, and make not provision for the flesh, to fulfil the lusts thereof'.] Nor did I choose to read anything more, nor had I occasion. Immediately at the end of this sentence, all my doubts vanished.

In this masterpiece AUGUSTINE'S literary powers appear at their best. The book is instinct with life, abounds in graphic touches, vivid terms, trenchant and memorable phrases. The language is occasionally too highly elaborated and sometimes is over exuberant but it vibrates with emotion and flows with musical rhythm.[1]

The main masses of AUGUSTINE'S literary labours were in part related to three important controversies, and in part to the explanation of Christianity as he understood it. So far as his controversial works are concerned he stands alone among early Christian writers in the consciousness of his own shortcomings. In these works, nine-tenths of which discuss psychological rather than theological questions, he modified his views as time went on, until he found himself unable to solve to problems he had propounded.[2]

He wrote seven works against the Manichaean beliefs he had shared before his conversion to Christianity, and from him the Manichaean heresy received its death blow.

The second Donatist schism roused him to the task of correcting errors in Christian teaching. OPTATUS of Milevi, fl. 365-378, condemned Donatism in *The Schism*, a Letter addresssed to PARMENIAN, the Donatist bishop of Carthage, 368. AUGUSTINE threw himself into the dispute with characteristic energy. He argued with the party leaders at Carthage, 411, and then wrote *Against the Letters of Parmenian and Petilian*. He prepared defensive books on the *Unity of the Church*, and the *Rite of Baptism*, and issued controversial pamphlets against Cresconius and Gaudentius who were

---

[1] R. E. Welsh, *Classics of the Soul's Quest*, pp. 28 ff.

[2] *Dictionary of Christian Biography*, Vol. II., p. 459.

outstanding schismatics. Other of his contributions to the contention were a *Colloquy with the Donatists,* and a *Letter to Boniface.*

A second literary warfare was waged over the teaching of PELAGIUS, 360-420, a British or Breton monk, who based his belief in the efficacy of Divine grace upon man's freedom of will, which, when reinforced by Christianity, could satisfy all the demands of God. His book on the *Trinity* had served as a text-book for students, and like his *Commentaries on St. Paul's Epistles* was irreproachable. But when he came to Rome teaching that "free will exists generally in all mankind" he opened the way for a fresh psychological examination of religion of which his mighty antagonist took full advantage. AUGUSTINE maintained a seven years controversy with Pelagianism until the Church accepted the doctrine of original sin and acknowledged that the human will is impotent for salvation.

JEROME wrote a *Dialogue against Pelagius,* "a model of irrational polemics"; PELAGIUS replied in two works, the first, *Nature,* issued before his acquittal in 415, the other entitled *Free Will,* issued soon after.

AUGUSTINE first answered PELAGIUS in *The Deserts and the Remission of Sins,* 412; he next took up the gage thrown down in *Nature* and replied to it in *Nature and Grace,* 415. He published two Letters against the acquittal of PELAGIUS by the synod of Diospolis, then in quick succession he wrote *The Origin of Sin, The Spirit and the Letter, Grace and Free Will,* and *Correction and Grace.* The latter two works were answers of assurance to those who regarded his teaching concerning irresistible grace with dismay. In the book on *Original Sin* he quotes PELAGIUS as saying:

> Nothing good and nothing evil . . . is born with us, but is done by us, for we are born not fully developed, but with a capacity for either conduct, we are

formed naturally without virtue or vice; and previous to the action of our own proper will, the only thing in man is what God has formed in him.

PELAGIUS vanished from the scene of controversy after his condemnation, leaving his cause to the care of COELESTIUS, who had joined him at Rome in 405 and shared in his condemnation at Ephesus in 431; and to JULIAN of Eclanum, 386-454, "the first, and until the sixteenth century the unsurpassed representative of a self-satisfied Christianity."

AUGUSTINE was on friendly terms with Julian's family as his letters show, but when JULIAN wrote letters on behalf of PELAGIUS, AUGUSTINE replied in *Against Two Letters of the Pelagians*, 419. JULIAN combatted AUGUSTINE'S book entitled *Marriage and Lust* by writing *Against Those Who Condemn Marriage and Assign its Fruits to the Devil*, 419. This subject was further debated by the two contestants in other works.

AUGUSTINE "found in JULIAN (a man of striking ability and an acute polemic) his peer in dialectic skill . . . . JULIAN was a sharp and vigorous as well as a fearless antagonist. He seized on the vulnerable points in AUGUSTINE'S theory and pursued him with questions and objections which the latter was unable to parry"[3] except with difficulty.

The semi-Pelagian views of COELESTIUS were adopted by VITALIS to whom AUGUSTINE sent a friendly *Epistle* describing the character of his error and the manifold disproofs of it.

VINCENT of Lerins, d. 450, indirectly opposed AUGUSTINE'S doctrine of irresistible grace in his first *Commonitory*, 434. "That celebrated treatise . . . which has so often been taken as the basis of the Anglican theory"[4] laid

---

[3] G. P. Fisher, *History of Christian Doctrine*, 2d. ed., p. 186.

[4] J. H. Newman, *Apologia pro Vita sua*, Oxford ed. (1913), pp. 289, 290.

down the well-known canon of orthodoxy: *"quod semper, quod ubique, quod ab omnibus creditum est."*

Also in the Catholic Church itself we take great care that we hold that which has been believed everywhere, always, by all. For that is truly and properly 'Catholic,' as the very force and meaning of the word show, which comprehends everything almost universally. And we shall observe this rule if we follow universality, antiquity consent.

PROSPER of Anquitane, 403-465, wrote as an Augustinian but with studied moderation. He was a controversialist even in his poetry; his most important poem *The Ingrates* is a piece of one thousand and two lines directed against the Pelagians and the semi-Pelagians. It gives an outline of the Pelagian doctrine, traces its reception in the Church, and describes the part played in connection with it by AUGUSTINE, "the light of the age." The temper of the poem is violent, harsh, melancholic and despondent.

Among his argumentative replies to various followers of PELAGIUS are Letters to the Gallic bishops, to the party of Vincent of Lerins, and a book *Against the Conferences* (of JOHN CASSIAN). In all these works he defends AUGUSTINE, upon whose writings he drew with sincere confidence in their truth. He also compiled a *Book of Sentences from the works of Augustine.* His independent writings were entitled *The Calling of all the Nations,* and a *Letter to Demetrias,* otherwise called a *Treatise on Christian Humility.*

PROSPER carried the case of the semi-Pelagian HILARY of Arles, 401-449, to AUGUSTINE in a Letter on the views held in Southern Gaul on the subject of Predestination. HILARY is said to have written Poems, Sermons and an *Exposition of the Creed;* but all his works were lost with the exception of a Letter and a *Biography of Honoratus* who preceded him as Bishop of Arles.

FAUSTUS of Riez, d. 492, another semi-Pelagian, received high praise for his various writings from his friend SIDONIUS APOLLINARIS, but equally strong censure from the staunch Augustinians. In *A Profession of Faith* directed against those who say that by the sole Will of God some are drawn to life, others pressed down to death, whom therefore FAUSTUS charges with asserting Fate with the Gentiles and denying Free Will with the Manichaeans, he repudiates Pelagianism but avoids supporting its extreme opposite. *The Epistle to the Presbyter Lucidus* is similar in purpose but fiercer in language. The same theme is handled again in the first part of *The Grace of God and the Free Will of the Human Mind.* The second part of this work contains discussions of various passages of Scripture; it contains the rare doctrine that the heathen know God naturally (chap x.).

The literary style of FAUSTUS may be seen in his *Sermon to Monks* in which he urges them to fulfil their calling rather than forsake it:

> The very birds love their nests. The wild beasts love the place in which they are nourished . . . . Use your will. Resist the devil. Cherish all graces especially obedience and humility. As much as we apply ourselves in study, by so much will He appoint (us) among the helpers. As much as we shall set ourselves to diligence by so much will He add to (our) glory. He who has to him shall be given.

JOHN CASSIAN whose monastic writings were of high importance, was the most conspicuous of those who sought a middle position between the extremes of Pelagianism and Augustinianism. He was a clear and forcible writer, generous in his theological views and anxious to avoid any teaching that set arbitrary limits to the work of salvation. His strong disapproval of AUGUSTINE'S doctrine of predestination was expressed in the thirteenth of his Collations.

His criticisms moved AUGUSTINE to write two works; the first on the *Predestination of the Saints,* the second on the *Gift of Perseverance,* 429.

The immense influence exercised by AUGUSTINE'S doctrinal writings was surpassed by his systematic treatise entitled *The City of God;* his pre-eminent apologetic, and in many respects his most significant work. It is from some points of view "the greatest book of the early Christian Church."

This solid contribution to the Christian philosophy of history contains the strongest statement of its author's theological opinions. He wrote it with considerable care; its publication was spread over thirteen years, 413-426. AUGUSTINE passed sentence almost with exultation upon the old world. "The terrestial city, whose eternity had been the theme of pagan history, had just fallen before Alaric's Goths," and AUGUSTINE "inflamed with zeal for the Lord's house" pictures the divine plan of the ages to "refute the mistakes of some and the blasphemies of others." The central idea of the work, that the City of God abideth forever even though earth's empires fall into ruin, became the ruling conception of mediaeval Catholicism.

> That most glorious society and celestial city of God's faithful, which is partly seated in the course of these declining times, wherein he that liveth by faith, is a pilgrim amongst the wicked; and partly in that solid estate of eternity, which as yet the other part doth patiently expect, until righteousness be turned into judgment . . . have I undertaken to defend in this work . . .

"Taking a rapid survey of the history of Rome, AUGUSTINE asks what the gods of heathenism had ever done for the prosperity of the state and for public morality. All the riches of learning are enlisted in the service of truth. . . .

He opposes the destinies of the world to those of the Church; and the city of men, such as it appeared to him four centuries after Christ, formed a dismal picture . . ." The work is really a running Christian commentary on Biblical and secular history leading up to the apocalyptic vision of the blessedness of the resurrection life in the heavenly Jerusalem.

As a theologian AUGUSTINE was the standard authority for a millenium. His work on *The Trinity*, 400-416, gave the final form to the doctrine, and although the thought is somewhat disconnected and the definition is blurred by interpolated speculations and discussions, yet "never perhaps was a deep subject handled more delicately or expounded more luminously, or each conclusion . . . respecting it expressed with more modesty and reserve."[5]

A little handbook, the *Enchiridion*, written in 421 for Laurentinus was his most serious effort to give his views systematic form. In a late work, the remarkable *Retractations*, 427, AUGUSTINE passed his opinions in review, corrected those he had come to think mistaken, made clear what seemed to be doubtful, and left a standard whereby all his earlier books must be judged.

> When I was still a presbyter, it happened that some of us were together at Carthage, and were reading the Epistle of the Apostle to the Romans. I was asked some questions by the brethren. I answered them as well as I could; and they expressed a wish that what I had said should . . . . be written down. (Cf. his *Exposition of certain Propositions from the Epistle to the Romans*, 394).
>
> I had not then inquired with sufficient care; nor had I yet discovered what is the nature of 'the election of grace' about which the same Apostle says 'the remnant' were saved 'according to the election of grace' . . . .

---

[5] *Dictionary of Christian Biography*, Vol. II., p. 460.

I then went on to say, For the same Apostle says, 'It is the same God who worketh all things in all'. Nowhere is it said It is God who believeth all things in all: and I then added, That we believe is our affair; that we do well is His affair, who gives to believers His Holy Spirit. I should certainly not have said this, if I had known that 'faith' itself is found among the gifts of God, which are given 'by the same Spirit'. Both indeed are our affair because of our free will . . . And whereas I said a little lower down Our part is to believe and to will: His part is to give, to those who believe and are willing, the power of doing well through the Holy Spirit . . . . Both are His affair, because he Himself prepares the will; and both are our affair, since it is not done except of our free will (*Retractations* I., xxiii.).

POSSIDIUS of Calama, d. 438, wrote a *Life of Augustine* which completes the story of the *Confessions*. "Though there have been few men whose lives are written in their own works more fully than that of AUGUSTINE has been by himself, yet history and the Church would have lost much if we did not also possess the simple, modest, and trustworthy narrative gathered in great measure from AUGUSTINE himself, which POSSIDIUS has left behind him."[6]

The age of AUGUSTINE was rich in Christian poetry not perhaps of the highest order but deserving of mention.

PONTIUS MEROPIUS ANICIUS PAULINUS of Nola, 353-431, was a pupil of the famous Ausonius, and then successively, a consul, a monk, and a bishop. He turned to Christian literature when about forty years old refusing thereafter to write any but sacred pieces. His correspondence with Alypius, Augustine, Aurelius, and other of the African clergy reveals his genuine interest in books.

He left thirty-six poems and about half a hundred Let-

---

[6] *Dictionary of Christian Biography*, Vol. III., p. 446.

ters. His Discourses have perished. He is noteworthy as a writer who sent with his Epistles and Poems gifts of a more substantial sort, a loaf of bread, a fragment of the true Cross, a dress, some ortolans, or some oysters.

His Poems include a rendering of the history of Suetonius, Christian prayers, Paraphrases of Psalms, an account of John the Baptist, a comparison of the Scriptural doctrines and the teachings of heathenism; but the majority of them sing the praises of Felix an earlier bishop of Nola. They are rich in stories of his wonder-working powers, his popularity, and of the miraculous virtues of his tomb.

The work of PAULINUS shows the changes that were taking place in the language and in poetic method, and it reflects the simple credulity of the peasant mind.

MAGNUS FELIX ENNODIUS, 474-521, was a native of Arles and a strong advocate of an undivided Church. The Gallic influence upon his writing is very marked. "Many of his Letters would seem to have proceeded from the pen of a heathen rhetorician, rather than of a Christian bishop. His illustrations are commonly drawn from Greek mythology. He speaks of divine grace as descending "de Superis," and sets the Fates side by side with Jesus Christ. His Letters addressed to the other sex breathe a spirit of gallantry, little in keeping with his sacred office."[7]

His style represents the debased classicism of the fifth century, the false rhetoric and stilted mannerisms of which came from a slavish imitation of Virgil. His prose works include twenty-eight Discourses, a *Panegyric of the King Theodoric, an Apology for the Synod* that acquitted Pope Symmachus, a *Life of that Most Blessed Man Epiphanius,* Bishop of Pavia, a *Life of St. Anthony the Monk,* and a *Eucharisticon of his Life* in which he penitently reviews his past.

CLAUDIUS MARIUS VICTOR, fl. 400-425, attempted to

[7] *Dictionary of Christian Biography,* Vol. II., p. 124.

render the story of Genesis into hexameter verse; this work is known as the *Alethia,* and is an expository version of the narrative with a few reflective comments. It is written in close imitation of the biblical record, except that, after the expulsion from Paradise, Adam assails the serpent with stones whereby a spark is struck from a flint and the resultant fire destroys the shelter of the fugitives. The fire also reveals the presence of metals in the earth, and by clearing the ground makes possible the production of grain.

CAELIUS SEDULIUS, fl. 450, anxious to win the heathen to the privileges of the Gospel, wrote the *Paschal Song* in some two thousand hexameter lines, singing of Christ the Passover offered for men. He wished to set forth the miracles of Jesus as something more wonderful than all the marvels of heathenism, and chose the poetical form because so little Christian verse existed.

SEDULIUS, however, translated his poem into prose in the *Paschal Work,* adding a few illustrations. This work is far below the literary level of his verse, but its colloquial language may have been an intentional concession to those critics who objected to the liberties he had taken with the sacred story in the Song.

He returned to the same theme in *The Elegy.* Two hymns of the Church have been taken from his *Triumphal Song concerning Christ, Arranged according to the Letters of the Alphabet;* one is translated by Ellerton:

> From east to west, from shore to shore
> Let every heart awake and sing
> The Holy Child Whom Mary bore,
> The Christ, the everlasting King.

The other, in Neale's translation, is:

> How vain the cruel Herod's fear,
> When told that Christi the King is near!
> He takes not earthly realms away,
> Who gives the realms that ne'er decay.

BLOSSIUS AEMILIUS DRACONTIUS, fl. 460, a citizen of Carthage, whose seeming want of loyalty to king Gunthamund was punished by imprisonment, wrote while in prison his thoughtful and interesting poem *The Praises of God*. "Its subject is God's mercy which led Him to create and then redeem mankind, and which leads Him always to direct human affairs for good, despite the wickedness of men."[8]

The greater part of the first book was soon published as a separate work under the title *The Six Days*, and held its place in high esteem for centuries. A poem of apology to the King, the *Satisfaction*, secured the unfortunate poet's release.

ALCIIMUS ECDICIUS AVITUS of Auvergne, 460-523, was the author of perhaps the most original of these early Latin poems based on the Bible narratives. This is *The Deeds of Spiritual History* which covers the period from the Creation, to the passage of the Red Sea. The first three divisions— the origin of the world, original sin, and the judgment of God—"constitute a veritable poem" having for its subject the loss of Paradise. AVITUS was one of the forerunners of JOHN MILTON who centuries later read his work.[9] He also wrote a consolatory poem *In Praise of Chastity*, beside some Homilies, and works against the Eutychian and Arian heresies.

It was however in MARCUS AURELIUS CLEMENT PRUDENTIUS, 348-413, a Christian, a Spaniard, and a Roman, that the Christian poetry of the age had its best exponent. In his work the Church Latin of the fourth century shows its finest characteristics.

After deep religious impressions received somewhat late in life he devoted himself to sacred verse "the earthen vessel of a rustic poet." Emotionally affected at the sight of the martyrs' memorials in Rome he there began to write

[8] H. O. Taylor, *The Classical Heritage of the Middle Ages*, p. 282.

[9] Guizot, *History of Civilization in France* (Bohn's ed.), Vol. II., pp. 146-157.

the fourteen lyrical ballads which are collected under the title *Concerning the Crown*. They describe the heroic careers of various confessors from Paul and Peter.

His dogmatic orthodoxy found voice in a work *Against Symmachus*, 404, written in verse so that Christian dogma might appear in an attractive form. Even more vigorous was the fiery rhetorical polemic called *The Apotheosis*. This poem opposed the chief heresies that misunderstood the nature of Christ. Its ambiguous title probably means The Deification—or Apotheosis—of Christ's Humanity.

> O Name most delightful to me,
> My hope, my adornment, my light,
> My stalwart protector in fight,
> My certain repose after toil.
>
> Like a delicate taste to the lips
> A sweet scent or a lifegiving spring
> Thou art mine! I Thy praises must sing
> Spotless Love, Fair Appearance, Pure Joy.

An even fiercer invective, *The Origin of Evil*, was written against MARCION "the blasphemous divider of the gods." This work is much indebted to the thought of TERTULLIAN, and is notable as giving for the first time in Latin poetry a large picture of the devil. The closing prayer may serve as an index to the spirit of the author:

> Be thou there O Cavern deep
> When the failing body needs thee
> When sad fires in Hell shall clasp me
> Or my soul in fumes shall steep.
>
> May the blaze to languor turn.
> When on some Thy light supernal
> Shines like victor's crown eternal,
> May my doom fires mildly burn.

The *Spiritual Combat* maintains the plea that as Abraham with his three hundred and eighteen servants freed Lot from the heathen kings, so the Christian, assisted by the Cross of Christ, may deliver his soul, win the Lord's blessing, and work that which is good. In this allegorical poem Faith defeats Idolatry, Modesty triumphs over Lust, Patience beholds Anger destroy itself, Pride is snared by Deceit and perishes leaving Humility unhurt, Self-Restraint puts Luxury to flight, Reason delivers the victims of Avarice, who is slain by Charity, and Discord after wounding Concord is killed by Faith.

The most popular work of PRUDENTIUS, *Day by Day*, includes twelve Hymns; the first six for different hours of the day, the others for various Church seasons. They are skilfully written and are fitting expressions of sincere religious feeling. *The Double Food*, or *Double Testament*, "is a wordy collection of forty-nine sets of four verses each on Old and New Testament scenes."

PRUDENTIUS was both varied and original, he used twenty different metres of which eleven seem to have been his own creation. He was especially the poet of dogma; his work has real theological value as a reflection of the mind of his age; it has equal literary value, for "he did not shrink from helping forward that great transformation of the Latin language, which it needed to undergo, now that it should be the vehicle of truths which were altogether novel to it." Perhaps the historical value of his work is greatest of all, for it is rich in information concerning social and ecclesiastical usages.

John Mason Neale has rendered one popular hymn:

> Of the Father's love begotten ere the worlds began to be
> He is Alpha and Omega, He the Source and Ending He,
> Of the things that are and have been
> And that future years shall see, evermore and evermore.

Edward Caswall has given a familiar translation of another:

> Earth has many a noble city; Bethlehem, thou dost all excel:
> Out of thee the Lord from heaven came to rule His Israel.
> Fairer than the sun at morning was the star that told His birth
> To the world its God announcing seen in fleshly form on earth.

Among the writers of prose it will be enough to recall
FABIUS CLAUDIUS GORDIANUS FULGENTIUS of Ruspe,
468-533, notorious for literary ability, deep knowledge of
Scripture, and theological learning. His bitter experiences at
the hands of the Arian Vandals failed to shake his devotion
to Catholic doctrine. He wrote first *A Book against the
Arians, Ten Answers to Ten Objections;* then *Three Books
to Thrasimund King of the Vandals,* in which he further
assailed the Arian doctrine. During a "second exile" he
wrote most of his Letters. These are concerned with weighty
theological problems and reveal his cordial agreement with
AUGUSTINE on such themes as predestination, grace, and the
remission of sin, in opposition to the semi-Pelagians of
Southern Gaul and North Africa. Among them is his well
known *Incarnation and Grace of our Lord Jesus Christ,*
which he wrote on behalf of his fellow exiles in reply to
the "brethren who had been sent to Rome from the East
in the cause of the Faith."

After his return from banishment he wrote his great
work *An Instrument of the Catholic Faith collected from the
Books of Fulgentius against the Works which Fabianus the
Heretic Falsely Fabricated against Him.* Less important writings were a *Little Book on the Trinity, The Sermon of Fas-
tidiosus,* a criticism marked by singular passion, a *Letter to
the Monks of Scythia,* and a discussion concerning *The Maker
of the Lower Creatures.*

CHAPTER XVIII

THE CONVERSION OF THE BARBARIANS

The life of AUGUSTINE closed amid the barbarian deluge that would have overwhelmed the Church as well as the Empire, had not the Gothic conquerors from Alaric to Theodoric been acquainted with Christianity. In some of the Sermons of MAXIMUS of Turin, fl. 388-455, the dismay and horror caused by the invasions are vividly reflected.

But the existence of the Faith was not seriously endangered. The Visigoths had been the objects of the missionary labours of ULPHILAS—Wolf—, 313-381, the son of captured Cappadocian Christians. He was brought up in the Arian faith and at the Synod of Antioch in 341 was consecrated bishop of the Goths. His supreme achievement in literature was the translation of the Bible into Gothic, for which he invented the Gothic written characters. To ULPHILAS therefore belongs the honour of being the father of vernacular translation in the Church, and also that of being the first writer to give the dignity of a written language to barbarian speech.

"What we possess in the Gothic language beside the *Bible of* ULPHILAS is insignificant; there is an interpretation of *St. John's Gospel* founded on Greek commentaries; a fragment of a Gothic *Calendar;* a few documents attested in Gothic; a Gothic toast in a Latin epigram and a few isolated words in Latin writings." The Gothic *Bible of* ULPHILAS is the oldest book written in a language like our own to which we can go back, it is also one of the finest extant specimens of ancient language.

147

AUXENTIUS of Milan, fl. 360-374, the Arian disciple and comrade of ULPHILAS wrote an authoritative account of his master's career.

SALVIAN of Marseilles, 400-495, gives a useful account of the conquerors' rule in his famous book entitled *The Governance of God*, or more correctly, *Present Justice*. This is a frank discussion of the question which AUGUSTINE had already raised in *The City of God*, viz., whether God ever removes His care from the world. In books one and two SALVIAN offers facts of experience and texts from Scripture to prove that the care of God is constant; in book three he undertakes to prove that the prevailing miseries of the Roman world were due to disobedience and sin.

He draws a striking contrast between the luxurious licentiousness of the Romans and the chastity of the Vandals, the piety of the Goths and the virtue of the Franks and Saxons to whom God was then giving the Empire.

> What is there like this among the barbarians? Where are there any Cirque-Games among them? Where are their theatres? Where is the abomination of all kinds of impurities? . . .
>
> But as to us . . . . We prefer plays before the churches of God. We despise altars and honour theatres. We love them all. We respect them all. 'Tis only God Almighty who seems little to us in comparison of them all . . . .
>
> If at any time it chances, which it often does, that on the same day there is a Church Festival and public plays, I desire to ask of every man's conscience which of the two places has the greater congregation of Christians in it: the seats of the public play, or the court of God, and whether all rather follow the temple or the theatre; and whether they love the word of the Gospel more, or those of the players; the words of

life, or the words of death; the words of Christ, or
the words of a mimical actor?

SALVIAN had previously attacked another widespread evil
in a tract on the perils of wealth entitled *The Church or
Against Avarice,* to which he makes reference in *The Govern-
nance of God.*

Over against the views of SALVIAN must be set those of
the Spanish presbyter OROSIUS, fl. 409-420, who not only
wrote an account of the religious parties in Spain, 413,
under the title *A Commonitory for Augustine,* but also at
AUGUSTINE'S suggestion wrote *Seven Books of Histories
against the Pagans,* to show that the calamities of Rome
were not special divine punishments but only the ordinary
distresses of mankind. Although a poor and feeble compilation this work was widely read in later times.

The spread of the Catholic Faith among the barbarians
was due in large measure to the missionary enterprises which
were inspired by the example of Irish monks whose illustrious leaders are well represented in Christian literature.

The Confession of ST. PATRICK, 372-493, and his *Letter
to Coroticus* are the oldest writings belonging to Christianity
in Ireland. *The Confession* is a naïve autobiography, written in a rude and barbarous Latin, but very precious as a
first hand record and as a faithful revelation of the author's
spirit.

I, Patrick the sinner, am the most clownish and the
least of all the faithful, and contemptible in the eyes
of very many . . . Nevertheless, although I am faulty
in many things, I wish my brethren and kinsfolk to
know what manner of man I am, and that they may
be able to understand the desire of my soul I
who was at first a clown, an exile, unlearned verily,
who know not how to provide for the future—but this
I do know most surely, that before I was afflicted I

was like a stone lying in the deep mire; and he that is mighty came, and in his mercy lifted me up, and verily raised me aloft and placed me on the top of the wall.[1]

The Letter to Coroticus is an appeal to the soldiery across the sea to cease their piratical raids on Irish Christians whom PATRICK "in countless numbers begot to God and confirmed in Christ." Although modern criticism regards the *Lorica* or *Breastplate,* so long attributed to the saint, as a pagan composition originally known as the *Cry of the Deer* it deserves quotation:

> I bind myself to day to a strong virtue, an invocation of the Trinity.
> I believe in Threeness with a confession of Oneness in the Creator of the Universe.
> I bind myself to day to the virtue of Christ's birth with His Baptism,
> To the virtue of his crucifixion with his burial,
> To the virtue of his resurrection with his ascension,
> To the virtue of his coming to the Judgment of Doom. . . .
>
> I bind myself to-day to God's virtue to pilot me
> God's Might to uphold me
> God's Wisdom to guide me
> God's Eye to look before me. . . . . .
>
> Christ with me, Christ before me, Christ behind me, Christ in me.
> Christ below me, Christ above me, Christ at my right, Christ at my left.
> Christ in breadth, Christ in length, Christ in height!
> Christ in the heart of every one who thinks of me,
> Christ in the mouth of everyone who speaks to me,
> Christ in every eye that sees me,
> Christ in every ear that hears me![2]

COLUMBAN, 543-615, sometimes called Columba the Younger and sometimes Columba of Luxeuil, who must be distinguished from COLUMBA of Iona, carried on mis-

---

[1] Newport J. D. White, *A Translation of the Latin Writings of St. Patrick.*
[2] *Irish Literature,* Philadelphia (1904), Vol. VIII., pp. 3244-3246.

sionary work among the people of the Vosges Mountains and at Bobbio in Italy. All his writings are connected with these enterprises. They include a *Rule for Coenobites, The Mode of Penances*, some *Psalms*, and a collection of fifteen addresses entitled *The Instructions of St. Columban*. These Instructions are written in old Greek metre and deal chiefly with moral and saintly virtues; *e.g.* mortifying vices and attaining virtues, hating the world, loving heavenly things, work, ideals of life, etc. Although necessarily cast in the monkish and allegorical moulds of its class this work of COLUMBAN is rich in ethical truths, striking expressions, and signs of the author's devout and earnest spirit. It quotes Juvenal in support of Gospel teaching, for COLUMBAN urged that the classical poets should be studied with as great diligence as was given to the early Church fathers.

COLUMBA of Iona, 521-597, called Columcille—the dove of the Church—travelled to heathen Scotland with twelve disciples. Tradition regarded him as the first of the Irish poets and ascribed to him a *Song of Trust* (in the King's judgment concerning a copy of the Psalter which he had transcribed). The verdict however was given against him and caused him to stir up rebellion against his royal judge.

The earliest story of COLUMBA, which was written in 657 by CUMINIUS, abbot of Iona, d. 669, is a tissue of miracles. It was enlarged by ADAMNAN, 624-704, and later on was edited by BEDE with brief but valuable notes.

In MAGNUS AURELIUS CASSIODORUS, 490-583, the West had "the greatest individual contributor to the preservation of learning" prior to the Middle Ages. Failing to establish a school in Rome he founded a library for his monks at Squillace in 431 and there he wrote two works, *The Institutes of Sacred and Humane Letters* and, *The Arts and Discipline of Liberal Letters*. As a connecting link between the world of classic Rome and that of the Middle Ages he played an important part in the literary history of Europe. In 519 he prepared a *Chronicon*, or abstract of history from the Deluge to 519, and soon afterwards began his important *History of the Goths*, upon which JORDANES, fl. 550, based his *Getica*. The original work of CASSIODORUS is now lost.

A treatise entitled *The Nature of the Soul*, 539, marked the beginning of the monastic career of CASSIODORUS at Squillace. In his retirement he also wrote a voluminous *Commentary on the Psalms*, and a more valuable, although incomplete, version of the *Notes on the Catholic Epistles* by CLEMENT of Alexandria. It was at his suggestion and with his help that EPIPHANIUS SCHOLASTICUS, fl. 510, produced his *Tripartite History*, by translating into Latin the ecclesiastical histories of SOCRATES, SOZOMEN, and THEODORET.

In VENANTIUS HONORIUS CLEMENTIANUS FORTUNATUS, 530-609, Latin poetry had its last representative in Gaul. The advancing tide of barbarism had submerged almost all the old classical culture; in the writings of FORTUNATUS the metrical forms of the vanishing pagan literature appear in Christian literature for the last time. His poems range from the liveliest social verse to the grandest hymns; they unite sincere feeling, rich imagination, and religious spirit, with a pedantic style, an imperfect taste, and many grammatical errors.

His work entitled *Miscellanies* is a collection of two hundred and forty-six pieces of verse without much literary value. The *Life of St. Martin of Tours* is a metrical version of the Life which SULPICIUS SEVERUS had written "in incomparably better prose." Under the inspiring direction of his friend, Queen Rhadegunda, he wrote of the men and events of his day in a political poem of three cantos. His other works are a *Group of Verses* and the *Lives of Eleven Saints*.

The subjects and style of his lesser poems may be seen in the following trifle:

> Surrounded by various delicacies, and all kinds of ragouts, sometimes I sleep, sometimes I eat; I open my mouth, then I close my eyes, and again I eat of everything; my mind was confused, believe it, dear ones, and I could not easily either speak with liberty, or write verses. A drunken man has an uncertain hand; wine produced the same effect upon me as upon other drinkers; methinks I see the table swimming in pure wine. However, as well as I am able, I have traced in soft language this little song for my mother and my sister . . .

His Hymns, of which less than a dozen survive, show him to much better advantage. In some of these he "rises to a rugged grandeur in which he has few rivals." His best known hymn is translated by Neale.

> The royal banners forward go
> The Cross shines forth in mystic glow;
> Where He in flesh, our flesh Who made,
> Our sentence bore, our ransom paid . . . . . .
>
> To Thee, Eternal Three in One,
> Let homage meet by all be done:
> As by the Cross Thou dost restore,
> So rule and guide us evermore.

GREGORY THE GREAT, 540-604, was an outstanding and vigorous champion of missionary work among the barbarian peoples. His enterprise in sending the monk Augustine to Britain in 596, and Paulinus in 601 was in accord with his aim to uproot paganism, and to purge the Church of heresy. He was the first monk to become Pope; his work constituted a bond between the earlier and the later schools of mediaeval thought; he was the unrivalled teacher of the Church until ANSELM; he set up the literary standard of his age, and he is remembered as the last of the four Doctors of the Latin Church.

He holds an important place in the literary history of Christianity because of the mass and the far reaching influence of his writings. That influence opposed the classic tradition to which he had an "implacable aversion." He thought it "most unfit that the words of the heavenly oracle should be subjected to the rules of the grammarian Donatus." Nevertheless had it not been for his zeal "there would have been no Aldhelm, no Benedict Biscop, no Bede, no Alcuin, no opening for the enormously important influence of Theodore of Tarsus and of Hadrian the Abbot."[3]

His shortened and simplified version of the *Sacramentary* of Gelasius became the basis of the Roman Missal. His *Book of Pastoral Rule*, addressed to Leander of Seville, enjoyed great popularity, especially after KING ALFRED translated it for the British clergy, and Charlemagne commended it to the Franks. It deals with the responsibilities of the pastoral office, the character of pastors, and the instruction suitable for the various classes of Church members.

Four books of Dialogues were only less popular; they were devoted to the praise of the lives and miracles of the Italian Fathers, and are astounding revelations of the excessive superstition that had grown up around the story of the past. GREGORY also left thirty-five books of biblical Expositions, twenty *Homilies on Ezekiel*, forty *Homilies on the Gospels*, and a large number of Letters. He thus wrote of the success of the British mission:

> The English race, situated in the far corner of the world has hitherto remained in unbelief, worshipping stocks and stones, . . . I made up my mind (it was God who prompted me) to send a monk of my own monastery to them to preach . . . . And now letters

---

[3] *Cambridge Mediaeval History*, Vol. III., chap. xix., p. 488.

have just arrived telling us of his safety and of his work . . . . And at Christmas last more than ten thousand English people, we are informed, were baptised by our brother and fellow bishop.

GREGORY'S exposition of the book of Job, commonly called *The Great Morality,* won its way to fame and is still an invaluable record of the theology of the sixth century in spite of the fact that the style is often barbarous, the thought superficial, the explanations frequently childish, and the plan without order.

> What I feel within, I lay open to my reader. In expounding I have not concealed what I think; in confessing I hide not what I suffer—I beg every reader to pray for me. If the value of his prayers and of my exposition be compared, he will have the advantage. He receives from me only words; but repays me with tears of supplication (Job conclusion).

The successor of GREGORY THE GREAT in the Western pontificate was ISIDORE of Seville, 560-636, the greatest man of his time in the Church of Spain, and the leading transmitter of knowledge in his century. In his massive works he showed that the literature of antiquity might yield much treasure for the enrichment of Christianity.

He gathered and condensed the results of his reading into *The Etymologies,* an uncritical and incomplete encyclopedia. The dryness and poverty of thought of this work "are outdone only by the absurdity of its etymologies."[4] In a work entitled *Differences* he discusses the different meanings of hundreds of words and the different characters of things. The second part of this book is really "a brief theological treatise on the doctrine of the Trinity, the power and nature

---

[4] H. O. Taylor, *Classical Heritage of the Middle Ages,* p. 51, note.

of Christ, paradise, angels, and men, under which is an elaborate definition of words . . ."[5] Other writings from his laborious pen are *Allegories of Certain Sacred Scriptures, The Birth and Death of the Fathers Extolled in the Scripture, Expositions of the Secrets of the Sacraments, The Catholic Faith from the Old and New Testaments against the Jews,* and *Three Books of Thoughts.* His better known and much quoted works are *The Ecclesiastical Office, The Great Chronicle,* and a *History of the Kings of the Goths, Wandals, and Suevi.* The last named still holds high rank as a historical source. In it ISIDORE expresses his aversion to the compulsory conversion of the Jews in Spain, as when he says of King Sisabut:

> He had a zeal of God but not according to knowledge. For he coerced by force those whom he ought to have provoked to faith by reason. But it is thus written 'Whether by opportunity or by truth Christ is preached, in this I rejoice and I will rejoice.'

Spain also gave MARTIN of Dumium, 530-580 to Christian literature. He wrote ethical tracts on *Pride,* and *Humility,* he collected a volume of *The Sayings of the Hermits,* and wrote on *The Paschal.* His *Instruction of Rustics* gives a notable example of the way in which Christian teaching was given to country children. It reappeared later in a Homily by CAESARIUS of Arles. MARTIN'S best known work is *The Formula for a Useful Life,* in which he gives a practical exposition of the four cardinal virtues.

About 600 the German national epic reached the highest point of its development. It was the swan song of a dying barbarism, which, like its Arian creed, was about to give way before the intellectual dominance of Rome and the spiritual authority of the Catholic faith.

---

[5] *Dictionary of Christian Biography,* Vol. III., p. 308.

The conversion of Germany is intimately connected with the life work of the Englishman WYNFRITH, 680-750, commonly called BONIFACE. Two of his fellow-countrymen, Wilfrid of York in 678, and Willebrord of Ripon in 689, had attempted and abandoned the task before BONIFACE organised a mission in 722 under the protection of Charles Martel.

At the monastic school which he established at Fulda in 742, BONIFACE composed several works which are more important for the insight they give into primitive German Christianity than for their intrinsic value. They included *The Eight Parts of Speech,* a collection of poems entitled *The Enigmata,* a *Penitential,* a Collection of Sayings and fifteen Sermons.

The literary influence of the conversion of the barbarians shows to excellent advantage in England where a distinctively Christian literature began with CAEDMON. GILDAS, 516-570, a monk of the school of Illudd wrote the first extant book belonging to the old British Church. This is *The Destruction of the British* in which GILDAS bewails the advent of the Angles and the Saxons. It reflects a mood of deep depression; it grieves over the Saxon devastations and the British vices; its style is "verbose, involved and obscure."

The Anglo-Roman Church that sprang from the mission of Augustine used the Latin tongue for its worship and the Rule of Benedict for its law. The transition from heathenism is reflected in what is known as *The Exeter Book,* where some of the poems have Christian additions, *e.g.* the "Wanderer," the "Sea-farer," the "Ruined Town," and the "Riddlers."

But CAEDMON, d. 680, the Anglo-Saxon Milton, bridged the gulf with a *Hymn of the World's Creator,* in which he proved that the Christian message could be sung in the heroic measures used by heathen bards to extol their favourite heroes.

> Now must we hymn the Master of heaven,
> The might of the Maker, the deeds of the Father,
> The thought of His heart. He, Lord everlasting,
> Established of old the source of all wonders:
> Creator all-holy, He hung the bright heaven,
> A roof high upreared, o'er the children of men;
> The King of mankind, then created for mortals
> The world in its beauty, the earth spread beneath them,
> He, Lord everlasting, omnipotent God.[6]

The so-called *Paraphrase,* often attributed to CAEDMON, is almost certainly the work of several writers. It retells in glowing poetry the stories of Genesis, Exodus, and part of Daniel.

ALDHELM of Sherborne, 640-709, holds a very important place in this early literature. He is associated with some of the biblical and legendary stories in the *Exeter Book,* but his authentic work is a volume *In Praise of Virginity,* and some of *The Hundred Riddles* which had great vogue as popular conundrums. These writings show that he had a considerable knowledge of books "and great facility in writing very involved and elaborate Latin."

The Hundred Riddles are often ascribed to CYNEWULF, fl. 750, with whom the second period of Old English poetry begins. He is the greatest of the Anglo-Saxon poets, a convert from heathenism whose awkward renditions of the *Legends of Juliana,* and *Guthlac* are far surpassed by his *Crist,* "Here, for the first time in his Christian work, he reaches originality, his true method and fit material." The material is taken partly from the Church liturgy, but more largely from the Homilies of GREGORY THE GREAT. "More than any poem in any language, *The Christ* reflects the spirit of early Latin Christianity."[7]

---

[6] "Caedmon's Hymn," Cook's version.

[7] William J. Long, *English Literature,* p. 37.

Ours was a sorry plight
Until at last we sailed unto the land
Over the troubled main. Help came to us
That brought us to the haven of salvation,
God's Spirit-Son, and granted grace to us
That we might know e'en from the vessel's deck
Where we must bind with anchorage secure
Our ocean steeds, old stallions of the wave.

CYNEWULF touched with a sure hand the notes of personal piety, of manliness, and of praise, both in *The Crist* and in the *Sequel to St. Guthlac,* the *Descent into Hell* and the *Elene.* Other works of his school are the *Fates of the Apostles,* and the *Andreas,* a picturesque version of the career of St. Andrew. The fine poems entitled *The Phoenix,* and *The Dream of the Rood,* are more freely Christian. The last named is the noblest extant example of Old English religious poetry. It is unnamed but is regarded by many as the work of CYNEWULF—"his last poem, his farewell." The Cross tells its own story in his dream.

I was hewed down in the holt, and wrought into shape, and set on a hill, and the Lord of all folk hastened to mount on me, the Hero who would save the world. Nails pierced me; I was drenched with the Hero's blood, and all Creation wept around me. Then His foes and mine took Almighty God from me, and men made His grave, and sang over Him a sorrowful lay.

In southern England whence all memories of the old British Church had disappeared, THEODORE of Tarsus, 602-690, laid new foundations on which the English Church has ever since rested. His one remaining book a *Penitential,* preserves a number of disciplinary canons.

The outshining and abiding glory of those days, too soon to be overshadowed by the Danish invasions, was BEDE,

673-735, a Northumbrian, who never left the monastery of Jarrow where his constant pleasure lay in learning, teaching, and writing. BEDE was the first great English scholar, the father of English learning, the founder of mediaeval history, and the first English historian.

Forty-five works bear witness to his untiring industry. His Sermons are modelled on monastic patterns with quotations from the Fathers and especially from GREGORY THE GREAT. His Expositions were gathered from earlier authorities "as from the pleasant meadows of far-flowing Paradise." In his *Histories of Saints* he "seems to have been the originator of a new type of *martyrologium*, in which the number of entries was much reduced but brief historical details were added concerning the saints who were commemorated."[8] He wrote *The Lives of the Holy Abbots of Weremouth and Jarrow*, and *The Life and Miracles of St. Cuthbert;* the latter was executed in both prose and verse and is a monument of credulity. Every chapter has its marvel:

> He presently fell upon some shepherds' huts, which . . . . were now deserted and ruinous. Into one of these he entered . . . . He then turned his thoughts to prayer, but suddenly, as he was singing a psalm, he saw his horse lift up his head and pull out some straw from the roof, and among the straw there fell down a linen cloth folded up, with something in it. When he had ended his prayers, wishing to see what this was, he came and opened the cloth, and found in it half a loaf of bread, still hot, and some meat, enough of both to serve him for a single meal (chap. v.).

The poetical side of BEDE'S nature found expression in Hymns of which nearly a dozen remain. It is however his *Ecclesiastical History of the English Nation* that gives him his place among the classics of all time. "The *Ecclesiastical*

---

[8] *Encyclopaedia of Religion and Ethics*, Vol. XI., p. 57.

History would be a treasure-house did it contain nothing but the charming tales of Alban and Augustine, of Edwin, Paulinus, Coifi, Caedmon, Cuthbert, Cedd and Aidan. But it holds far more than this. It presents the whole dramatic situation, not only in England, but in the civilized world. We contemplate the cosmopolitan power of the Church Catholic, pouring her riches with generous largesse into the little island of the North."[9]

After Caedwalla had possessed himself of the kingdom of the Gewissae, he also took the Isle of Wight, which till then was entirely given over to idolatry, and by cruel slaughter endeavoured to destroy all the inhabitants thereof, and to place in their stead people from his own province; having bound himself by a vow, though he was not yet, as is reported, regenerated in Christ, to give the fourth part of the land, and of the booty, to our Lord, if he took the island, which he performed by giving the same for our Lord to the use of Bishop Wilfrid, who happened at the time to have accidentally come thither out of his own nation. . . . .

Here I think it ought not to be omitted that the first fruits of the natives of that island who, by believing, secured their salvation, were two royal youths, brothers to Atwald, king of the island, who were honoured by the particular grace of God (chap. xvi.).

---

[9] Vida D. Scudder, *Intro. to the Eccles. History* (Dent's Everyman's Library), p. viii.

CHAPTER XIX

THE MENACE OF THE MOSLEMS

Scarcely two centuries had elapsed since Attila's successes when an even worse invasion threatened the Christian world.' After Muhammad, 568-633, decided to use the sword as an instrument of conversion, the spread of the Moslem power was amazingly swift. In 634 Bostra, the stronghold of Roman Arabia, fell to the arms of Islam; then followed in rapid succession, Jerusalem 637, Syria 641, and Alexandria 643. Africa was occupied in 647, Armenia in 654, Carthage in 698, and thus the whole southern seaboard of the Mediterranean came under the sway of the Crescent.

Damascus became the capital of an Empire which stretched from India to Spain under the Umayyad rule, 661-750. It dominated the Christian populations of Syria, Persia and Egypt, and even though Christians could attain to responsible offices, yet the progress of the Faith was retarded and Christian culture declined. Christian literature continued to be written wherever the milder rule of the victors tolerated the existence of the Church.

A certain PAULUS, who became bishop of Sidon after it had been captured by the Saracens, defended Christianity against the arguments of the victors in *A Letter to a certain Muhammadan on what the Christians Think of Muhammad and of the Truth of the Christian Religion.* He also wrote *An Epitome of Theology, The Coming of Messiah to the Jews,* and *The Trinity and the Incarnation.*

A more notable figure is GEORGE of Pisidia, fl. 610-640. Part of his work is historical, and his historical temper

162

shows itself in a *Hymn to the Virgin Mary, 626,* thanking her for the victory gained over the Avars. His religious writings consist of Sermons and Poems. "He is a court poet, writing with an eye to his patrons, and profuse in his praises of them." His most elaborate piece is the *Hexaemeron,* a poem of the Creation in nineteen hundred lines. The *Vanity of Life* is a short moral poem; in a work called *Against Severus* he contests the heresy of the Monophysites as it was held by the bishop of Antioch.

The Sermons are for the greater part fulsome and extravagant eulogies of the Virgin Mary; they reveal tendencies that were developed in the works of ANDREW of Crete, 660-732, who holds his place in literary history as the inventor of the Canons. Eight of these forms of Christian song are attributed to him, the most celebrated being the *Great Penitential Canon,* an ode of prodigious length and considerable beauty. In it the soul reviews various characters of the Bible, compares itself with the sinners and contrasts its own unworthiness with the virtues of the saints. He also wrote a *Canon on Lazarus,* a *Triode for Palm Sunday,* and various *Idiomela.* The Hymn for times of temptation has become universally popular in the version of J. M. Neale.

> Christian, dost thou see them on the holy ground,
> How the hosts of darkness compass thee around?
> Christian, up and smite them, counting gain but loss;
> Smite them by the merit of the holy Cross.

Forty of the Homilies of ANDREW are extant; seventeen of them are especially interesting as indications of the growth of the cultus of Mary. They contain some of the earliest examples of the extravagant titles which became so familiar in later years—"Diadem of Beauty," "Rod of Aaron," "Sceptre of David," "Refuge of all Christians," "Queen of our Race," "Temple of Christ."

GERMANUS of Cyzicus, 635-733, carried on his work

under the scrutiny of the Moslems. He convened a synod that met during the first siege of Constantinople, and during another siege he is said to have secured the break-up of the besiegers' fleet by his prayers to the Virgin. He left some Sermons and a few religious Poems devoted to the praise of Mary. He defended the orthodoxy of GREGORY of Nyssa in a *Treatise of Lawful Retribution.* Three of his Letters remain; they were the sources of "the anathemas pronounced by the second Council of Nicaea against those who refused to worship images."

It was in JOHN of Damascus, 680-764, that the Eastern Church under the Muhammadan regime had its most illustrious representative, its last great theologian, and the greatest of its religious poets. He was known among the Arabs as Mansur, *i.e.,* ransomed, and among his admirers as Chrysorrhoas, *i.e.,* the golden current. He became the highest authority in the theological literature of the Greeks. His book *The Fountain of Knowledge* gave the first comprehensive exposition of Christian Doctrine, and made the Damascene the true father of the Church's philosophy in the Middle Ages.

This great work was a compilation in three main divisions. The first part connected the logic of Aristotle with Christian theology, the second part reproduced and continued the work of EPIPHANIUS on Heresies, the third and most valuable part was "An accurate Exposition of the Orthodox Faith." This contains an elaborate and complete system of theology based on the writings of the early Fathers and the Canons of the great Councils. In its final form it dates from the year 743.

JOHN took a prominent part in the Iconoclastic controversy by writing three *Orations concerning the Images,* as protests against the edicts of the Emperor Leo, 727 and 730, forbidding the use of icons in churches. At the end of each

Oration JOHN gives extracts from earlier Christian writers in support of his views, and as a conclusion to the third he quotes Galatians i.8, and adds "shut your ears for I shrink as yet from saying what the divine apostle said: *Let him be accursed.*"

His *Book of Right Thoughts* is a formal profession of the true faith and the rejection of certain forms of heresy. He wrote *Against the Jacobites, Against the Manichaeans,* and *Against the Saracens,* as well as a curious treatise *Dragons and Vampires,* in which he discountenances the current superstitious belief in these creatures. His *Epistle on the Trisagion* defends the original form against all additions.

JOHN of Damascus was a real poet in spite of his tendencies to over-refinement and his "elaborate tricks of expression." He abandoned the popular simplicity of ROMANOS, 491-525 fl., who had carried Eastern hymnology to its highest perfection; with COSMAS THE MELODIST, d. 760, his friend and fellow poet, the Damascene went back to the 'classical' style of GREGORY NAZIANZEN. His *Golden Canon* is "the grandest piece in Greek sacred poetry. Nowhere are the best characteristics of the Greek Canon exhibited so splendidly." The first Ode of this Canon has won universal favour.

> The Day of Resurrection Earth tell it out abroad
> The Passover of gladness; the Passover of God!
> From death to life eternal, from earth unto the sky,
> Our Christ hath brought us over with hymns of victory.

JOHN's disciple THEODORE ABUKERA prepared a useful work on Christian apologetics with the title *Questions and Answers between a Barbarian and a Christian.*

The name Theodore also belongs to that eminent figure in Christian history, THEODORE of the Studium, 759-812, famous for his advocacy of a reformed monasticism and for his defence of image worship. He was noted for his fine penmanship, and his zeal in securing copies of manuscripts.

His two important works are *The Greater* and *The Lesser
Catecheses,* addressed to the brethren of the great monastery
of the Studium.   The Polemical Discourses are valuable for
the history of the Iconoclastic controversy in which he
played so active and stormy a part.   They were preached to
defend the use of images in Christian worship, and their
arguments are those in common favour in the eighth century.
During the peaceful years 787-813, that intervened between periods of stress and persecution, the monastery of
the Studium became the home of hymnography, and THEO-
DORE was not the least successful of the hymn writers there.
A Hymn for the first Sunday in Lent, "A song, a song of
gladness," probably celebrates the temporary success of the
advocates of the icons.   Another of his poems, "That fear-
ful day, that day of speechless dread," has been called "the
grandest judgment hymn of the Church" prior to the composition of the "Dies Irae" some four centuries later.

The presbyter EULOGIUS of Cordova, c. 818-859, left a
*Memorial of the Saints, or Three Books of the Martyrs of
Cordova,* a work which honours the Spanish confessors of
the period and furnishes an important source of information
concerning the condition of the Church in Spain.   He was
also responsible for *An Exhortation to the Martyrs,* a little
work of encouragement to the virgin confessors Flora and
Mary.

After the year 850 the lenient policy of Moslem rule
towards Christianity was reversed.   Many Christians suffered in consequence.   Their persecutors misinterpreted their
devotion which EULOGIUS defended in *An Apology for the
Martyrs against their Calumniators,* written to deny the
slander that Christians wantonly sought death as the reward
of their faith.

ALVAR of Cordova, the friend and biographer of EULO-
GIUS, reinforced this Apology in a work of his own.   His

loyalty to the Faith and his fears for the youth of his day appear in his *Brilliant Revelation*, in which he declared "all our Christian youths who are winning a name for themselves by their talents, know the language and the literature of the Arabs alone." His fears for the future were however unfulfilled; by the eleventh century Christianity had won complete ascendency in Spain.

CHAPTER XX

THE HISTORY OF THE FAITH

On the threshold of the Carolingian era which marked the definite victory of Christianity in Europe, it will be well to review the historical writings that had been composed in the interest of the Faith during the first eight centuries of its existence. These are a vital element in the Christian story. "From the first, Christianity had a philosophy of history. Its earliest apologists sought to show how the world had followed a divine plan in its long preparation for the life of Christ. From this central fact of all history, mankind should continue through war and suffering until the divine plan was completed at the Judgment day. The fate of nations is in God's hands; history is the revelation of His wisdom and power."[1]

The first Church historian after the close of the New Testament era was HEGESIPPUS, 120-185, a Hebrew Christian. In his *Reminiscences,* he attempted to preserve the more useful records of literature, doctrine, paganism, contemporary heresies, and Hebrew Christianity. He wrote five books on the Apostolical Preaching, *i.e.,* probably, *Commentaries on the Testimonies,* with illustrations and explanations of the teaching involved. To him is due the preservation of the story of the martyrdom of St. James the Just, the account of the arrest of certain members of Christ's family, etc.:

> . . . . many bore the name of James, but this one was holy from his birth. He drank no wine or intoxi-

[1] *Encyclopaedia Britannica,* 11th ed., Vol. XIII., p. 529.

cating liquor, nor did he eat flesh; no razor came upon his head; he did not anoint himself with oil, nor make use of the bath. He alone was permitted to enter the holy place: for he did not wear any woollen garment, but fine linen only. He alone was wont to go into the Temple: and he used to be found kneeling on his knees, begging forgiveness for the people—so that the skin of his knees became horny like that of a camel's by reason of his constantly bending the knee in adoration to God, and begging forgiveness for the people (*Commentaries*, Bk. V.).

The great story of the final struggle between the Faith and the State was told from the Christian standpoint in *The Deaths of the Persecutors,* an accurate and trustworthy record ascribed to LACTANTIUS (see page 42).

"Christian history begins with the triumph of the Church," and the father of Christian history in the full sense of the term was EUSEBIUS of Caesarea, 264-340, with whom the apologetic pamphlets of the age gave way to a reasoned review of three centuries of Christian progress. He was the first to attempt a united and complete history, into which he introduced large quotations from other authors. He owed much to the noted Pamphilus whose fine library and literary friendships were placed at the service of the historian.

EUSEBIUS wrote an account of the *Martyrs of Palestine* in two rescensions of which the longer seems to have been the original. The shorter version was written later as an Appendix to his *History of the Church.* He also gathered and edited a *Collection of Ancient Martyrdoms,* in which later writers found much material for their pious legends and literary fictions. His *Chronicon,* with its introductory epitome of universal history down to 325, is a famous example of the chronological computations which Christians were led to make by their studies of prophecy and by the necessity of confuting the plea that heathenism was older than Christianity. JULIUS AFRICANUS was the first Christian writer who attempted "to embody in a single history the most important facts recorded either in Scripture or by secular historians", so arranged that the facts appeared in their proper relative places. His epitome provided EUSEBIUS with a foundation for *The Chronicon,* a work that opened a new path in historical writing. The original perished, but not before GEORGE SYNCELLUS of Constantinople, fl. 785-810, had copied large portions of it into his *Chronicle.* JEROME also made a Latin translation of the original work, and an anonymous Armenian of the fifth century rendered it into his own language.

The enduring fame of EUSEBIUS will always rest upon his *Ecclesiastical History,* nine books of which were written in 313, and the tenth in 324. This is the last great literary monument of the period which it describes.

> . . . . it is my purpose to record the successions of the holy apostles, together with the times since our Saviour, down to the present, to recount how many and important transactions are said to have occurred in ecclesiastical history, what individuals in the most noted places eminently governed and presided over the church, what men also in their respective generations, whether with or without their writings, proclaimed the divine word; to describe the character, times, and number of those who, stimulated by the desire of innovation, and advancing to the greatest errors, announced themselves leaders in the propagation of false opinions, like grievous wolves, unmercifully assaulting the flock of Christ; as it is my intention, also, to describe the calamities that swiftly overwhelmed the whole Jewish nation, in consequence of their plots against our Saviour; how often, by what means, and in what

times, the word of God has encountered the hostility of the nations; what eminent persons persevered in contending for it through those periods of blood and torture, beside the martyrdoms which have been endured in our own times; and after all, to show the gracious and benign interposition of our Saviour. . . .

(Bk. I., chap. i.).

The *Life of Constantine* by EUSEBIUS is an extravagant eulogy, in which legend and truth are so intermingled as to be almost inseparable. Among his apologetic writings he left a rich literary treasure *The Preparation for the Gospel*, which justifies the separation between Christianity and Greek philosophy, as its sequel the *Demonstration of the Gospel*, 312, justifies the change from pagan habits and ideals to those of the new religion.

GELASIUS of Caesarea in Palestine, 320-394, continued the *Ecclesiastical History* in a brilliantly written but now lost work.

That tireless translator RUFINUS TYRANNIUS, 340-410, made the Church of the West familiar with the Greek fathers in Latin versions. As a theologian he wrote, in defence of the orthodoxy of ORIGEN, *A Dissertation on the Adulteration by Heretics of the Works of Origen*, which he prefixed to his translation of an *Apology on Origen's Behalf* written by PAMPHILUS. When his own orthodoxy was questioned he defended himself in an *Apology to Pope Anastasius*. His work entitled the *Explanation of the Symbol* consists of a comparison between the Nicene Creed and the Confession of Aquilea, his native city.

As a historian he is inaccurate, biased, and credulous. He in part translated and in part created an *Ecclesiastical History* based on the work EUSEBIUS. *The History of the Egyptian Hermits*, a biographical account of thirty-three monks of the Nitrian desert, was his own original work.

Arianism had its historian in PHILOSTORGIUS, 368-425, whose *Ecclesiastical History* ranks among the best works of its kind, although according to the contemptuous criticism of PHOTIUS it is marred by faults of stiffness, coldness, and obscurity, and according to GIBBON its credibility is discounted by passion, prejudice, and ignorance. Like a similar work by PHILIP of Side, fl. 420, it is now almost entirely lost.

The substantial and interesting *Church History* of SOCRATES, 380-440, has fortunately been preserved in its entirety. He was a lawyer of Constantinople with definite leanings toward the Novatian heresy. In his use of a great mass of valuable material he exercised a critical judgment and discriminated between what was probable, what doubtful, and what fictitious. He cultivated a simple, unadorned, and unreflective style in order to set forth the facts as faithfully as he could.

> I come now to speak of the cause which led them (the Abyssinian people) to become converts to Christianity. Meropius, a Tyrian philosopher determined to visit (their) country . . . . Having taken with him, therefore, two youths to whom he was related. . . . . Meropius arrived at that country by ship. The Indians (*i.e.* Abyssinians) . . . . having seized the philosopher and those who sailed with him, killed them all except his two young kinsmen, but sparing them from compassion for their tender age, they sent them as a gift to the king. . . . .
>
> The king dying soon after left them free, ... and the queen, seeing her son thus left in his minority, begged the young men to undertake the charge of him until he should become of adult age.
>
> They therefore accepted the commission and entered on the administration of the kingdom, the chief author-

ity being in the hands of Frumentius who began anx-
iously to enquire whether among the Roman merchants
trafficking with that country there were any Christians
to be found; and having discovered some, he informed
them who he was, and exhorted them to select some
appropriate places for the celebration of Christian worship (*History*, I., xix.).

With the work of SOCRATES in his hand, SOZOMEN, 400-
443, a Jewish lawyer practising in Constantinople, prepared
a *Church History* of the century 323-423.   In writing this
he used not only SOCRATES but also the works of EUSE-
BIUS, RUFINUS, ATHANASIUS, SABINUS PALLADIUS and
OLYMPIODORUS.   His *Epitome* of events from the beginning of the Christian era to the year 323 is among the many
lost books of the Church.

> When the day came round for giving money to the
> troops . . . . Julian reflected that soldiers are natu-
> rally thoughtless and simple, and disposed to be covet-
> ous of money, and therefore concluded that it would
> be a favourable opportunity to seduce them to the wor-
> ship of the gods. . . . .
> It is related that as some of those who had ignorantly
> fallen into sin were seated at table and drinking to each
> other, one among them happened to mention the name
> of Christ.   Another of the guests immediately ex-
> claimed: 'It is strange that you should call upon
> Christ when, but a short time ago, you denied Him.
> for the sake of the Emperor's gift, by throwing incense
> into the fire'.   On hearing this they all became sud-
> denly conscious of the sin they had committed. . . . .
> They then presented themselves before the Emperor,
> threw back his gold, and besought him to put them to
> death (*History*, V., xvii).

Another link in the chain of records is *The Religious His-*

tory by THEODORET of Cyrrhus, 386-458. This work covered the years 390-457, and gave an account of the lives of
the Syrian monks, especially of one named Jacob who lived
as a hermit near Nisibis. It is a monument of religious credulity amazing in so well-read and so intellectual an author.
During the year 416-417 the Spaniard, PAUL OROSIUS,
fl. 409-420, prepared a historical treatise *The History of
the World,* to confirm by facts the doctrine maintained by
AUGUSTINE in his *City of God.* Written in an attractive
style and of convenient size this became the popular historical manual of the Middle Ages. A free abridged translation
by ALFRED THE GREAT is extant and testifies to its widespread popularity.

The succession was maintained by ZACHARIAS, bishop of
Melitene, fl. 540, commonly called Rhetor, who described
the events of the period 451-491, in an *Ecclesiastical History*
in Syriac. For the material of this work he borrowed from
SOCRATES and from THEODORET. The story of the century 420-520 by THEODORUS the Reader, is now almost
wholly lost. The *Chronography* of JOHN of Antioch, surnamed MALALAS, fl. 600, holds a celebrated place in English
literary history. In the first place it was the first Byzantine
work edited by English scholarship, and in the second place
it was the subject of the celebrated letter of Bentley to Mill.
The work is in eighteen books; the first nine deal with the
history of the world before the Incarnation; the others treat
of Christian times. Much material not found elsewhere is
preserved in this *Chronography;* thus it says that Evodius.
the second bishop of Antioch, fixed upon the believers the
title of Christians (cp. Acts xi.26).

PROSPER of Aquitane, whose other writings have already
been noticed (page 136), left a *Chronicle* in three parts.
Part one extends from the earliest age to 326; part two from
326 to 378; part three carries the story down to 455, when
Rome was taken by the Vandals.

After the death of Maximus, there followed immediately the captivity of the Romans, a thing worthy of many tears. The city was left undefended, and Gaiseric got possession of it. The holy bishop Leo went forth to meet him outside the gates, and his prayers, by God's help, so softened him, that, though all was in his power, as the city had been handed over to him, he refrained from fire and slaughter and punishment. So for fourteen days they were free and at liberty to search. They spoiled Rome of all its wealth, and many thousand captives, according as age or beauty took their fancy, they carried off to Carthage, including the Empress and her daughters.

EVAGRIUS the Scholar, 536-c.600, is known only by his *History* which was written as a continuation of the works of EUSEBIUS, SOCRATES, SOZOMEN, etc.:

that the famous deeds which slumbered in the dust of forgetfulness might be revived; that they might be stirred with his pen, and presented for immortal memory; . . . . that no worthy act, by reckless security and languishing slothfulness, the sister of oblivion, might be put clean out of remembrance (Preface).

The kinsman of EVAGRIUS, JOHN of Asia, 505-590, a Monophysite leader of the Syriac-speaking Church, was one of its earliest and most serviceable historians. His *Ecclesiastical History* began with Julius Caesar and carried the story down to 585. The first part however is now lost; the second part is known only by meagre quotations in the *Chronicon* of DIONYSIUS; the third is a record of the years 571-585, and as a contemporary and largely autobiographical narrative it has very high importance. JOHN was also the author of *The Biographies of the Saints*, 569.

The honour of producing the first real history written

in the Middle Ages falls to GREGORY of Tours, 538-594, who compiled an *Ecclesiastical History of the Franks to the year 584* from many previous histories, episcopal lists, lives of saints, legends, annals, and traditions. This work is almost our only source of information for the period that it covers. Its attractiveness and its mastery of the art of narration won for GREGORY the title of "the Herodotus of the Barbarians." He is "the last of the Ciceronians, the first of the chroniclers." His Latin was becoming French, it shows an ignorance of grammar for which he apologised. but the occasional passages that are wrought with poetry and grace redeem it from utter rusticity.

A serious decline in historical writing took place after EVAGRIUS, and for three centuries this department of Greek Christian literature produced little more than a few *Chronicles*. In the West the history of the Church became an integral part of the history of the world, and thenceforward the historian found his proper place outside the limits of specifically Christian literature.

PART V

THE MEDIÆVAL AGE
(800-1500)

CHAPTER XXI

THE CAROLINGIAN REVIVAL

An event of capital importance for civilisation and Christianity in Europe took place on Christmas Day, 800, when Charlemagne, 742-814, was crowned Emperor of the Romans by Pope Leo III, 795-816. Here we are concerned only with his encouragement and patronage of Christian literature.

The Church had shown that it was alive to its own interests when it accepted the so-called *Donation of Constantine.* "This pious falsehood was perhaps first devised by Stephen II when he was on his famous visit to King Pipin at Paris in 754 . . . . the document itself seems to have been concocted somewhat later . . . by some clever papal notary." (In 777 it) "was for the first time openly and officially cited, Hadrian entreating Charles to "become a new Constantine." Its value as a historical document does not of course consist in the legends that it preserves, but in the fact that . . . "although a portentous falsehood, it is the most unimpeachable evidence of the thoughts and beliefs of the priesthood which framed it."

> We hand over and relinquish to the most blessed Pontiff and universal Pope Sylvester, our palace, the city of Rome, and all the provinces, places, and cities of Italy, and the western regions, and we ordain that they shall be governed by him and his successors and shall remain under the authority of the holy Roman Church.[1]

[1] H. B. Cotterill, *Medieval Italy,* pp. 302, 304.

179

The new Emperor gathered about him some of the best intellects of the West, schools were founded, and monasteries became nurseries of religious culture. His circular letter to the Frankish clergy *The Cultivation of Literature,* 787, has been called the "constituent charter of modern thought."

> Charles, by the aid of God, king of the Franks and Lombards, and prince of the Romans, to the high ministers of religion throughout our dominions: Having it near at heart that the state of the churches should more and more advance towards perfection, and being desirous of restoring by assiduous care the cultivation of letters, which have almost entirely disappeared from among us, in consequence of the neglect and indifference of our ancestors, we would excite by our own example all well-disposed persons to the study of the liberal arts. To this purpose, we have already by God's constant help, accurately corrected the books of the Old and New Testaments, corrupted by the ignorance of the copyists.

His decree of 789 to secure religious uniformity evoked the earliest German prose writings—translations of the baptismal vow, the Creeds, the Lord's Prayer, etc. Other religious writings soon developed from these, and in their turn furnished material for the sermons that Charlemagne ordered the clergy to preach.

The literary movement which had passed from Ireland to Iona, and from thence to Jarrow and York, now spread to Aix where Charlemagne sought to make his court a Christian Athens. Three successive phases marked the revival which had thus begun.

i. The first was due to PAUL THE LOMBARD, c. 720-790, and to PETER of Pisa, whose common reverence for AUGUSTINE attracted the attention of the Emperor. PAUL turned his gift for narration to account and continued the *History* of Eutropius with the addition of many stories which he told with real zest and a keen delight in heroic deeds. He also wrote *The Lives of the Bishops of Metz*, a *Life of Gregory the Great*, some Homilies and Poems.

ii. The second period saw ALCUIN, 735-804, and his Anglo-Saxon colleagues in the ascendant. ALCUIN was the foremost theologian, philosopher, and teacher of his age, in whom commences the alliance of love of pagan literature with sincerity of Christian faith and eagerness to fathom its mysteries. Although "no real poet" and too often dull and spiritless, he showed his literary tendencies while master of the school of York, 766-780, by writing *Verses on the Fathers, Kings, and Saints of the Church of York*. This is the best of his Latin poems. A section in prose translation reads:

> The learned Aelbert gave drink to thirsty minds at the sources of various sciences and studies. To some he was eager to communicate the art and rules of grammar; for others he made flow the waters of rhetoric. He exercised these in the combats of jurisprudence, and those in the songs of Adonia. Some learned from him to sound the pipes of Castalia, and to strike with a lyric foot the summits of Parnassus. To others he taught the harmony of heaven, the works of the sun and the moon, the five zones of the pole, the seven wandering stars . . . . the nature of men, of beasts, and birds, and the inhabitants of woods . . . he taught how to calculate with certainty the solemn return of Easter; and, above all, he explained the mysteries of the holy scripture (1431-1447).

As the guide of the revival he digested into dialogues various standard works; *e.g.* on Grammar, Orthography, Rhet-

oric, and Logic.   The following passage gives an example
of his method:

> What is life?
> Happiness for the happy, misery for the miserable;
> the expectation of death.
> What is death?
> An inevitable event, a doubtful journey, a subject of
> tears for the living, the confirmations of wills, the
> robber of men.
> What is man?
> The slave of death, a passing traveller, a guest in his own
> abode.

As a defender of the Faith he combatted the Adoptionist
heresy in a work entitled *The Trinitarian Faith*, which in
the main is plagiarised from AUGUSTINE'S work *The Trinity*.   As a theologian he wrote Commentaries on various
books of the Bible.   These were intended to unfold the
allegorical meaning of the text and to determine the moral
sense.   His work entitled *The Virtues and Vices* concludes
with this generous affirmation:

> For as the beatitude of the kingdom of God is preach-
> ed to all without distinction, so the entry to the king-
> dom is open equally, with only a distinction as to
> merits, to each sex, to all ages, to all ranks: there no
> heed is taken as to whether a man on earth has been a
> layman or priest, rich or poor, young or old, master
> or slave, but eternal glory crowns each according to
> his works.

The three hundred and eleven Letters that remain of his
correspondence with Charles and the most important personages in England and Europe, "have the best right to
the name of literature."   They give a most valuable survey
of the humanism of the age.

In 796 ALCUIN, wearied with his labours, retired to the abbey of St. Martin of Tours where he taught until, in 801, he resigned his offices and prepared himself for death.

AGOBARD of Lyons, 779-840, who played an outstanding part in the political and religious life of his day, left some practical works on doctrine and discipline. One, entitled *Bishop Bernard on the Rights and Privileges of the Priesthood*, was an able and useful work; another more contentious book, called *Pictures and Images*, 824, was widely known and freely contradicted. It urged the abolition of the cult of image worship. A third book from his pen was *The Truth of the Faith*, in which he made an evangelical appeal to the people of Lyons.

As a preface to a work called *The Correction of the Antiphony*, he wrote *On Divine Psalmody*, criticising AMALARIUS who had objected to the changes introduced into church music by AGOBARD. He returned to the same subject in *A Book against the Four Books of Amalarius*.

The great treatise of AMALARIUS, *The Ecclesiastical Offices*, "is one of the most curious documents which those who are especially occupied with the liturgy and the emblematic significance of the ceremonies of the Church should consult."

iii. The third period of the revival found native scholars predominant. EINHARD or Eginhard, 770-840, Charlemagne's friend and secretary, wrote the Emperor's biograpy in *The Annals of Einhard*, 830. He went to the Palace School from the monastery at Fulda, but retired in disgust at the rivalries and quarrels of the Court where he acquired the name of the Ant because of his tireless industry. His *Life of Charlemagne*, 821, is a character sketch rather than a real biography, and although true to life is lacking in many details. It took its place among the most widely read books of the Middle Ages.

A less trustworthy treatise *The Translation and Miracles of S. S. Marcellinus and Peter*, with a parallel *Poem of the Passion of the Christian Martyrs S. S. Marcellinus and Peter*, have some historical value. His work entitled *The Adorable Cross* is now lost.

THEODULPH of Orleans, c.751-821, "a Goth by nature and an Italian by birth," fell under the royal displeasure for writing *A Collection of the views of the Fathers on the doctrine of the Procession of the Holy Ghost*. He was more fortunate as a poet, his best works are the poems that won for him the title of the Pindar of the Royal school. His exultant hymn for Palm Sunday is sung the world over.

> All glory, laud, and honour
> To Thee, Redeemer, King,
> To Whom the lips of children
> Made sweet hosannas ring!
> Thou art the King of Israel,
> Thou David's royal Son,
> Who in the Lord's name comest,
> The King and Blessed One.

Tradition says that it was first sung by its author from behind his prison bars at Angers in 820 and secured his release. His services to religious culture are attested by his Sermons, as well as by a *Treatise on the Vices* (the Cardinal Sins), a work *On Baptism*, an *Exhortation to Prelates*, and a poem of nine hundred and sixty-five verses entitled *An Exhortation to Judges*, intended to instruct magistrates as to the discharge of their duties. It ends on a generous note:

> Mortal, always be prepared to treat mortals with mildness; the law of nature is the same for them and for thee. However different may be thy course here below, thou and they start from the same point; it is to the same point that you tend . . . . The Author of life died for them as well as for thee, and he will extend his gifts to each according to his merits. Let us

here fold the sails of my book, and let the anchor retain my ship on this shore.

In Ireland FOTHAD, d.819, is remembered for his "canon" absolving all priests from military service.

The Church of the living God, let her alone, waste her not,
Let her right be apart, as best it ever was.
Every true monk, who is of a pure conscience,
For the Church to which it is due let him labour like every
        servant,
Every soldier from that out, who is without rule or obedience,
Is permitted to aid the great Aedh, son of Niall.
This is the true rule, neither more nor less:
Let every one serve in his vocation without murmur or complaint.

The far reaching effects of the new literary spirit are also visible in the Saxon poem *The Saviour*, Heiland or Heljand—a didactic piece of some six thousand alliterative lines, "written by a Saxon priest with the avowed purpose of opening the obdurate ears of his countrymen to the message of Christianity." It dates from 830, when its author was indebted to Louis the Pious for suggesting the theme. The poem has been praised beyond its merits as "the only real Christian epic," and "the most sublime work which Christian poetry has ever produced," a less immoderate criticism regards it as representing "the most complete absorption of the Christian tradition by the German mind . . . before the time of Dürer." [2]

Then became enraged the swift sword-thane Simon Peter; his wrath welled up, he could not speak a word, so deeply it grieved him that they wanted to bind the Lord. Fiercely he went, the bold thane, to stand in front of his liege lord . . . At once he drew his sword from his side and smote the foremost of the foes with full force so that Malchus was reddened with the

---

[2] Kuno Francke, *History of German Literature*, 7th impression, pp. 38, 39.

sword's edge on the right side, his ear hewn off, his cheek gashed, blood leaped forth, welling from the wound. And the people drew back fearing the sword bite.

The spirit of the revival moved in Germany's first native teacher MAGNENTIUS HRABANUS MAURUS, 776-856, a pupil of the two schools of Fulda and Tours. He was in his own estimation "something of a collector," and gathered from far and wide material for Encyclopaedias and Biblical Commentaries. About 820 he compiled a *Commentary on Matthew*, to which he added a preface from a similar work by BEDE, with a frank confession of his methods which certainly had the merit of keeping open the avenues of ancient knowledge. In this way he served the needs of his age. He prepared a collection entitled *Passages of Scripture bearing on Virtues and Vices*, a series of *Extracts from the Grammar of Priscian*, Commentaries on most of the books of the Old and New Testaments, and two collections of Sermons—one for private reading, the other for pulpit use by the clergy.

MAURUS was probably the moving spirit behind the work of translating a Latin *Life of Christ* into German. His most popular work was *The Praises of the Holy Cross*, an allegorical poem with prose notes intended as explanations. It lacks both form and meaning. He was quite alive to the perils attending the use of allegory, and vainly tried to reduce the method to a system in a book called *The Allegories in the whole Sacred Scriptures*. He encouraged CANDIDUS, fl. 790-830, whom he placed at the head of the school of Fulda in 822, to undertake literary work. Acting on the suggestion CANDIDUS wrote *The Life of St. Eigil*, in one book of prose and one book of verse. Besides this he composed some expository Homilies, *A Little Work on the Passion of the Lord*, and *An Answer to a Monk*. In the last named book he considered the question whether Christ could see God bodily with His bodily eyes. The answer is in the negative, and forms an appeal for the cultivation of purity of heart as the only means of seeing God.

HAYMO of Halberstadt, 778-853, an English relative of BEDE, was the foremost representative of clerical learning among the Germans of the ninth century. He was with HRABANUS MAURUS both at Fulda and Tours, and imitated his methods of quotation and allegorising; a large proportion of his books consists of extracts from the Fathers. One hundred and fifty-four Homilies remain as samples of his labours.

> We are not only unable to perfect any good, without divine grace and mercy preceding and following us, but not even to think any. For the grace of God prevents us, that we may be willing, and follows us, that we may be able. Every good thing that we have, the good will, and the good work, is not from ourselves but from God.

WALAFRID STRABO of Reichenau, 808-849, laid the foundation of mediaeval exposition in a work of extraordinary popularity, *The Ordinary Tongue,* which won the title of the *Tongue of Scripture,* and "remained for some five hundred years the most widespread and important quarry of mediaeval biblical science." All later writers consulted it. It became "the workshop of the ecclesiastical mind." *An Exposition of the Four Evangelists* is also attributed to him. His Poems are concerned with the Lives and Visions of various saints—Gall, Wettin, etc. The last named poem was based on a rather Dantesque prose account of the *Vision of St. Wettin,* 823, by HETTO, 763-836, whom Charlemagne first elevated to be bishop of Basle, and afterwards to be abbot of Reichenau. HETTO'S account of his mission to Constantinople is now lost; but a *Book of Rules* for those having spiritual charge in his diocese remains, in addition to *A Vision of St. Wettin* which describes a journey in the spirit to the underworld.

SERVATUS LUPUS of Ferrieres, 805-862, a devotee of the classics and an ardent collector of books, excelled his contemporaries in clearness of exposition, grasp of essentials, and appreciation of the vital issues in matters of controversy. He foreshadowed one of the great disputes of his age in a work called *The Three Questions*. These questions were the freedom of the will, twofold predestination, and the range of Christ's redemption.

> Since many reject it as a blasphemous assertion, as an assertion which greatly detracts from the merits of our Redeemer, to say that he did not redeem all men, we will, therefore, holding fast only to the faith that God has redeemed by the blood of Christ all whom he willed, leave the matter so far undetermined as to allow that if it could be shown that the blood of the Redeemer had somewhat benefitted even the damned in the mitigation of their punishment, we would not only not oppose it, but even gladly adopt their opinion; for, if the sun, though it cannot enlighten, still gives warmth to the blind, why may not that mightier sun though it does not save those who are blinded and lost by their own guilt, still make them experience, in the mitigation of their sufferings, the influence of so great a ransom?

Another of the pupils of HRABANUS MAURUS was OTFRID of Weissenberg, 800-870, whose *Book of the Gospels*, 868, gave the laity a "devotional" commentary in the vernacular. The narrative is interspersed with reflections and personal applications which often rise to heights of eloquence, and also with musical and pleasing Hymns. The prose is often feeble, diffuse, and out of touch with the theme. One interesting chapter is headed—"Why the author wrote this work in German."

The possibility of arguing on the Three Questions which SERVATUS had pointed out was exploited by GOTTSCHALK, 808-867, a monk of Fulda and a friend of WALAFRID STRABO. His work on *Predestination* attempted to define what AUGUSTINE had left indefinite. It affirmed that as God decrees eternal life to the elect, and the elect to eternal life, so also does He decree everlasting punishment to the reprobate, and the reprobate to everlasting punishment. Although a vigorous and original thinker, GOTTSCHALK was a rather reactionary theologian; his teaching was in essence a form of fatalism foreign to the genius of Christianity. His book has disappeared, and is only known from the criticisms of its opponents, but its main thesis was defended by its author in both a *Longer,* and a *Shorter Profession of Faith.*

The *Predestination* raised a tremendous controversy in which many took part. GOTTSCHALK was condemned as a heretic, 849, degraded from the priesthood, ordered to be beaten with rods, imprisoned and forced to cast his book into the fire. He died in prison firmly maintaining the truth of his views.

"Only within recent times have certain lyrics of his been brought to light . . . Yet more recently GOTTSCHALK has been accepted as the author of a poem very famous for six or seven centuries after him, the *Eclogue of Theodulus"* (Theodulus Gottschalk *i.e.* God's slave, in Greek). This Eclogue is a colloquy between Truth and Falsehood, with Reason for an umpire. Falsehood cites a number of incidents from pagan mythology, giving a quatrain to each. Truth caps each incident with a citation from Scripture. The verdict is a foregone conclusion. In length and subject the poem was admirably fitted to be a school book, and as a school book it survived well into the Renaissance period.[3]

An even more important and certainly a more lasting con-

---

[3] *Cambridge Mediæval History,* Vol. III., p. 529.

troversy sprang from *The Sacrament of the Body and Blood of Christ*, 831, written by RADBERT PASCHASIUS, d. 860. This is the first systematic treatise on the doctrine of the Eucharist in Christian literature, and it contains the first dogmatic statement of the idea of transubstantiation. In 844 PASCHASIUS presented to Charles the Bold, 823-877, a revised and popular version of the work with the title *The Body and Blood of Christ*. The mood of the age welcomed the idea of a fleshly element in the Eucharist and the treatise became "in the subsequent period the authoritative exposition of the rite." But Augustinianism, to which the idea was repugnant, was still strong, and an interminable discussion began in which RATRAMNUS was the leading opponent of the new teaching. His book bearing the title *The Body and Blood of the Lord*, was written at the request of Charles the Bold.

Many disputants entered into the fray without reaching agreement. The controversy continued for centuries, and, throughout the later history of Christian literature, works constantly appear either to oppose or to defend the thesis of PASCHASIUS.

Among so much that is technical the examples of pure literature are most welcome. The ninth century witnessed the first use of rhyme in Germany; this use connects with the writing of Christian hymns in imitation of popular Latin poetry. The cult of literature spread among women and Charlemagne's daughters joined the company of scholars.

The nun HROTSUIT, commonly called ROSWITHA, 935-990, who belonged to the nunnery of Gandersheim wrote a *Life of Otto the Great*, and a famous series of sacred legends and plays with various titles, *Gallicanus Dulcitius, Abraham,* etc. These are characterised by rapidity of action, frequent change of scene, and interplay of conflicting feelings. Their one theme is the "battle of vice and virtue, the triumph of Christian martyrdom over the temptations and sins of the world." They are noteworthy as being the first dramatic attempts in the literatures of modern Europe, and they were honoured by being among the first books printed in Southern Germany.

> I, the strong voice of Gandersheim, have not hesitated to imitate in my writings a poet (Terence) whose works are so widely read, my hope being to glorify, within the limits of my poor talent, the laudable chastity of Christian virgins in that self same form of composition which had been used to describe the shameless acts of licentious women . . . .
>
> I have been at pains, whensoever I have been able to pick up some threads and scraps torn from the old mantle of philosophy, to weave them into the stuff of my book, in the hope that my lowly ignorant effort may gain more acceptance through the introduction of something of a nobler strain.[4]

[4] *The Plays of Roswitha*, trans. by Christopher St. John, The Mediaeval Library (1923), pp. xxvi., xxix.

CHAPTER XXII

THE RISE OF SCHOLASTICISM

The impetus of the Carolingian revival did not bring about a great development of pure literature. From the tenth to the sixteenth century, German literature, for example, was at its lowest ebb. The poetry of the ninth century was forgotten by the twelfth. This condition was, in great measure, due to the growing interest in problems of philosophy and Christian doctrine. The Scholastic movement had begun.

JOHN of Damascus is regarded as the founder of the scholastic type of thought; but as Greek was almost unknown in the West the early Scholastics nourished their minds on translations and on such philosophy as they could find in *The Satyricon* of MARTIAN of Capella, fl. 400-435, in *The Arts* of CASSIODORUS, *The Origins* by ISIDORE of Seville, and the writings of AUGUSTINE.

Foremost among the makers of the mediaeval ecclesiastical philosophy stands JOHN SCOTUS ERIGENA, c.800-880, the great Irish divine. He was head if the Palace School for thirty years, 845-875, during the short-lived revival of literature under Charles the Bold. His rare knowledge of Greek enabled him to read Aristotle, the early Church Fathers, and some of the neo-Platonists who affected him deeply. He was *"the* metaphysician of the ninth century."

His first known work controverted the teaching of PAS-CHASIUS and advanced the view that the Eucharist is symbolical and commemorative only. Having been officially appointed to refute GOTTSCHALK he wrote *The Divine*

Predestination, 851, which aroused the deepest suspicions of his own orthodoxy. It begins thus:

> Since, in earnestly investigating and attempting to discover surely the reasons of all things, every means of attaining to a pious and perfect doctrine lies in that science and discipline which the Greeks call *philosophy,* we think it necessary to speak in a few words of its divisions and classifications. 'It is believed and taught,' says St. Augustine, 'that philosophy, that is, the love of wisdom, is no other than religion; and what proves it is, that we do not receive the sacraments in common with those whereof we do not approve the doctrine.' What, then, is the object of philosophy but to set forth the rules of true religion, whereby we rationally seek and humbly adore God, the first cause and sovereign of all things? From thence it follows that true philosophy is true religion, and conversely, that true religion is true philosophy.

Philosophy or reason was thus given the fundamental or primary place, and religion was regarded as derived and secondary. This aspect of his work was seriously challenged by FLORUS of Lyons whose book opens thus:

> In the name of the Lord Jesus Christ, against the follies and errors of a certain presumptuous man named John, on predestination and divine prescience, and the true liberty of human thought.

JOHN then undertook, at the request of Charles the Bold, the task of translating the works of pseudo-DIONYSIUS the Areopagite. His great work however was entitled *The Division of Nature.* This is written in dialogue form, and offers a more or less pantheistic interpretation of the universe. Nature is divisible into four realms, of which the first is God as the origin of all things, the second and third are

the created universe in which God manifests Himself, the
fourth division is God as the final end of all.
The practical religious issues of his philosophy are clear.

What, then, God, the Word made flesh, said to His
Disciples, 'It is not you who speak, but the Spirit of
your Father which speaketh in you,' true reason com-
pels us, in other similar things, similarly to believe, to
speak, to understand. It is not you who love, who see,
who move, but the Spirit of your Father, who speaketh
truth in you concerning me and my Father, and Himself. He loves me, and sees me and my Father and
Himself in you, and moves Himself in you, that you
may love me and my Father.

"The last book of the treatise . . . is, in many respects,
the most striking of the five. There are passages in it of
very high philosophical eloquence. The tone of it is freer
and more exalted. (It contains) the full exposition of the
doctrine that all things are to return to God, that He is to
be all in all."[1]

In the East the ripe and gifted scholar PHOTIUS, 820-
891, far surpassed every contemporary in learning, literary
power, and force and versatility of intellect. He gathered
into a *Library* or *Myrobiblion*, extracts and abridgements
from two hundred and eighty classical works which he reviewed and criticised. This work preserves the condensed
substance of many lost treasures of secular and religious
literature.

A more important book, *The Amphilochia*, addressed to
Amphilochius of Cyzicus, contains a collection of questions
and answers relating to more than five hundred Biblical
difficulties. PHOTIUS, who is remembered in ecclesiastical
history as the champion of the liberties of the Eastern Church
against the claims of Rome, wrote a digest of Canon law

---

[1] Frederick Denison Maurice, *Mediaeval Philosophy* (1870), p. 75.

entitled *The Nomocanon,* some Commentaries on books of
the Bible, Homilies, Letters, and a tract *Concerning Those of
Ancient Rome Who Say That the Holy Ghost Proceeded
from the Father Only and Not also from the Son.*
The names of GREGORY of the Isaurian Decapolis, c.731-
817, CHRISTOPHER of Alexandria, fl. 800, and GEORGE
of Nicomedia, d.800, are recalled in connection with a few
Sermons in which the growing adoration for the mother of
Jesus found expression.

A composition vastly more significant than Sermons or
songs in praise of Mary made its appearance in the West
during the pontificate of Nicholas I, 858-867. An editor
calling himself ISIDORE MERCATOR, fashioned the *Isidorian
Decrees*—usually known as *The False Decretals.* This is a
collection of various genuine papal letters and authentic decrees of Councils, with a large number of spurious documents; there are sixty forged letters purporting to be written
by popes earlier than Nicholas, and many pretended canons
of Church councils. In these spurious documents many of
the pressing problems of the ninth century are represented as
having been settled by papal authority in the previous centuries.

The author was ingenious in his work. About sixty per
cent of the letters falsely ascribed to different bishops of Rome
were his own creation. He took over the bulk of *The His-
pana,* a collection of the decrees written and issued in Spain
by ISIDORE of Seville. To these main masses he added the
spurious *Donation of Constantine* and a few smaller items.
The completed compilation contained thirty forged letters
bearing the names of the popes from Sylvester, 314-335, to
Damasus, 366-384, and the genuine Decretals of Rome down
to Gregory the Great, with a letter of Gregory II, 715-731.

The production of this amazing work falls between 847,
when the false Capitularies in it were forged, and 858, when
SERVATUS LUPUS knew of it. Accepted at its face value,

it became the instrument of an immense ecclesiastical authority which was accepted and obeyed until Nicholas of Cusa, 1401-1464, and John of Torquemada, 1388-1468, began to discredit it.

The Book of Pontiffs—Liber Pontificalis—also belongs to this period. In its latest form it is a composite biographical record of all the bishops of Rome down to Stephen VI, *i.e.* 885. ANASTASIUS, the librarian of the Roman Church during the years 860-885, was credited with the larger part of it, but as the first version of it probably dates back to 700 he must have built on another man's foundation.

The Book divides into two parts, of which the first covers the period from the beginning to 514, and the second to 867; in the later editions it reaches to 885. The first part was probably the work of a converted Goth whose Latin was imperfect; the rest was composed by various hands, generally "contemporary with the popes whose lives are recorded." The material came from the so-called *Liberian Catalogue,* 354, documents from the archives of Rome, and various Apocrypha connected with the papal controversies of the fifth and sixth centuries.

The work was intended to glorify Rome at the expense of Constantinople by representing the pope as having exercised supremacy over the whole Church from the first.

These dark blots on the page of the story are offset by the bright light shed by the labours of King ALFRED THE GREAT of England, 848-901, who educated half a nation, salvaged a noble literature, and created the first English prose.

The harrying of England by the Northmen began in earnest in 860, and the terror was at its height in 871. Christianity was swept from Northumbria in 867, three years later a similar fate had overtaken Mercia, and in 874 only Wessex remained unconquered. ALFRED was victorious over the oppressors in 878 when better days began, and in 901 the Church of England entered upon the third period of its influence.

ALFRED'S patronage of letters promoted the growth of a vernacular literature to which Plegmund of Canterbury, Asser of Sherborne, Werfrith of Worcester, Grimbald, and Athelstan, lent their aid. ALFRED became "the father of English prose." His first work, 888, was a now lost religious *Commonplace, or Hand Book*. Then followed translations of *The Dialogues of Gregory the Great,* and of GREGORY'S *Pastoral Care*, 890. The preface to the latter book is from ALFRED'S own hand and it is the beginning of English prose literature. At the end the King added some verses—perhaps the first verses that he wrote. They are paraphrased by Stopford. A. Brooke:

> Some shut up this stream of wisdom in their mind so that it flows not everywhere in vain, but the well abides in the breast of the man, deep and still. Some let it run away in rills over the land, and it is not wise that such bright waters should, noisy and shallow, flow over the land till it becomes a fen. But now draw near to drink it, for Gregory has brought to your doors the well of the Lord. . . .

The *Universal History* of OROSIUS, in 890, and *The Ecclesiastical History* by BEDE, in 891, were given to the people from the Latin at ALFRED'S suggestion and under his supervision. In 897 *The Consolation of Philosophy* by Boethius, "the most popular philosophical manual of the Middle Ages," was translated very freely, with the addition of considerable material taken from earlier editors.

> Reason! . . . . Indeed thou knowest that no man can show forth any craft; can order, or guide any power, without tools or material—material, that is, for each craft, without which a man cannot work at

that craft. This then is the material of a king and his tools, wherewith to rule—That he have his land fully manned, that he have prayer-men, and army-men, and workmen. Indeed thou knowest that without these tools no king can show forth his craft.

The last of the good king's works was entitled *Blossoms*. It was an anthology gathered from the *Soliloquies* of AUG-USTINE and various other sources. "The last words of it . . . . form a fitting epitaph for the noblest of English kings."

Therefore he seems to me a very foolish man, and very wretched, who will not increase his understanding while he is in the world, and ever wish and long to reach that endless life where all shall be made clear.

For a full century after ALFRED, literature in England was practically at a standstill, it awaited the impulse and the culture necessary for a new and greater art.

The spirit of continental Christianity is reflected in a military song written for the Modenese soldiers as they guarded their city walls against the Hungarians, about the year 924.

Let us adore the Godhead of Christ,
Let us sing for Him our songs of jubilee
Relying on His powerful guard,
Let us watch and sing our songs of jubilee.
O Christ, King of the world take into thy powerful keeping
These camps in which we watch.
Be Thou our impregnable rampart,
Be Thou the terrible enemy of our enemies.
No force can hurt us whilst Thou keepest guard,
For Thou puttest to flight the armies of the warlike.
Do Thou O Christ gird in our walls.
Do Thou defend them with Thy powerful lance.

CHAPTER XXIII

THE POWER OF THE PAPACY

By the year 1000, when popular superstition looked for the end of the world, Europe was nominally Christian. The papacy had fallen on evil days prior to Pope Sylvester II, 999-1003, with whose primacy a betterment began. It was however with GREGORY VII—HILDEBRAND—1053-1085, that the papal power took on new forms of self assertion. He sought to strengthen the spiritual authority of the Holy See, so that it might hold supremacy over all other sovereignties in the Western nations. His efforts provoked the bitter Investiture Controversy in which a hundred and sixty publicists, legalists, and canonists took part between the eleventh and the sixteenth centuries.

The struggle for papal supremacy may be separated into four eras.

i. 1075-1124.

HILDEBRAND'S view of the Church is given in a Letter to his friend Hugo of Cluny.

> The Oriental church fallen from the faith, and attacked from without, by the infidels. Casting your eye over the West, South or North, you find scarcely anywhere bishops who have obtained their office regularly, or whose life and conversation correspond to its requirements, and who are actuated in the discharge of their duties by the love of Christ and not by worldly ambition; nowhere, princes who prefer God's honour to their own, and justice before gain.

Among other reforms he proposed to insist upon the celibacy of the clergy. PETER DAMIAN, 1007-1072, gave vehement support to the proposal in *The Book of Gomorrah* and in seventeen minor works. GERHOH of Reichersberg, 1093-1169, also cordially endorsed the change in a book on the tenth Psalm. On the other hand DIETERIC of Verdun, Cardinal BENNO, HENRY of Speier, and WALTRAM of Naumberg strenuously opposed it.

LAMBERT of Aschaffenberg left a *History of Germany* in which the story of these contentions is told from the side of the supporters of GREGORY whom he calls

> a man much admired both for eloquence and for knowledge of the sacred writings . . . . most famous in the whole Church for every kind of virtue.

The domestic issue was soon overshadowed by the vastly larger question of Investiture, concerning which HILDEBRAND in a Letter to King William I of England asserted that sovereigns must be invested by the action of the Church.

> That kingdoms may be ruled after God by the care and ordinance of the apostolical dignity.

To Hermann of Metz he was more explicit:

> Who does not know that kings and princes have their origin from those, who, not knowing God, proud, plunderers, false, man-slayers following almost every crime, obviously moved by the prince of the world, the devil, have grasped at lordship over their equals, namely men, by a foul cupidity and an intolerable presumption.

His policy of making the Church supreme had the written support of ANSELM of Lucca, BERNOLD of Constance, and GERHOH of Reichersberg. The genuine interest of GERHOH in church politics appears in several works written during the course of the strife. He laid at the feet of Pope Eugene

III an *Essay on the confusion between Babylon and Jerusalem*. From this grew his later book *The Corrupt State of the Church* or *Exposition of Psalm sixty-four*, written, as he says:

> With this intention, that the Roman *Curia* may in part attend to itself and at the same time to the whole Church which it ought to rule, that it may be busy to show itself separate from the Babylonian confusion without spot or wrinkle, for it does not appear to be destitute of this wrinkle, that it is now called the Roman *Curia* which before was called the Roman Church.

Other works from his hand are *The State of the Church under the Emperors Henry IV, Henry V, and Gregory VII with Some Consequences to the Roman Pontificate, The Building of God, An Enquiry Concerning Anti-Christ, A Dialogue on the Differences between the Secular and the Regular Clergy.*

Under the name of GREGORY there are a "number of brief maxims relating to the laws and government of the church, called his dictates (dictatus). Although these maxims did not by any means proceed from himself, still, they contain the principles which he sought to realize in his government of the church, the principles of papal absolution . . . . Most of these maxims may be confirmed by passages from his letters."[1]

The concession of lay investiture forced from Pope Paschalis in 1112 was the subject of much heated argument. The name of Paschalis was handed down as that of "the man who had cowardly betrayed the liberties of the Church." GOTT-FRID of Vendome bitterly upbraided him in his Letters. JOACHIM of Calabria said "the servitude of the Church began with him." On the other hand HILDEBERT of Mans

---

[1] Neander, *Church History* (Bohn's edition), Vol. VII., p. 165.

and IVO of Chartres excused his action "because it was done under compulsion." Thus IVO wrote to John of Lyons:

> God has permitted the greatest and holiest men, when they have given way to a necessity which seemed to exculpate them or have descended to a prudent accommodation, to fall into such weaknesses, in order that they might thereby be led to a knowledge of their own hearts, learn to ascribe their weaknesses to themselves, and to feel their indebtedness to the grace of God for all the good that is in them.

In the midst of the strife PLACIDUS of Nonantula wrote *A Book concerning the Honour of the Church*, in which he took up a middle position between those who defended lay-investiture in the interests of the state and those who maintained the absolutism of the papacy. This was the attitude of HUGO of Fleury, fl. 1110-1120, in the book entitled *The Royal Power and Sacerdotal Dignity*, which he addressed to Henry II of England. He denied the claim of GREGORY that the monarchy was not founded on a divine order, and he advocated that bishops should be elected without secular interference, and after election receive their secular priviliges at the hands of the king. Even GOTTFRID of Vendome, fl. 1070-1100, an ardent devotee of the principles of GREGORY, urged the same plea in a pamphlet addressed to Pope Calixtus II, and also in a tract, *The Ordination of Bishops and the Investiture of Laymen*, written to Cardinal Peter of Leonis.

> If thou sayest what have I to do with the king; then call not the possessions thine; for thou hast renounced the only right by which thou *canst* call them thine. Whence does he possess whatsoever he does possess? By any human right? For by the divine right of the Lord is the earth and its fulness his. God

has made the poor and the rich of one blood and one earth supports both rich and poor.

ii. 1124-1198.

Both PETER THE VENERABLE of Cluny, 1092-1157, and BERNARD of Clairvaux, 1091-1153, who were keen antagonists on other issues, supported Innocent III in his contest against Anaclete II for the papacy. BERNARD wrote his last work, *Meditation,* to win over the French Church to the side of Innocent. The book was as strong in rebuke as it was conciliatory in purpose, and was without result. BERNARD brought the chief opponent of Innocent to submission and ended the lamentable schism by a spectacular use of the bread of the Sacrament.

GRATIAN'S *Harmony of Discordant Canons—the Decretum*—1149, carried more weight than BERNARD'S *Mediation.* It was a new collection of the sources of the canon law with thirty-six specimen cases for solution, and a statement of the law respecting Church ritual and the Sacraments. It brought the old and the new ecclesiastical laws together, discussed their differences, and attempted their reconciliation. It gave fresh impetus to the study of canon law, but, as PETER CANTOR complained in his *Short Word:*

> Dismissing liberal arts and heavenly disciplines everybody reads the Codex and enquires after the legalities so that they may go begging for glory and lucre (Chap. 51).

iii. 1198-1261.

Papal claims and papal rights were ably championed by INNOCENT III, 1198-1216, who insisted that the Lord left to Peter the governance not of the Church only but of the whole world.

Even as God the Creator of the universe has placed two great lights in the firmament of the heavens, a larger one to rule over the day, a smaller one to rule over the night, in like manner has he placed in the firmament of the universal church two great offices, a larger one to rule over the souls, a lesser one to rule over the bodies, the papal and the imperial authority. And even as the moon receives its light from the sun, so the imperial power receives the splendour of its office from the papal dignity (Regest I., 401).

In earlier life he had written *The Contempt of the World,* which had been translated into English under the title *The Mirror of Man's Life.* Many of his Sermons, "inspired by a high moral earnestness," and his *Exposition of the Psalter* still exist. His Letters with their revelations of the depths of iniquity into which some of the bishops had sunk are, in the opinion of Hallam, "full of unprovoked rudeness."

These literary achievements however fade before the magnificent *Stabat mater dolorosa* and another masterpiece of Latin sacred poetry that are attributed to him by common tradition.

The *Stabat mater* has been called "the most pathetic hymn of the Middle Ages." It describes the weeping mother at the Cross with a vividness of presentation and a tenderness of feeling to which the beauty of the verse is exquisitely adapted. It has often been translated.

> Near the Cross her vigil keeping,
>   Stood the mother, worn with weeping,
>   Where He hung, the dying Lord:
> Through her soul, in anguish groaning,
> Bowed in sorrow, sighing, moaning,
>   Passed the sharp and piercing sword.

His second Hymn often called "The Golden Sequence," has a stately grace and a perfect rhythmic melody that are

transfigured by the glow of devotion into "the loveliest . . . .
of all the hymns in the whole circle of Latin sacred poetry."

> Come, Thou Holy Spirit, come,
> And from Thy celestial home
> Shed a ray of light divine;
> Come, Thou Father of the poor,
> Come, Thou source of all our store,
> Come, within our bosoms shine:
>
> Heal our wounds; our strength renew;
> On our dryness pour Thy dew;
> Wash the stains of guilt away;
> Bend the stubborn heart and will;
> Melt the frozen, warm the chill;
> Guide the steps that go astray.

Reaction set in after the death of INNOCENT III. The
secularising of the Church was carried to great lengths,
although it met with a resistance, to the brilliant energy of
which a brief era of German poetry bears witness. HEINRICH
VON MOLKE, fl. 1150, represented this resistance in some
effective pieces. He was a poet of real talent, the Juvenal of
Chivalry, and the earliest German satirist.

In ROBERT GROSSETESTE, 1175-1253, the church in
England had a zealous champion of its rights, who threw
all his learning and influence on the side of the Emperors
against the extreme claims of the papacy. His *Remonstrance,*
1253, written to oppose the acts of the papal commissioner,
is preserved in the *Major Chronicle* of MATTHEW PRIOR.
His thesis entitled *The Difference between a Monarchy and
a Tyranny,* met with the enthusiastic agreement of Simon
de Montfort. His name is also associated with some Anglo-
Norman Songs. His famous Epistle contained the germs
of reformation truths which exercised long enduring influence.

Our Saviour Christ saith, whosoever is not with me
is against me. Our lord the pope appears to be his
type and representative. It is impossible then that the

sanctity of the apostolical See can be repugnant to the authority of Jesus Christ. The NON OBSTANTE clause overflows with uncertainty, fraud, and deceit, and strikes at the root of all confidence between man and man. Next to the sin of Antichrist, which shall be in the latter time, nothing can be more contrary to the doctrine of Christ, than to destroy men's souls, by defrauding them of the benefit of the pastoral office. . . . No man, faithful to the said See, can, with an unspotted conscience, obey such mandates, even if they were seconded by the high order of angels themselves; on the contrary, every faithful Christian ought to oppose them with all his might.

iv. 1261-1305.

The power of the papacy waned, and after the Sicilian Vespers, 1282, it engaged in a series of contests with France which left it defeated and powerless, 1303. Religious poetry was one of the best solvents of the strict traditions of the Church, and the English *Cursor Mundi,* 1270, an epic of twenty-four hundred lines aided the work of disintegration. The author made use of many earlier works; his poem is a storehouse of mediaeval legend as well as of biblical history, designed to show "the whole dealing of God with man from Creation to Domesday." Among many other legends it contains the story of the discovery of the true Cross by a condemned Jew and its miraculous identification by the Empress Helena.

He fand tua crosses and that ilk	*i.e.* the true one
Bot yeit ne wist thai quilk was quilk,	which
The quilk moght be the lauerd tre	Lord's
And quilk it moght the theves be.	
Wit mikel joi and mikel gle	With much
Unto the tun bar thai thaa tre	town those

Thar war thai don als in mide place
For to abide ur lauerd grace   our
Abute the time o middai or mar   or more
A ded man bodi forth thai bar;
Sant Eline mad hir praier thar,   there
And sua did all the folk was thar,
That Crist suld tham sum-quat scau, somewhat shew
His aun dere tre to knau.   own
With aither tre the cors on-ran, the corpse they touch
Bot allwais lai it still as stan;
The thred thai toched til his hide thick skin
And up he ras wit-uten bide, without delay
And spak wit a blithful voice,
The tre thus hailsand o the croice.[2] hailing cross

The supreme literary interest of the period centres in the immortal and inexhaustible Florentine DANTE (Durante) ALIGHIERI, 1265-1321, who, on the border line of mediaeval and modern times, poured the mind of the past into his visions of eternity, and created new channels for the spiritual thought of the world.

About 1292 he voiced his platonic passion for Beatrice di' Portinari, d.1290, the ideal of his soul, in a splendid confessional work entitled *The New Life.* This is "the first great example of Italian prose, the first revelation of the genius of the greatest mediaeval poet, and the incarnation of that romantic conception of ideal love by which the Middle Age might fairly claim to have augmented the heritage bequeathed by antiquity."[3]

In the *Banquet,* 1295, Beatrice appears as an allegory of divine philosophy, and DANTE becomes a philosopher striving to fashion a hand-book of universal knowledge which he left unfinished. DANTE also left unfinished a literary work in Latin, *The Vulgar Tongue,* 1304, written for those

---

2 *Cursor Mundi,* ed. R. Morris, 1877-92, lines 21533-21552.
3 Richard Garnett, *Italian Literature,* p. 32.

who despised the vernacular. In 1311 he issued *The Monarchy,* "at once the epitaph of a dead ideal and the prophecy of a more glorious future." It was an attempt to show that

> Man has need of a two-fold directive power according to his two-fold goal; the Sovereign Pontiff to lead the human race to eternal life in accordance with revealed truth, and the Emperor to direct him to temporal felicity in accordance with philosophic teaching.

It raised "the cry of indignant protest against the degradation of divine offices to human ends, upholding at the same time the divine origin and essential independence of the temporal State."

In the *Divine Comedy,* austere and magnificent, yet alive with the instinct of beauty, he added to Christian literature a sublime and unparalleled epic of man as the pilgrim in the Way of salvation. He described its purpose to Can Grande: "The object of the whole work is to make those who live in this life leave their state of misery, and to lead them to a state of happiness." The three parts of the work, The Inferno, The Purgatory, and The Paradise, therefore represent "stages in the passage of the blessed soul from the slavery of the present corruption to the liberty of eternal glory."

The Inferno represents the various punishments allotted to the various sins included in the three groups—sins of incontinence, sins of malice, and sins of gluttony. The Purgatory describes the seven circles of purgative discipline applied to those who are guilty of the seven sins; pride, envy, anger, sloth, avarice, gluttony, and lust. The Paradise accepts the theory of ten heavens, nine of which move round the earth, the tenth being the motionless Empyrean encircling all. In these heavens various degrees of bliss are enjoyed by 'religious' whose vows were broken under compulsion, seekers after fame, lovers, theologians, warriors for the faith, righteous kings, thinkers, Christ in His triumph, and the angelic hosts. The visible presence of God pervades the Empyrean.

As a narrative the *Divine Comedy* is simple and intelligible, but DANTE compressed meaning within meaning into the Visions seen by the two travellers beyond the gates of death until his poem became "a mystic unfathomable song." It is capable of four interpretations. Literally it shows the passage of the poet "from sin and death, through penitential suffering to newness of life blessed and eternal." As an allegory it pictures man on his earthly pilgrimage, experiencing all the common fortunes of the race. Morally interpreted it shows man moving from the inferno of vice through all the stages of ethical progress to the paradise of virtue. Spiritually it describes man's soul on the upward way from a state of sin to a state of glory.[4]

No single formula can describe the involution of DANTE'S mind which turned to account for its high purposes a masterly knowledge of "history, contemporary astrology, surviving classical culture, Aristotelian philosophy, scholastic theology, the economy of Church and State, the Romantic poetry of chivalric love, and mystical experience."

DANTE drew into the deep channel of his genius tributary streams from many Christian sources; from AUGUSTINE, the pseudo-DIONYSIUS, GREGORY THE GREAT, PETER DAMIAN, BERNARD of Clairvaux, and RICHARD OF ST. VICTOR; and through the rich current of these mingled streams ran the pervading influence of THOMAS AQUINAS.

---

[4] Cp. R. E. Welsh, *Classics of the Soul's Quest*, p. 81.

CHAPTER XXIV

THE NEW MONASTICISM

A change in the character of monasticism began to take place after the publication of the so-called Augustinian Canon. Although AUGUSTINE did not compose a Rule in the technical sense, some of his writings were used as the basis of three separate Rules. In his Epistle 211 he gave counsel to a group of nuns, and in two of his Sermons, 355 and 356, he described his own life among his clergy at Hippo.

One of the Rules based upon these works is a fairly complete Canon and is commonly known as *The Rule of St. Augustine*. Under its regulations there arose a new Order of clerical Friars who left very definite impressions on Christian literature.

During the Crusades the military Orders and the Orders of Ransom were established and for centuries they have influenced the songs and romances, the sermons and the hymns of Western Christendom. But it was the mendicant Friars who brought fresh inspiration to literature, and opened practically limitless fields of literary romance.

The Franciscans were founded in 1210, the Dominicans in 1215, the Servites in 1233, the Carmelites in 1245, and the Augustinian Hermits in 1256.

To JOACHIM of Floris, 1132-1202, belongs the honour of having roused the better spirits of the age to a sense of the religious needs of new populations crowding into cities where the old parochial system of the Church had broken down. His three chief works are *The Book of Concord of the New and Old Testaments, An Exposition in the Apoc-*

alypse, and *An Instrument of Ten Strings.* In these books he attempted to explain various prophecies of the Bible in relation to the history and the prospects of the Church as he knew it.

He is, however, much better known by *The Everlasting Gospel* (cf. Rev.xiv.6), a work in which he struck at the very roots of the papal system. He divided time into three periods corresponding to the three Persons of the Trinity. The age of the Father was the age of power and fear, and is reflected in the Old Testament. Peter is its Christian representative. The age of the Son, represented by Paul, is the age of the Catholic Church, the age of the divine wisdom. A third age will come, the age of the Spirit; it is represented by John. This third age will be a dispensation of universal love, the letter of the Gospel will be transcended, and the Church will become unnecessary.

> Some have so exalted the church in Rome, that a man was held up as a heretic who did not visit the threshold of Peter. Their guilty mistake lay in this, that they bid men visit the holy material temple, when the truth is, that in every place every Christian is a temple of God, if he leads a good life.[1]

From JOACHIM came the chief influences that shaped the character and purposes of FRANCIS of Assisi, 1181-1226, who soon overshadowed his teacher. Legends of the most touching grace grew around the person of this most lovable of all the saints. He became the hero and the idol of a literature which has almost completely eclipsed his own writings.

FRANCIS is the author of two versions of a Rule, of *The Testament, Spiritual Admonitions, The Canticle of the Spirit, The Song of the Creatures,* and Letters. These titles are often varied and the works ascribed to FRANCIS are some-

---

[1] Neander, *Church History* (Bohn's Edition), Vol. VII., p. 307.

times called *A Canticle of the Sun, A Seraphic Keepsake, or a Talisman against Temptation Written for Brother Leo by St. Francis of Assisi,* and *Words of Counsel and Praise of God Most High.*

RENAN pronounces the *Song of the Creatures* to be "the most perfect expression given by the modern world of its feeling for religion." It has been thus translated by Matthew Arnold.[2]

> O most high, almighty, good Lord God, to thee belong praise, glory, honour, and all blessing!
>
> Praised be my Lord God with all his creatures, and especially our brother the sun, who brings us the day and who brings us the light; fair is he and shines with very great splendour: O Lord, he signifies to us thee!
>
> Praised be my Lord for our sister the moon, and for the stars, the which he has set clear and lovely in heaven.
>
> Praised be my Lord for our brother the wind, and for air and cloud, calms and all weather by which thou upholdest life in all creatures . . .
>
> Praised be my Lord for all those who pardon one another for his love's sake, and who endure weakness and tribulation: blessed are they who peaceably shall endure, for thou, O most Highest, shalt give them a crown.
>
> Praised be my Lord for our sister, the death of the body, from which no man escapeth. Woe to him who dieth in mortal sin! Blessed are they who are found walking by thy most holy will, for the second death shall have no power to do them harm.
>
> Praise ye and bless the Lord, and give them thanks unto him and serve him with great humility.

THOMAS of Celano one of the earlier disciples of the saint was probably his first biographer. He wrote a first *Life of St. Francis,* in 1228, and a second Life, supplementary to the first, about 1245. These are not formal biographies, but rather collections of the most characteristic and important incidents in the Saint's career, grouped with great skill in

---

[2] *Essays in Criticism, First Series,* 1883.

such a way as to illustrate the main features of his character. JOHN FIDANZA, 1221-1274, whom FRANCIS surnamed BONAVENTURA, wrote *The Legends,* 1260, which ultimately became the official Life. This book is the work of a loving disciple; and, "charmed by it, Dante drew the picture of the Saint in the Paradiso."

> Humility, the guardian and glory of all virtues, abounded in rich fulness in the man of God. In his own estimation, he was nought but a sinner, whereas in very truth he was the mirror and brightness of all saintliness. In humility he strove to build himself up, as a wise master-builder laying the foundation that he had learnt of Christ. . . . .
> This too he was wont to say 'A man's worth is what he is in the sight of God and no more' (Part II., chap. 6).

The Mirror of Perfection, ... "is a compilation edited by one of the Spirituals of the Porziuncula . . . . and completed about 1318." The method adopted to describe the many virtues of the Saint is to take some point of his teaching or some trait of his character, and after stating it to illustrate it by an incident from his life.

The author of the anonymous *Little Flowers of the Glorious Messer St. Francis and of his Friars,* 1340, has been identified with "a certain UGOLINO BRUNFORTE, 1262-1348. His book is a "collection of the sayings and doings of the whole Franciscan Brotherhood in its early days as developed and distorted by popular religious tradition." The tales range from the most realistic records to the wildest fairy stories.

To meet the needs of the educated classes, DOMINIC, 1170-1221, founded the Order that has ever since been known by his name. His successor as master-general was JORDAN of Saxony, d. 1237, who wrote *The Life of St. Dominic.*

WILLIAM of St. Amour questioned the sincerity and denounced the mission of the Order in the *Perils of the Last
Times*, 1255. He reasserted his distrust in later Sermons
and Letters, and again, in a *Manifesto* written after pope
Clement IV had deposed and exiled him.

His strictures led BONAVENTURA to write, in defence of
the monastic Orders, a book entitled *Boundaries about the
Rule of St. Francis*, in which he says:

> because sins in the Church were continually on the in-
> crease, and bishops, occupied with external things,
> could not turn their attention to spiritual affairs; be-
> cause few shepherds resided with their churches, but
> the majority committed the guidance of souls to hire-
> ling vicars, who were for the most part ignorant, negli-
> gent, and impure in their lives, therefore the pope, on
> whom devolves the care of the whole Church, has called
> us to the assistance of the clergy and the communities.

In an *Apology for the Poor* (*i.e.* for the Friars Minor)
BONAVENTURA recalls his brethren to perfection through
entire detachment from all earthly things.

THOMAS AQUINAS, in a work entitled *Against the Enemies of Religion*, maintained, in sympathy with BONAVEN-
TURA, that the ignorance of the parish priests had made the
work of the friars indispensable. He saw evidence of the
divine appointment of the Friars in their success in uprooting
heresies, reclaiming unbelievers, and teaching the uneducated.
The founder of the Sorbonne, ROBERT, 1201-1274, in a
work on *Conscience*, imitated BONAVENTURA in begging the
Friars to be strictly moral in order that they might escape
criticism.

On the other hand PETER CANTOR, d. 1197, rebuked
those who criticised others while they themselves were not
free from suspicion. His *Summary of the Sacraments and
of the Spirit of the Councils* develops at length the moral

aspect of the Sacraments; it is still precious for its varied information on the institutions and religious customs of the time. His book called *Distinctions* is a theological dictionary. It is by his *Short Word* that he is best remembered; in it he shows the spirit of a reformer who is at war with the ecclesiastical abuses of his age. Because he writes for the guidance of young men who consecrated themselves to the service of the Church, PETER says:

> Not therefore clamouring in theological disputes, nor discussing frivolities, but, as Seneca says, discuss with me, justice, piety, thrift, and modesty, both of the mind and of the body.

Two outstanding literary movements aided the activity of the mendicant Orders. The first was the marked development of preaching and the consequent increase of the Homiletical literature of Christianity. In these departments France held the premier position during the 12th century.

The twenty-four existing Sermons of IVO of Chartres, 1040-1116, are good types of lively, vital speech used by a sound thinker with a fresh imagination. IVO was a conspicuous canonist, whose *Panormia*, 1095, is a handy and well arranged collection of canon law, for which he had made preparation by an earlier *Decretum* in seventeen books. The Sermons connected with the name of ANTHONY of Padua, 1195-1231, are rich in natural familiar illustrations. He is credited with the power to attract and to sway great multitudes.

Mediaeval Germany's greatest preacher BERTHOLD of Regensburg, 1220-1272, left seventy Sermons in the vernacular. These Sermons are the chief existing monument of Middle High German prose; they contain material from which an excellent picture of the age may be constructed. BERTHOLD was a true man of the people one "who knew how to appeal to the instincts of the common man, how to enliven his oratory with allusions to every-day occurrences, how to illustrate even the supernatural by graphic and striking imagery."[3]

Of the glory of God we can speak only in images. For all that we could ever say about it, that is just as though the unborn babe . . . were to tell of the beauty and glory of the world, of the shining sun, of the shining stars, of the powers and manifold colours of precious metals, of the power and perfume of noble spices, of the beautiful things made of silk and gold, of all the sweet voices of the world, of the sound of harps and of the variegated colours of the flowers. As little as the babe in the mother's womb which never saw either good or bad and never felt a single joy, could talk of this, so little can we talk of the unspeakable delight which is in heaven or of the beauteous face of the living God.

GUIBERT of Novigentium prefaced his *Exposition of Genesis* with a dissertation on "The Method of making Sermons," in which he besought preachers to make their discourses simple and ethical. HUBERT of Romanis wrote a book on *The Education of Preachers,* and INNOCENT III showed his interest in the work of preaching by writing *The Mysteries of the Mass.* HONORIUS SCHOLASTICUS, d. 1150, prepared a collection of Homilies entitled *The Mirror of the Church* for the use of priests, "that the bride of Christ may see what is displeasing to the Bridegroom in her and may conform herself to His image." By the help of this work and the patristic writings, WERNER of Ellerbach, d. 1126, prepared his contribution to sermonic literature, *Flowers plucked from the Fathers.* CONRAD the priest, broke away from the common usage of writing sermons in

---

[3] Kuno Francke, *History of German Literature*, p. 108.

Latin, and issued *Sermons for Common and Popular Priests and Those Lacking Books,* in the old German dialect. This contained a full set of discourses for the Church year, and for many of the Saints' days.

In England collections of Homilies were abundant in the twelfth century but they were usually anonymous and undated. As far back as AELFRIC, 955-1025, Homilies had been prepared for the use of the priests. He was an industrious worker in this department, and wrote two series of *Catholic Homilies,* 992, and a series of *Passions,* or *Lives of the Saints,* 977. The great homilist WULFSTAN, fl. 1002-1023, is inseparably associated with AELFRIC in literary labour for the advancement of the work of the pulpit.

AILRED of Revesby, 1109-1166, who was a writer of some importance in his day, left some Sermons, besides more formal theological works and histories. Six Sermons, "quite crudely and insipidly written," by PETER of Blois, a Frenchman in the service of Henry II of England, still remain.

The second literary revival coincident with the work of the Friars was associated with Hagiology, *i.e.* the work of compiling and publishing *Legends of the Saints.* The beginnings of Hagiology are very obscure, but they were very early. *A Vision of St. Paul,* written before 400, is one of the earliest existing examples, and is probably the first sacred romance devoted to things beyond death. "In its primitive meaning the legend is the history that has to be read, *legenda,* on the feast of a saint." [4] It was never a purely literary work, it was always intended for edification, but it provided "infinitely good reading."

"The work of the hagiographer may be historical, but it is not necessarily so. It may assume any literary form suitable to the glorification of the saints, from an official record adapted to the use of the faithful, to a poetical composition

---

[4] Père H. Delehaye, *The Legends of the Saints,* trans. by Mrs. V. M. Crawford, (1907), p. 10.

of the most exuberant character wholly detached from reality."[5]

The makers of Legends were generally very careless about evidences and probabilities. Some of their characters result from misconstructions of antiquity; some of their incidents are memories of pagan myths, others are founded on parables. Many legends arose from the extravagant devotions connected with the cult of Mary the mother of Jesus. In the great majority of the legends however there is a historical nucleus, but "the confusion between history and legend was never ending. History, in the Middle Ages, meant everything that was told, everything that was written in books."

"Hagiographic literature treats of a large and varied assortment of personages who do not all possess equally valid claims on public veneration. There are, in the first place, those whose cultus has been canonically established by the Church and has received the sanction of centuries. . . Next to them come those real personages devotion to whom was in the first instance irregularly established, whatever consecration it may have acquired through length of usage . . . . yet a third category, relatively few in number . . . . the imaginary personages to whom a real existence has ultimately been attributed."[6]

Collections of Saints Legends thus brought into being, became the reading books in church schools; they furnished the romances that were read in abbeys and castles; they formed the popular literature of the multitude.

Apart from a *Life of St. Leger*, a *Passion*, a rude translation of a *Sequence in honour of St. Eulalia*, dating from the tenth century and a *Life of St. Alexis* in the eleventh century, the history of French legends begins only after the year 1100. But the number of Anglo-Norman legends written in metre is very large. There are extant seventy-

[5] *Ibid.*, p. 2.
[6] *Ibid.*, pp. 108, 109.

five poems in the French language, although written in England, "dealing with the lives or the miracles of about fifty different saints or biblical characters." During the same period the writing of Latin legends was carried on with equal zeal. "At the end of the eleventh century the fluent GOSCELIN was perhaps the best known writer of Saints Lives in England. He prepared Legends of Augustine of Canterbury, of St. Swithin, St. Werburgh, of Mildred of Kent, Edith and Ives, "all of which enjoyed great and lasting renown."[7]

The immense popularity of Saints Legends in the thirteenth century was due in large measure to JACOB of Voragine, 1230-1298, who issued a generous selection in *The Lombardic History*, or *Legends of the Saints*, a work universally known as *The Golden Legend*. It mirrors every aspect of the age—its mental conceits, childish superstitions, delight in the miraculous, theological pedantry, and literary taste. It represented the thirteenth century in the same way that *The Ecclesiastical History* of EUSEBIUS represented the fourth, and *The Glory of the Martyrs* by GREGORY of Tours, the sixth. "These three great collections mark well defined stages in the history of the legend, and each is worthy of praise according to its kind."[8]

Another excellent example of the work of the hagiographers is found in the writings of GONZALO de Berceo, 1198-1268, the first poet of Castile whose name reaches us. Nine of his poems and three of his Hymns survive. The subjects of the poems are, *The Life of St. Oria, Virgin, The History of Senor St. Millan of Cogalla, The Life of St. Dominic of Silas, The Sacrifice of the Mass, The Martyrdom of St. Lawrence, The Praises of Our Lady, Signs visible before the Judgment, The Miracles of Our Lady, The Virgin's Lament on the Day of the Passion of Her Son Jesus Christ.*

[7] Gordon Hall Gerould, *Saints Legends*, pp. 131, 134-136, 140.
[8] *Ibid.*, p. 54.

"He was not . . . . a great poet. But in his own way he was, if not an inventor, the chief of a school, and the necessary predecessor of such devout authors as LUIS DE LEON and ST. TERESA."[9]

Hookham Frere translated parts of the Life of St. Millan.

> He walked those mountains wild, and lived within that nook
> For forty years and more, nor ever comfort took
> Of offer'd food or alms, or human speech or look;
> No other saint in Spain did such a penance brook.
>
> For many a painful year he passed the seasons there,
> And many a night consumed in penitence and prayer—
> In solitude and cold, with want and evil fare,
> His thoughts to God resigned, and free from human care.
>
> Oh! sacred is the place, the fountain and the hill
> The rocks where he reposed, in meditation still
> The solitary shades through which he roved at will:
> His presence all that place with sanctity did fill.

About 1340 the industrious compiler JOHN of Tynemouth published a great collection entitled *The Legends of the Saints of England,* which was "the most complete collection of the lives of saints in any way connected with Great Britain and Ireland that had ever been attempted." The latter part of the fourteenth century saw the beginning of the most brilliant period of the work of English hagiographers. This period, which ended at the middle of the fifteenth century saw the production of CHAUCER'S *Second Nun's Tale,* the *Christina* of WILLIAM PARIS, the *Vision* of TUNDALE, the *Life of St. Cuthbert,* in verse, *St. Robert of Knaresborough,* and *St. Alexis.*

JOHN LYDGATE, 1370-1451, the most celebrated English legend writer of the fifteenth century, "is characteristically mediaeval—mediaeval in his prolixity, his platitude, his want of judgment and his want of taste; mediaeval also in his pessimism, his Mariolatry and his horror of death." His

---

[9] J. Fitzmaurice-Kelly, *Spanish Literature,* p. 59.

most important Legend is *The Life of Our Lady*, 1410; other similar poems are *St. George, St. Margaret, St. Edmund, St. Alban*, 1439, and *The Miracles of St. Edmund*, 1444.

The *Legends of the Saints* gradually gave place to more dramatic works which soon escaped from the control of the Church. Religious festivals offered opportunities for the making of a Christian drama, for which biblical characters and lives of saints supplied the subjects, until, in the natural course of development, secular themes claimed notice, the plots became more elaborate, and the regular drama came to its own.

CHAPTER XXV

SCHOLASTICISM

The supreme aim of Christian thought during the mediaeval period was the effort to build a rational system of Catholic theology that should satisfy the demands of the intellect and at the same time be loyal to the traditions of the Church.

ANSELM, 1033-1109, marks the beginning of Scholasticism proper, although he had several heralds and forerunners. His working principle, "I believe in order that I may know," was as valuable as its counterpart, "I would know in order that I may believe." All his work bears witness to the sincerity of his religious life. His books were not "hard dogmatical treatises written in cold blood, to build up a system or to vanquish opponents. They were actual guides to the doubter; attempts, often made with much reluctant modesty, to untie knots which worthy men found to be interfering with their peace and with their practice."[1]

His Sermons are certainly inferior to his theological writings; they are remarkable neither for eloquence nor for originality of thought. On Matthew xiv. 22, he says:

> In this lection, according to its mystical interpretation, we have a summary description of the state of the Church from the coming of the Saviour to the end of the world. For the Lord constrained his disciples to get into a ship when he committed the church to the government of the apostles and their followers; and thus to go on before him unto the other side, that is,

---

[1] Frederick Denison Maurice, *Mediaeval Philosophy* (1870), p. 97.

to bear onward towards the haven of the celestial country, before he himself should entirely depart from this world.

It was by his theological and philosophical works that he won his place as "the Augustine of his age." At Bec he wrote three Dialogues on the ideas of *Truth, Free Will,* and *Sin.* In 1070 he met one of the problems of the day with *The Monologue on the Essence of Divinity,* in which he set forth his famous *a priori* proof of the existence of God, the proof that finds the idea of God implicit in human experience. The book answers the question:

> seeing that there are innumerable good things, the great diversity of which we experience with the sense of our body and discern with the reasoning of our mind, are we to believe that there is some one thing, in virtue of which one all good things are good, or are they good, some for this cause, some for that?

This *Soliloquy,* as ANSELM called it because it is a man's discourse with himself about God, was followed by a companion work *The Proslogion* or *Exhortation concerning the Existence of God* which takes the form of a supplication to God to be a teacher concerning Himself. "The object of the reasoning is to show that the existence of God is in fact an immediately evident truth. Uncertainty about God's existence is possible only so long as we are unaware of the true meaning of the word *Deus.*"[2] By "God" ANSELM understood "that than which nothing greater can be conceived." The argument of the book is the first complete statement of what is known as the "ontological" argument.

A monk GAUNILO, d. 1083, criticised the book in his *Apology for the Fool,* and urged his well known plea that the idea of the lost Isle of the Blest does not prove that it exists or ever has existed. ANSELM replied with *An Apolo-*

---

[2] *Encyclopaedia of Religion and Ethics,* Vol. XII., p. 267.

getic Book Against Gaunilo's Answer for a Fool, and in a second book entitled *A Fool Refuted.*

Against the monistic teaching of ROSCELLIN, 1050-1122, the founder of Nominalism, whose writings are lost, AN-SELM issued *The Trinitarian Faith,* 1098, to show that the individual and the universal are not mutually exclusive. He compares the triune Godhead of the orthodox faith to the Nile which is at once a fountain, a river, and a lake. He also wrote a book on *The Will,* and a *Dialogue on the Harmony of the Divine Foreknowledge with Free Will.*

Notwithstanding their importance and notoriety these works proved to be much less influential upon Christian thinking than his famous treatise *Cur Deus Homo?*—Why the God-Man?—1096, of which he says in the Preface:

> I . . . . have divided it into two books. The first of these contains certain objections of unbelievers who reject the Christian faith because they think it contrary to reason, with the answers of the faithful; and, finally, setting Christ aside, (as though He had never been) proves by logical arguments that it is impossible for any man to be saved without Him.
>
> In a like manner, in the second book (as though nothing were known of Christ) it is shown no less plainly by reason and in truth, that human nature was made to this end, that at some time man in his completeness, *i.e.* in body and soul, should enjoy a blessed immortality; and that it is necessary that, what man was made for, to that he should come: but that only by one who is man and God, and of necessity by all which we believe of Christ, could this be done.

The pith of the argument of the book is stated thus:

> God will not do it (*i.e.* make satisfaction for sin) because He ought not and man will not, because he cannot; therefore that God and man may do this, it is

needful that the same person shall be perfect God and perfect man, who shall make this satisfaction; since he cannot do it unless he be very God, nor ought, unless he be very man (Part II., chap. 7).

The work opened a new era in the discussion of the doctrine of the Atonement by denying the universally accepted theory that, in the sacrifice of the Cross, Christ was offered to the devil as a ransom price for man.

ANSELM was a poet of no mean order. He has left among other poetical pieces a series of prayers for the 'hours.'

AT TIERCE (BEFORE CONFESSION)

O gentle master who by birth
Mysterious camest once on earth
This our confession now receive
And with us Thy forgiveness leave.

Thou that in time didst generate
The Father's Offspring Uncreate
Oh by Thy merits may we be
Released from mortal pravity.

"Fairest and most fragrant, daintiest and most delicate perhaps of all the flowers that blow in the garden of the Mother of God, is the modest and yet queenly Mariale, a poem of five hundred and thirty-nine stanzas, long attributed to St. Bernard of Clairvaux, but which may now with somewhat more of probability be assigned to the saint of Le Bec."[3]

Every day
To Mary pay
Soul, thy tribute, praises high.
All her glory
All her story
Celebrate and magnify.
Contemplate
Her lofty state,

---

[3] J. M. Rigg, *St. Anselm of Canterbury*, p. 96.

Thyself with lowly awe possessed.
Mother! hail her,
Neither fail her
To salute as Virgin Blest.
Oh! adore her
And implore her
Thee from sin to liberate.
Her to aid thee
When invade thee
Passion's whirlwinds, supplicate.
By this maiden
Bounty laden
God to earth did once incline.
Queen of Heaven
She hath given
To her children, grace divine.
Now thy burden
Tongue the guerdon
Of her maiden-motherhood.

. . . .

Eve's offending
Far descending
Barred the Gate of Paradise.
Mary's credence
And Obedience
Ope the portals of the skies.
'Twas by reason
Of Eve's treason
Sentence stern on man was passed;
By her holy
Hearkening lowly
Mary leads him home at last.

PETER ABELARD, 1079-1142, did posterity a notable service when he composed his *History of Calamities,* in which he tells the story of his studies under ROSCELLIN, and William of Champeaux, of his professorial triumphs in the provinces and in Paris, of his love for Heloise, and of all the dire consequences of his passion. The letters that passed between him and Heloise still remain, they are "written with the most perfect freedom, and in the maturity of the character, intellect, and misfortunes of both."

ABELARD was a lecturer rather than an author, a critic of authority, and a spiritual outlaw; nevertheless he produced some memorable writings. His first tractate, entitled *The Divine Unity and Trinity*, was expanded later into a *Christian Theology*, which brought him under censure, and which he was compelled to burn in public with his own hands.

The key-note of his method was struck in *So and Not So* —Sic et Non—in which he illustrated his principle that "by doubting we are led to question, by questioning we arrive at the truth." The book contained one hundred and fifty-eight theses for each one of which ABELARD gathered from the writings of the Fathers apparently contradictory statements, *e.g.*

That God is threefold and the contrary.

That sin is displeasing to God and the contrary.

That nothing happens by chance and the contrary.

That no one can be saved without the baptism of water and the contrary.

That it is lawful to lie and the contrary.

ABELARD made no comments on the passages that he collected, but in his preface to the book he defended himself from misunderstanding.

Even if the sayings of the Fathers do not agree, it is not to be judged that they are untrue. The seeming disagreement may come from our lack of ability to understand them, not from their mistakes.

He left a work entitled *Know Thyself*, a book on *Ethics*. a *Conversation between the Philosopher, the Jew, and the Christian*, an *Epitome of Christian Theology*, and thirty-four Sermons that add little if anything to his fame.

His pupil PETER LOMBARD, 1100-1160, the master of Sentences, lives in literary history by his one great work, *Four Books of Sentences*, 1148. This famous theological

handbook is "primarily a collection of opinions of the
Fathers." Its basis is the aphorism of AUGUSTINE—every
doctrine is either of things or of signs. The first book treats
of God; the second of creation; the third of the Incarnation, redemption, and the virtues;[4] the fourth of the seven
Sacraments, and of the last things. The work definitely asserted the doctrine of seven Sacraments, and described a Sacrament as "a sign of a sacred thing capable of conveying the
grace of which it is the sign."

"The *Sentences* soon attained immense popularity, ultimately becoming the text-book in almost every theological
school, and giving rise to endless commentaries, over 180 of
these being written in England."[5]

PETER was by no means a mere dialectician as his theology
shows.

> We must not so conceive of the reconciliation of man
> with God, brought about by Christ, as if God then,
> for the first time, began to love those who were before
> objects of his hatred, as an enemy is reconciled to his
> enemy. God did not first begin to love us when he
> became reconciled with us through the blood of his
> Son; but he loved us before the world was, and before
> we were. We were, only on account of sin, at enmity
> with him, who ceased not to love us even when we were
> his enemies. We were at enmity with him as sin and
> righteousness are at enmity.

The great age of Scholasticism, 1193-1280, began with
the work of ALBERT of Bollstadt, 1193-1280, universally
known as ALBERTUS MAGNUS. Under the influence of
JORDAN of Saxony he entered the Dominican Order in 1221

---

[4] His theory of redemption was that of a pious fraud:
What did the Redeemer do to the despot who had us in his
bonds? He offered him the Cross as a mouse-trap, and put his
blood on it as bait (*Sentences*, Bk. III., div. 19).
[5] *Encyclopedia Britannica*, 11th ed., Vol. XXI., p. 293.

or 1223, and began the systematic study of theology. "He may pass for the most fertile writer in the world." He reproduced the whole philosophy of Aristotle in a form adapted to the Christian faith. He felt it to be his task to give every branch of human learning its proper place and its proper work, and then to show that it depends upon theology for its very life.

He wrote a *Commentary* on the *Sentences* of PETER LOMBARD, and also arranged the *Sentences* in a systematic work called a *Summary of Theology*. His scientific researches were gathered up into a *Summary of Natural Philosophy*, commonly known as *The Philosophy of the Mendicants*. Some of his minor works *e.g. On Holding to God*, and his commentaries on the writings of the pseudo-DIONYSIUS, show his religious affinities to the mystics. His hold on the popular mind however was gained by his interest in alchemy whereby he was supposed to be in touch with the supernatural world.

In his pupil THOMAS AQUINAS, 1227-1274, "a finer, even if not a more powerful intellect than ALBERT," Scholasticism reached the zenith of its perfection and power. His belief that reason and faith agree, even though the truths of reason and the mysteries of faith spring from different sources, made him the incarnation of the Scholastic spirit.

He published a *Discussion of Peter Lombard's Sentences;* prepared a Commentary on the Gospels—*The Golden Collection*—by summarising the teaching of the Fathers; and discussed the religious questions of the day in *Twelve various Discussions*, and in a work called *Disputed Questions*. He had also to his credit an *Exposition of all the Epistles of the Holy Apostles*, and some elucidations of Isaiah, Jeremiah, and the Psalter.

After these immense preparations AQUINAS undertook the stupendous task of arranging the world of knowledge into a rational system ruled by the Catholic faith. The result was the *Summa Theologiae, The Sum of the Catholic Faith against the Heathen,* one of the most remarkable achievements of the human mind.

The method of the work is to state a proposition, to assail it with every objection, then to defend it, and to reach a conclusion by the help of the accepted standards of the Church. "From first to last" AQUINAS "was thinking of all that could be said on both sides of the question he was discussing; chiefly of what might be said in favour of the opinion which he did *not* hold, and which he was ultimately to annihilate. . . . The reasoner against almost any tenet of the Catholic faith may be furnished at a short notice with almost any kind of weapons out of the armoury of *the* great Catholic doctor."[6]

The method of this monumental classic may be illustrated from the reply given to the mystical theory of JOACHIM of Floris (cf. p. 210):

> It seems that the New Law will not last till the end of the world. . . . . I Cor. xiii. 10; John xvi. 13. . . .
>
> I answer that The state of the world may change in two ways. In one way, according to a change of law and thus no other state will succeed this state of the New Law. . . . Heb. x. 19–22.
>
> In another way the state of mankind may change according as man stands in relation to one and the same law more or less perfectly. . . .
>
> Nevertheless we are not to look forward to a state wherein man is to possess the grace of the Holy Ghost more perfectly than he has possessed it hitherto, especially the Apostles who *received the first fruits of the Spirit.*
>
> The Old Law corresponded not only to the Father

---

[6] F. D. Maurice, *Mediaeval Philosophy* (1870), p. 188.

but also to the Son, because Christ was foreshadowed in the Old Law. Hence our Lord said, 'For had ye believed Moses, ye would have believed me: for he wrote of me' (John v.46). In like manner the New Law corresponds not only to Christ but also to the Holy Ghost according to Romans viii. 2.

Hence we are not to look forward to another law corresponding to the Holy Ghost.[7]

The Dominicans and the Augustinians accepted the *Summa* as the authoritative statement of theology, but the Franciscans demurred. WILLIAM LAMARRE published *Refutations of Brother Thomas*, 1285, but the chief critic was JOHN DUNS SCOTUS, 1270–1308. His strength lay rather in acute negative criticism of the teaching of others, than in the positive elaboration of his own. "In many respects DUNS SCOTUS is the most important Christian thinker of the Middle Ages. . . . it has been said with much truth that "in Scotus, great Schoolman as he was, Scholasticism overreached itself, and entered upon a subtlety which was the beginning of its decline!"[8] He won the title of "the subtle Doctor." His works were *A Commentary on the Sentences of Peter Lombard*, and *Questions of Sorts;* they belong to the literature of philosophy rather than to that of Christianity. With him began the division of the later scholastics into the rival camps of Thomists and Scotists.

[7] *The Summa Theologica* (1915), literally trans. by Fathers of the English Dominican Province, Part II., First Part, Third Number. Q. Q. xc-cxiv. pp. 287-290.

[8] *Ency. of Religion and Ethics*, Vol. XI., p. 247.

CHAPTER XXVI
PRE-REFORMATION MYSTICISM

Reaction from the formal dialectics of Scholasticism to the emotionalism of the Mystics was almost inevitable. When the Scholastic philosphy had exhausted its original impulse, it was bound to give way to the enthusiasm that tried to grasp reality by intuition, and to gain an immediate experience of God by direct vision.

"Mysticism is religion in its most concentrated and exclusive form; it is that attitude of mind in which all other relations are swallowed up in the relation of the soul to God."[1]

Neo-Platonic mysticism exercised an early influence on Christian thought. VICTORINUS, converted from neo-Platonism in 360, carried his mysticism into his new found faith. All his writings are intensely obscure. JEROME says of them, "He wrote in a dialectical style some very obscure books, intelligible only to the learned." These books are treatises of controversial theology, *On the Generation of the Divine Word, Against Arius, Three Hymns on the Trinity, To Justin the Manichaean against the Two Principles of the Manichaeans and of the True Body of Christ,* and a curious work entitled *The Morning and Evening Make One Day.*

For his use of neo-Platonic ideas as moulds in which to cast his Christian thought, VICTORINUS deserves credit as a pioneer in claiming for Christianity the products of philosophy.

---

[1] Edward Caird, *Evolution of Theology in the Greek Philosophers* (1904), Vol. II., p. 210.

MAXIMUS the Confessor, 580–622, wrote a *Commentary on Dionysius,* as a disciple of the school of Proclus, the neo-Platonist; but he was at the same time a fairly orthodox representative of the speculative activity of the Greek Church. His Expositions of the Lord's Prayer and of the Sermon on the Mount are rich in practical theology, as is also the collection of Aphorisms gathered from his writings. In his *Thoughts concerning Charity* he says:

> He who has genuine faith in Christ, has within him all the charismata collectively. But since, by reason of our inactivity we are far from that active love towards him, which unveils to us the divine treasures which we bear within our own souls, so we justly believe that we are without the divine charismata. If, according to St. Paul, Christ dwells in our hearts by faith, and in him are hid all the treasures of wisdom and knowledge, then all the treasures of wisdom and knowledge are hidden in our hearts. But they reveal themselvs to the heart in proportion as the heart becomes pure, through obedience to the divine commands.

GREGORY THE GREAT showed a mystical tendency in many scattered passages of his writings; so also did JOHN CLIMASUS, d. 605, in his *Ladder of Paradise,* which records his own experiences of the spiritual life, and gives guidance to those who seek the higher degrees of holiness. The book was dedicated to JOHN of Raithu who composed a Commentary on it.

The really creative impulse towards Christian mysticism was given when JOHN SCOTUS ERIGENA translated the works of the pseudo-DIONYSIUS of Areopagus into Latin. This was by far his most notable and influential piece of work.

The first mention of the Areopagite's works occurs in a defence of Monophysitism by some Severian sectaries in Constantinople in 533. Their fame grew steadily in the Greek Church. MAXIMUS wrote notes on them, 600; THEODORUS defended them; LEONTIUS of Byzantium, 590, SOPHRONIUS of Jerusalem, 638, and JOHN of Damascus, 730, all showed their interest in them. In the West the earliest notice of them occurs in the writings of GREGORY THE GREAT. They are quoted in a letter written by Pope Adrian I to Charlemagne, and in 827 the Emperor Michael the Stammerer sent a copy of them to Louis I, the Pious, 778–840, who deposited them in the abbey of St. Denis, where their reception was believed to have been marked by the occurrence of a number of miracles.

Their translation by JOHN SCOTUS ERIGENA brought him trouble. Pope Nicholas I addressed a letter to the Emperor Charles the Bold, 865:

> It has been reported to our apostleship that a certain John, of Scotch origin, has lately translated into Latin the work which the blessed Dionysius wrote in the Greek language, on divine names and celestial orders. This book ought to have been sent to us, according to custom, and approved by our judgment; the more so, that this John, though he is cried up as posessed of great knowledge, has not always, it is everywhere said, been sound in his views upon certain subjects. We recommend, therefore, very strongly, that . . . you do not permit him any longer to reside at Paris, in the school of which he is stated for a long time to have been the chief, in order that he may no longer mingle his tares with the wheat of the holy word, giving poison to those who seek for bread.

The sequel is given in the *Chronicle* of MATTHEW of Westminster under the date 883:

> In consequence of this reproach, this same John

quitted France and came into England, where, some years after, he was stabbed to death by his own pupils with their styles, and died in great agony.

The translation that had such tragic issues was so literal that "the interpretation almost needs an interpreter." Commentators went eagerly to work on it. HUGO of St. Victor treated *The Heavenly Hierarchy*, 1120; ROBERT GROSSETESTE reviewed all the books, 1235; THOMAS AQUINAS discussed *The Divine Names*, 1255; ALBERTUS MAGNUS in 1260, and DIONYSIUS THE CARTHUSIAN in 1450 also dealt with the illimitable theme. New translations were made by JOHN SARRACIN in the twelfth century, and by AMBROSE of Camaldul in the fifteenth century.

The writings which exercised this wide and profound influence were the work of an unknown author of the fifth century. They included *The Heavenly Hierarchy*, *The Ecclesiastical Hierarchy*, *The Divine Names*, *Mystical Theology*, *Theological Outlines*, *Symbolical Theology*, *The Soul*, *The Just Judgment of God*, *The Objects of Intellect and of Sense*, and some Hymns.

Of these some are now lost and some are not essential to the main scheme of the writer. The exposition of the Dionysian system is contained in the first four. That system teaches that "to bring us to Himself, God . . . . makes use of signs and symbols, and of intervening orders of ministers, by whose means we may be gradually raised to nearer communion with him." These symbols and ministers constitute a Hierarchy, or order, of which the various books give their account.

According to his use of the term,

A Hierarchy is a sacred order, and science, and activity, assimilated as far as possible to the godlike, and elevated to the imitation of God proportionately to the

Divine illuminations conceded to it (*Heavenly Hier.*, i.2).

It consists of Seraphim, Cherubim, Thrones, Dominations, Powers, Authorities, Princedoms, Archangels and Angels in descending order; the Angels bringing the powers of heaven into connexion with the beings of earth.

There was one sovereignty over all, and it was to this that the angels presiding over each nation according to the Divine order led those who followed them (*Heavenly Hier.*, ix.3).

The Heavenly Hierarchy is the type of an earthly or Ecclesiastical Hierarchy the form of which however is unlike that of heaven.

The beings and ranks above us are incorporeal; their Hierarchy is intellectual and supramundane; but ours, in due relation to ourselves, is furnished with a manifold array of sensible symbols, by which, according to the divine order, after the right measure of our powers, we are raised to God and divine virtue, that we may be made like Him in the one way (*Ecc. Hier.*, i.2).

To be made divine is to be made like God, as far as may be, and to be made one with Him. This is the common end of every hierarchy, the continuous devotion of love to God, and the things of God, wrought by sacred means in a godly and single fashion; and as a preliminary to this, the complete and unhesitating abandonment of all that is contrary to it, the recognition of things as they are, the sight and knowledge of sacred truth, the godly participation in the one mode of perfectioning, participation in the One Himself, as far as may be, the feast of the beatific vision which nourishes intellectually, and makes divine every one who strains aloft to behold it (*Ecc. Hier.*, i.3).

The treatise *On the Divine Names* is the longest and most important of the series. It gathers together what may be known of God from the descriptive titles given to Him in Scripture, it contains much technical theology, and forms a sequel to the *Theological Outlines.*

God is

> the life of all things that live, the being of all things that exist, the beginning and cause of all life and all being, through His goodness, whereby He calls into being the things which are and sustains them while they are (*Divine Names*, i.3).

Evil is

> a deficiency, a weakness, a want of harmony, a failure; bereft of aim, of beauty, of life, of mind, of reason, of end, of basis, of course; without limit, issue, effect, strength, order, symmetry; infinite, dark and essenceless; by itself, having nowhere and in no case any existence (*Divine Names*, i.30).

The *Mystic Theology* professes to present the esoteric teachings of Christianity; the teachings whereby the devout soul is led step by step to higher things until it is

> released from the objects and the powers of sight, and penetrates into the darkness of un-knowledge, which is truly mystic, and lays aside all conceptions of knowledge and is absorbed in the intangible and invisible, wholly given up to that which is beyond all things, and belonging no longer to himself nor to any other finite being, but in virtue of some nobler faculty is united with that which is wholly unknowable by the absolute in operation of all limited knowledge, and knows in a manner beyond mind by knowing nothing (*Mystic Theol.*, i.3).

The theological school of St. Victor eagerly welcomed and enthusiastically spread the new teaching until the whole of the latter part of the twelfth century was pervaded by it.

HUGO of St. Victor, 1096–1141, was by birth a Saxon, and by repute the Augustine of his time. His fame even exceeded that of BERNARD among the aristocrats of contemplative piety, because he disdained everything outside the limits of the soul's companionship with God. His *Ark of Noah*, written with the charm of spiritual refinement, leads seekers after religious knowledge to the God who dwells within, either as knowledge or as love.

> The way to ascend to God, is to descend into oneself.

All the sixty various writings attributed to him are not his, but he was a copious author whose books have the pure mystic strain. *The Ecclesiastical Ceremonies, Sacraments, Offices and Observances*, like *The Sacraments of the Christian Faith*, was designed to explain and to regulate the rites of the Church. *A Collection of the Sentences*, was the fruit of his scholastic training, but like his *Rules for Study* which was prepared for his monks, shews the generosity of his mind. In the Rules he gives the advice:

> Study everything; thou wilt afterwards see that nothing is superfluous.

But he also gives the warning:

> It is impossible to arrive at anything great, without commencing with the little. It is impossible to become a grammarian without beginning with the alphabet.

The *Soliloquy of the Earnest Soul, Contemplation and its Works*, the *Golden Book of Meditation*, the *Vanity of the World*, and the *Love of the Bridegroom for the Bride*, are all of the true mystic type.

Three eyes have been given to man: the eye of sense, for the sensible objects lying without him; another eye, whereby the soul is enabled to know itself, and what is within itself—the eye of reason; a third eye, within itself, to perceive God and divine things—the eye of contemplation.

RICHARD of St. Victor, d. 1173, was a Scotchman more scholastic in mind than his master HUGO, and, like him, a devoted student of the pseudo-DIONYSIUS. DANTE esteemed him as one of the greatest teachers of the Church. He was a true mystic who sought personal religion apart from the formal theology and sacramentarianism of the age.

If thou wishest to search out the deep things of God, search out the depths of thine own spirit.

He wrote a sprightly book, entitled *Benjamin,* in which he distinguished between active contemplation that seeks the object of its desire, and passive contemplation that attracts it. He gave some prominence to ecstasy in his teaching, and traced the tendencies that lead to it, and the conditions that control it. There are three stages of religious development: that in which God is seen by faith; that in which He is known by reason; that in which He is beheld by contemplation.

To the first and second stages men may ascend; but to the third they can never arrive except by ecstatic transportation of the spirit above itself. The soul raised above itself, beholds things too high for reason in the light of the Godhead, where the thinking reason retires back.

His mystical works are *The State of the Interior Man, The Preparation of the Soul for Contemplation, The Grace of Contemplation, The Steps of Contemplation,* and *The Nuptial Secret.*

In the first of these he claims that good intention is the source of all virtue.

> What the body is without life, that a deed is without good intention. As life proceeds from the heart, and spreads itself through every member, so also good intention rises from deliberation and has accustomed a lively virtue to animate works to merit (Bk. I., chap. 7).

In the second he says:

> He knows not how all the glory of the world lies under his feet, who has not learned to estimate the dignity of his own nature. If thou art not yet capable of entering into thyself, how wilt thou be capable of exploring what is within thee and above thee (chap. 6).

> The rational mind, finds, without doubt, in itself the most excellent mirror wherein to see God. For if God's invisible essence may be known from His works, where can we find those marks more clearly stamped than in that which is His own image? Every one therefore, who longs to see God, should cleanse the mirror of his own spirit (chap. 72).

WALTER of St. Victor, d. 1180, was more aggressive in his opposition to Scholasticism. His *Four Labyrinths of Gaul,* was a vehement criticism of ABELARD, PETER LOMBARD, PETER OF POITIERS, and GILBERT DE LA POREE.

In ADAM of St. Victor, 1110-1172, the Middle Ages had their greatest poet. He was "the most prominent and prolific of the Latin hymnists." His works are spoken of as being "charged and saturated with the great facts, the very inmost, the most recondite and spiritual meanings of Scripture, with its mystical and symbolical meanings and interpretations, and are in musical and flowing verse, clothed with the magnificent imagery and descriptions of the prophets and of the book of Revelations." The best known of the 106 Hymns and Sequences that remain of his poems, is perhaps that translated:

> Jesu, Word of God Incarnate,
> Of the virgin mother born.
> On the Cross Thy sacred body
> For us men with nails was torn.
>
> Cleanse us by the blood and water
> Streaming from Thy pierced side;
> Feed us with Thy body broken,
> Broken in death's agony.

The school of St. Victor was only one of several sources of the pre-Reformation mysticism. Many students of the mystical theology were independent of its aid. Among such was the ever illustrious BERNARD of Clairvaux, 1091–1153. He was many men in one, a rigid and disciplined ascetic, a vigorous theologian, a preacher of the Crusades, a keen man of affairs, a mystic, and an ardent defender of orthodoxy. The sincerity of his mysticism is revealed in the saying:

> To lose thyself in some sort as if thou wert not . . . to be emptied of thyself and almost annihilated—is heavenly conversation.

He led the way toward a romantic type of mysticism in which Christ was worshipped as "the bridegroom of the soul." "The romantic side of Mysticism, for good and for evil, received its greatest stimulus in BERNARD'S Poems and in his Sermons on the Canticles."[2] Some of the Poems are widely used in translations. *The Joyful Rhythm of St. Bernard on the Name of Jesus,* is dated 1150 when the author was in retirement after the failure and shame of the Second Crusade. "It is the finest and most characteristic specimen of St. Bernard's 'subjective loveliness,' and in its

---

[2] W. R. Inge, *Christian Mysticism,* 5th ed. (1921), p. 140, note 2.

honeyed sweetness vindicates his title of the Mellifluous Doctor. It has been called "the sweetest and most evangelical hymn of the Middle Ages."[3] Caswall translates it:

> Jesus, the very thought of Thee
> With sweetness fills my breast;
> But sweeter far Thy face to see,
> And in Thy presence rest.
>
> Nor voice can sing, nor heart can frame,
> Nor can the memory find
> A sweeter sound than Thy blest name,
> O Saviour of mankind.

Other poems almost as universally admired are the Sequence beginning,—"Full of gladness, Let our faithful choir," and the *"Rhythmical prayer to any one of the members of Christ, suffering and hanging on the Cross."* This is divided into seven parts which are addressed to the Feet, Knees, Hands, Side, Breast, Heart, and Face. The last part was most powerfully rendered into German by GERHARDT from whose version comes the English:

> O Sacred head, now wounded,
>   With grief and shame weighed down;
> Now scornfully surrounded
>   With thorns Thine only crown;
> How art Thou pale with anguish,
>   With sore abuse and scorn;
> How does that visage languish,
>   Which once was bright as morn!

The *Sermons on the Song of Songs* mark an epoch in mystical thought, both by their romanticism and by their consistent use of symbolism as an aid to the interpretation of the Bible. To BERNARD the Church is the bride of Christ, and the symbolism of marriage is very freely used in developing the meaning of the Canticles, but without the extravagance that marked later developments.

[3] Cf. Julian's *Dictionary of Hymnology*, 2d ed., p. 585.

How fair Thou appearest to me, even in my own form, Lord Jesus! not solely on account of the divine miracle, but also on account of the truth, meekness, and righteousness. Blessed is he who narrowly observeth Thee, so as Thou walkest as a man among men, and, according to his ability, striveth thus to be thine imitator (Sermon 25).

In a treatise *On Loving God,* he deals with the four stages of the soul's progress to the highest perfection, concerning which he humbly says:

I do not know if the fourth is perfectly attainable in this life by any man, that a man may love himself for the sake of God alone. If they who have experience do assert this, to me, I confess, it seems impossible.

The books entitled *Meditations,* addressed to pope Eugenius, are of great beauty. They breathe the spirit of holy liberty, but express the fear lest feebleness of faith shall follow an undue sense of power in the Church.

GUIGO THE CARTHUSIAN, d. 1137, wrote with a beauty of spirit and a sincere piety for which he has always been praised. BERNARD appreciated the liveliness as well as the nobility of thought in the Letters he received from GUIGO's pen. Six Letters are extant as well as a *Life of St. Hugh of Chateau Neuf,* and a book of *Meditations*—short, solid, noble thoughts forcefully expressed.

WILLIAM of Thierry, 1085–1148, the compiler of the first book of *The First Life* of BERNARD, also fed the mystic flame.

The prince of mystical theologians was JOHN FIDANZA, 1221-1274, familiarly known as BONAVENTURA. All his writings emphasise the craving of the naked passive soul for union with the Eternal in the depths of the divine darkness.

The mind must be dark to all phantasms and images in order that it may see God.

BONAVENTURA gave a new vocabulary to his successors through the riotous exuberance of his language. He threw all his ardour, eloquence, fluency, and persuasiveness into the effort to bring all that is worth knowing into union with the divine. He was the greatest scholastic among the mystics, and the greatest mystic among the scholastics. His teaching was characterised by the doctrine of 'illumination'—reason can discover some truths, but the highest truth can be known only through illumination.

His scholasticism appears in his *Commentary on the Sentences,* and in *The Reduction of the Arts to Theology.* The conclusion to the last named work is as follows:

> Thus it is manifest . . . how the multiform Wisdom of God is hidden in every kind of knowledge, and in all nature. It is manifest also how every kind of knowledge ministers to Theology. . . . And this is the fruit of all sciences, that in all, Faith should be built up, God should be honoured, manners should be softened and harmonised, and those consolations imbibed which come from the union of the Bridegroom and the Bride. . . .

In the Commentary he says concerning the knowledge "in which the affection is set on fire":

> In my opinion, this manner of knowledge is to be sought by every just man in this life. If God shall perform aught beyond this, it is a special privilege, not the common law.

His chief mystical writings are *Meditations on the Passion of Christ, The Three-fold Way, A Short Word, A Soliloquy, The Seven Ways of Eternity,* and above all *The Journey of the Mind to God.* It is in the *Journey* that he gives his famous description of the divine as "wholly within all things, and wholly without . . . . the sphere of which the centre is everywhere and the circumference nowhere."

"The beauty of his Latin Hymns captivated admirers of literature, and touched the heart of the pious . . . . in majestic verses BONAVENTURA manifested the religion which found help for action and ease for trouble in contemplation of the Cross of Christ."

> In your toiling and your resting,
> In your weeping and your jesting,
>   When you smile and when you smart,
> Going forth or home returning,
> Comforted or with pain burning,
>   Keep the Cross within your heart.

Under the influence of the writings of JOHN SCOTUS ERIGENA, there grew up in Paris a mystical school led by AMALRICH of Bena, d. 1207, whose teaching that humanity is essentially divine brought about his condemnation in 1205. His persecuted followers were scattered far and wide; those who found shelter in the Rhineland united as the Brothers of the Free Spirit.

Mysticism attained its zenith in the thirteenth century. Many German women lent their influence to spread the teaching. MATHILDE of Magdeburg, 1210-1285, wrote *The Streaming Light,* the first work of its kind in Old German. In it she describes the marriage of the soul to the heavenly bridegroom, using an exalted rhetoric which at times passes into rhyme. MECHTILDE of Hackeborn, 1240–1298, MARGERIE KEMPE, d. 1290, and ANGELA of Foligno, 1248–1309, represent a type of mysticism in which spiritual aspiration is blended with the desire to reform social and ecclesiastical abuses.

The desire to emancipate mysticism from traditional religion took definite shape in the mind of JOHN (or HEINRICH) ECKHART of Cologne, 1260-1327. Of all the mystics he was "the most clear and explicit in regard to the relation of God and man. His fundamental position was 'God and Being are one and the same thing.' " But his theology was far from being of the orthodox type. "How utterly impossible it is to reconcile with orthodox theology such sayings as these":

> In the moment that God was, the world was created.
> God created the world and I with Him.
> Before the creatures were, God was not God.
> God is in all things: all things are God.
> The Father begets me His son without cessation; I say more: He begets in me Himself and in Himself me.
> The eye with which I see God is the same eye with which God sees me.
> My eye and God's eye are one eye.

The character of his mysticism may be seen in his theology.

> God and Godhead are as distinct as earth is from heaven.
> The Godhead has left all things to God: It owns nought, wills nought, requires nought, effects nought, produces nought.
> Thou shalt love the Godhead as It truly is: a non-God, non-Spirit, non-Person . . . . a sheer pure, clear One, severed from all duality: let us sink down into that One, throughout eternity, from Nothing into Nothing, so help us God.

ECKHART was the most gifted of the German mystics. By the help of his associates he created a national vocabulary for the mystical philosophy; his writings are however almost all lost, only a few pamphlets and some Sermons remain. RICHARD ROLLE of Hampole, 1290-1349, who is the father of English mysticism, also belongs to the company of those who exalt piety of mind above ecclesiasticism. His desire was "to compose or write something by which the Church of God might grow in divine delight." He wrote *The Pricke of Conscience,* a long, rather lifeless religious poem, in short couplets, dealing with the transitoriness of human things, with death and judgment, heaven and hell. He made three translations of the Psalter, one in metre and two in prose, and furnished the prose versions with Commentaries. He also wrote *The Contemplation of the Fear and the Love of God, The Remedy against the Troubles of Temptation, The Amendment of Life,* and *The Fire of Love.*

> Therefore truly long I after love, the fairest of flowers, I am inwardly burned by the flame of fire. Thus it warms, a man thinks not how, save that he feels solace in himself, the heart singing ditties and taken captive with the charge of charity. Soothly this that I thus receive is most mercy, and I nearly die while it is thus made steadfast with burning love. Now grant my best Beloved, that I may cease; for death, that many dread, shall be to me as heavenly music. Although I am sitting in the wilderness, yet I am now as it were stable in Paradise, and there sweetly is sounding a loving song in the delights that my love has given me.

WALTER HYLTON, d. 1396, described the progress of the spiritual life in *The Scale or Ladder of Perfection,* a book that was "chosen to be the guide of good Christians in the courts of kings and in the world." The steps of the Ladder are first, a knowledge of the facts of religion, then the feeling of grace, then knowledge with love.

> In the third stage of contemplation, reason is turned into light, and will into love.
> Christ is lost, like the piece of money in the parable; but where? In thy house, that is, in thy soul. Thou

needest not run to Rome or Jerusalem to seek Him. He sleepeth in thy heart, as He did in the ship; awaken Him with the loud cry of thy desire. Howbeit, I believe that thou sleepest oftener to Him than He to thee.

JULIANA of Norwich, 1343-1443, is an English representative of erotic mysticism, the mysticism that expresses the desire of the soul for God in terms of the love betwen man and woman. Her point of view finds expression in the sentence:

I saw Him, and sought Him, I had Him and I wanted Him.

JULIANA is remembered in literature by her *Revelations of Divine Love Recorded by Julian, Anchoress at Norwich.* There are sixteen Revelations describing her experiences after she had reached the age of thirty. They satisfied her desire to see Christ on the Cross.

All this was showed by three parts—that is to say, by bodily sight, and by words formed in my understanding, and by ghostly sight.

She saw

. . . . that it is more worship to God and more very delight that we faithfully pray to Himself of His goodness, and cleave thereto by His grace, with true understanding and stedfast by love, than if we made (use of) all the means that heart can think.

. . . . that in every soul that shall be saved there is a godly will that never assented to sin, nor ever shall;

. . . . (our Lord) scorning the fiend's malice, and noughting his unmight.

In 1350 that universally famous hand-book of mystical devotion, *The German Theology,* was issued anonymously by the Friends of God at Frankfort.   The only clue to its origin is given in an introductory note.

> This little book hath the Almighty and Eternal God spoken by the mouth of a wise and understanding, faithful, righteous man His Friend, who aforetime was of the Teutonic Order, a priest and warden in the house of the Teutonic Order in Frankfort, and it giveth much precious insight into Divine truth and especially teacheth how and whereby we may discern the true and upright Friends of God from those unrighteous and false teachers who are most hurtful to the holy Church.

LUTHER translated and published it in 1516, criticising its crabbed words and bad style, but confessing his deep indebtedness to its message.   The vital principle of the teaching of the book is the need of abolishing selfishness.   Religion should exclude the creature glory of "I" and "Mine," so that God may be all in all.

> All things have their being more truly in God than in themselves.
> I can do nothing of myself but simply yield to God so that He alone may do all things in me.
> I would fain be to the Eternal Goodness what his own hand is to a man.

The Friends of God from whose community *The German Theology* came, included some well known mystics.   JOHN TAULER, 1300-1361, the great doctor and master of Holy Scripture, was their outstanding preacher.   In him Mysticism attained its sanest and most humane form.   The religious oratory of Germany before LUTHER reached its culminating point in his Sermons, which are "close analytical studies of Christian experience" cast into expository moulds.   He discarded scholastic forms in favour of the more loosely constructed forms of the earlier Homilies.   His style is lively and popular; he uses many illustrations and much fresh, piquant, and impressive imagery. The tone and temper of these Sermons is evangelical, sincere, lofty, and pure. "It may be justly said of him, that he first gave to prose that direction in which Luther afterwards advanced so far." His whole soul flames up when he depicts the spiritual life which in one passage he likens to a wilderness:

> In this wilderness are found the lilies of chastity, and the white roses of innocence; and therein are found too the red roses of sacrifice, when flesh and blood are consumed in the struggle with sin, and the man is ready, if need be, to suffer martyrdom—the which is not easily to be learned in the world. In this wilderness, too, are found the violets of humility, and many other fair flowers and wholesome roots, in the examples of holy men of God.

HENRY SUSO, 1295-1365, a disciple of TAULER, looked upon mysticism as "an intimate personal adventure." He was a poet and man of letters rather than a theologian and a preacher; he stands in the succession of the minnesingers, but he wrote in prose and transferred the language of earthly love to spiritual devotion. His *Autobiography* is a gem of mediæcal literature, it records his experiences as a servitor of the heavenly wisdom—experiences of terrible austerity, soaring speculation, contemplative vision, and inner dereliction. SUSO embodied his own principle:

> A man of true self-abandonment must be unbuilt from the creature, inbuilt with Christ, overbuilt into the Godhead.

His viewpoint is stated in the following declaration:

> I set before my inner eyes myself in all my being, with body, soul, and all my faculties, and placed around

myself all creatures which God ever created, in heaven, on earth, and in all the elements, the birds of the air, the beasts of the forests, the fishes of the water, the leaves and the grass of the land, and the countless sand of the sea, and thereto all the little dustflakes which shine in the rays of the sun, and all the little water-drops which ever fell or fall from dew, snow, or rain, and wished that each of these things had a sweetly swelling sound of harps, well prepared from the innermost recesses of my heart, so that there would rise up from them a new jubilant hymn of praise to the beloved gentle God from evermore to evermore.

RULMANN MERSWIN, 1308-1382, perhaps the most representative writer among the Friends of God, was a layman whose devotion to literature led him to write sixteen books in a rather diffuse and uninteresting style, full of repetition. He "unites the dying strain of Middle High German love-poetry with the first tones preluding the Reformation." His *Book of the Nine Rocks* describes the ascent of the soul from earth to the Creator.

BRIDGET of Sweden, 1303-1373, "that flower of the North transplanted to the Eternal City," began to dictate her wonderful *Book of Revelations* in 1344, when the spirit of prophecy fell upon her. It "is at once a spiritual autobiography, a collection of epistles, a record of graces and visions, a denunciation of the corruption of the times."[4] She was deeply concerned about the evils that crept into the two Orders of Friars, about the state of the Church, and especially about the ignominious position of pope Urban at Avignon.

In this deep concern CATHERINE of Siena, 1347-1380, was at one with her. Both visited the pope and strove to persuade him to return to Rome. CATHERINE's great literary work is *The Dialogue*, first published in 1472. There

---

[4] Edmund G. Gardner, *St. Catherine of Siena*, p. 44.

is also ascribed to her a short treatise, *Consummate Perfection*, "a kind of spiritual conversation between the soul and her Creator upon the complete abnegation of self and the perfect fulfilling of the will of God."

The *Dialogue* or *Treatise of the Divine Providence*, "seems to be properly divided into six treatises or tracts; an Introduction, The Treatise of Discretion, The Treatise of Prayer, The Treatise of Tears, The Treatise of the Divine Providence and the Treatise of Obedience."[5] The opening passage, on the possibility of the soul's union with God in love, contains the very essence of mysticism:

> When a soul lifts herself up athirst with very great desire for the honour of God, and the salvation of souls, she exercises herself for a while in habitual virtue and dwells in the cell of knowledge of self, in order better to know the goodness of God; for love follows knowledge, and when she loves, she seeks to follow and to clothe herself with the truth. But in no way does the creature taste and become illumined by this truth as much as by means of humble and continuous prayer based on knowledge of self and of God.

In the Netherlands the father of mysticism was JAN VAN RUYSBROECK 1294-1381, the ecstatic doctor, whose books carry the mystical impress in their very titles. His mysticism was less profound than that of ECKHART and less practical than that of TAULER, but his insight into things spiritual is so deep that it has been said of him, "his marvellous ignorance rediscovers the wisdom of buried centuries and foresees the knowledge of centuries unborn." In *The Ladder, or Seven Grades of Love*, he defines the course of the mystic's progress as being through goodwill, voluntary poverty, purity, lowliness of mind, desire for God's glory, and Divine contemplation, to the nameless transcendence of all knowledge and

---

[5] *Ibid.* p. 354.

thought. *The Adornment of Spiritual Marriage* indicates an even more elaborated progress from another viewpoint. The Active Life meets the Bridegroom in the ways of humility, love, and justice. The Inner Life rising above the Active Life apprehends Him with the Affection, advances towards Him by the Will, and craves Him with the Affection. Finally the Contemplative Life, by a living immersion and by melting into the unknown Dark, enables the soul to sink into the Godhead, *i.e.* into the Abyss in which the Persons of the Trinity transcend themselves.

The sum total of the writings of RUYSBROECK is large. In addition to the two works already mentioned he wrote *The Book of the Twelve Beguines, The Mirror of Eternal Salvation, The Book of the Spiritual Tabernacle, The Sparkling Stone, The Book of Supreme Truth, The Book of the Seven Castles, The Book of the Kingdom of the Beloved, The Book of the Four Temptations, The Book of the Twelve Virtues, The Book of Christian Faith,* seven Letters and two Hymns.[6]

A devoted admirer of RUYSBROECK, GERHARD GROOT, 1349-1384, in company with FLORENTINUS RADEWYN, 1350-1400, planned to establish the College of the Brothers of the Common Lot at Derventer. The College was built and inhabited in 1400. This brotherhood was remarkable for the attention it gave to the cultivation of knowledge. Their schools were "the first genuine nurseries of literature in Germany, so far as it depended on the knowledge of languages . . . ." They copied good books and lived in common on the income from their work; they published Collections of Aphorisms from the New Testament, from AUGUSTINE, ANSELM and BERNARD.

GROOT became missionary preacher of the diocese of Utrecht in 1379, but in spite of his immense popularity his

---

[6] Maurice Maeterlinck, *Ruysbroeck and the Mystics,* trans. by Jane T. Stoddart, 2d ed. (1908), p. 32.

work was prohibited because he exposed and denounced the sins of the clergy. In a *Public Protestation* he insisted in vain upon the evangelical character of his labours.

Most famous of the Brothers is THOMAS HAEMERLEIN, 1380-1471, universally known as THOMAS A KEMPIS. His loyalty to GROOT was shown in his biography *The Life of the Great Gerard,* but his literary immortality rests on his devotional classic *The Imitation of Christ.* In this work A KEMPIS adopted the three stages of spiritual ascent indicated by earlier mystics, but he did not express that passionate longing for the Ineffable which is the confessed motive of their upward striving.

The Imitation is "the ripe fruit of mediæval Christianity as concentrated in the life of the cloister." It represents the religious life as a life of moral discipline under which the soul is controlled by purity, veracity, obedience, brotherliness, and charity. It is formally a cluster of short treatises of which the second and fourth were originally called Church Music— a common name for works of its kind. It was written in rhyming metre with a musical lilt that expressed the emotion of the writer. Its form is that of an antiphony between God and the soul.

> The glory and privilege of a good man consists in the testimony of his own mind; for this is a perpetual feast and triumph. It sets him above the power of fortune, and makes the sharpest afflictions not only an exercise of his invincible patience, but a matter of undisturbed joy to him. Whereas even prosperity itself cannot procure ease and content to a guilty and self-condemning breast.
>
> Wouldest thou then enjoy a sweet and uninterrupted tranquility? Keep all at peace within, and give thy own thought no cause to reproach thee (Bk. II., chap. 6).

The last of the scholastic mystics appeared in PETER D'AILLY, 1350-1425, and in JEAN CHARLIER, 1363-1429, who is better known as JEAN GERSON. These French representatives lacked the emotional fervour of the Dutch and the German mystics.

GERSON in his *Mystical Theology* tried to make mysticism simple and systematic, but with him and his contemporaries the great age reached its term. The passion of the mediæval mystics was thereafter subdued to the enthusiasms of daily devotion. The spirit had fled.

PART VI

THE REFORMATION PERIOD
(1300-1600)

CHAPTER XXVII

THE CHILDREN OF THE FUTURE

The *Divine Comedy* of DANTE ALIGHIERI not only crowned the Middle Ages with a consummate expression of their spirit, but it also opened the new age by its aspirations and ideals. On the threshold of that new age, GIOVANNI BOCCACIO, 1313-1375, touched the heart of the world with a *Decameron* of short stories that pictured the lamentable humiliation of clerical Christianity, and the consequent laxity of life and morals.

"Under pope John XXII, 1313-1334, things were bad." ALVARUS PELAGIUS, in *The Lamentation for the Church*, said:

The gold which is the holiness of virtues has grown dim in the Church. Ordinations and the sacraments are bought and sold for gold. Whenever I entered the apartment of the chamberlain of our Lord the Pope I saw brokers and tables full of gold and clerics counting and weighing florins.[1]

But a new day was at hand. FRANCESCO PETRARCH, 1304-1374, greeted the new day with a fresh voice, and his coronation with the poetic laurel of Rome in 1341 began a literary revival. "From that day the history of modern literature as a recognised power may be said to date." Although his genius was entirely lyric, his literary labours were not restricted to lyrical poetry. Religion was a forceful element in his character, and some of his moral writings re-

---

[1] Edmund G. Gardner, *St. Catherine of Siena*, p. 27.

veal the earnestness of his soul. He addressed two metrical
Epistles to Benedict XII, 1334-1342, exhorting him to
leave Avignon and return to Italy, and he offered a similar
appeal to Clement VI, 1342-1352. In three terrible
Sonnets against Avignon he painted for all time the state
of the society that gathered about the exiled popes' throne.
His *Untitled Epistles* contain even more frightful pictures
of the corruption of the papal court.

> What difference is there between those enemies of
> Christ who betrayed Him with a kiss and bent the knee
> before Him in mockery and the Pharisees of our time?
> That same Christ, whose name they exalt night and
> day with hymns of praise, whom they robe in purple
> and gold, whom they load with jewels, whom they
> salute and adore prostrate—that very same do they
> not buy and sell on earth like merchandise? As it
> were blindfold that He may not see, they crown Him
> with the thorns of their impious wealth, they defile
> Him with their impure spittal, and assail Him with
> viperous hissing; they strike Him with the spear of
> their poisonous deeds, and so far as in them lies, mocked,
> naked, poor, and scourged, they drag Him again to
> Calvary and nail Him again to the Cross.

PETRARCH'S interest in the character of AUGUSTINE
moved him to write a eulogy of the solitary life entitled
Contempt of the World, 1343. The praise of monasticism
was also the subject of *The Solitary Life* and *The Ease of
the Religious*. The most important of these religious
pamphlets is the *Remedies for both kinds of Fortunes*, 1356,
in two books, the first treating of the snares of prosperity,
the second arming the soul against adversity. His tract
His Own and Others Ignorance, gives a lively representation
of the struggle between the humanistic scholar and the orthodox Christian.

A sterner spirit than that which stirred in Italian humanism found incarnation in the English WILLIAM LANGLAND,
1332-1400, who preached the equality of man, pleaded for
justice in social life, and urged the betterment of religion, in
his poem *The Vision of Piers Plowman,* or, as the title
should probably be, *The Book concerning Piers the Plowman.* This is "a calm, allegorical exposition of the corruptions of the State, of the Church, and of social life," designed to reveal to the people the "true causes of the evils
under which they were suffering, and to secure the reformation of those grievous abuses."

> Heremites on an heep With hoked staues,
> Wenten to Walsyngham and here wenches after;
> Grete lobyes and longe that loth were to swynke,
> Clotheden hem in copis to ben knowen fram others;
> And shopen hem heremites here ese to haue.
> I fonde there Freris alls the foure ordres
> Preched the peple for profit of hem-seluen,
> Glosed the gospel as hem good lyked.
> For coueitise of copis construed it as they wolde . . .
> There preched a Pardonere as he a prest were
> Brouzte forth a bulle with bishopes seles,
> And seide that hym-self myzte assoilen hem alle
> Of falshed of fastyng of vowes ybroken.

But by far the most powerful English figure of the four-
teenth century was JOHN WICLIF, 1324-1384, the morning
star of the Reformation. Inspired by the prophecies of
JOACHIM of Floris, and distressed by the corruption of the
Church, he issued his first book, *The Last Times of the
Church.* He contributed *A Certain Resolve concerning
Authority,* 1374, to the controversy between King John
Lackland and the Pope about the payment of tribute. Two
years later he read to his students a treatise on *Civil Lord-
ship,* in which he advanced his famous principle "that righteousness is the sole indefensible title to dominion and prop-
erty"; in other words "dominion is founded on grace."

In 1378 with the help of members of his circle, he made the first English translation of the *Vulgate*. This was completed in its earlier form by NICHOLAS HEREFORD, and in 1388 was revised throughout by JOHN PURVEY.[2] This translation, together with his Sermons and Tracts, made WICLIF the founder of English prose. It is impossible to over-estimate the influence of his work on the life and literature of England.

> Ye beleven not, for ye ben not of my scheep. My scheep heren my vois, and I knowe hem, and thei suen me. And I gyve to hem everlastynge life, & thei schulen not perische, withouten end; and noon schal rauysche hem fro myn hond. That thing that my Fadir gaf to me, is more than alle thingis: & no man may rauysche from my Fadris hond. I & the Fadir ben oon (John x.26-30).

A *Defence*, sixty pages in length, appeared in the later editions in explanation of his method.

> First it is knowe that the best translation is out of Latyn into English, to translate after the sentence, and not oneli after the wordis, so that the sentence be as opin, either openere in English as in Latyn, and go not fer fro the lettre.

WICLIF was a copious writer, more than two hundred works are ascribed to him, many of them being of a political or semi-political character. He wrote *The truth of Holy Scripture, The Church, The Office of King, The Papal Power, The Great Sentence of Excommunication Explained,* and *Confessions.* In *A Feigned Contemplative Life* he condemned those who gave up the work of preaching for the life of the cloister. His *Fifty Heresies and Errors of Friars,*

---

[2] Cf. Margaret Deanesly, *The Lollard Bible and other Medieval Biblical Versions* (1920).

1384, denounced the hypocrisy, pride, and covetousness that prevailed in the mendicant Orders.

His greater books are the *Exposition of the Decalogue,* the *Eucharist,* 1381, and the *Trialogus.* The *Eucharist* contains twelve conclusions against the doctrine of transubstantiation of which he says:

> As a man leeves for to thenk the kinde of an ymage whether it be of oke or of ashe, and settys his thought in him in whom is the ymage: so myche more schuld a man leve tho thenk on the kynde of brede, but thenk upon Christ; and with alle cleness, alle devotion, and alle charitye that God wolde gif him worschippe he Crist, and then he receives God ghostly more needfully than the prist that syngus the masse in less charity.

The brilliant *Trialogus* was the best known and the most influential of all his works. It was the first of his books to be printed, 1525. In it he summarised his opinions on theology and philosophy in a three-sided discussion between Truth, Falsehood, and Wisdom.

The spirit aroused by WICLIF was challenged by the only great English theologian of the fifteenth century, REGINALD PECOCK, 1395-1459, in a masterly work *The Repressor of Over-much Weeting* (blaming) *of the Clergie,* 1455. His other writings include the *Book or Rule of Christian Religion,* the *Book of Faith or the Donet,* and the *Folewer to the Donet.* The *Donet* is "an introduction to the chief truths of the Christian faith in the form of a dialogue between father and son." His views, however, brought him into conflict with the authorities, for he regarded Scripture as the only standard of right and wrong, and exalted the authority of reason, wishing

> bi cleer witte drawe men into consente of trewe feith otherwise than bi fire and swerd or hangement.

CARDINAL MORTON, 1486-1500, in his *Pastorals*, also crossed swords with WICLIF; he insisted upon the dignity and seriousness of the priest's office although he would have it reformed in some minor things. The *Trialogus* was specifically answered by one WIDEFORT, a Franciscan, who "dedicated his laboured reply to archbishop Arundel."

WICLIF'S doctrinal influence soon waned in England, but in Bohemia his views were raised to the dignity of a national religion. MATTHIAS of Janow may be regarded as the man who introduced the new teaching into Bohemia. He was a widely travelled scholar who had spent six years in the University of Paris. In a book entitled *The Abomination of the Flesh of Priests and Monks*, he recounts the story of his own spiritual deliverance, but the work from which the clearest insight into his spirit and influence is gained is *The Rule of the Old and New Testaments*, which seems to be a collection of several independent treatises composed between 1385 and 1390.

> The Lord Jesus instructed me how to write all this which relates to the present condition of priests, that is, the carnal ones, and which throws light on the character of these times; but what the end is in which all this is to result, he only knows who set me to work. And he sent me his spirit who shoots the fire into my bones and into my heart, leaving me no rest till I expose the hidden shame of the mother of harlots.

In the work called *The Kingdom, People, Life and Manners of Antichrist*, he wrote:

> All holy Scripture predicts, that before the end of the world the church of Christ shall be reformed, renovated, and more widely extended; that she shall be restored to her pristine dignity, and that, still, in her old age, her fruitfulness shall increase.

The work of MATTHIAS and the spirit of STANISLAUS of Znaim left deep impressions upon JOHN HUS, 1369-1415, who, together with his friends, met the opposition to Wiclifism expressed by STEPHEN of Dolan who wrote, 1408, *Marrow of the Wheat, or Anti-Wiclif*. STEPHEN continued his attacks in other books, *e.g., Anti-Hus, A Winged Dialogue between a Goose and a Sparrow* and *A Book of Letters to the Hussites.*

HUS was stirred by some fictitious miracles, which served the greed of the clerics, to write his first book, *The Glorification of the Blood of Christ.*

"The years 1412-1414 were the years of HUS'S greatest literary activity. . . . . To the earlier part of this period if not to a yet earlier date belong the two treatises entitled . . . . *The Mirror of Sin,* an almost literal translation of the work entitled *Speculum Peccatoris* that has been attributed to AUGUSTINE, and a similar shorter work entitled . . . . the *Shorter Mirror.* To . . . . 1412 belong a series of Expositions dealing consecutively of the faith, the Commandments, and the Lord's Prayer, and a short work entitled the *Daughter.* . . . He here and everywhere maintains the mediæval theory of the superiority of maidenhood to the state of a matron.

"Of greater interest than any of these writings is the short book entitled *On Simony,* written early in 1413; for it deals with the real cause of the Bohemian troubles of this period . . . ."

As simony is heresy, and as the evil denounce good men as heretics, I wish—as an admonition and confirmation for the good, and also for the correction of the evil—to define first of all what heresy is, that people may know whether those are heretics to whom they give the name, or whether they are themselves tainted with heresy.

"Hus defines three sources from which heresy springs; they are apostacy, blasphemy, and simony . . . . To 1413 belongs also another of Hus's most valuable Bohemian works . . . . the *Postilla* . . . . afterwards greatly venerated as his "testament" or "last will."[3]

Hus compiled a work called *The Church* from two works of Wiclif,—the *Church,* and the *Power of the Pope.* He handled the Bohemian controversy in *The Refutation of the Eight Doctors,* and the *Answer to Master Stanilaus.* His doctrinal views were explained in *The Trinity, The Body of Christ,* and *The Elucidation of his Faith.* In a Letter written to the Bohemian nation the night before his execution, 1415, he said:

> I beg of the nobility to remember the poor, I beg of the citizens to conduct their business honestly. I beg of the artisans to do their work well and to use it properly. I beg of the servants to serve their masters and mistresses honestly.

A certain Master Jenseintz issued a *Defence of the Cause of John Hus;* Andrew of Broda, replied in *An Answer to the Epistle Sent out by John Hus.* The followers of the reformer however separated into Taborites and Calixtines, and in 1457 a third party arose and called themselves The Church of the Brotherhood.

This Church of the Brotherhood (Unitas Fratrum), found their guide and rule in the writings of their leader Gregory. His works included *Seven Letters to Rokyczana,* 1468-1470, a *Tract on the Holy Church,* a *Treatise on the Narrow Way to Christ,* and *The Two Kinds of Work, One Founded on Sand and the Other on Rock,* 1471.

Gregory was succeeded by Lucas of Prague, 1490-1528, who provided the Brotherhood with a *Constitution,*

---

[3] Count Lutzow, *The Life and Times of John Hus,* pp. 186-188, 197.

a *Rule of Faith,* a *Hymn book,* 1501, and a *First Cate-chism,* 1502. Next to KOMENSKY he was "the most volu-minous writer of the Unity." Sixty-eight theological works are attributed to him. After his death the Church of the Brotherhood came into close touch with LUTHER who fur-nished a preface for their *Statement of Faith,* 1533.

The ruin of the evangelical cause of Bohemia, 1620, led to a general exodus under the guidance of the one surviving bishop, JOHN AMOS COMENIUS, 1592-1670, "the herald of the humanistic and religious training of the young." Of the one hundred and forty-two works ascribed to him the greatest is the allegorical tale entitled *The Labyrinth of the World;* perhaps the most famous work in the Bohemian tongue.

The death of COMENIUS closes the first part of the story of the tradition of WICLIF.

Italy had a forerunner of the Reformation in GIROLAMO SAVONAROLA, 1452-1498, who "died because he was a preacher of righteousness in an age and Church at the depths of unrighteousness." While a young man of twenty he wrote a poem entitled *The Ruin of the World,* and followed it with a prose work *The Contempt of the World.* During his novitiate he composed *The Ruin of the Church* as a com-panion work to his first poem. These earlier pieces show the bent of his mind when he pondered upon religious things in connection with his own age.

He left the world to "enter religion" because "first, the great misery of the world, the iniquities of men, the ravish-ing, the adultery, the pride, the idolatry, the cruel blasphe-mies; for the age has come to such a pass that not one is found who acts rightly . . . ."

His preaching during the Lent of 1481 made little impres-sion; but in 1485 he proclaimed some of his prophetic views, and again with greater power in 1486. By a "ter-rible sermon" on August 1, 1490, he won a great notoriety

in Florence. Thereafter his preaching rang with three notes;
the Church would be scourged, it would be renewed, and
these prophecies would soon be fulfilled. His fame spread
like wildfire.

> Tell me, ye who contradict, did you ever in your
> times see a man preach in one city, and his voice run
> through all Italy and beyond Italy?

Ten courses of his Sermons exist: viz., on 1 John,
1491; Psalm 73, 1493; the Ark of Noah, 1494; Haggai,
1494-5; the Psalms, 1495; Job, 1495; Amos and Zech-
ariah, 1496; Ruth and Micah, 1496; Ezekiel, 1496-7;
Exodus, 1498. "Though the magic of the preacher's personality has passed away, and we are dependent upon re-
porters, ... enough remains to enable us to realize the
terrible quality of Savonarola's eloquence, his apocalyptic
fire and religious fervour, his zeal for righteousness, his fear-
lessness of men, and the profound emotion that these discourses must have stirred in his audience."[4]
In his writings SAVONAROLA gives more orderly and formal expression to the teaching which his Sermons proclaimed in popular eloquence. He described the visions that
had inspired his religious and political prophecies in a book
entitled *A Compendium of Revelation*, 1495. His leading
principles are explained in his four favourite works. *The
Simplicity of the Christian Life*, 1496, defines Christian living as the imitation of Christ in obedience to His teaching.
The Christian life is established on the grace of God; it is
nourished by the Eucharist and disciplined by Penance.
The True Faith in the Triumph of Christ's Cross, 1497,
the only one of his works which he wrote in Italian as well
as in Latin, is really an apology suited to the age of the
Renaissance. It maintains that the Christian faith has the
aid of human reason as well as that of divine revelation. A

---

[4] Edmund G. Gardner, *Ency. of Religion and Ethics*, Vol. XI., p. 217.

Dialogue concerning Prophetic Truth, 1497, defends the author as an accredited prophet of reform. He claims a special divine revelation in addition to the directions given by Scripture, reason, and experience. *The Treatise concerning the Rule and Government of the City of Florence,* 1497, pleads for the maintenance of a republic as the most suitable form of government for the city.

SAVONAROLA left many smaller treatises on mystical and ascetic themes. Among them are two works written in the year 1492 which are still widely read: a *Treatise of Mental Prayer,* and a *Treatise of the Love of Christ.*

"Best known of all . . . . are the meditations on the Psalms 50-51, and 30-31, written by SAVONAROLA in prison a few days before his death. The first is purely devotional in treatment, closing in the vision of the future renovation of Zion and the writer's oblation of himself as a victim upon the Cross of Christ. In the second, which was left unfinished, a more personal note is struck; it depicts the struggle between hope and despondency in SAVONAROLA'S own soul, ending with the vindication of his revelations as 'divine illuminations' and the utterance of his trust in the Lord and in His name."[5]

In Holland the growing discontent with the condition of Christianity found voice in JOHN WESSEL, 1420-1489, who won the surnames of The Light of the World and The Master of Contradictions. LUTHER acknowledged his worth when he said, "Had I read WESSEL sooner my enemies would have said that I had borrowed my whole doctrine from him."

WESSEL'S writings were collected and edited by LUTHER in 1521. They included works on *Providence, The Cause and Effects of the Incarnation and Passion, Ecclesiastical Dignity and Power, The Sacrament of Penance, What is the true Communion of the Saints?* and *Purgatory.* In spite of

---

[5] Edmund G. Gardner, *Ency. Religion and Ethics,* Vol. XI., p. 218.

the fact that his theology was mediæval in type, a long series of charges was brought against him, and from fear of the Inquisition he recanted; but with something of the spirit of Galileo he said to the court; "If Christ were now present and ye were to treat Him as ye do me He might be condemned by you as a heretic. However He would get the better of you by His acuteness."

JOHN PUPPER of Goch, d. 1475, anticipated LUTHER'S doctrine of justification by faith; he wrote a work entitled *Christian Liberty,* and a Dialogue concerning the growth of the ecclesiastical law. JOHN RUCHRAT of Wesel, 1419-1481, also stands in the goodly succession of reformers before the Reformation. His books on the *Ecclesiastical Power,* and on the troubled question of *Indulgences,* brought him under condemnation and they were burned as heretical.

CHAPTER XXVIII

THE DAWN OF THE NEW DAY

The century that witnessed the rebirth of culture, literature, and liberty was also the witness of the fall of Constantinople, 1453, the consequent dissolution of the Eastern
Empire, and the recovery of peace in Italy, 1530, after
nearly forty years of war.

The fall of Constantinople made Italy the sole heir to
the ancient Grecian civilisation which committed its treasures and its scholars to her care. Through the Italian wars
these treasures became known to France, Spain, and Germany, where they exerted their refining and quickening influence.

In Italy the renaissance of learning was almost entirely
literary and artistic, unrestrained by morality and religion.
Vanity Fair, as JOHN BUNYAN pictured it in his *Pilgrim's
Progress*, fairly represents the Rome of the Renaissance. But
amid the careless multitudes there were some conspicuous
representatives of the spiritual interests of the revival. FRAN-
CESCO FILELFO, 1398-1481, roused the whole of Florence
to wondering admiration of his learning. MARSILIUS FI-
CINUS, 1463-1499, wrote a book entitled *The Christian
Religion*, 1474, and eight years later issued his *Platonic
Theology*, "a beautiful but too visionary and hypothetical
system of theism, the groundworks of which lay deep in the
meditations of ancient Oriental sages." The illustrious
JOHN PICUS of Mirandola, 1463-1494, published an exposition of Genesis i., based upon his researches into the Jewish Cabala. He called it the *Heptaplus of John Picus of*

271

Mirandula concerning Six of the Sevenfold Days in the Story of Genesis, 1490. This was the fruit of his transformation from "the proud vaunter of universal knowledge into the humble student of the Bible." Some Letters of his remain, and four sets of verses entitled, *Twelve Rules, partly Exciting and partly Directing a Man in Spiritual Battle, The Twelve Weapons of Spiritual Battle, The Christian's Affection towards Jesus Christ,* and *A Prayer of Pico Mirandola to God.* SIR THOMAS MORE translated them.

> Consider, when thou art movèd to be wroth,
>   He who that was God and of all men the best,
> Seeing himself scorned and scourgèd both,
>   And as a thief between two thieves threst,
>   With all rebuke and shame; yet from his breast
> Came never sign of wrath or of disdain,
> But patiently endurèd all the pain! . . . .
>
> Think on the very lamentable pain,
> Think on the piteous cross of woeful Christ,
>   Think on his blood, beat out at every vein,
>   Think on his precious heart carvèd in twain:
> Think how for thy redemption all was wrought.
> Let him not lose, what he so dear hath bought.

That greatest of Italian humanists, "the most brilliant classical scholar of his age," ANGELO AMBROGINI, 1454-1494, opened to the poets of Italy a career of epic and lyric fame. He is better known as POLITAN, and is universally recognised as the chief exponent of the new classical culture.

In Spain the spirit of the renaissance stirred in RAYMOND of Sabunde, fl, 1434, who became a professor of theology at Toulouse. His *Book of Nature or of the Creatures,* 1434-1436, denied the view that reason and faith, philosophy and theology, are opposed and irreconcilable. As MONTAIGNE says, "he undertaketh by humane and natural reasons, to establish and verifie all the articles of Christian religion against Atheists."[1]

---

[1] *Essays* (Florio's trans.), Bk. II., Chap. 12, "An Apology for Raymond Sebond."

There are two books given to us by God: that is the book of the universe of the creatures, or the book of nature, and the other is the book of sacred Scripture . . . The first book, *i.e.* nature, cannot be falsified, nor obliterated, nor falsely interpreted . . . . But the second can be falsified and falsely interpreted and understood amiss.

The first effect of this return to classical study was to make the forms of Christian literature seem mean and worthless, and its subjects difficult and unmanageable in comparison with those of the *literae humaniores*. The second result was that the literature of Europe began to branch out into national literatures each with its own individuality.

In Germany and northern Europe generally, the purely literary interest of the Renaissance gave place to that of religion. Foremost among the men who led this development was JOHN REUCHLIN, 1455-1522, a scholar, a jurist, and a student of the Hebrew language. His mystical writings *The Marvellous Word*, 1494, and *The Cabalistic Art*, 1517, tried to interpret Christian teaching by the aid of the Jewish Cabala. His *Book of Aphorisms on the Art of Preaching* was a pioneer work in modern homiletics.

But REUCHLIN'S influence depended far less upon his writings than upon his labours as a student of Hebrew; he was the father of Hebrew philology among Christians. MELANCTHON went so far as to say that his *Rudiments of Hebrew* entitled him to the highest praise from all living and future believers.

The chief apostle of the tolerant and scholarly spirit of humanism in Germany was DESIDERIUS ERASMUS, 1466-1536, whose student years at Deventer, 1475-1484, gave him an early acquaintance with its aims. His first book was a small volume of *Poems*, 1495. This was followed by *Adages*, 1500, which in its enlarged edition, *A Thousand*

Proverbs, 1508, won a literary reputation for its author. In its last edition it contained as many as 4151 Adages. It is "a rich repository of anecdotes, quotations, and historical and biographical sketches. . . . . It formed an introduction to the Greek and Latin classics and it furnished eloquent declamations against kings and monks, war and priestcraft."

The *Handbook of a Christian Soldier,* 1500, a Christian knight's manual, is the finest of his lesser works. "The Lord of Vere had a wife of remarkable piety. He himself was . . . . the worst of profligates, and given to association with abandoned women. He despised all religious teachers except me," says ERASMUS "and his lady, in alarm for his soul, asked me to write something which might bring him to a sense of his condition . . . So I did what she desired."[2] The result is "one of the first unmistakable attempts in modern history to make reason the basis of religious experience."

> Reason is a king, a divine counsellor of man. Enthroned in its lofty citadel, mindful of its exalted origin, it does not admit a thought of baseness or impurity.

Stirred by abuses in the Church he sent out in 1511 *The Praise of Folly,* the wittiest and most effective of all his writings. "Folly in cap and bells is made to mount the rostrum and sing her own praises. She is shown as the laughing goddess whose very appearance lightens men's hearts and spurs them to greater achievements than the calculations of reason. . . . As he continued Erasmus' mood changed. He had started lightly but his sense of the real folly of mankind overcame his lightness. His mocking banter passes into stern arraignment. . . . . But the Moria ends as it had begun with mockery; from a satire it passes back to an oration, and Erasmus whimsically proves that Solomon,

---

[2] J. A. Froude, *Life and Letters of Erasmus,* Lect. 5.

St. Paul, even Christ Himself sang the praises of Folly . . . "[3]

The crown of immortal fame came to ERASMUS when he issued the *New Testament* with a revised Greek text, a fresh Latin translation, and a preface and notes for each book, 1516. Thus on I Corinthians xiv.19 he says:

> St. Paul says he would rather speak five words with a reasonable meaning in them than ten thousand in an unknown tongue. They chant nowadays in our churches in what is an unknown tongue and nothing else, while you will not hear a sermon once in six months telling people to amend their lives.

In point of time ERASMUS had been forestalled, for the first Greek text ever printed was sent out from the press of Alcala de Henares in 1514. But the *New Testament* of ERASMUS contained a revised text and was vastly better than any edition hitherto attempted. The famous *Complutensian Polyglot* followed in 1520.

ERASMUS was now launched on the full tide of literary activity. He contributed prefaces and dedications to a Patristic series, prepared a work on rhetoric entitled *The Twofold Abundance of Words and Things*—the *Copia*— 1511, and wrote a *Sketch of His Life*. In 1524 he issued his famous *Colloquies,* a master-piece of unsparing denunciation of the abuses of the Church and the habits of the clergy, who are consistently represented as idle and corrupt. Professedly designed for the instruction and amusement of the young, it slighted the fasts of the Church, virginity, monkery, pilgrimages, and other well established usages. It is rich in portraiture; "bishops and abbots, monks and parish priests, lords and commoners, French grisettes, soldiers of fortune, treasure-seekers, quacks, conjurors, tavern-keepers,

---

[3] *The Praise of Folly,* trans. by John Wilson (1668), ed. with intro. by Mrs. P. S. Allen, Oxford, Clarendon Press (1913).

there they all stand, the very image and mirror of the time."[4]

In 1524 ERASMUS published a treatise entitled *Free Will,* to which Luther replied in a work called *Slave Will.* The controversy was ended by ERASMUS who wrote *Hyperaspistes,* a book that greatly delighted his friend SIR THOMAS MORE. In reply to ULRICH VON HUTTEN who had charged him with being uncertain in his welcome to the work of Luther, ERASMUS produced a pamphlet *The Sponge,* wherewith he claimed to wipe up his critic completely. His tract entitled *The Purity of the Church,* 1536, shows that, in spite of his vacillation, ERASMUS was in cordial sympathy with many of the ideals of the Reformer.

"The Epistles of Erasmus," says Hallam, "are a vast treasure for the ecclesiastical and literary history of his times."[5]

ULRICH VON HUTTEN, 1488-1523, one of the young poets of the University of Erfurt, bright, witty, and wayward, was drawn into a controversy that arose when REUCHLIN refused to endorse the suggestion of JOHN PFEFFERKORN of Cologne, 1469-1522, that all Hebrew books with the exception of the Old Testament, should be burned. The friends of REUCHLIN published a volume of *Letters of Well Known Men to J. R.* in which they endorsed his refusal. REUCHLIN, quiet and retiring though he was, threw down the gauntlet to the whole system of clerical learning in some polemical works, among which were *The Eye Glass,* and *The Defence against the Calumniators of Cologne.*

The youth of Erfurt banded themselves together into the 'Order of Mutianus' and issued the famous *Letters of Obscure Men.* These were addressed to ORTWIN GRAES of Cologne and satirised and ridiculed the opponents of REUCHLIN without remorse. They were written in the student slang

---

[4] J. A. Froude, *Life and Letters of Erasmus,* Lect. 11.
[5] *Literature of Europe,* Boston (1864), Vol. I., p. 359.

of the day, and, together with a "farrago of questions on grammar, etymology, graduation precedence, life in a country parsonage, and scholastic casuistry," they contained descriptions of the Cologne doctors,—their ignorance of the classics, foolish controversies, deep arguments about trifles, quarrels, and even of their confidential confessions of amours and convivialities. These merciless caricatures were based on real knowledge of their victims, but "the spirit of many allusions which delighted or offended that age is now lost."

JOHN JAEGER of Drontheim (CROTUS RUBEANUS), 1480-1539, the originator of the Letters, wrote most of the first series of forty-one, 1516. ULRICH VON HUTTEN was responsible for the major part of the second series of sixty-two Letters, 1517. His lofty seriousness, his pathos, and his better style were, however, not altogether to the advantage of the scheme. But the victory over public opinion was so decisive "that from this time the study of Greek and Hebrew became general among the German youth; and the cause of the Reformation was identified in their minds with that of classical literature."[6]

HUTTEN had a literary career apart from the Letters. In 1517 he received the poet's crown. He was a rare controversialist as he proved in *The Gallic Disease*, the *Ciceronian Orations*, the *Pamphlet against Phalarismus*, and the Letters of 1519. His two volumes of Dialogues 1520-1521, attacked the papacy with biting wit from the standpoint of German patriotism; from an artistic point of view they were his most important contribution to the literature of the Reformation.

> Three things uphold the Roman authority; the papal power, relics, and indulgences. Three things are brought home by those who make a pilgrimage to Rome: a bad conscience, a sick stomach, and an empty

---

[6] Hallam, *Literature of Europe*, Vol. I., p. 299.

purse. Three things are killed at Rome: a good conscience, religion, and a binding oath. Three things the
Romans sneer at: the example of the ancients, St.
Peter's memory, and the Last Judgment. Three things
are banished from Rome: simplicity, continence, and
honesty. Three things are for sale at Rome: Christ,
spiritual offices, and women *(The Roman Triad)*.

After 1520 he wrote in German instead of in Latin, and
gave some rousing songs to the religious struggle, as in his
reply to the papal excommunication of Luther:

> Oh, hither come, ye freemen all
> Our common cause and good now call!
>   The flame of war spreads fast.
> Assemble all who freedom love!
> Here shall the tyrant's yoke remove,
>   His bondage cease at last.

The Renaissance was delayed a full century before making its due impression in France, but the delay served to
cement the alliance between the Revival and the Reformation. The century, 1500-1600, witnessed the achievements
of FRANCOIS RABELAIS, 1483-1552, CLEMENT MAROT,
1495-1544, PIERRE DE RONSARD, 1524-1584, the illustrious band of The Pleiade, and of MICHEL DE MONTAIGNE,
1533-1592.

In Spain CALDERON, 1600-1681, expounded Church
theories in his dramas, and earned the title of "the poet of
the Inquisition" by expressing the views of the hierarchy in
his poems. His genius is seen to best advantage in his *autos
sacramentales,* a dramatic form peculiar to Spain.

"The word *auto* is first applied to any and every play;
then, the meaning becoming narrower, an *auto* is a religious
play, resembling the mediæval Mysteries. . . . Finally, a
far more special sense is developed, and an *auto sacramental*
comes to mean a dramatized exposition of the Mystery of

the Blessed Eucharist, to be played in the open on Corpus Christi Day. . . . . The true *auto* has no secondary interest, has no mundane personages: its one subject is the Eucharistic Mystery exposed by allegorical characters . . ."[7]

England gave the Renaissance a ready welcome and a generous opportunity. The pioneer was Duke Humphrey of Gloucester, 1391-1447, whose protégé THOMAS BECKYNTON, 1390-1465, names some active humanists of the day in his Letters. JOHN COLET, 1466-1519, began to expound the New Testament in the new light even before ERASMUS gave himself to the task. He expressed his views on some of the current ecclesiastical abuses in *A Serious Protest Against Auricular Confession,* and in a book entitled *Absolution.* His sincere piety is shown in a little work on *Daily Devotions,* and especially in *A Right Fruitfull Admonition concerning the Order of a Good Christian Man's Life,* which passed through many editions during the sixteenth century:

> But in especial is it necessary for thee to know that God of his great grace has made thee his image, having regard to thy memory, understanding, and free will, and that God is thy maker, and thou his wretched creature, and that thou art redeemed of God by the passion of Jesus Christ, and that God is thy helper, thy refuge, and thy deliverance from all evil.

Another man of Oxford, THOMAS MORE, 1478-1535, threw his influence on the side of light for a time, but afterwards "went violently back to the extreme of maintaining the whole fabric of superstition." He was the author of the only work of genius that England can boast in this age, the UTOPIA, 1516, *a jeu d' esprit,* written to satirise existing institutions. "The point of the UTOPIA consisted in the contrast presented by its ideal commonwealth to

---

[7] J. Fitzmaurice-Kelly, *Spanish Literature,* pp. 327, 328.

the condition and habits of the European commonwealths of the period."[8] "Beneath the veil of an ideal communism, into which there has been worked some witty extravagance," there lies a powerful and original study of social conditions unlike anything that had appeared before in literature.

MORE'S definitely Christian writings included *A Dialogue against Luther and Tyndale*, 1528, *The Supper of the Lord*, first part 1532, second part, 1533, and *A Dialogue concerning Comfort against Tribulation.*

[8] Frederic Seebohm, *The Oxford Reformers*, chap. xii., **3.**

CHAPTER XXIX

THE REFORMATION

(i. IN GERMANY)

The spirit of. liberty evoked by the revival of classical learning entered into the realms of theology and Church government in the north of Europe, where it produced the Reformation. From the standpoint of Christian literature the Reformation appears as a religious development of the Renaissance. Humanism attained spiritual completion among the sincerities of the Reformed faith.

Germany was the scene of the beginning of this religious change, and MARTIN LUTHER, 1483-1546, was the protagonist of the reform. His first overt literary act took place when he set forth his now famous *Ninety-five Theses*, 1517, "those ninety-five sturdy strokes at a great ecclesiastical abuse which was searing the consciences of many." The *Theses* are plain and easily understood; they gained sympathy from all the simple evangelical believers, and from all those who were leaning towards the non-ecclesiastical piety that was rapidly gaining ground on all sides.

COUNT WIMPINA undertook to answer them in a book called *Counter Theses*. JOHN MAYR of Eck, 1486-1543, usually referred to as ECK, repudiated LUTHER'S propositions in a pamphlet entitled *Obelisks*, 1518, to which LUTHER made answer in *Asterisks*. These discussions quickened the excitement and caused LUTHER to explain and defend his views. This he did in the most carefully written of all his works, the defence called *Resolutions*.

Thus began a pamphlet warfare which "raised the German prose dialogue to the rank of a recognized branch of literature," and which "may almost be said to have created the German book trade." The period, 1518-1530 was given up to discussion. Hitherto printed books in German had been few and insignificant; they were popular chapbooks and almanacs, herbals and books of folk-lore, and a few songs, and tales, and lives of saints. "But in the years 1518-1523 they increased enormously, and four-fifths of the increase were controversial writings prompted by the national antagonism to the Roman Curia."[1]

One such booklet, *The New and the old God,* 1521, had an immense circulation. "It attacked the ceremonies, the elaborate services, the obscure doctrines which had been thrust on the Church by bloody persecutions." JOHN EBERLIN of Gunzburg, wrote fifteen pamphlets during 1521: they became known as *The Confederates,* and included such titles as: *Of the Forty Days' Fast before Easter and Others which Pitifully Oppress Christian Folk, An Exhortation to all Christians that They Take Pity on Nuns, How Very Dangerous it is that Priests Have Not Wives, Why There is No Money in the Country, Against the False Clergy, Bare-footed Monks, and Franciscans.*[2]

JOHN COCHLAEUS, d. 1552, wrote a series of *Commentaries on the Acts and Writings of Martin Luther,* during the years 1517-1546, and JOHN FABER, d. 1561, published his *Hammer for Heretics* in 1523. In 1518 LUTHER issued *The Sacrament of Penance,* and after his disputation with ECK at Leipsic on the primacy of the Pope he reasserted his new found principles in Sermons, including some on the sacraments of Repentance and Baptism and on Excommunication. His popular Account of his disputation with ECK, 1519, brought increasing sympathy to his side.

The alarm spread to Italy where SYLVESTER MAZZOLINI

---

[1] T. M. Lindsay, *History of the Reformation,* Vol. I., p. 300.
[2] *Ibid.,* p. 304.

of Prierio, 1460-1523, attacked the reformer in *A Dialogue on the Presumptuous Conclusions of Martin Luther concerning the Power of the Pope*, 1518, to which LUTHER made a written reply. MAZZOLINI defended the papacy in three serious works: *An Epitome of Answers to Luther*, 1519, *Errors and Arguments of M. Luther*, 1520, and *The Constitution and Irrefragable Truth of the Roman Church and Roman Pontiff*, 1520.

The literary labours of LUTHER multiplied rapidly. While under examination at Augsburg he issued his *Appeal from the Pope Ill-informed to the Pope Well-informed*, 1518, and an *Appeal to the General Council*, 1518. After his return to Wittenberg he described the interview with Cardinal Cajetan, 1470-1553, the papal Legate, in a work entitled *Acta Augustana*, 1518. The first edition of his memorable *Commentary on the Epistle to the Galatians* was printed in 1519; it was revised and much improved in 1536.

These are the points of doctrine which ought to be explained to the people; and in the very order in which the apostle lays them down in this epistle. For example; let a man first learn to despair of his own strength; let him hear the word of evangelical faith; hearing, let him believe it; believing, let him call upon God; calling upon him, let him find, as he will find, that he is heard; being heard of God, let him receive the spirit of love; receiving this spirit, let him walk in the same, and not fulfill the lusts of the flesh; but let him crucify them; lastly, being crucified with Christ, let him rise from the dead, and possess the kingdom of heaven.

In 1520, believing that he had broken with Rome, he issued his three primary works, which set forth "what is truly vital and permanent in his doctrine." The earliest of these, *The Address to the Nobility of the German Nation*, or, *Of the Bettering of the Christian Estate,* was written in June, and was a terrible philippic calling upon the laity to deliver religion from "the miserable, heathenish, unchristian regimen of the Pope, the devil and anti-Christ at Rome," where, he declared:

> vows are annulled; where a monk gets leave to quit his cloister; where priests can enter the married life for money; where bastards can become legitimate, and dishonour and shame may arrive at high honours. . . . . There is a buying and selling, a changing, blustering, and bargaining, cheating and lying, robbing and stealing, debauchery and villainy, and all kinds of contempt of God, that Antichrist himself could not reign worse.

In October he issued *The Babylonian Captivity of the Church,* a work less violent in language, but nevertheless a scathing denunciation of the sacramental system that put such spiritual power into the hands of the hierarchy.

> Good God! it is horrible to look upon the temerity of the tyrants of Rome, who thus, according to their caprices, at one time annul marriages and at another time enforce them. . . . And what do they sell? The shame of men and women, a merchandise worthy of these traffickers, who surpass all that is most sordid and most disgusting in their avarice and impiety.

KING HENRY VIII, of England answered this work in a pamphlet, *The Seven Sacraments,* which gained for him and his successors on the English throne the title of Defender of the Faith.

The third primary work, also issued in October, 1520, was *The Liberty of the Christian Man,* "a very small book so far as the paper is concerned but one containing the whole sum of the Christian life." It maintains the principle that "neither Pope nor bishop nor any other man has the right to prescribe a single syllable to a Christian without his consent"; the priesthood of all believers is its theme.

> Here you will ask, 'If all who are in the Church are priests by what character are those whom we now call priests to be distinguished from the laity?' I reply, 'By the use of those words *priests, clergy, spiritual person, ecclesiastic,* an injustice has been done, since they have been transferred from the remaining body of Christians to those few who are now, by a hurtful custom, called ecclesiastics. For the Holy Scripture makes no distinction between them, except that those who are now boastfully called Popes, Bishops, and Lords, it calls ministers, servants, and stewards, who are to serve the rest in the ministry of the Word, for teaching the faith of Christ and the liberty of believers.'

In 1520, he also issued his tracts entitled *Martin Luther against the Execrable Bull of Antichrist,* and *A Defence of the Articles of Martin Luther.* The following year saw the publication of other tracts, *e.g. On Penance, Against Private Masses, Against Clerical and Cloister Vows,* and *The German Postille.*

LUTHER'S greatest literary achievement, perhaps the greatest literary event of the sixteenth century, was the translation of the New Testament into High German, 1522. As many as fourteen High German translations of the *Vulgate* had been made between 1466 and 1518, "until there came into existence a German Vulgate, which was used indiscriminately by those who adhered to the mediæval Church and those who were dissenters from it."[3] The work of LUTHER practically superseded these; in twelve years it

---

[3] *Ibid.,* p. 150.

passed through sixteen revisions and was reprinted more than fifty times.

This work permanently fixed the literary language of Germany and helped to pave the way for modern German literature.

For the larger work of translating the Old Testament, LUTHER enlisted the services of other scholars; the result of their united labours was issued in parts until 1532, when a complete copy was published in one volume. A translation of the Apocrypha followed in 1534.

During the same year in which he completed the translation of the New Testament he sent out various tracts, of which the most elaborate was called *Martin Luther, against the Order, Falsely Called the Ecclesiastical Order, of Popes and Bishops.* In this work he styles himself simply the Preacher, and declares:

> In one word, Sirs, this is my resolution. As long as I live my attacks on your abominations shall grow bolder and fiercer. I will make no truce with you. And if ye slay me, ye shall still be farther from peace. As the prophet Hosea says, I will be unto you "as a lion, as a leopard by the way." My most earnest wish is, that ye should repent; but if ye will not repent, there must be perpetual war between us.

The Church of the Reformation was in being, and LUTHER developed the spiritual side of his leadership by preparing *The Order of Public Worship,* and by issuing the first German *Hymn Book,* 1524. LUTHER was the first evangelical hymnist. He wrote in all thirty-seven Hymns, twenty-one of which belong to the year 1524. Some of them are immortal, especially the triumphant war-cry of the Reformation which is best known in Carlyle's translation:

A safe stronghold our God is still,
    A trusty shield and weapon;
He'll help us clear from all the ill
    That hath us now o'ertaken.
The ancient prince of hell
Hath risen with purpose fell;
Strong mail of craft and power
He weareth in this hour;
On earth is not his fellow.

All his hymns are characterised by simplicity and strength
and a popular churchly tone, and breathe a bold, confident,
joyful spirit of faith. The first of them was evoked by the
first martyrdom for the evangelical cause in 1523; it closed
with the "prophetic words":

Summer is even at our door,
The winter now hath vanished,
The tender flowerets spring once more,
And He who winter banished,
Will send a happy Summer.

The *Eight Song Book* of 1524 contained four of his
Hymns. In the *Erfurt Hand Book*, 1524, eighteen of its
twenty-five Hymns were from his pen. The *Spiritual Song
Booklet* of the same year was composed of twenty-four
Hymns by LUTHER, and eight other pieces. Some of his
Hymns are translations, others are adaptations of earlier
songs, others again are paraphrases of Scripture or versions
of Psalms; eight are altogether original.

The New Prophecy, which was a millenarian and holiness
movement, under the leadership of CARLSTADT, provoked
LUTHER to write *Against the Heavenly Prophets*, 1525, and
the peasants rising drew from him the book *Against the
Robber-murdering Peasants*, in the same year. The peasants
explained their many grievances in Twelve Articles, and peti-
tioned the Reformer to secure their removal by the proprietors
and princes. He gave a carefully considered judgment. To
the proprietors he said:

> Put then bounds to your exactions, pause in your hard tyranny, consider them as intoxicated, and treat them with kindness, that God may not kindle a fire throughout Germany which none will be able to extinguish . . . Some of the twelve articles of the peasants are so equitable that they dishonour you before God and the world; they cover you with shame.

To the peasants he said:

> You want the free preaching of the Gospel to be secured to you. God will assist your just cause if you follow up your work with conscience and justice. In that case you are sure to triumph in the end . . . You must not take justice into your own hands; that is also the prescription of the natural law. Do you not see that you put yourself in the wrong by rebellion.

His counsels however were rejected. The Peasants Revolt broke out, and in his wrath he sent forth his savage denunciation, which in spite of an attempted justification entitled *A Dispatch concerning the Hard Booklet against the Peasants*, 1525, has left upon his memory the stigma of a betrayal of the cause of social reform. His better mind is unfolded in his *Exhortation to Peace, a Reply to the Twelve Articles of the Peasants of Suabia*, 1524, from which the above quotations have been taken.

In all his works LUTHER shows himself a master of racy vernacular; he thought with the learned but talked with the people; at times his writing is clumsy, and at times it is coarse, but it is always clear. It is vital, emotional, and full of vigour.

During LUTHER'S seclusion in the Wartburg, ANDREAS RUDOLF BODENSTEIN, 1480-1541, who is better known as CARLSTADT, took charge of the reformed interests in Wittenberg. Following LUTHER'S example he answered ECK'S

Obelisks in a "series of theses maintaining the supremacy of the Holy Scriptures . . . . over ecclesiastical tradition and the authority of the fathers, and asserting the liability of general councils to error." After a public disputation with ECK he issued three violent polemical treatises against his opponent; in these he insisted upon "the doctrine of the exclusive operation of grace in the justification of believers," 1519. He also published a dramatic work *Eck Trimmed,* 1520. Eccius means the corner, the title is therefore sometimes translated *The Corner Trimmed off.*

CARLSTADT'S name was coupled with LUTHER'S in the papal bull of excommunication issued in 1520; he retaliated by exposing the corrupt condition of the papal court. This was the subject of his book with the caustic title, *The Holiness of the Pope.* In three other works he criticised the Roman doctrine—*The Holy Sacrament, Celibacy,* and *The Real Presence,* 1524.

After a year of banishment he returned to Thuringia, 1525, but being unable to agree with "Dr. Martin's opinions on the sacrament," he was obliged to fly in order to escape imprisonment. He then joined the followers of ZWINGLI. LUTHER made another vehement attack upon him in the work *Against the Heavenly Prophets and Carlstadt.* He answered this work in *A Declaration of Several Chief Articles of Christian Doctrine,* in which he gave full exposition of his views.

CARLSTADT was a pioneer of the Reformation and he was also "the first of modern biblical critics, denying the Mosaic authorship of the Pentateuch and classing the Scriptures into three categories of different value in accordance with the degrees of certainty as to their traditional origin."[4]

JOHN OECOLAMPADIUS, 1488-1531, followed CARLSTADT into the Zwinglian camp. He wrote *The Seven Last Sayings of our Lord on the Cross,* and *A Protest against the*

---

[4] *Encyclopedia Britannica,* 11th ed., Vol. V., p. 348.

Use of Humorous Stories in Easter Sermons, 1518, and later on appeared as a champion of LUTHER in a work called *Unlearned Ecclesiastics,* which won from ERASMUS the eulogium "OECOLAMPADIUS has the upper hand among us." His more celebrated treatise *On the Genuine meaning of our Lord's words 'This is my body,'* moved ERASMUS to say to the senate of Basle: "it is a learned, eloquent, and elaborate performance. I should be disposed to add, it is a pious performance, if anything could be pious which opposes the judgment and consent of the Church."

It was LUTHER'S closest friend, the pliable PHILIP MELANCTHON, 1497-1560, who gave the first work of systematic theology to the Reformation in his famous *Loci Communes of Things Theological,* 1521, which LUTHER called MELANCTHON'S "invincible theological tracts." His *Instructions,* 1522, described the "tumultuous deeds" in electoral Saxony, and it was probably sent to LUTHER to induce him to leave the Wartburg and give aid to stay the trouble, which he did in March 1522.

From 1522 to 1524 MELANCTHON was busily helping in the work of translating the *New Testament,* and in publishing Commentaries on some of its books. In 1524 he prepared a *Summary of the doctrines of Luther.* After the Diet of Spiers, 1526, had appointed twenty-eight commissioners to visit the reformed states and to regulate the constitution of Churches, he compiled a *Book of Visitation for the Leaders of Churches outside of Germany,* for the commissioners' use. He was the scribe of the Reformation. It was his pen that composed the *Confession of Augsburg.* This was what it claimed to be, a statement of "opinions and grievances," and does not pretend to be a full exposition of doctrinal tenets. It is divided into two parts, the first of which states the views held by those who signed it, whilst the second describes the errors against which they protested. It begins with an appeal to the Elector:

Inasmuch as the Churches among us dissent in no article of faith from the Holy Scriptures or the Church Catholic, and only omit a few of certain abuses which are novelties, and in part have crept in, in part have been introduced by violence, and contrary to the purport of the Canons, have been received by the fault of the times, we beg that your Imperial Majesty would clemently hear both what ought to be changed, and what are the reasons that people ought not to be forced against their consciences to observe those abuses.

He also wrote the noble and learned *Apology for the Augsburg Confession*, which is about seven times longer than the declaration it defends. The sincerity of his humanistic sympathies had been shown in his introductory lecture as professor of Greek at Wittenberg, entitled *Reforming the Studies of Youth*, 1518. His loyalty to his great leader is fully expressed in his *History of the Life and Acts of Luther*, 1545. His orthodoxy is expressed in *An Exposition of the Nicene Symbol*. His abundant learning fully justified the title given to him, "The Preceptor of Germany."

The Protestant spirit of enquiry and reform found its way into the field of historical research, where the critical labour of MATHIAS FLACIUS, 1520-1575, and his colleagues, resulted in the first general history of the Christian Church written from the Reformation point of view. This was *The Magdeburg Centuries* as the work is commonly called; the original title was *A History of the Church of Christ*. It was first published at Basle, 1559-1574, translated into German, 1560-1565, and issued in Latin, 1562.

The popular name *Centuries* is due to the division of the narrative into sections of one hundred years each, down to 1400. The work rivalled the secular histories of the age by its criticism of authorities and its repudiation of untrustworthy records.

Protestant literature did not escape the satire of virile and powerful opponents. NICHOLAS MANUEL, 1484-1530, and ERASMUS ALBERUS, 1500-1553, were conspicuous in their efforts to overwhelm the Reformation movement with ridicule. They were both outdone by THOMAS MURNER, 1475-1537, a Franciscan of Alsatia, whose *Exorcism of Fools* consisted of a series of pictures representing typical fools, with explanatory verses accompanying the plates. This was succeeded by *The Great Lutheran Fool*, 1537, the most unscrupulous satire of the age, written in rhymed couplets on a clever but carelessly constructed plan.

After MURNER the tone of these satirical jibes improved. BARTHOLOMEW RINGWALD, 1530-1599, pointed to better things in his poems entitled *Heaven and Hell*, and *Christian Knighthood*. These were rich in satirical passages, but they were richer still in descriptions of things religious. The works of GEORGE ROLLENHAGEN, 1542-1609, were also indicative of the better spirit.

The only Protestant who could rival MURNER in ability and power was JOHN FISCHART, 1550-1591. Less eloquent and popular than LUTHER, he was the second stoutest controversialist on the side of reform. His *Prognostic*, 1572, was harmless enough, but his work grew in effectiveness and power. The most famous and forcible of his satires was a paraphrase of the first book of RABELAIS' *Pantagruel*, which he expanded and adapted with many exaggerations of style into *A History of Gargantua*, 1575, a chaotic mass of comic allusions, digressions, puns, anecdotes, jingling rhymes, perverted proverbs, and piled up synonyms, intended to ridicule the manners of the age, and the monasticism, education, and philosophy of Rome.

He wrote an ironical *Book of Comfort in Gout*, 1577, and a most wholesome *Little Book of Marriage Discipline*, 1578. In *The Bee-hive for the Swarms of Holy Rome*, 1579, he was violently satirical at the expense of popery, as he was caustically critical of the Jesuits, whom he hated with inveterate hatred, in *A Little Guard for Jesuits*, 1580. He had a keen wit, a raciness of satire, and an exuberance of style linked with rectitude of purpose and a full understanding of human life.[5]

The spirit of the Reformation affected the Drama through men like PAMPHILUS GEGENBECK, who wrote *Plays for Shrove Tuesday*, 1515; BURKARD WALDIS, the author of *The Lost Son*, 1527; and SIXT BIRCK, who published *Susannah*. HANS SACHS of Nuremburg, 1494-1576, was the most popular, the most fertile, and the most artistic of these lesser poets and playwrights. The bewildering succession of songs, dramas, stories, and hymns that came from his pen revealed the prevailing lack of culture and low standard of taste.

His *Pamphlets concerning Luther*, whom he called "the Nightingale of Wittenberg," were concerned with the popular controversies which the reformed teaching had aroused. After 1535 he devoted himself to the work of producing Scriptural dramas, but the Reformers discouraged this type of popular literature—represented later by the crude folk-tale, *Doctor John Faustus*, 1587—as unworthy of the cause it professed to support.

[5] Cf. Kuno Francke, *History of German Literature*, pp. 167-169.

CHAPTER XXX

THE REFORMATION

(ii. BEYOND GERMANY)

MARTIN LUTHER was one of three outstanding reformers. HULDREICH ZWINGLI, 1484-1531, was another. He represented the reformed faith among the people of Switzerland, and, as became a pupil of the great Pico della Mirandola, he carried his love of humanism into the closest relationship with his religious teaching.

As early as 1516, "before he had heard of LUTHER, he began to preach the Gospel at Zurich, and to warn the people against relying upon human authority." He has recounted the story of his emancipation from the traditional theology in these words:

> . . . . when seven or eight years ago I gave myself up to the study of the Bible I was completely under the power of the jarring philosophy and theology. But led by the Scriptures and the Word of God I was forced to the conclusion: you must leave them all alone and learn the meaning of the Word out of the Word itself.

His earliest reformation writing appears to be *A Defence of Martin Luther by Christ our Lord, addressed to the City of Rome, 1520.* This was an appendix to a Latin pamphlet which was entitled *Advice of One who desires with his Whole Heart that Due Consideration be paid both to the Dignity of the Pope and to the Peaceful Development of the Christian Religion.* The Defence, which is in ZWINGLI'S

294

handwriting, although not at all in his style, is a terrible arraignment of the bishop of Rome.

In justification of some members of his congregation who did not observe the Lenten fast of 1522, he published a sermon entitled *Selection or Liberty respecting Foods; on Offence and Scandal; whether there is any Authority for forbidding Meat at Certain Times.* After a discussion of several texts of the New Testament he reaches the conclusion:

> I say that it is a good thing for a man to fast, if he fasts as fasts are taught by Christ. . . . But show me on the authority of the Scriptures that one cannot fast with meat. . . .
>
> These points have forced me to think that the church officers have not only no power to command such things, but if they command them, they sin greatly.

His first Reformation treatise of any length was the *Archeteles*, "the beginning and the end," 1522, in which he defended himself against various charges brought by the bishops against him. He resolved "by one blow to win his spiritual freedom," and therefore exposed in a thoroughly ruthless fashion the unscriptural nature of the episcopal claims and practices. During the same year he issued two sermons. The first was *On the Perspicuity and Certainty or Infallibility of the Word of God;* the second was entitled *The Perpetual Virginity of Mary the Mother of Jesus Christ Our Saviour.*

What ZWINGLI had done for the learned in his Latin treatise the *Archeteles*, he did for the people in *The Sixty-Seven Articles.* In this work he gave a summary of his teaching in German; later in the same year, 1523, he published an *Exposition and Proof of the Conclusions or Articles.* This clear but somewhat discursive defence "is full of per-

sonal allusions," and "contains ZWINGLI'S first printed assertion of his relation to LUTHER. . . ."[1]

With the hope of preventing any abuses of the Reformation doctrine of liberty he published a practical tract on *Divine and Human Righteousness,* 1523, of which he says in
the preface:

> The Gospel of Christ is not hostile to rulers, nor does
> it occasion any disturbance to temporal affairs, rather
> it confirms the authority of rulers, instructs them in the
> right performance of their duties and how to be in
> harmony with the people, if they act in a Christian
> manner according to the divine precepts.

In a work on *The Canon of the Mass,* 1523, "he enunciates
the doctrine, now so commonly associated with his name,
that the Eucharist is not a mystery but a ministry, the atmosphere is not awe but love, the result is not infusion of grace
but of enthusiasm; we remember Christ, and the thought of
His presence stirs us to fresh exertion in His service."[2] At
the end of the same year he prepared for the Council of the
city of Zurich *A Short Christian Introduction,* to be sent to
the pastors and preachers under its authority. It treats of
sin, of law, of the Gospel, of "the removal of the Law," of
images, and of the mass. Of images he says:

> If any one wishes to put historical representations on
> the outside of the Churches, that may be allowed, so
> long as they do not incite to their worship. But when
> one begins to bow before these images and to worship
> them, then they are not to be tolerated anywhere in the
> wide world; for that is the beginning of idolatry, nay,
> is idolatry itself.

---

[1] Samuel Macauley Jackson, *Huldreich Zwingli,* 2d ed. (1900), p. 197.

[2] *Ibid.,* p. 201.

A small work entitled *The Shepherd* was published in 1524, and a lengthy defence entitled *Antibolon*. (Antibolon is a late Greek word meaning a formal reply.) It contained an attack upon a work written by JEROME EMSER during the previous year with the title *Defence of the Canon of the Mass against Huldreich Zwingli.*

The Swiss Reformer's best known work is his lengthy *Commentary on the True and False Religion*, 1525, which covers most of the subjects of practical theology, and gives the most comprehensive summary of his mature teaching. The much canvassed subject of Baptism next engaged his attention, and he devoted several tracts to the exposition of the views he held, and to the denunciation of the Catabaptists, *i.e.* the drowners. During 1530 he issued some expository works—*A Clear Instruction concerning the Last Supper, The Providence of God,* and, in 1531, *the Exposition of the Christian Faith,* was published posthumously. His general theological position appears in one of his later works, the *Reckoning of the Faith of Ulric Zwingli,* which is dated July 3, 1530, and was laid before the Emperor Charles at the Diet of Augsburg.

> Briefly the Spirit breathes wherever He wishes. . . . Thus the Truth spake. Therefore, the Spirit of grace is conveyed not by this mersion, not by this draught, not by this anointing; for if it were thus it would be known how, where, whence, and whither the Spirit is given.
>
> For if the presence and efficacy of grace are bound to the sacraments, they work where these are conveyed; and where these are not applied all things languish.

The Anabaptist movement troubled both LUTHER and ZWINGLI. BALTHASAR HUBMAIER, 1480-1528, was first drawn to the Reformation by the writings of LUTHER; he afterwards became a follower of ZWINGLI; and finally, in

1525, an Anabaptist. He left a "really beautiful address, vigorous and acute in argument," entitled *The Sum of the Truly Christian Life,* 1525. MENNO SIMONS, 1492-1559, the founder of the Mennonite sect, also became an Anabaptist after his conversion from the Roman communion. His first piece of literary work was *The Horrible and Gross Libel of John of Leyden,* in which he protested against the use of physical force in the service of religion. Thirty-two other works followed this, the chief of them being *The Foundation of the Christian Doctrine,* 1539, in which he explained the main principles of his faith.

ZWINGLI'S successor at Zurich was HENRY BULLINGER, 1504-1575, whom the influence of PETER LOMBARD had led by way of the writings of AUGUSTINE and CHRYSOSTOM to a first-hand study of the Scriptures. He had made himself acquainted with the works of LUTHER, and in 1521, had lectured on the *Loci Communes* of MELANCTHON in the cloister school of Cappel. His writings are in the main controversial. He wrote against the Lutheran view of the Lord's Supper, and joined with CALVIN in 1549 in the conclusions of the Consensus Tigurinus on the same theme. He is best known to English readers by his Sermons, of which there are four volumes of translated selections. Among these a series of fifty, divided into groups of ten, was entitled *The Decades;* they were rendered into English during the reign of King Edward VI, and soon took their place as a manual for the training of the Anglican clergy.

LEO JUD or JUDAS, 1482-1542, succeeded ZWINGLI at Einsiedeln, and became known as an assiduous preacher of the reformed doctrines. He was one of the earliest translators of the Bible into German; in fact his version was printed at Zurich in 1529, before LUTHER'S rendering was completed.

In France, the father of the Reformation, and "the first scholar to preach Christ from the sources," was JACQUES

LEFEVRE D'ETAPLES, 1455-1537, commonly called FABER STAPULENSIS. He began his literary career with translations. His version of the *Vulgate* was prohibited by the Parliament of Paris in 1525, and was therefore printed at Antwerp. "The French Bible of Louvain, which is that of FABER, revised by the command of Charles V, appeared as a new translation in 1550."

He bears a high character among contemporary critics for his theological and his philosophical writings, but his dread of leaving his mother Church lessened his literary influence among reformed circles. His appeal *To the Christian Readers of Meaux,* shows the spirit of his mind.

> And why should we not wish to see our century brought back to the image of the primitive Church, because then Christ was receiving purer homage, and the glory of His name was more widely spread? . . . May this extension of the Faith, may this purity of the cult, now that the light of the Gospel reappears, be accorded to us by the One who is blessed above all others.

In WILLIAM FAREL, 1489-1565, the reformed doctrine found an advocate who led an organised band of missioners to devote themselves to the evangelisation of western or French-speaking Switzerland. He was the author of *The True Cross of Jesus Christ,* and of *Thirteen Theses* which he defended in a public discussion in Basel, 1524; but his lasting glory is the fact that under his persuasion JOHN CALVIN made his home in Geneva.

The spread of the Reformation was materially helped by colporteurs in France who carried their books in a pack on their backs and hawked them in villages and towns. Many were seized and thus their titles are known. They include *The Colloquies* of ERASMUS, *The Fountain of Life* (selected passages of Scripture in French), *The Book of True and*

Perfect Prayer (selections from the works of LUTHER), *The Catechism of Geneva, Ecclesiastical Prayers with the Manner of Administering the Sacraments, A Christian Alphabet,* and *A Christian Instruction.*[3]

Against such works as these CARDINAL CARRERO issued the warning "It is specially needful to have a care of these little books. They are like a charm thrown by an enemy who is unable to harm by the spoken word."

The influence of all such works was however immeasurably surpassed by the great text book of Protestant theology, *The Institutes of the Christian Religion,* 1535, written by JOHN CALVIN, 1509-1561. CALVIN had already proved his scholarship and his moral temper in a *Commentary on The Clemency of Seneca,* 1532. His wide and minute knowledge of Greek and Latin classical authors shows to advantage in his notes, and his plea for tolerance is made "in language as lofty as Milton employed in his *Areopagitica.*" He had also shown his interest in matters theological in a famous treatise entitled *Psychopannychia,* 1534, "which he levelled against those who taught the sleep of souls until the day of judgment," and in which he maintained "that the souls of the elect go immediately to heaven and the souls of the reprobate to hell."

During his stay in Paris CALVIN had written the Rectorial Address for Nicholas Cop in 1533. His subject was *Christian Philosophy,* with Matthew v.3, as the text. "The discourse was an eloquent defence of Evangelical truth . . . When the people discovered that Calvin was the real author he had to flee from Paris and eventually found refuge in Basel, 1535, where he finished his *Institutes of the Christian Religion.*"[4]

The *Institutes* is a work of 'monumental severity,' with no aesthetic beauty to adorn its rigid logic; but the clarity

---

[3] T. M. Lindsay, *History of the Reformation,* Vol. II., p. 152.
[4] *Ibid.,* Vol. II., pp. 98, 99.

of its thought, the definiteness of its language, and the depth and range of its vision make it one of the greatest presentations of Evangelical teaching ever given to the world. It is the first work of its order written in French prose, and it has been one of the most powerful forces in human history.

It was originally designed to show that the Reformers were not Anabaptists. In a prefatory letter of protest against the persecution of Protestants in Paris that took place in October, 1534, CALVIN describes his purpose in writing the *Institutes:*

> First that I might vindicate from unjust affront my brethren whose death was precious in the sight of the Lord, and next, that some sorrow and anxiety should move foreign peoples since the same sufferings threatened many.

In the dedication To His Most Gracious Majesty, Francis, King of France, and his sovereign, he says:

> I exhibit my confesstion to you that you may know the nature of that doctrine which is the object of such unbounded rage to those madmen who are now disturbing your kingdom with fire and sword. For I shall not be afraid to acknowledge that this treatise contains a summary of that very doctrine which, according to their clamours, deserves to be punished with imprisonment, banishment, proscription, and flames, and to be exterminated from the face of the earth.

CALVIN took the Apostles Creed . . . . "and proceeded to show that when tested by this standard the Protestants were truer Catholics than the Romanists . . . . "

"For the *Institutes* is an expansion and exposition of the Apostles' Creed, and of the four sentences which it explains." It contains six chapters: i. The Law. (*i.e.* the Ten Commandments); ii. The Faith (*i.e.* the Apostles' Creed); iii.

Prayer; iv. The Sacraments; v. False Sacraments; vi. Christian Liberty. The first edition in Latin was printed in 1535 and published in 1536. It was much enlarged and improved in the later editions of 1539 and 1559, and also in the French edition of 1541.

During his establishment in Geneva, 1536-1539, CALVIN wrote some less important works—*Flight from the Religion of the Impious, The Overthrow of the Papal Power,* and a condensed summary of the *Institutes,* entitled *The Instruction and Confession of Faith for the Use of the Church of Geneva,* 1537. His exile in Strassburg, 1539-1541, gave him leisure to revise the *Institutes,* to write a *Commentary on Romans,* and to issue a *Tract on the Lord's Supper.* After his reinstatement in Geneva, 1541, he issued *A Confession of Faith,* which was a simpler work than the earlier *Instruction.* He controverted the romanist ALBERT PIGHIUS in a work on *Free Will,* and therewith secured his conversion to the reformed doctrine. After the death of MICHAEL SERVETUS, 1511-1553, for heresy, CALVIN issued *A Faithful Exposition of the Errors of Servetus,* and an *Apology for the Punishment of Heretics by the Civil Magistrate,* 1554.

The Spanish physician SERVETUS gave himself with eager zest to theological enquiry, and although outwardly a conforming Catholic, was a speculative unitarian and an Anabaptist. His crude but original *Seven Books on the Errors of the Trinity,* 1531, and the *Two Books of Dialogues concerning the Trinity,* 1532, were read and highly praised by many of his contemporaries. During 1545 or 1546 he engaged in a perilous correspondence with CALVIN on matters theological, and in 1553 he issued his fatal *Restoration of Christianity,* which brought him to the stake as a blasphemer.

A reply to CALVIN'S *Exposition of the Errors of Servetus,* was issued under the assumed editorship of MARTIN BELLAY.

An answer to the *Apology for the Punishment of Heretics* was published by THEODORE BEZA, 1519-1605, who however was sufficiently loyal to CALVIN to write his *Life*, and a work entitled *Little Traits of M. Jean Chauvin.*

In the Life he relates the story of FAREL'S call to CALVIN to settle in Geneva.

> You have no other pretext for refusing me than the attachment which you declare you have for your studies. But I tell you, in the name of God Almighty, that if you do not share with me the holy work in which I am engaged he will not bless your plans, because you prefer your repose to Jesus Christ.

BEZA had a literary career independent of theological controversy. Between 1565 and 1600 he edited no less than ten translations of the New Testament, and his talent for poetry led him to unite with CLEMENT MAROT, 1497-1544, in rendering the Psalms into French metre. The translations of MAROT were issued in 1541; they were the first to be published in France, and in the judgment of Hallam[5] "are among his worst performances." Notwithstanding this, his version of Psalm 68 became the battle-song of the Huguenots.

In England the Reformation of the Church coincided with the domestic difficulties of KING HENRY VIII, 1491-1547. HENRY won the title of "Defender of the Faith," 1521, by his book entitled *The Seven Sacraments against M. Luther,* to which LUTHER made answer in *Luther's Answer to the Abusive Epistle of the King of England,* 1527. The king's final repudiation of papal jurisdiction was less an assertion of doctrinal independence than one of national autonomy in church government.

THOMAS CRANMER, 1489-1556, was "the first Protestant Archbishop of this kingdom, and the greatest instrument under God, of the happy Reformation of this Church of

---

[5] *Literature of Europe*, Vol. I., pp. 418, 419.

England: in whose piety, learning, wisdom, conduct, and blood the foundation of it was laid."[6] In 1534 he issued a pastoral letter of Instructions for the clergy, bidding them keep silence concerning masses for the dead, prayers to saints, pilgrimages, and the celibacy of the clergy, but urging:

> That from henceforth all preachers shall purely, sincerely, and justly preach the Scripture and Word of Christ, and not mix them up with man's institutions, nor make them believe that the force of God's law and man's law is like; nor that any man is able or hath power to dispense with God's law.

The Institution of a Christian Man, 1537, popularly known as *The Bishop's Book*, was revised and reissued in 1543 as *A Necessary Doctrine and Erudition for any Christian Man*, which, being published by royal authority, was called *The Kings Book*. It contained an exposition of the orthodox faith as the English bishops understood it. A much more important step in the way of reform was taken in 1545 by the publication of *The Primer*, a little collection of prayers for private use but containing the Litany which "apart from its literary charm . . . . has proved so admirable a vehicle for religious devotions and aspirations that its phrases have won their way into the hearts and minds of millions who do not profess and call themselves members of the English Church."[7]

In 1543 CRANMER submitted to Convocation a number of Homilies which failed to win approval, he however published *The Book of Homilies*, 1547, containing at least three of his own Sermons in which he explained the right use of Scripture, and urged the practice of good works and of charity. This work was issued as an antidote to 'rash preaching.' In the "Homily of Salvation" he says:

---

[6] Strype, *Life of Cranmer*, 1694.
[7] A. F. Pollard, *Thomas Cranmer and the English Reformation*, p. 175.

. . . . faith does not exclude repentance, hope, love, dread and the fear of God, to be joined with faith in every man that is justified, but it excludeth them from the office of justifying . . . . Nor that faith also doth not exclude the justice of good works, necessarily to be done afterwards of duty towards God . . . . but it excludeth them, so that we may not do them to this intent, to be made good by doing of them.

The *Book of Injunctions* followed the *Book of Homilies* in the same year, and was "even more largely concerned with conduct" than its forerunner.

An outburst of Protestant literature took place in England in 1548, similar to that which had occurred in Germany during the years 1521-1525. Between twenty and thirty books controverting and ridiculing the Roman doctrine of the mass are known to have been issued, "some of them respectable arguments, but most appeals to the crowd couched in coarse and ribald terms."

This year also witnessed the final stage in the evolution of *The Boke of the Common Praier and Administration of the Sacramentes and other Rites and Ceremonies of the Churche after the Use of the Churche of England.* This was essentially CRANMER'S work when it was laid before Parliament; when it emerged from the ordeal of amendment it was a work of compromise between the two parties, and therefore a real disappointment to the thoroughgoing reformers, but an Act of Uniformity, 1549, imposed it upon the Church of England. The work was revised in 1552 and this revised form is substantially *The Book of Common Prayer* of the present day.

CRANMER'S views of the Eucharist were severely criticised by RICHARD SMITH. The Archbishop made a reply, and then in *A Defence of the True and Catholic Doctrine of the Sacrament,* 1550, proceeded to show that the Protestant view was correct. STEPHEN GARDINER, 1493-1555, who had written against the reformed doctrine in a book entitled *Detection of the Devil's Sophistry*, 1546, was then in prison, but he answered CRANMER in *An Explication and Assertion of the True Catholic Faith Touching the Most Blessed Sacrament of the Altar with Confutation of a Book Written against the Same*, 1552. CRANMER was busy with a reply when martyrdom cut short his work. He had maintained:

> As for the real presence of Christ in the Sacrament, I grant that he is really present . . . . that is to say in deed, and yet but spiritually. Doth not God's word teach a true presence of Christ in spirit where he is not present in his corporeal substance? As when he saith: 'where two or three be gathered together in my name, there am I in the midst of them' . . . . Was it not a true presence that Christ in these places promised? And yet can you not of this true presence gather such a corporeal presence of the substance of Christ's manhood as you unlearnedly contrary to the Scriptures go about to prove in the Sacrament.

England became a refuge to many whose reformed principles exposed them to peril on the Continent. Such was BERNARDINO OCHINO, 1487-1564, whose remarkable Sermons in Venice, 1539, and equally important *Seven Dialogues*, made flight from the Inquisition the only way of safety. During a stay at Geneva he published six volumes of Tracts, 1544 and an *Exposition of Romans;* at Augusburg he issued a similar *Exposition of Galatians*, 1546. It was while he was in England that he issued his chief work *A Tragedy, or Dialogue, of the Unjust Usurped Primacy of the Bishop of Rome*, 1549, now known in a translation, "a splendid specimen of nervous English," by Bishop John Ponet.

OCHINO assailed CALVIN'S view of predestination in the

course of a discussion of free will, entitled *The Labyrinth,* and then at Zurich unloosed a storm of opposition by publishing *Thirty Dialogues,* 1563, in which, it was said, he advocated polygamy, anti-trinitarianism, and easy divorce.

The most influential of the foreign divines in England was MARTIN BUCER, 1491-1551, the learned, zealous, and wide-minded disciple and friend of MELANCTHON. In 1530 he had prepared the *Confessio Tetrapolitana,* and in collaboration with MELANCTHON had compiled the *Pia Consultatio* in 1543, the influence of which is seen in the Baptismal Office of the *First Book of Common Prayer.* He went to England in 1549 and taught divinity at Cambridge. In the following year he issued his *Kingdom of Christ* in which he urged:

> . . . . those are not to be listened to who will that
> the religion of Christ be thrust upon men only by
> proclamation and by laws, and who say that it is
> enough if the sacred services of Christ are said to the
> people it matters not how.

In his *Censorship* he insisted that the *First Book of Common Prayer* needed revision; and to him "has sometimes been ascribed the determining influence in the matter," although the changes in the *Second Book* went farther than BUCER recommended.

The Florentine scholar PETER MARTIRE VERMIGLI, 1500-1562, better known as PETER MARTYR, accompanied OCHINO to England and there became Regius Professor at Oxford. He gave help in the revision of the *Prayer Book;* and wrote some twenty theological works, most of which were Commentaries, and discussions of the Lord's Supper.

JOHN A LASCO, 1499-1560, a refugee Pole, gained fame as a writer, a commentator, and an organiser of Churches. JEAN VÈRON, d. 1563, left his mark on Christian literature by writing *Five Abominable Blasphemies Contained in the Mass,* 1548.

These birds of passage have been almost forgotten because of the greater names and greater works of English
writers whose books and deeds shed lasting lustre on this
stormy time.

WILLIAM TYNDALE, 1484-1536, resolved to produce a
translation of the New Testament in the vernacular. But
finding "that there was no place to do it in all Englonde,"
he fled to the Continent in 1524 and began to print his work
at Cologne. Driven thence by peril he carried his unfinished
book to Worms, where an edition of six thousand copies was
completed in 1526. The sheets were then smuggled over
to England where everything was done to suppress the work.
But TYNDALE'S version won ready welcome; it put the
Bible into the homes of the common people; it set a standard of good English, and much of it was incorporated in
CRANMER'S edition—the *Great Bible* of 1539.

> And Jesus answered and sayde to him: happy arte
> thou simon the sonne of Jonas, for fleshe and bloud
> have not opened unto the that, but my fater which ys
> in heven. And I saye also unto the, that thou arte
> Peter,[1] and upon thys roocke I wyll bylde my congre-
> gacion: and the gates of hell shall not preveyle ageynst
> it (Matthew xvi.17, 18).

[1] Peter in the greke sygnifyeth a stoone in englysshe. This confession is the rocke. Nowe is simon barjona or simon jonas sonne, called
Peter because of hys confession. Whosoever then this wyse confesseth of
Christe, the same is called Peter. Nowe is this confession come too all
that are true christen. Then ys every christen man and woman peter.

In *The Parable of the Wicked Mammon*, published at
Marburg, 1528, he dealt with the crucial doctrine of justification by faith; and in *The Obedience of the Christen Man
and How Christen Rulers ought to Govern*, 1528, he taught
that the Scriptures are the supreme authority in all matters
of religion, and the king is authoritative in all matters of
government. He thus refuted the common charge that the

reformers were politically lawless. His *Practyse of Prelates,*
1530, made a strong indictment of the bishops, of Wolsey,
and of the king, in connection with the royal divorce. In
reply to SIR THOMAS MORE'S *Dialoge,* 1529, TYNDALE issued *An Answere unto Sir Thomas More's Dialoge,* which
called forth other pamphlets from MORE in 1532 and 1533.
The reformer also wrote *A Briefe declaration of the Sacraments,* 1533, a work on *Marriage,* and some *Expositions.*
Few as his writings were they gave TYNDALE a place as "one
of the greatest forces of the English reformation."

"Rough" HUGH LATIMER, 1490-1555, having won a
popular preacher's reputation under the king's protection,
appealed to his patron to allow the free circulation of the
Bible. In *An Address* "of almost unequalled grandeur" he
declared that the Faith need not be defended by force.

> for God will not have it defended by man or man's
> power, but by His Word only, by which He hath ever-
> more defended it, and that by a way far above man's
> power and reason.

After his breach with Rome his Sermons exposed the corruptions in civil and ecclesiastical life, and they are quite
invaluable for their racy sketches of social conditions and
contemporary character.

> For if ye bryng it to passe, that the yomanry be not
> able to put their sonnes to schole (as in dede vniuersi-
> ties do wonderously decaye all redy) and that they be
> not able to mary their daughters to the auoidyng of
> whoredome, I say ye plucke saluation from the people
> and vtterly distroy the realme" (*Seven Sermons
> Preached before Edward VI,* 1549; Sermon i.).

> Where the Deuyl is residente and hath his plough
> goinge: there awaye with bokes and vp with candelles,
> awaye wyth Bibles and vp with beades, awaye wyth

the lyghte of the Gospel, and vp with the lyghte of
candells, yea at noone dayes. Where the Deuyll is resi-
dente, that he maye preuaile, vp wyth al superstition
and idolatrie, sensing, peintynge of ymages, candles,
palmes, asshes, holye water, and newe seruice of menes
inuenting . . . ." (*Sermon on the Ploughers,* 1549).

His brother in the faith and companion in martyrdom,
NICHOLAS RIDLEY, 1500-1555, left writings of excellent
quality, the work of his days in prison. He criticised the
doctrine of transubstantiation in a *Treatise on the Lord's
Supper;* he defended the principles of the Reformation in
The Lamentation for the Change in Religion; and in *Two
Farewell Addresses* he unburdened his soul.

With these literary warriors whose books were battles,
the constructive theologians must be associated. MATTHEW
PARKER, 1504-1575, was the first of a remarkable band of
men of letters to whom the Anglican Church has ever since
been indebted. PARKER was a pioneer, and although he
wrote well on *The Antiquity of the Church* and edited
early Chronicles, like those of Asser and Matthew Paris, his
most valuable service was rendered by his collection of MSS.

JOHN JEWEL, 1522-1571, began his career as a stout reformer, but modified his views on his return to England,
where he became the chief apologist of Anglicanism. His
classic *Apology for the Anglican Church,* 1562, was "the
first methodical statement of the position of the Church of
England against the Church of Rome."

THOMAS HARDING, 1516-1572, wrote a bitter *Answer
to the Apology,* 1564, to which JEWEL made a *Reply,* 1565.
To HARDING'S objection that he appealed too much to negative authority he answered:

> This kind of argument is thought to be good, when-
> soever proof is taken of God's word; and is used not
> only by us, but also by St. Paul, and by many of the

Catholic Fathers. St. Paul saith, God said not unto Abraham, 'In thy seeds all the nations of the earth shall be blessed:' but, 'In thy seed, which is Christ': and thereof he thought he made a good argument . . . . Such arguments Origen and other learned Fathers thought to stand for good, whatsoever misliking Master Harding hath found in them (*Reply to M. Harding's Answer*, Art. i. Div. 29).

HARDING returned to the fray with a *Confutation*, 1566, to which JEWEL made answer in *A Defence*, 1567.

The controversy gave JEWEL an assured place as a standard authority on ecclesiastical matters in the English Church. His doctrines were made authoritative by order of ARCHBISHOP BANCROFT, who commanded that a copy of the Apology should be placed in every Church.

A series of Sermons on the Epistles to the Thessalonians exists with other discourses. His famous *"challenge Sermon,"* 1559, was to the effect "that if any one could prove the essential Romanist doctrines as to the papacy, purgatory, masses, transubstantiation, ... by Scripture or by any church teacher for six hundred years after Christ, he, JEWEL, would subscribe to it and renounce Protestantism."

THOMAS STERNHOLD, 1500-1549, essayed to do for England what CLEMENT MAROT had done for France—to supersede "obscene ballads" with translations of the Psalter. The results of his effort should be judged as popular ballads rather than as poetry, although his work was well up to the standard of the age. The first edition is undated and bears the title, *Certayne Psalmes, Chose out of the Psalter of Dauid and Drawe into Englishe Metre*. It contains nineteen Psalms. The second edition, 1549, contains thirty-seven. Other writers contributed to the completion of the whole Psalter in the work now known as *The Old Version*, but published in 1562 with the title *The Whole Book of Psalms*, *collected into English Metre by T. Sternhold, John Hopkins and others.* Parts of his rendering still appear in the Hymn books of Christendom.

O God my strength and fortitude,
Of force I must love Thee;
Thou art my castle and defence
In my necessity;

My God, my Rock, in Whom I trust,
The worker of my wealth,
My refuge, buckler, and my shield,
The horn of all my health.

(Psalm 18.)

CHAPTER XXXI

PURITANISM

The effort to reform the Church of England on conservative lines was complicated by the attitude of the thoroughgoing Protestants, commonly called Puritans, whose two outstanding principles were personal piety and full liberty in civil and religious affairs. Their history falls within the period marked by the two Acts of Uniformity, 1559 and 1662.

Puritanism emerges into the history of Christian literature with the publication of *The Admonitions to Parliament,* 1570 and 1572. The *Admonitions* were the work of THOMAS CARTWRIGHT, 1535-1603, THOMAS WILCOX, 1549-1608, and THOMAS FIELD. They demanded the equal standing of all ministers of religion in the eyes of the law, the election of ministers by congregations, the appointment of elders and deacons, the use of civil authority to suppress heresy and superstition, and the abolition of prescribed prayers. The resolute language in which these demands were advanced was the expression of the Puritans' refusal to conform to the established Church.

> Neither is the controversy between them and us for a cap, a tippet, or a surplice, but for great matters concerning a true ministry and regiment of the Church, according to the Word. Which things once established, the others melt away of themselves.

JOHN WHITGIFT, 1530-1604, published *An Answer to a certain Libel Intituled An Admonition to Parliament,*

1572. The second *Admonition*, which was written by CARTWRIGHT, insisted that the Bible was the only authoritative standard of Christian doctrine, discipline, and Church government. WHITGIFT in a *Defence*, 1574, urged the need of expediency with extraordinary bitterness and unwisdom; and CARTWRIGHT not only issued a *Second Reply* in two parts, 1575 and 1577, but also an *Examination of Whitgift's Censures*, 1575.

This controversy gave rise to the notorious *Martin Marprelate Tracts*, 1588-1589, a series of virulent, abusive pamphlets which upbraided, cursed, and vituperated the Anglican prelates with violent vulgarity. In spite of these characteristics it has been not untruly said: "The *Martin Marprelate Tracts* belong not more to the history of our ecclesiastical life than to the history of our literature. They are now recognized as prose satires of quite extraordinary genius. Criticism has not succeeded in solving the problem of their authorship; but it has established their claim to a permanent place among English classics."[1]

A little tract of 67 pages, called *The State of the Church of England, laide open in a conference between . . . . a Byshop, ... a Papist, an vsurer, ... an Inn-keeper, and . . . . a preacher of the worde of God*, may be regarded as being, for substance, the pioneer of the famous series. The immediate occasion of the Tracts was a huge book by JOHN BRIDGES, d. 1618, entitled *A Defence of the Government established in the Churche of Englande for Ecclesiasticall matters*, in which answers were made to WALTER TRAVERS' *Ecclesiastical Discipline*, and BEZA'S *Judgment*.

The pseudonymous MARTIN put forth in 1588, a thin quarto with a lengthy title beginning *Oh read ouer D. Iohn Bridges, for it is a worthy worke: Or an Epitome of the fyrste Booke of that right worshipfull volume written against*

---

[1] C. S. Horne, *Popular History of the Free Churches*, 6th ed., p. 54.

the Puritans, ... The aim of this attack upon the clergy was:

> to proue that you ought not to be maintained by the authoritie of the magistrate in any Christian Commonwealth: Martin is a shrewd fellow and reasoneth thus. Those that are pettie popes and pettie Antichrists, ought not to be maintained in anie Christian commonwealth. But everie Lord B. in England . . . . all the Bb. in England, Wales and Ireland, are pettie popes, and pettie Antichrists. Therefore no Lord B. . . . . is to be tollerated in any christian commonwelth.

THOMAS COOPER, 1517-1594, bishop of Winchester, replied to this Tract in *An Admonition to the People of England:* . . . . 1589. In this work he gives the following sketch of the growth of the Puritan movement:

> At the beginning, some learned and godly preachers, for private respects in themselves, made strange to wear the surplice, cap, or tippet: but yet so that they declared themselves to think the thing indifferent, and not to judge evil of such as did use them. Shortly after rose up other, defending that they were not things indifferent, but distained with antichristian idolatry, and therefore not to be suffered in the Church. Not long after that came another sort, affirming that those matters touching apparel were but trifles, and not worthy contention in the Church, but that there were greater things far of more weight and importance, and indeed touching faith and religion, and therefore meet to be altered in a church rightly reformed. As the Book of Common Prayer, the administration of the Sacraments, the government of the Church, the election of ministers, and a number of other like. Fourthly, now break out another sort, earnestly affirming and

teaching, that we have no church, no bishops, no ministers, no sacraments; and therefore that all that love Jesus Christ ought with all speed to separate themselves from our congregations, because our assemblies are profane, wicked, and antichristian. Thus have you heard of four degrees for the overthrow of the state of the Church of England. Now lastly of all come in these men, that make their whole direction against the living of bishops and other ecclesiastical ministers that they should have no temporal lands or jurisdiction (*Admonition*, p. 160).

MARTIN issued at almost the same time another *Tract*— a broad-sheet containing thirty-seven propositions for the prelates to defend. He then turned to answer the *Admonition* of BISHOP COOPER and wrote a pamphlet of fifty-eight pages with a London street cry for its title: *Hay any worke for Cooper: or a briefe Pistle etc. . . . .*

Other *Tracts* followed at brief intervals, and answers were made to them by several well-known writers: *Countercuffe, An Almond for a Parrot, The Return* and *Pasquil's Apology* are attributed to THOMAS NASH, 1567-1601, *Pappe with an Hatchet*, to JOHN LYLY, 1553-1606, and *Plain Perceual*, to RICHARD HARVEY, d. 1623.[2]

If Martin will fight Citie fight, wee challenge him at all weapons, from the taylors bodkin to the watchmans browne bil. If a field may be pitcht we are readie: if they scratch, wee bring cattes: if scolde, we will bring women: if multiplie words, we will bring fooles. . . . . (*Pappe with a Hatchet*).

JOHN PENRY, 1559-1593, who had much to do with the

---

[2] H. M. Dexter, *Congregationalism* . . . . *as Seen in Its Literature* (1880), pp. 131-203.

printing of the *Tracts* was charged with their authorship, but this he denied and the identity of Martin has yet to be revealed.

A more worthy statement of Puritan principles appeared when WALTER TRAVERS, 1548-1635, put forth *A Full and Plaine Declaration of Ecclesiasticall Discipline owt off the Word off God, and off the Declininge off the Churche off England from the Same,* 1574, a work that became the "recognised text book of puritanism." A brief *Book of Discipline* was "drawn up about 1580 on the basis of Travers' work and widely used by Puritan clergymen in the effort to reform the English Church from within, and to make it Presbyterian in government and discipline. An English translation of it was found among Cartwright's papers and published in 1644."[3]

The honours of the literary controversy with Puritanism will ever rest with RICHARD HOOKER, 1553-1600, whose book entitled *Of the Laws of Ecclesiastical Polity,* 1592, is perhaps "the noblest piece of controversial literature in the English language." This classic monument of real learning "so handled its theme that no scholar would dream of superseding it or of building on any other foundation than that which HOOKER laid down." It is written in a noble style, and bears the marks of clear thinking, and of an admirable spirit of moderation and calmness.

> It is no part of my secret meaning to draw you hereby into hatred, or to set upon the face of this cause any fairer glass than the naked truth doth afford; but my whole endeavour is to resolve the conscience, and to shew as near as I can what in this controversy the heart is to think, if it will follow the light of sound and sincere judgment, without either cloud of prejudice, or mist of passionate affection . . . .

---

[3] A. C. M'Giffert, *Protestant Thought before Kant* (1917), p. 126n.

I have for that cause set down in the first place an introduction on both sides needful to be considered: declaring therein what law is, how different kinds of laws there are, and what force they are of according unto each kind.

This done, because ye . . . . are drawn to hold it as the very main pillar of your whole cause, 'That Scripture ought to be the only rule of all our actions' . . . . I have spent the second Book in sifting of this point . . . .

Whereunto the next in degree is . . . . 'that in Scripture there must of necessity be found some particular form of Polity Ecclesiastical, the Laws whereof admit not any kind of alteration.'

The first three Books being thus ended, the fourth proceedeth from the general grounds and foundations of your cause unto your general accusations against us, as having in the orders of our church (for so you pretend) corrupted the right form of church-polity with manifold popish rites and ceremonies, ... (Preface, chap. vii. 1-5).

HOOKER'S argument is to the effect that the Puritans were in error in believing that no law not expressly laid down in Scripture can be of permanent force; and equally in error in holding that no law contained in Scripture can be merely temporary. Therefore "in laying down the distinction between natural and positive law, and affirming the former alone to be immutable, he prepares the way for denying the main position of the Puritan antagonism, that all things contained in Scripture are of perpetual obligation. It is his doctrine that, where God has not declared a positive command to be perpetual, it may be dispensed with by lawful human authority; and, in the third book, he in express words asserts this of ecclesiastical government."[4]

---

[4] Hallam, *Literature of Europe*, Vol. II., pp. 124, 125.

Thus we see how even one and the selfsame thing is under divers considerations conveyed through many laws; and that to measure by any one kind of law all the actions of men were to confound the admirable order, wherein God hath disposed all laws, each as in nature, so in degree, distinct from other.

Wherefore that here we may briefly end: of Law there can be no less acknowledged, than that her seat is the bosom of God, her voice the harmony of the world: all things in heaven and earth do her homage, the very least as feeling her care, and the greatest as not exempted from her power: both Angels and men and creatures of what condition soever, though each in different sort and manner, yet all with uniform consent, admiring her as the mother of their peace and joy.[5]

HOOKER was the first great English writer to break away from scholastic methods; although a few European writers like Machiavelli, 1469-1527, Bodin, 1530-1596, and Montaigne, 1532-1592, had exercised a similar liberty. His work was "the first great effort made in modern times to give the full theory of a great institution, to show the ideal principles on which it was founded, and to indicate its substantial agreement with that ideal."

The spirit of HOOKER was an inspiration to LANCELOT ANDREWES, 1553-1626, the most learned linguist of his age, whose works of controversy with Rome have been overshadowed by his works of practical divinity.

In 1609 he published *Tortura Torti*, as an answer to BELLARMINE'S *Mattheus Tortus*, in which the learned Roman controversialist had attacked the pamphlet of king JAMES I, entitled *An Apology for the Oath of Allegiance*, 1607. BELLARMINE replied to ANDREWES in *An Apology*,

---

[5] *Ecclesiastical Polity*, Keble's ed., Bk. I., chap. xvi., pp. 7, 8.

to which ANDREWES made answer with *A Response to the Apology of Cardinal Bellarmine*, 1610. He also wrote *A First Answer to Cardinal Perron*, 1629, because PERRON had disputed the king's right to the title 'Catholic.' "But to answer such writers was a thankless task chiefly because the general literary judgment of the age was as yet unqualified to distinguish good evidence from bad, apparent victory from real."[6]

The enduring fame of ANDREWES rests upon his seventeen *Sermons on the Nativity*, which were preached before the Court at Advent, 1605-1624. These are still read for their weighty thought and their exhaustive treatment, their quaint conceits and whimsical fancies.

> Now then: this is the rule of reason, the guide of all choice, evermore to take the better and leave the worse. Thus would man doe . . . . Here then commeth the matter of admiration: notwithstanding these things stand thus, betweene the angels and Abraham's seed: (they, spirits, glorious, heavenly, immortall;) yet tooke He not them; yet, in no wise, took He them; but the seed of Abraham. The seed of Abraham, with their bodies, vile bodies, earthly bodies of clay, bodies of mortalitie, corruption and death; these He tooke, these He tooke for all that (on Hebrews ii.16).

By order of King Charles I ninety-six of his Sermons were published in 1628. ANDREWES keeps his high place in Christian affection by his *Manual of Private Devotions*, as well as by the aid of his Sermons. The *Manual* consists of a number of prayers composed for his own personal use; the first part of the work was written in Greek and the second in Latin. The MS remained unpublished until Drake translated it in 1648, since when the work has taken so eminent a place in general esteem that "there is nothing in the

---

[6] R. L. Ottley, *Lancelot Andrewes* (1894), p. 155.

whole range of devotional literature to be set beside" it.
ANDREWES was incredibly ingenious in enumerating objects
of intercession; he covered the whole field of prayer with a
fullness and a minuteness of claim that make his *Manual*
unique.

GILES FLETCHER, 1588-1623, gave to English literature
its most notable religious poem since *Piers Plowman*, in
Christ's Victory and Triumph, 1610. His imagery of the
Bower of Vain Delight is one of the outlines that MILTON
adopted and filled in.

> Through this false Eden, to his leman's bowre
> (Whome thousand soules devoutly idolize)
> Our first destroyer led our Saviour;
> Thear in the lower roome, in solemne wise,
> They daunc't around, and powr'd their sacrifice
>   To plumpe Lyaeus, and among the rest,
>   The jolly priest, in yvie garlands drest,
> Chaunted wild orgialls, in honour of the feast . . . .

> Thus sought the dire Enchauntress in His minde
> Her guilefull bayt to have embosoméd;
> But He her charmes disperséd into winde
> And her of insolence admonishéd;
> And all her optique glasses shatteréd.
>   So with her sire to Hell shee took her flight,
>   (The starting ayre flew from the damnéd spright,)
> Whear deeply both aggriev'd plungéd themselves in night.

GEORGE WITHER, 1588-1667, was a Puritan poet
"whose irrepressible Muse made herself heard even amid the
din of civil war." He wrote *Prince Henries Obsequies*, 1612,
and in 1613, the "stinging and patriotically outspoken"
poem entitled *Abuses Stript and Whipt*. A *Satyre to the
King*, 1615, was followed by "a noble piece of fiery and
idiomatic English, and manly pleading for respect to popular rights and liberties," named *The Voice of the Common
Folk*. His *Exercises upon the First Psalm*, 1620, was a herald of the first hymn book in the English language, which
WITHER issued and to which he gave the title *Hymns and*

Songs of the Church, 1623. Later on he published *The Psalmes of David* 1632, and another hymn book entitled *Hallelviah or Britain's Second Remembrancer,* 1641.

The Puritans were no farther behind their Anglican contemporaries in the literature of devotion than they were in poetry. RICHARD BAXTER, 1615-1691, the busiest man of his age and the chief of the Protestant schoolmen, left one hundred and sixty-eight treatises. Among these are works "without parallel in the history of English theological literature." They are the products of an incisive pen, they are written in a forceful style, and are often characterised by grim irony and courteous dignity. *The Saints Everlasting Rest,* 1650, surpassed them all in popularity; it is a work almost of inspiration. In it "BAXTER reveals a spirit of catholicity and noble sympathy far in advance of the average spirit . . . . In his description of the beatitude of heaven he dwells with special satisfaction on the fact that 'we shall rest from all our sad divisions.' "

> Oh, how canst thou find it in thy heart, if thou bear the heart and face of a Christian, to be bitter or injurious against thy brethren, when thou dost but once think of that time and place where thou hopest in the nearest and sweetest familiarity to live and rejoice with them for ever! . . . Alas! that Turk and Pagan can agree in wickedness better than Christians in the truth! That bears and lions, wolves and tigers can agree together, but Christians cannot. That a legion of devils can accord in one body, and not the tenth part of so many Christians in one Church!

After service with the Parliamentary army BAXTER went back to his Presbyterian charge at Kidderminster, where he resumed his literary labours with undiminished zeal. His *Aphorisms of Justification,* 1649, aroused a hot theological discussion. *The Reformed Pastor,* 1656, is a classic of pastoral theology, but after *The Saints Everlasting Rest,* the book entitled *A Call to the Unconverted,* 1657, was his most influential work. *The Life of Faith,* 1670, is now no longer remembered, but the apologetic work called *Reasons for the Christian Religion,* 1672, still retains an honourable place in the literature of Christian evidences. The now forgotten work on *Catholic Theology,* 1675, like the *Christian Theology,* 1681, belonged to the same category, and gave their author a place next to the illustrious GROTIUS in that "long line of apologetic writers who have sought to establish the truth of Christianity by a systematic exhibition of the arguments in favour of its divine origin." The famous and valuable *Reliquiae Baxterianae,* 1696, is a vivid and vivacious narrative of his own life and times.

Both by training and by conviction JOHN OWEN, 1616-1683, was eminently fitted to represent the doctrinal aspect of the Puritan movement. He first became widely known by a spirited defence of rigid Calvinism entitled *A Display of Arminianism, being a Discovery of the Old Pelagian Idol Freewill with the New Godless Contingency,* 1643. He was then a Presbyterian, but in his next work, *A Country Essay for the Practice of Church Government,* 1646, he showed signs of sympathy with the Independents, and soon afterwards he became pastor of the Congregational Church at Coggeshall. His doctrinal views however were still Calvinistic, and he again attacked Arminian teaching, this time in *The Death of Death in the Work of Christ,* 1647, over which he and BAXTER had a long controversy.

Under the Cromwellian régime he became dean of Christ Church, Oxford; he there wrote *Divine Justice,* 1653, to maintain the thesis that divine forgiveness is impossible apart from an atonement. *The Doctrine of the Saints Perseverance,* 1654, was his final attack upon Arminianism.

Several works of practical divinity attest his interest in religious experience, *e.g. The Mortification of Sin in Be-*

lievers, 1656, *Communion with God*, 1657, *Schism*, 1657, and, *Of Temptation*, 1658. The last of these was "an attempt to recall Puritanism to its cardinal attitude from the jarring anarchy of sectarianism and the pharisaism which had followed on popularity and threatened to destroy the early simplicity."

He was deprived of his deanery in 1660, and retired to his birth-place where he wrote a laborious history of theology, *The Theologoumena Pantodapa*. In *Animadversions*, 1662, he refuted the Roman theories of a work entitled *Fiat Lux*, 1661, by VINCENT CANE.

The first part of his vast work *Exercitations on the Epistle to the Hebrews*, was written in 1668. The work was in four volumes, the final volume being published in 1684, posthumously.

An intolerable attack on the nonconformists by SAMUEL PARKER, 1640-1688, called *A Discourse of Ecclesiastical Polity*, 1670, provoked OWEN to reply in *Truth and Innocence Vindicated*. ANDREW MARVELL, 1621-1678, took part in the controversy that followed, and finally silenced PARKER by writing *The Rehearsal Transposed*, 1672-3.

OWEN drew a sorry picture of the state of religion after the Restoration in his book, *On Apostasy*, 1676. His valuable and long cherished *Pneumatology, or a Discourse concerning the Holy Spirit*, 1677-8, and his work of exposition, *The Doctrine of Justification*, 1677, represent pronounced aspects of his richly religious character. His most important work, *A Treatise on Evangelical Churches*, reflects "his latest views regarding Church government." "His style is far from admirable; his argumentation is terribly discursive, wordy, and tedious; yet there are powerful, terse, and memorable passages and pages . . . ."

Great opportunities for service neglected and great gifts not improved are oftentimes the occasion of plunging the soul into great depths. Gifts are given to trade withal for God; opportunities are the market-days for that trade; to napkin up the one and let slip the other will end in trouble and disconsolation. Disquietments and perplexities of heart are worms that will certainly breed in the rust of unexercised gifts. God loseth a revenue of glory and honour by such slothful souls, and He will make them sensible of it. I know some at this day whose omissions of opportunities for service are ready to sink them into the grave (*Exposition of Psalm* 130).

JOHN HOWE, 1630-1705, the Platonic Puritan, one of the most gifted and eminent of the nonconformists, left a lasting impress on personal religion by his writings on practical divinity. The Act of Uniformity, 1662, compelled him to resign his charge, and for years he led a wandering and penurious life. Want obliged him to publish *The Blessedness of the Righteous*, 1668, but the reputation it gave him opened hospitable doors, and encouraged him to produce the most eloquent of his shorter treatises, *The Vanity of Man as Mortal*, and, *Of Delighting in God*, 1674. His best and most famous work is *The Living Temple of God*, 1675-1702. "The matter of his works is vastly better than the manner; endless digressions render most of his works wearisome, his sentences are unwieldy, and his argument is but rarely illumined by lighter touches."

The Puritan problem of church government received the clearest possible definition from ROBERT BROWNE, 1550-1633, whose tract entitled *A Treatise of Reformation without Tarying for Anie, and of the Wickednesse of Those Preachers, which will not Reforme till the Magistrate Commaunde or Compell Them*, 1582, was the original charter of the Separatists and the "first clear exposition of the freedom of the Church" from state control.

My kingdom, saith Christ, is not of this world, and they would shift in both bishops and magistrates into his spiritual throne to make it of this world; yea to stay the church government on them, is not only to shift but to thrust them before Christ. Yet under him in his spiritual kingdom are (I Cor. xii.) first Apostles; secondly Prophets; thirdly teachers, etc. Also helpers and spiritual guides: But they put the magistrates first, which in a commonwealth indeed are first, and above the preachers, yet have they no ecclesiastical authority at all, but only as any other Christians, if so be they be Christians.

In the same year, 1582, BROWNE also issued *A Booke which sheweth the Life and Manners of all True Christians, ... Also the Pointes and Partes of all Diuinitie . . . .* This work assumes that the Church is a company of saints, called out of the world and set apart from it, hence:

Christians are a company or number of believers who, by a willing covenant, made with their God, are under the government of God and Christ, and keep his laws in one holy communion.

BROWNE issued *A Treatise upon the Twenty-third of Matthew, both for an Order of Studying and Handling the Scriptures, and also Auoyding the Popishe Disorders,* etc. 1582, and followed it with *A Trve and Short Declaration,* etc. 1584, in which his church theory is again emphasised.

The kingdom of God is not to be begun by whole Parishes, but rather by the worthiest were they never so few.

His views were received slowly, although a few eager spirits tried most eagerly to spread them. HENRY BARROW, 1550-1593, and JOHN GREENWOOD, 1560 (?)-1593, re-

plied to the *Briefe of the Positions holden by the newe Sec-
terie of Recusants*, by sending forth from prison *A Briefe An-
sweare to such Articles as the Bishopps haue giuen out in
Our Name*, etc. 1589. They also collaborated in writing
*A True Description, out of the Word of God, of the Visible
Church*, 1589. "During 1590 the printed fruits of the labor
of the two men together were astonishing, when the difficulties under which they wrought are taken into the account.
We have . . . . *A Collection of certaine Sclanderous Articles gyuen out by the Bishops* . . . . etc. . . . . and *A
Collection of certaine Letters and Conferences* . . . . etc.
. . . . Then we have a black-letter quarto of seventy-four
close pages, entitled *An Avnswer to George Giffords Pretended Defence of Read Prayers* . . . . etc. . . . . Further
we have, chiefest of all, BARROWE'S *A Brief Discouerie of the
False Church* . . . . In the following year, 1591, the two
men jointly sent forth . . . . another, and extremely effective, refutation of GIFFARD'S arguments against the Separation: *A Plaine Refutation of Giffard's Short Treatise
Against the Donatists, etc.*"[7]

JOHN PENRY, 1559-1593, who had been involved in the
production of the *Martin Marprelate Tracts*, not only defended himself from the charges laid at his door, but also
wrote *An Exhortation vnto the Gouernours and People
. . . . of Wales, to Labour Earnestly to Have the Preaching of the Gospel Planted among them*, 1587, and *A Viewe
of Some Part of Such Publike Wants and Disorders as Are
in the Service of God*, 1588.

Persecution drove the Separatists to Holland from whence
FRANCIS JOHNSON, 1562-1618, issued a *Confession of
Faith*, "on a single quarto sheet," which R. ALISON controverted in *A Plain Confutation of a Treatise of Brownism*,
1590. In this work he took under review the *Description*

---

[7] H. M. Dexter, *Congregationalism . . . . as Seen in Its Literature*,
pp. 234, 235.

of the Visible Church, and the two *Collections* prepared by
BARROWE and GREENWOOD.

The Separatists in England united with those in exile to
send out *A True Confession of Faith and Humble Acknowledgement of the Allegiance which we Falsely Called Brown-
ists do hold toward God,* 1596. The unity was but short
lived. The Amsterdam community was torn asunder by
faction, its membership was divided into groups, and each
group went its way. The group at Leyden rejoiced in the
ministry of JOHN ROBINSON, 1575-1625, "the Galahad of
the theological and controversial tourneys," whose extant
writings are "chiefly occupied with those matters which lay
nearest to his heart as a Separatist."

JOSEPH HALL, 1574-1656, who claimed to be the first
English satirist:

> I first adventure, follow me who list
> And be the second English satirist—

wrote *A Letter to M. Smith and M. Robinson Ringleaders
of the Late Separation at Leyden,* 1608, in which he "censured and advised them."

> The God of heaven open your eyes, that you may
> see the injustice of that zeal which hath transported
> you; and turn your heart to an indeavour of all Chris-
> tian satisfaction: otherwise, your souls shall find too
> late that it had been a thousand times better to swal-
> low a ceremony, then to rend a chvrch . . . .

ROBINSON replied in *An Answer to a censorious Epistle,*
1610. He then wrote his first full-grown volume, *A Justification of Separation from the Church of England.
Against Mr. Richard Bernard his Invective Intitvled; The
Separatists Schisme,* 1610.

> But this I hold, that if iniquity be committed in the
> Church, and complaint, and proof accordingly made,

and that the Church will not reform, or reject the
party offending, but will on the cotrary maynteyn pre-
sumptuously, & abet such impiety, that then by abet-
ting that party & his sin, she makes it her own by imputation, & enwrapps her self in the same guilt with
the sinner. And remayning irreformable . . . .
wypeth herself out the Lords Church-rowl, and now
ceaseth to be any longer the true Church of Christ.

Other treatises of a less militant character followed; *e.g.*
Religious Communion Private and Public, 1614, *The Peo-
ple's Plea for the Exercise of Prophecy*, 1618, *A Just and
Necessary Apology*, 1619. There is "one considerable trea-
tise" upon the doctrines of theology, viz., *A Defence of the
Doctrine Propovnded by the Synode at Dort*, 1624, "which
serves to show the harmony of doctrinal view between the
Separatists and the Puritan movement in general."

Who is able to understand the manner of God's
working, in giving the Holy Ghost to man, and in directing the tongues and pens of the prophets infallibly,
and so as they could not err? Much less discernible
is God's manner of working in, and about the creature's sinful actions. And because many take offense at
this doctrine of truth and work of God, I will, the
Lord assisting me, plainly and briefly as I can, prove
that all events, even those most sinful, in regard of
the creature's work in, and of them, come to pass necessarily, after a sort, in respect of God's providence,
as being a hand steady and which swerveth not, in
ordering the creature in and unto the same.

The spirit of ROBINSON'S life is well illustrated by a passage from his *Observations Divine and Morall*, 1625.

He that strives for errour, strives for Satan against
God: He that strives for victorie, strives for himself

against other men: But he that strives for truth
against errour, helps the Lord against God's, and his
own enemie Satan, The Father of Lyes; and this especially, if withall he handle God's cause according unto
God.

With the blessing of ROBINSON upon them the men of
the Mayflower crossed the Atlantic, and a vigorous offshoot
of European Christian literature soon took root in the new
colony. "About the year 1639 the new English Reformation resolving upon a new translation (of the Psalms), the
chief divines in the country took each of them a portion
to be translated."[8] Among them were RICHARD MATHER,
1596-1669, THOMAS WELDE, 1590-1662, and JOHN
ELIOT, 1604-1690. The Psalms thus turned into metre
were issued in 1640 under the title *The Whole Book
of Psalms Faithfully Translated into English Metre*. This
was the first book to be printed in New England, and is
popularly known as *The Bay Psalm Book*. Its many imperfections are perfectly obvious, but it is an honourable
piece of pioneer work.

> I in my streights cal'd on the Lord
> and to my God cry'd: he did heare
> from his temple my voyce, my crye,
> before him came, unto his eare.
>
> Then th' earth shook & quak't and mountaines
> roots moov'd, and were stir'd at his ire
> Up from his nostrils went a smoak,
> and from his mouth devouring fire:
> By it coales inkindled were.
>
> (Psalm xviii. 6, 7, 8.)

In the second edition a few spiritual songs were added
and the versification was improved.

The discussions of the Westminster divines during 1643
stirred up ROGER WILLIAMS, 1604-1684, to publish his

---

[8] Cotton Mather in the *Magnalia*.

Queries of Highest Consideration, 1644, in which he affirmed that there should be no national Church. Soon afterwards he sent out *The Bloody Tenet of Persecution for Cause of Conscience,* 1644, "a book of strong, limpid, and passionate argument, glorious for its intuitions of the world's coming wisdom."[9] JOHN COTTON, 1585-1652, replied to this contention in *The Bloody Tenet Washed and Made White in the Blood of the Lamb,* 1647, wherein he "vigorously opposed religious freedom." WILLIAMS took up the challenge of this book and wrote against it *The Bloody Tenet Yet More Bloody by Mr. Cotton's Endeavour To Wash it White in the Blood of the Lamb,* 1652. "This book is the most powerful of the writings of ROGER WILLIAMS. There are three principal matters argued in it—the nature of persecution, the limits of the power of the civil sword, and the tolerance already granted by Parliament."[10]

Popular esteem set MICHAEL WIGGLESWORTH, 1631-1705, above all other writers of his time. He was "a poet who so perfectly uttered in verse the religious faith and emotion of Puritan New England that for more than a hundred years his writings had universal diffusion there and a popular influence only inferior to that of the Bible and the Shorter Catechism."[11]

In connection with a serious drought he wrote *God's Controversy with New England,* 1662, and another work of the same order was *Meat out of the Eater, or, Meditations concerning the Necessity, End, and Usefulness of Afflictions unto God's Children,* 1669. His most popular effort was the poem entitled *The Day of Doom, or A Poetical Description of the Great and Last Judgment,* in which he "attributed to the Divine Being a character the most execrable and

---

[9] Moses Coit Tyler, *A Manual of American Literature,* ed. by Theodore Stanton (1909), pp. 15, 16.

[10] *Ibid.,* p. 16.

[11] *Ibid.,* p. 21.

loathsome to be met with, perhaps, in any literature, Christian or pagan."[12]

The second generation of New England writers moved in the wake of the first. THOMAS SHEPHERD, 1605-1649, JOHN NORTON, 1651-1716, INCREASE MATHER, 1639-1723, and COTTON MATHER, 1663-1728, were all preachers whose Sermons are "the most authentic and characteristic revelations of the mind of New England" during the seventeenth century. COTTON MATHER was attracted by the Pietist movement in Europe, and for several years carried on a correspondence with some of its representatives. In 1715 he published a small pamphlet entitled *Good News from a Far Country, A Brief Account of Some Good and Great Things Adoing for the Kingdom of God in the Midst of Europe.*

> The World begins to feel a Warmth from the Fire of God which thus flames in the Heart of Germany, beginning to extend into many Regions; the whole World will ere long be sensible of it.

New England Puritanism culminated in the personality, the theology, and the writings of JONATHAN EDWARDS, 1705-1759, the "one figure of real greatness in the intellectual life of colonial America." EDWARD'S literary fame rests upon three books: *A Treatise Concerning Religious Affections,* 1746; *A Careful and Strict Inquiry into the Modern Prevailing Notions of That Freedom of the Will Which is Supposed to be Essential to Moral Agency,* etc. 1754; and *The Great Christian Doctrine of Original Sin Defended,* 1758.

The *Treatise on Religious Affections* was not only a defence of the great spiritual revivals of 1735 and 1740, but it "was designed to lay the foundation for more solid and

---

[12] *Ibid.,* p. 21.

successful labor in the field of practical religion by removing
the obscurity which overhung the nature of true religion."[13]

> Unless men may come to a reasonable solid persua-
> sion and conviction of the truth of the gospel by in-
> ternal evidences in the way that has been spoken, viz.,
> by a sight of its glory, it is impossible that those who
> are illiterate and unacquainted with history should
> have any thorough and effectual conviction of it at all.

The work *On the Freedom of the Will* is a classic of the
New England theology. In it EDWARDS argued for a system of moral philosophy that was avowedly a system of
necessity, and tried "to prove that necessity is not inconsistent with liberty."

> The plain and obvious meaning of the words free-
> dom and liberty in common speech is the power, op-
> portunity, or advantage that any one has, to do as he
> pleases. Or in other words, his being free from hin-
> drance or impediment in the way of doing or conducting
> in any respect as he wills.

"The old Calvinism had had no place for any ability to
good, and this had been the paralyzing influence of the early
days. EDWARDS introduced an ability, which in process of
time became a *true* ability, under which revival preaching
arose."[14]

> . . . . Scripture abundantly teaches that grace in
> the soul is so the effect of God's power that it is fitly
> compared to those effects which are farthest from being
> owing to any strength in the subject, such as a being
> begotten, or being raised from the dead. So it was
> with the cases of particular persons recorded in the New

[13] F. H. Foster, *History of the New England Theology*, p. 56.
[14] *Ibid.*, p. 78.

Testament. They were not effected in that silent, secret, gradual and insensible manner, which is now insisted upon; but with those manifest evidences of a supernatural power wonderfully and suddenly causing a great change, which in these days are looked upon as certain signs of delusion and enthusiasm.

These works are the only enduring monuments of the strength of New England Puritanism; they were the achievements of the last of the colonial Puritans, for New England idealism was begotten by the mind of JONATHAN EDWARDS.

His immediate follower was JOSEPH BELLAMY, 1719-1790, from whose pen issued treatises entitled *The Half Way Covenant, There is but One Covenant. . . . .* and a work on justification called *Theron, Paulinus,* and *Aspasio.* He is best remembered by his *True Religion Delineated,* in which he describes religion as conformity to the law of God and a compliance with the Gospel of Christ. He followed up the teaching of EDWARDS with the paradox:

The more unable to love God we are, the more are we to blame.

And he argued:

There is not one title in the Old Testament, or in the New, in the law or in the gospel, that gives the least intimation of any deficiency in our natural faculties. The law requires no more than all our hearts, and never blames us for not having larger natural capacities. The gospel aims to recover us to love God only with all our hearts, but makes no provision for our having any new natural capacity; as to our natural capacities, all is well. It is in our temper, in the frame and disposition of our hearts, that the seat of all our sinfulness lies.

In 1758 he passed into a new field of theological effort where he wrote a treatise on the *Permission of Sin,* in order to show that a good God can permit the presence of evil in the world. He "thus began that long line of effort culminating . . . in the so-called New Haven Theology." The work was answered by S. MOODY in *An Attempt to point out the Evil and Pernicious Consequences of Rev. Joseph Bellamy's Doctrines concerning Moral Evil,* 1759, to which BELLAMY made answer in *A Vindication,* 1760, and also in *A Blow at the Root of the Refined Antinomianism of the Present Age,* 1763.

A second follower of EDWARDS was SAMUEL HOPKINS, 1721-1803, who formulated the first "system" of New England theology. His system was his own, and was set forth in a series of controversial writings, and finally gathered together in *A System of Doctrines,* 1793. In this he showed that he had adopted the new theory of the atonement; God was no longer regarded as "the offended party," but as the Governor of the world whose rectorial justice demanded the exemplary sufferings of Christ.

Both BELLAMY and HOPKINS were influential in modifying the extreme doctrine of man's moral inability; ASA BURTON, 1752-1836, completed the change. The tendency to exalt the agency of God, whilst reducing man to the position of a mere moral puppet, was arrested by his *Essays on Some of the First Principles of Metaphysicks, Ethicks, and Theology,* 1824, which is "one of the classics of New England theology, and one of the great influential philosophical books of the world."[15]

The Puritan movement in England had its popular exponent in JOHN BUNYAN, 1628-1688, whose life is a vivid illustration of the religious individualism which marked the close of the English reformation. His literary activity began with a work against the Quakers, entitled *Some Gospel*

---

[15] *Ibid.,* p. 243.

Truths Opened, 1656. A prominent Quaker, EDWARD BUR-
ROUGH, replied to his strictures and thereby roused BUNYAN
to write *A Vindication of Gospel Truths Opened*. During
the twelve years, 1660-1672, which he spent in gaol as 'a
prisoner of the Lord', BUNYAN composed *Profitable Meditations, Praying in the Spirit, Christian Behaviour*, and that
masterpiece of religious autobiography the *Grace Abounding
to the Chief of Sinners*, 1666.

After three months of freedom came a second imprisonment during which England's one great allegory, the immortal *Pilgrim's Progress*, was partly written. This "unparalleled monument of creative literature" is "remarkable amongst
all the allegories of the world" in that it has a strong human
interest. The first part was finished soon after BUNYAN'S
release, 1678. It was followed by the realistic character
study, *The Life and Death of Mr. Badman*, 1680, and by
the imaginative allegory of the struggle between God and the
devil for man's soul, entitled *The Holy War*, 1682. The second part of the *Pilgrim's Progress* was published in 1684;
other works such as *The Jerusalem Sinner Saved, The Heavenly Footman*, followed until nearly sixty publications stood
to BUNYAN'S credit.

The primary document for his religious experience and
his literary masterpiece, the *Grace Abounding*, was written
with lovable modesty and sincerity to encourage believers to
stand firm in times of persecution. It is "a drop of that honey
that he had taken out of the carcass of a lion."

> Presently after this I changed my condition into a
> married state, and my mercy was to light upon a wife
> whose father and mother were counted godly; this
> woman and I, though we came together as poor as poor
> might be, not having so much household stuff as a
> dish or spoon betwixt us both, yet this she had for
> her part, *The Plain Man's Pathway to Heaven*, and

The Practice of Piety, which her father had left when he died. In these two books I sometimes read, wherein I found some things that were somewhat pleasant to me; but all this while I met with no conviction. . . . . Wherefore these books, though they did not reach my heart to awaken it about my sad and sinful state, yet they did beget within me some desires to reform my vicious life, and fall in very eagerly with the religion of the times . . .

The *Pilgrim's Progress* however took the premier place in popular esteem. It was woven of a captivating dramatic interest, enriched with masterly character sketches. It summed up the evangelical theology of the age in a series of personal adventures which gave vitality to the doctrines and made it easy for even the simplest minds to grasp their meaning. "Every reader," said Macaulay, "knows the straight and narrow path as well as he knows a road in which he had gone backward and forward a hundred times. This is the highest miracle of genius, that things which are not should be as though they were, that the imaginations of one mind should be the recollections of another. And this miracle the tinker has wrought."[16]

GEORGE FOX, 1624-1691, against whose views BUNYAN'S first book had been written, imitated his opponent by writing a most remarkable spiritual autobiography, his *Journal,* or *Historical Account,* first published in 1694. FOX issued one or two pamphlets during his lifetime, *e.g. A Testimony of the True Light of the World,* 1656, and *The Great Mystery Unfolded,* 1659, but he was a preacher rather than an author. His "letters . . were lumpy and ungrammatical, whilst his bodily presence was powerful and awe-inspiring." His characteristic doctrine is unfolded in the Testimony:

---

[16] *Essay on John Bunyan* (Dec., 1831).

> Every one coming into the world, having a light
> that comes from the way, lets him see the way, and
> a light from the life lets him see the life, and a light
> from the truth lets him see the truth, and a light from
> the word lets him see the words, and lets him see the
> Word that was in the beginning before the world was.

He tells the story of his great spiritual experience in the
Journal:

> Now was I come up in Spirit through the flaming
> sword into the paradise of God. All things were new
> and all the creation gave another smell unto me than
> before, beyond what words can utter. I knew nothing
> but pureness and innocency, and righteousness, being
> renewed into the image of God by Jesus Christ, to the
> state of Adam, which he was in before he fell.

ROBERT BARCLAY, 1648-1690, resisted his early inclina-
tion to become a Roman Catholic and followed his father
into the Society of Friends, 1667. He soon became prominent among them as a controversialist, and issued *Truth
Cleared of Calumnies,* 1670, and *William Mitchell Un-
masqued,* 1672. The latter book was the outcome of a controversy with a neighboring minister on the subject of the
Quakers' doctrines.

BARCLAY issued *A Catechism and Confession of Faith,*
1673, as a positive contribution to the movement. In a series
of fifteen *Theological Theses,* 1675, he discussed many of
the questions at issue between the Friends and their critics,
A little work entitled *The Anarchy of the Ranters,* 1676,
was designed to clear the Quakers of the charge of sympathy
with civil insubordination.

His most important and most enduring work is *An
Apology for the True Christian Divinity, as the Same is
set forth and preached by the People Called in Scorn Quakers,*

1678; this work had appeared in Latin in 1676, entitled *Theologiae verae Christianiae Apologia.* "The *Apology* is remarkable as the standard exposition of the principles of (the) sect, and is . . . impressive in style, grave, logical and often marked by the eloquence of lofty moral convictions. The essential principle (expressed in the scond proposition) is that all true knowledge comes from the divine revelation to the heart of the individual. (Barclay) infers that the authority of the Scriptures gives only a "secondary rule" subordinate to that of the inward light by which the soul perceives the truth as the eye perceives that the sun shines at noonday."[17]

The *Apology* was "one of the most important theological writings of its century, and is still perhaps the most important manifesto of the Quaker Society." Barclay defended its position in a later work *The Apology Vindicated*, 1677, and he reaffirmed his central doctrine in *The Possibility and Necessity of an Inward and Immediate Revelation*, 1686.

ISAAC PENINGTON, 1616-1679, became a Friend in 1657 and in later years described his spiritual experiences in two books; the first was *A Brief Account of my Soul's Travel toward the Holy Land*, the second was *A True and Faithful Relation in Brief concerning Myself in reference to my Spiritual Travails and the Lord's Dealings with Me*. This was written during his imprisonment in gaol at Aylesbury, 1667.

Previous to these works he had already written in support of the Quaker teaching. He expounded his doctrine of evil in *The Great and Sole Troubler of the Times, Represented in a Map of Misery: or a Glimpse of the Heart of man . . . . Drawn with a Dark Pencil, by a Dark Hand, in the Midst of Darkness*, 1649. In 1658 he collaborated with EDWARD BURROUGH and GEORGE FOX in writing *The Way of Life and of Death Made Manifest*. The next year he issued *The Scattered Sheep Sought After*, and *The Jew Outward; Being*

---

[17] *Dictionary of National Biography*, Vol. III., p. 169.

a Glasse for the Professors of This Age. He discussed one
of the characteristic features of the new teaching in a book
entitled *The Great Question concerning the Lawfulness or
Unlawfulness of Swearing under the Gospel,* 1661.

In the heat of controversy during 1675 an anabaptist,
THOMAS HICKS, misquoted and misrepresented PENINGTON
in *A Dialogue between a Christian and a Quaker.* PENING-
TON replied in a statement of doctrine entitled *The Flesh and
Blood of Christ . . . . with a Brief Account of the People
called Quakers,* 1675. His views were stated in a book primarily intended for the conversion of Papists, and published as *The Everlasting Gospel of Our Lord Jesus Christ,
and the Blessed Effects thereof Testified to by Experience,*
1678.

A more notorious and a more prolific writer on behalf
of the Friends was the famous WILLIAM PENN, 1644-1718,
the founder of the State of Pennsylvania. His friendship
with JOHN OWEN and his pupilage under MOISE AMYRAUT
doubtless influenced his religious thinking. He openly announced his agreement with the Quakers in 1667.

PENN'S literary life began soon after his conversion. "His
first book, *Truth Exalted,* 1668, was violent and aggressive
in the extreme." So also was his answer to *A Guide to the
True Religion* written by JOHN CLAPHAM; issued with the
title *A Guide Mistaken, and Temporizing Rebuked,* 1668.
During the same year he suffered imprisonment in the Tower
of London because of the views he had maintained concerning the doctrine of the Trinity, in a book called *The Sandy
Foundation Shaken,* 1668. He secured release and defended
his orthodoxy in *Innocency with Her Open Face,* 1669.
However, his most popular work, *No Cross, No Crown,*
1669, was written during his imprisonment. It is a learned
and eloquent discourse on the Christian duty of self sacrifice, and at the same time it offers a strong defence of the

Quaker teaching, and severely criticises the lax lives of many of the Anglican clergy.

PENN was a most valiant champion of the religious liberties of Christian believers. The Conventicle Act of 1665 found a real enemy in him; he directed against its operation his book entitled *The People's Ancient and Just Liberties Asserted, in the Trial of William Penn and William Mead,* 1670; a second work *The Truth Rescued from Imposture,* 1670, also dealt with the same trial.

The range and variety of his religious interests are seen in the three books which he issued in 1671; they are entitled, *A Seasonable Caveat against Popery, A Serious Apology for the Principles and Practices of the People Called Quakers,* and *The Great Case of Liberty of Conscience.*

In 1675 PENN bcame one of the three Masters of West Jersey, and his life thereafter was devoted to the interests of the colony for whose welfare he became responsible. His literary labours were continued in America until he had as many as thirty-nine various books on the list of his writings. Some of these were of a political character; the most famous of the religious works being *The Fruits of Solitude,* written in 1692.

The *Journal* of JOHN WOOLMAN, 1720-1772, belongs to the great religious autobiographies; it reveals the Quaker mystic at his best, and has far surpassed his Essays in popular esteem.

In Scotland the Protestant movement brought reformation to the Church and revolution to the State. JOHN MAIR—MAYOR—1469-1548, was less a reformer than an inspirer of reformers. His most memorable work is a *History of Greater Britain,* 1521, written in crabbed school Latin. MELANCTHON characterised his *Commentary on the Third Book of Peter Lombard's Sentences,* 1517, as a wagon load of trifles, and his *Exposition of Matthew's Gospel,* 1518, is little better; but he fired the spirit of John Knox, Patrick Hamilton, and George Buchanan.

SIR DAVID LYNDSAY, 1490-1555, disquieted by the general corruption of Catholicism became the poet of the Scottish Reformation. His religious business "was to make rulers uncomfortable by telling them unpleasant truths in the form of poetry." His rude effective satires became enormously popular; he lashed the vices of the clergy, pictured the times in racy speech, and described his subjects with humour or with sympathy. He exhorted ministers of the Gospel:

> To preiche with unfeignit intentis,
> And treulie use the sacramentis;
> Efter Christis institutiounis
> Leuing their vane traditiounis
> Quhilk dois the sillie scheip illude,
> Quhome for Christ Jesus sched his blude. . . .

LYNDSAY'S first poem *The Dreme*, was written about 1528. The prologue is the most poetical of all his pieces; the poem itself being a rather tedious survey of hell, of heaven, and of earth, especially of Scotland, from which John the Commoun Weill had been driven away. *The Testament and Complaynt of our Soverane Lordis Papyngo*, (popinjay), 1530, was a timely reforming tract. It was especially hard on monks and friars. *Kitties Confessioun*, 1541, is a satire on auricular confession.

His most notable work, *Ane Pleasant Satyre of the Thrie Estaitis*, 1539, the only existing specimen of the old vernacular Scottish morality-play, satirises the clergy, the nobles, and the merchants, with gross and pungent humour.

> My patent Pardouns, ye may see,
> Cum fra the Cam of Tartarie,
> 　　Weill seald with oster-schellis.
> Thocht ye have na contritioun,
> Ye sall have full remissioun,
> 　　With help of buiks and bellis.

Quha ever he be heiris this bell clinck,
Gif me ane ducat for till drink,
He sall never gang to hell,
Without he be of Baliell borne:
Maisters, trow ye, that this be scorne!
Cum win this Pardoun, cum.

PATRICK HAMILTON, 1504-1528, in his one book, *Common-places*, generally known as *Patrick's Places*, was the solitary representative of Lutheranism in the Scotch Reformation. His book was a collection of various Theses drafted for the first academic Disputation at the new Evangelical University of Marburg. The Theses were afterwards translated into Scots vernacular by John Firth. The three brothers WEDDERBURN,—JAMES, 1495-1533, JOHN 1500-1556, and ROBERT, 1510-1556, fostered the new spirit by their works. One of these was a satirical Morality against clerical abuses. A rudimentary song book, entitled *The Gude and Godlie Ballatis*, was published in 1545. In an improved form it was issued as *Ane Compendious Book of Godly Psalms and Spiritual Songs*, 1578, probably by JOHN WEDDERBURN. "The edition of 1578 is in four parts: i. The Catechisme . . . ii. Spirituall Sangis, 16 in number. . . . iii. Ballatis of the Scripture, 20 in number. . . . . iv. Psalms of David with uther new pleasand Ballatis Translatit out of Enchiridion Psalmorum to be sung. These include twenty-two Psalm versions . . . and (various) other pieces, in all sixty-nine."[18] Some of the pieces are amended ballads, and some are scurrilous denunciations of priests, monks, and nuns, *e.g.* "Quho is at my windo, quho?" "Johne kis me nowe"; "Hay nowe the day dawis"; "Welcum Fortoun." One of the most popular was "The Paip."

The Paip, that pagane full of pryde,
He hes vs blindit lang:

---

[18] Julian, *Dict. of Hymnology*, 2d ed., p. 1021.

For quhair the blind the blind dois gyde,
    No wonder thy ga wrang:
Lyke prince and king he led the ring
    Of all iniquitie:
Hay trix, tryme go trix,
    Vnder the grene-wod tree.

Bot his abominatioun
    The Lord hes brocht to licht;
His Popische pryde, and thrinfalde crowne,
    Almaist hes loist thair micht;
His plak pardounis ar bot lardounis   (deceits)
    Of new found vanitie:
Hay trix, ...

The Complaynte of Scotland, attributed to ROBERT
WEDDERBURN, is a puzzling book; the plan and arrangement
are mainly those of a famous old French poet's work, the
Quadriloque Invectif of ALAIN CHARTIER, 1386-1458.
"The long passages of the *Complaynte* are mere translations,
with occasional adaptations." It was an exhortation to the
three estates to be vigilant for the good of the commonwealth,
with many warnings against the discord, the self-seeking,
and the indolence that bring down the curse upon nations.

The outstanding leader of the reformation in Scotland
was JOHN KNOX, 1505-1572, who in spite of his absorption in the practical affairs of Church and State, holds his
place in the history of literature as the author of twenty-nine
works.

His first pamphlet, written on board the galley Notre
Dame, 1548, was *An Epistle to the Congregation of the
Castle of St. Andrew's, with a Brief Summary of Balnaves
on Justification by Faith.* HENRY BALNAVES composed in
prison the *Treatise on Justification,* and a book entitled *The
Works and Conversation of a Justified Man.* KNOX read
these while a prisoner in the galley, and was so pleased with
them that he edited them with an Introduction, "not so
much to illustrate the work . . as . . to give my confession of the article of justification therein contained." In

1550 he published *A Vindication of the Doctrine that the Sacrifice of the Mass is Idolatry*, to which he wrote a supplement entitled *A Summary according to the Scriptures of the Sacrament of the Lord's Supper*, 1550, to set forth his positive views of the Sacrament. On the death of King Edward VI., 1553, KNOX fled to Geneva, pausing at Dieppe to send *A Godly Letter of Warning or Admonition to the Faithful in London*, 1554. On his way back to England he sent *Two Comfortable Epistles to his Afflicted Brethren in England*, 1554, and one of his most slashing messages, *A Faithful Admonition to the Professors of God's Truth in England*, 1554. This is "in the form of a commentary on the miracle of Christ walking on the water and its purpose is to warn professing Christians against the sin of attending Mass, "under pretence that they may keep faith secretly in the heart and yet do as idolaters do."[19]

The original form of his *Letter to the Queen Dowager Regent* of Scotland, 1556, is a good example of his style:

> I doubt not, that the rumouris, whilk haif cumin to your Grace's earies of me, haif bene such, that (yf all reportis wer true) I wer unworthie to live in the earth. . . . I am traduceit as ane heretick, accusit as a fais teacher, and seducer of the pepill, besydis uther opprobries, whilk (affirmit be men of warldlie honour and estimatoun) may easelie kendill the wrath of majestratis, whair innocencie is not knawin.

The Letter was delivered to the Queen, who glanced at it with a careless air and gave it to the archbishop of Glasgow, saying, 'Please you, my lord, to read a pasquil. The report of this vexed KNOX who issued a second edition in which he gave free play to his wrath, 1558.

His famous *First Blast of the Trumpet against the Monstrous Regiment of Woman*, 1559, was a bitter and unen-

---

[19] James Stalker, *John Knox, His Ideas and Ideals*, p. 100.

lightened protest against the anti-reformation policy of Queen Mary of England. "It is essentially an ill-considered performance, as he himself, indeed, came to admit—undigested and ill-reasoned, violent without being powerful, and with few of those great strokes which abound in the work on which his reputation as a writer must mainly rest." The first sentence and chief proposition is:

> To promote a woman to bear rule, superiorite, dominion, or empire above any Realm, Nation, or City is repugnant to Nature, contumelie to God, a thing most contrarious to His revealed will and approved ordinance, and finally it is the subversion of good order, of all equity and justice.

KNOX supported this contention by arguing that nature intended the female sex for subjection, not superiority, to the male; that the divine law, announced at the creation of the first pair, had expressly assigned to man the dominion over woman; that female government was not permitted among the Jews; that it is contrary to apostolical injunctions; and that it leads to the perversion of government, and other pernicious consequences.[20]

The *Blast* drew forth several answers. *An Harborowe for Faithful and Trewe Subjects against the Late Blowne Blaste concerning the Government of Wemen*, 1559, by JOHN AYLMER was the most important. It was written to secure the favour of Queen Elizabeth for the Protestant exiles on the continent.

KNOX had intended to blow three Blasts, but in view of the commotion and opposition aroused by the first he gave up his design. Before his return to Scotland he addressed a general Council and the nobility against "false prophets, flattering friars and other such venomous locusts" in *The*

---

[20] Thomas M'Crie, *Life of John Knox*, first complete American ed. (1905), p. 142.

*Appelation from the Sentence Pronounced to the Bishops
and Clergy . . 1558.* He also wrote *A Letter addressed to
the Commonalty of Scotland,* 1558, on the same occasion.
Other Letters and controversial pamphlets followed in rapid
succession until *The Book of the Common Order,* 1564,
which shews that KNOX had reached security; and *The History of the Reformation of Religion within the Realm of
Scotland,* which shews that the victory had been won. This
last work is KNOX'S masterpiece. He first wrote Books two
and three which give an account of events up to the arrival
of Mary Queen of Scots. To this he added Book one, to
explain the historical beginning of the Reformation. In
1565 he added Book four. The last Book was added by an
editor from the papers which KNOX had left unfinished.

> Yf your Grace please to frequent the publict sermonis,
> then doubt I nott but that ye shall fullie understand
> boyth what I like and myslike, als weall in your Ma-
> jestie as in all otheris. . . But to waitt upoun your
> chalmer-doore, or ellis whair, and then to have no
> farther libertie but to whisper my mynd in your Grace's
> eare, or to tell to you what otheris think and speak
> of you neather will my conscience nor the vocatioun
> whairto God hath called me suffer it. . . . . And the
> said Johne Knox departed with a reasonable meary
> countenance; whairat some Papistis offended said, 'He
> is not effrayed'. Which heard of him he answered,
> 'Why should the pleasing face of a gentill woman
> effray me? I have looked in the faces of many angrie
> men, and yit have nott bene effrayed above measure.'
> And so left he the Quene and the Court for that tyme
> (Book IV).

"KNOX was taunted by his Catholic opponents with an
unpatriotic tendency to Anglicise in his literary style as
well as in his doctrine. The Catholic writers, including the

compiler of *The Complaynt of Scotlande*, strove to write what they thought their national tongue without English admixture." NINIAN WINYET, 1518-1592, a modest reformer who remained loyal to the Catholic faith, won royal patronage by his *Certain Tractis for Reformation of Doctryne and Maneris*. QUINTIN KENNEDY, 1520-1564, was an even more strenuous defender of the papal cause. He issued a *Compendious Treatise* . . . . *to establish the Conscience of a Christian Man*, in which he repeated the points concerning which he had publicly disputed with KNOX at Mayence.

GEORGE BUCHANAN, 1506-1582, was the humanist of the Scottish Reformation. Before he had openly joined the Protestant party, he had been moved by the impudence and hypocrisy of the Franciscan monks in Scotland to write a satirical poem against them entitled *Sleep*, 1538. They carried their case to King James V, who however encouraged BUCHANAN to write another poem on the same theme. The first fruits of this encouragement was *The Palinodia*, which was followed by the unpublished *Franciscans and Brothers*, 1539.

The Scotch Church in its various branches made rich contributions to Christian literature. SAMUEL RUTHERFORD, 1600-1661, is an excellent example of the breadth of interest and the spiritual temper of his age, "combining as he did the character of the love-sick mystic with those of the militant ecclesiastic and the laborious theologian." His *Apologetic Exercises for Divine Grace*, 1636, was so sternly Calvinistic in its opposition to Arminianism that it cost him his pastoral office, and led to his banishment from Anwoth to Aberdeen. During the two years of this interdict he wrote two hundred and twenty of his immortal *Letters*. "The *Letters* were the products of a fresh personal religious experience and are mostly sustained chants in praise of Christ." They are fashioned of scriptural fragments and phrases and abound in metaphor. "There is . . . perpetual iteration of Christ's kisses, wooing, 'love-embracements', of marriage with Him, even of being dandled on His knee, of the smell of His breath and of His garments." Thus in a Letter to the Countess of Kenmure in 1630 he says:

> For this is the house of wine, where ye meet with your Well-Beloved. Here it is where He kisseth you with the kisses of His mouth, and where ye feel the smell of His garments; and they have indeed a most fragrant and glorious smell. Ye must, I say, wait upon Him, and be often communing with Him, whose lips are as lilies, dropping sweet-smelling myrrh, and by the moving thereof He will assuage your grief; for the Christ that saveth you is a speaking Christ; and the Church knoweth Him by His voice, and can discern His tongue amongst a thousand. . . .

RUTHERFORD plunged into ecclesiastical controversy with the zest of a "very gladiator." His *Peaceable and Temperate Plea for Paul's Presbyterie in Scotland*, 1642, with its sequel, *The Due Right of Presbyteries*, 1644, roused the wrath of MILTON who counted their author among the New Forcers of Conscience. In 1644 RUTHERFORD issued his masterly *Lex Rex, a Dispute for the Just Prerogative of King and People*. This was intended as a reply to the advocates of an absolute monarchy. It did much to popularise the principle of the liberty of subjects. After the Restoration in 1661 it was burned by the common hangman in London. RUTHERFORD followed it up with *The Divine Right of Church Government and Persecution*, 1646, and with *A Free Disputation against Pretended Liberty of Conscience*, 1648, a work which Bishop Heber calls "perhaps the most elaborate defence of persecution which has ever appeared in a Protestant country."

RUTHERFORD was profoundly pious as *The Trial and*

Triumph of Faith, 1645, and *Christ Dying and Drawing
Sinners to Himself,* 1647, clearly prove, but he was also
rashly controversial. In reply to JEREMY TAYLOR'S *Liberty
of Prophesying* he wrote a *Treatise,* 1648, denying the
thesis of that landmark of religious freedom. In 1651 he
wrote *Divine Providence,* to refute the doctrinal views of
Jesuits, Socinians, and Arminians. RICHARD BAXTER, characterised this pamphlet as "the worst piece he had ever read."
RUTHERFORD'S last work, *Influences of the Life of Grace,*
appeared in 1659.

GEORGE GILLESPIE, 1610-1648, one of the most outstanding of the 'Westminster divines', had an important
share in drafting the *Westminster Confession of Faith,* and
the *Shorter Catechism.* His original and masterly work entitled *Aaron's Rod Blossoming,* 1646, states the high Presbyterian claim for spiritual independence.

> This controversy reacheth up to the heavens, and
> the top of it is above the clouds. It doth highly con-
> cern Jesus Christ himself, in his glory, royal preroga-
> tive, and kingdom, which he hath and exerciseth as
> Mediator and Head of his Church. The crown of
> Jesus Christ, or any part, privilege, or pendicle thereof,
> must needs be a noble and excellent subject. This truth
> that Jesus Christ is a king, and hath a kingdom and
> government in his Church distinct from the kingdom
> of this world and from the civil government, hath this
> commendation and character above all other truths, that
> Christ himself suffered to the death for it, and sealed
> it with his blood.

JAMES GUTHRIE, 1612-1661, drew up a shrewd little
work on *Elders and Deacons,* and shared in the production of
The Causes of God's Wrath against Scotland, 1651, a work,
which, together with other labours, led to his martyrdom.
WILLIAM GUTHRIE, 1620-1665, a "great melancholian",

published a "spiritual day-book of all the passages between the Spirit of God and the soul in its work of regeneration," entitled *The Christian's Great Interest*, 1659. ROBERT LEIGHTON, 1611-1684, towered above most of his contemporaries in intellect and piety. During his Presbyterian period, 1641-1661, he wrote *Devout Exercises*, and preached the sermons afterwards published in his remarkable and still valuable *Commentary on I Peter*.

The bitterness and wrath of reformation were also displayed in the literature. ROBERT CALDER, 1650-1723, wrote a scurrilous satire *The Scotch Presbyterian Eloquence, or the Foolishness of their Teaching Discovered from their Books, Sermons, and Prayers*, 1692, which pilloried the weaknesses and foibles of its victims in an exuberance of mockery. The 'Cameronian' sect said good-bye to meekness and gentleness in their *Apologetical Declaration*, 1684, and the distressing records of *The Cloud of Witnesses*, 1714, showed the disastrous results of their appeal to force. In 1685, Claverhouse and the Royalists took up the challenge, and the bloody consequences are variously described in *The Informatory Vindication*, 1687, *The Hind Let Loose*, 1688, and in DANIEL DEFOE'S, 1659-1731, *Memoirs of the Church of Scotland*, 1717.

The supreme and immortal masterpiece of Puritan literature was the work of JOHN MILTON, 1608-1674, whose "soul was like a star and dwelt apart." He linked the culture of the Renaissance with the tremendous moral earnestness of the Puritan faith. He wrote sublimely because he dwelt among sublime things.

During his college days he began the poem *On the Morning of Christ's Nativity*, and wrote the first draft of it on Christmas Day, 1629. His unfortunate experiences of marriage led him to write *The Doctrine and Discipline of Divorce, Restored to the Good of both Sexes from the Bondage of Canon Law and other Mistakes*, 1643, and another work on the same theme the *Tetrachordon: Expositions upon the Four Chief Places of Scripture which speak of Marriage,* 1644.

While King Charles I awaited the death penalty, there appeared the *Eikon Basilike* (the King's Image), describing his virtues and piety. This book moved MILTON to produce a written reply entitled *Eikonoklastes,* (the Image-Breaker), 1649. He justified the Puritan cause for compassing the King's execution in a work on *The Tenure of Kings and Magistrates,* 1649, and in spite of failing eye-sight he issued a magnificent *Defence of the Anglican People,* 1652, one of the most splendid works in English controversial literature.

MILTON'S magistral poetry was the fruit of his blind years. *Paradise Lost,* 1667, a colossal epic of the human race and the most honoured poem in the whole range of English literature, cost him seven years of toil. The sequel entitled *Paradise Regained,* was published in 1671, and in the same year MILTON also issued the *Samson Agonistes,* a pure tragedy, in some respects the most convincing of his works. That these greater works were in his mind years before they were written is shown by his words in the *Reason of Church Government urged against Prelatry,* 1641:

> Neither do I think it shame to covenant with any knowing reader that, for some years yet I may go on trust with him toward the payment of what I am now indebted, as being a work not to be raised from the heat of youth or the vapours of wine . . . . but by devout prayer to that eternal Spirit, who can enrich with all utterance and knowledge . . .

In 1673 he sent out *A Treatise of True Religion, Heresy, Schism, Toleration, and the Best Means to Prevent the Growth of Popery;* but a *Treatise of Christian Doctrine* that he left unpublished shows that his views changed from puritan orthodoxy to an essentially unitarian theory, and from a strict Calvinism to the Arminian doctrine of free-will, although he did not give up the evangelical doctrines of Sin and Atonement.

The temporary purpose and the controversial character of his prose writings have tended to obscure them, so that their noble passages are not well known. The *Areopagitica, a Speech of Mr. J. M. for the liberty of Unlicensed Printing, to the Parliament of England,* 1644, is probably the most widely read. It has been called "the noblest plea for liberty of thought in the English language"; through it MILTON gave the death blow to the licensing and censorship of the press.

> . . . . unless wariness be used, as good almost kill a man as kill a good book: who kills a man kills a reasonable creature, God's image; but he who destroys a good book kills reason itself, kills the image of God, as it were, in the eye. Many a man lives a burden to the earth; but a good book is the precious life-blood of a master-spirit, embalmed and treasured up on purpose to a life beyond life. . . . . We should be wary, therefore, what persecution we raise against the living labours of public men, how we spill that seasoned life of man, preserved and stored up in books. . . .

CHAPTER XXXII
THE COUNTER REFORMATION

The success of the Reformation was not suffered to pass unchallenged by the great Church whose very existence was imperilled by it. The broken forces were rallied and during the period through which the Council of Trent held its sittings, 1542-1563, "the Church of Rome having lost a large part of Europe not only ceased to lose but actually regained nearly half of what she had lost."

A vigorous effort was made to re-establish Rome as the centre of European culture. The Vatican press was set up, and the Index of forbidden books—the Index Expurgatoribus—was sanctioned and applied.

As early as 1501 the papacy had instructed the Universities of Köln, Mainz, Trier, and Magdeburg, to issue none but licensed books. In 1515 the Lateran Council approved the papal declaration that all books printed in Rome must be expressly approved by the Master of the Palace. After 1543 the Inquisition in Rome undertook the work of censorship.

Lists of prohibited books were drawn up by many civil authorities outside the States of the Church, and in 1559 the first papal Index was drafted. "Its very severity prevented its success." It was considered by a Commission appointed by the Council of Trent under whose direction the new Index was issued in 1564. A Congregation of the Index was established in 1571. Various revisions were undertaken until 1596, when the Index Expurgatoribus was sanctioned by a papal bull.

354

Critics of this censorship of literature were not lacking. AONIUS PALEARIUS, 1500-1570, who is known by a philosophical poem on *The Immortality of the Soul*, and by a work on *The Benefit of Christ Crucified for Christians*, pleaded in vain for liberty. The German Jesuit PETER CANISIUS, 1521-1597, pointed out that the people must have books, and that the Church ought to supply them. But the work of the Index was very thoroughly done. Italian scholarship was slain so far as Italy was concerned, and that of Spain and Portugal was also destroyed.[1]

The Council of Trent laid the dogmatic and disciplinary basis of the Counter Reformation. The story of the work of the Council belongs to ecclesiastical history and to the history of doctrine, but the contemporary records of the great assembly must be mentioned here. PIETRO SARPI, 1552-1623, who surnamed himself Paolo, began his literary life by republishing some of the tracts of GERSON. When the ecclesiastical liberties of his native Venice were threatened by papal aggression he wrote *The Reply of a Doctor of Theology*, in which "he laid down principles which struck at the very root of the Pope's authority in secular things." He continued his literary defence of the spiritual freedom of the republic of Venice in *Considerations upon the Censures*, and in *A Treatise of the Interdict*. The quarrel was composed in 1607 and SARPI returned to his cloister where he wrote *A History of the Inquisition in Venice*, 1615, and also his chief literary work *The History of the Council of Trent*, 1619, which became the text-book of Protestantism on the subject. Hallam says that his *Treatise on Benefices* is "a model in its way . . . . it can never be read without delight and admiration of the author's skill."[2]

A rival and apologetic *History of the Council of Trent*, 1656-57, was prepared by PIETRO SFORZA PALLAVICINO,

---

[1] T. M. Lindsay, *History of the Reformation*, Vol. II., pp. 603-605.
[2] *Literature of Europe*, Vol. II., p. 384.

1607-1667. A similar work had been attempted by TER-
ENZIO ALCIATI, and PALLAVICINO continued his unfinished
task with the aid of many sources which were not accessible
to SARPI. His criticisms of SARPI'S work however make
little or no difference to the substance of the anti-papal story.

CHARLES BORROMEO, 1538-1584, connects the Roman
Church of the Renaissance with that of the Counter Reformation. As Archbishop of Milan he edited *The Vatican
Nights,* a series of memoirs of learned academicians whose
company he cultivated. His only original works are Homilies, Discourses—such as his Instructions for Pastors, Sermons and Letters. He holds his place in literary history as
the editor of *The Roman Catechism* which was drawn up
by the Council of Trent under his superintendence.

Although hindered by the operations of the Index,
CAESAR BARONIUS, 1538-1607, wrote an enormous work
entitled *Ecclesiastical Annals,* 1588-1593, to offset the influence of the protestant *Magdeburg Centuries.* He is the
first modern Church historian. He surpassed the Centuria-
tors by the mass of his collection of sources for which he had
access to material hitherto unused for scientific history. He
tried to prove that the Church of Rome was an unbroken
unity that had kept itself pure. His vast work, "shapeless
and destitute of every trace of eloquence" though it is, transferred "to the Catholic party the preponderance in the field
of learning which ever since Erasmus had been on the side of
the innovators." He kept his work free from theological
bias, but he cited "apocryphal or disputable documents as of
equal value with those that were authentic." BARONIUS
carried his Annals down to the end of the twelfth century;
it was brought down to 1566 by RAINALDUS during 1646-
1663.

ISAAC CASAUBON, 1559-1614, the last of the great
scholars of the sixteenth century, settled in England in 1610
by invitation of King James I. There he consumed the four

years until his death "in the defence of his royal patron
against the Jesuits, and in writing *Animadversions on the
Annals of Baronius;* works ill suited to his peculiar talent."
His criticisms however were not unjust. In one of his letters
he says:

> Nevertheless Baronius is better than Bellarmine, a
> man skilled in artifices, sophistries, lies, and fit for noth-
> ing else. The rule of this man is not the sacred Scrip-
> tures but the lust of the pope who stands like God in
> the earth; he lies as wickedly as he does frequently.

Again, he wrote that he could by certain reasons demon-
strate all BELLARMINE'S positions false; but when he came
to the chapter on the Sacraments:

> I can most certainly prove that those of our writers
> who have attempted to show that the Fathers hold our
> views have egregiously wasted their time and been
> blind in broad daylight (*Epistle 1043*).

The epic of the Counter Reformation was written by
TORQUATO TASSO, 1554-1595, a young Italian poet who
won attention at the age of eighteen as the most promising
poet of his day. His pastoral drama, *Aminta*, "of exquisite
lyrical charm," was published in 1573, and in 1574 he issued
his *Jerusalem Delivered*, "a very great poem, the greatest of
all the artificial epics after the *Aeneid* and *Paradise Lost*."
The subject is the First Crusade with Godfrey as the hero
and the adventures of three lovely pagan women to provide
the element of affectionate sentiment. Tasso "thought, and
with justice, that he had written a truly religious poem and
he now found the ecclesiastical reaction demanding . . . .
that it should be adapted to the reading of monks and nuns."
Mental unsettlement led to years of misery, restraint, and
ill-health, but during his imprisonment as a madman, 1579-
1586, he wrote many Dialogues on philosophical and ethical

subjects. After his release he wrote a dull poem entitled *Mount Olivet*, 1588. In 1592 he revised and ruined the *Jerusalem* which he now renamed *Jerusalem Conquered;* he also prepared *The Seven Days*, "a dreary amplification of the first chapter of Genesis" in Italian blank verse, "chiefly remarkable for its evident influence upon the style and versification of Milton."

The *Jerusalem Delivered* has been translated by Edward Fairfax:

> The sacred Armies and the godly Knight
> That the Great Sepulcher of Christ did free
> I sing: much wrought his valour and foresight
> And in that glorious warre much suffred he:
> In vaine gainst him did hell oppose her might,
> In vaine the Turkes and Morians armed be:
>   His soldiers wilde, to braules and mutines prest,
>   Reduced he to peace, so heaven him blest.
>
> O heavenly Muse that not with fading baies
> Deckest thy brow by th' Heliconian spring,
> But sittest crowned with starres immortall raies,
> In heaven where legions of bright Angels sing;
> Inspire life in my wit, my thoughts upraise,
> My verse ennoble and forgive the thing,
>   If fictions light I mix with truth divine,
>   And fill these lines with other praise than thine.

The greatest of the Dutch poets and one of the greatest religious poets of the Counter Reformation was JOOST VAN DER VONDEL, 1587-1679. His earlier poems and plays show that Biblical dramas had displaced the mediæval Moralities, and all his work is instinct with the spirit of devotion to God and the Fatherland.

An attack upon Prince Maurice and the preachers made under the thin disguise of a classical tragedy, *Palamedes*, 1618, brought him within the power of the law; having gained freedom he won popularity by writing a series of satires against the Calvinists. The best of these satires are popular songs such as *The Beggars' Vesper for Sick Folks'*

Comfort; The Rumbling Pot of the Hen Roost; etc. In *The Horrible Decree* he denounced the Calvinistic doctrine of the eternal perdition of infants, and in *The Antidote to the Poison of the Spirit-fanatics,* 1626, he "ranges himself against the supporters of the doctrine that the private spirit is a source of inspiration and instruction equal or superior to the written Word." *The Curry Comb* and *The Harpoon* are pleas for the cessation of theological strife and hatred.

VONDEL passed into the Roman communion in 1641, and his "more purely Roman Catholic sentiments found expression in lyrico-didactic poems; an impassioned didactic poem on *The Sacrament of the Mass,* a work on *The Glory of the Church,* and one on *The Attributes of God.*"[3]

In Germany MARTIN VON BOBERFELD OPITZ, 1597-1639, is esteemed as the father of the modern German language of poetry in respect at least of its form. By means of his epoch-making *Book of German Poetry,* 1624, he gave to German verse the form it still retains. His taste for religious verse led him to write paraphrases on the *Lamentations of Jeremiah,* 1626, and *The Canticles,* 1627.

In 1628 he published a number of hymns entitled *The Epistles for Sunday and the chief Feasts . . . . in verse.* These hymns are certainly the best of his religious poems. A collection of his hymns, Psalm versions, etc., was published in 1638 with the title *Spiritual Poems.*

As a supporter of the Counter Reformation OPITZ wrote some poems in praise of von Dohna, who, in 1628, led the Catholic reaction in Silesia by means of force and persecution. OPITZ also translated a work by MARTIN BECANUS entitled *A Manual for the Conversion of the Erring,* 1631.

The Spaniard FRANCISCO SUAREZ, 1548-1617, represents the philosophical side of the anti-Protestant movement. In a *Tract concerning the Laws and Legislation of God,* he lays down the principle that all legislative, as well as all

---

[3] *Ency. of Religion and Ethics,* Vol. XII., pp. 637-640.

paternal, power is derived from God. He describes law in general; defines eternal, natural, and national law; discusses human or civil law; and considers the ecclesiastical law. He then studies the differences and the interpretations of human law, the laws of custom and of privilege; and finally discusses the divine law in relation to the old and the new dispensations. His definition of eternal law is:

> . . . . eternal law is the free determination of the will of God, ordaining a rule to be observed, either, first, generally by all parts of the universe as a means of a common good, whether immediately belonging to it in respect of the entire universe, or at least in respect of the singular parts thereof; or, secondly, to be specially observed by intellectual creatures in respect of their free operations.

Concerning the divine right of kings as a hereditary right he maintans:

> that such an opinion has neither authority nor foundation. . . . This is a certain conclusion, being common to all our authorities . . . . all of whom agree that the prince has that power of law-giving which the people have given him. And the reason is evident, since all men are born equal, and consequently no one has a political jurisdiction over another nor any dominion; nor can we give any reason from the nature of the thing why one man should govern another rather than the contrary.

In a *Defence of the Catholic Faith against the Errors of the Anglican Sect*, 1613, he denounced the oath against Catholicism that had been won from James I of England.

Philosophy was also represented by NICHOLAS MALEBRANCHE, 1638-1715, who wrote *Nature and Grace*, 1674, and *Christian Conversations*, 1677. During the years,

1684-1688, he carried on a written controversy with ARNAULD of Port Royal.

RICHARD SIMON, 1638-1712, was the Catholic exponent of Biblical criticism. In his *Critical History of the Old Testament*, he gathered up the results of critical inquiry in order to make the Protestants realise that their appeal to a textually infallible Bible could not be sustained. All his labour was of this character. He prepared *A Critical History of the Text of the New Testament*, 1689, *A Critical History of the Versions of the New Testament*, 1690, *A Critical History of the Principal Commentators of the N. T. from the Beginning*, 1693, and finally *New Observations on the Text and the Versions of the N. T.*, 1695.

These writings aroused great opposition. The Benedictine monks were especially bitter in their animosity, and with the help of BOSSUET secured a decree of the Council of State against him. His *Critical History* was confiscated and destroyed, but was republished in Holland in 1685.

SIMON'S strictures on ARNAULD'S *Perpetuity of the Faith* had provoked hostility among the Port Royalists who threw their influence against him. JEAN LE CLERC, 1657-1736, fell foul of both parties in his *Sentiments of certain Theologians in Holland concerning the Critical History of the Old Testament composed by P. Richard Simon*, 1685. In this work he not only pointed out what he believed to be the faults of the critic, but also made what he regarded as some positive contributions to the true understanding of the Bible. SIMON answered him in a *Response*, 1686, to which LE CLERC replied in *A Defence of the Sentiments*. SIMON made a final reply in a new *Response*.

In 1693 LE CLERC began an important series of Biblical *Commentaries* through which he exercised an enduring influence on the critical study of Scripture; the series was not completed until 1731.

The Counter Reformation was materially aided and

strengthened by the labours of JOHN MABILLON, 1632-1707, who gathered and arranged saintly traditions in *The Acts of the Benedictine Saints with Historical Introductions, showing the Relation of the Saints, the Church, and the State,* 1668-1672.   In the *Prefaces,* which were printed separately, "these lives were for the first time made to illustrate the ecclesiastical and civil history of the early middle ages"; they show that MABILLON had been richly endowed with the spirit of literature and the devotion of scholarship.

His masterpiece is the work *On Diplomacy,* 1681, which soon took its place as an indispensable guide to its subject. It enshrined the ideals of the Maurists, who maintained a school of history and criticism from which "an enormous number of colossal works of erudition" were issued during the years 1645-1780.   His *Supplement* to a revision of the *Diplomacy,* 1704, was the first work to lay down "the principles for determining the authenticity and date of mediæval charters and manuscripts.   It practically created the science of Latin palaeontology, and is still the standard work on the subject."

The labours of MABILLON and the Maurists were extended by the Bollandists—a group of Belgian Jesuits guided by JOHN BOLLAND, 1596-1665—who devoted themselves to the publication of *The Deeds of the Saints (Acta Sanctorum).*

HERIBERT ROSWEYDE, 1569-1629, had proposed in 1607 to publish the annals of the Saints from MSS. in the Belgian Library, and in 1615 had issued *The Lives of the Fathers,* "a veritable masterpiece" for that age.   His death left his plans barely begun, and the unfinished task fell into the hands of JOHN BOLLAND under whose supervision the first two volumes of the stupendous work appeared in 1643. The process of publication went on irregularly until 1788 when the labours of the Bollandists ceased.   There are now three editions of this colossal enterprise, which, if it had been completed, would have included 25,000 lives.

Other similar undertakings were inspired by this great work of the Bollandists. THIERRY RUINART, 1657-1709, published *The True Deeds of the Martyrs*, 1689. The Benedictines, D'ARCHERY and MABILLON, compiled *The Acts of Saints of the Order of St. Benedict*. THOMAS MESSINGHAM, d. 1638, compiled *A Florilegium of the Island Saints for Scotland and Ireland*, 1624, in which he included an interesting treatise on *St. Patrick's Purgatory in Lough Derg*. MESSINGHAM had previously published, 1620, *The Offices of SS. Patrick, Brigid, Columba*, and other Irish Saints.

The Counter Reformation was immensely assisted by the Society of Jesus, a missionary Order begotten of the militant spirit of IGNATIUS LOYOLA, 1491-1556. This Society was founded in 1534, was fully approved as an Order in 1540, and soon wrote itself deeply into the literary history of Christianity, especially during its second period which was characterised by a desperate effort to gain possession of the realms of letters and learning.

IGNATIUS LOYOLA owed his conversion from a worldly life to a life of aggressive Christian service to books like *The Life of Christ*, by RUDOLPH THE CARTHUSIAN, and *The Flowers of the Saints*. He naturally turned to literature and in 1521 wrote *The Spiritual Exercises*, an epoch making work which originated in his own religious experiences, and "was intended to serve as a perpetual introduction to the mysteries of the spiritual life." The earliest extant text is that of the year 1541, but we know that LOYOLA worked at it from 1522 to 1548 when it was approved by Pope Paul III.

"The book is simple enough, but it contains such a variety of subjects treated with such vivacity that the interest of the reader is never allowed to flag, and the peculiar skill of the author is shown by the way in which he makes the reader use his imagination as a tonic to his will."[4]

> The first point is to see by the imagination the vast fires of the lower regions, the souls enclosed in a kind of corporeal fires as in a slave prison. The second to hear with the imagination, the plaints, laments, cries and blasphemies roared out from that place against Christ and his Saints. The third with the imagination even to perceive by smell the fume, sulphur, and rank odour as of drugs or dung or putrefaction. The fourth to taste likewise the bitterest things, as tears, putridity, and the worm of the conscience. The fifth to touch in the same way those fires by the touch of which those souls are burned (from the *Fifth Exercise*).

There is a *Directory to the Spiritual Exercises* which shows that the meditations are for twenty-five days and that they are concerned with four great subjects, viz., sin and conscience, the earthly kingdom of Christ, the Passion of Jesus, and the Love of God with the Glory of the Risen Lord. According to the purpose of LOYOLA these meditations were intended to be made once in a lifetime in their fullness, but in part they may be made once a year.

In *The Kingdom of God*, as also in *The Two Standards*, the great leader gave his views of Christianity as a warfare against unbelief. *The Constitutions*, 1553, were model ordinances for the Society, and together with *A Letter on Obedience*, 1553, have ever since determined its constitution and enterprise.

> More easily may we suffer ourselves to be surpassed by other religious Orders in fasting, watching, and other austerities of diet and clothing which they practise according to their rule, but in true and perfect obe-

---

[4] Leighton Pullan, *Religion Since the Reformation*, p. 19.

dience and the abnegation of our will and judgment, I greatly desire, most dear brethren, that those who serve God in this Society should be conspicuous" *(Letter on Obedience).*

LOYOLA dictated his *Autobiography* to LUIS GONZALEZ DE CAMARA; this must ever retain the first place among the sources of our knowledge of his character and mission.

> On his way (to a Church near Manresa) he sat down facing the stream which was running deep. While he was sitting there, the eyes of his mind were opened so as to understand and comprehend spiritual things. . . . . with such clearness that for him all these things were made new. If all the enlightenment and help he had received from God in the whole course of his life . . . . were gathered in one heap, these all would appear less than he had been given at this one time.

JEROME NADAL drew up a proposal for the instruction of exercitants entitled *The Studies of the Society of Jesus, 1548-1552.* In 1559 this work was re-issued as *The Reason and Institution of the Studies of the Society of Jesus;* and under its system their work of education has been carried on ever since.

The devotional spirit among the Jesuits was nobly represented by FRANCIS DE SALES, 1567-1622, who in 1923 was proclaimed to be "the patron of Christian writers." His failure to attract audiences to his preaching led him to print his *Sermons.* He revised and re-issued them as *The Controversies,* 1672. *The Defence of the Banner of the Crucifix,* 1600, had a local and temporary value, but *The Introduction to a Devout Life,* 1609, "that new Imitatio for the use of the worldly," won universal and enduring fame as a spiritual classic. Its charming and seductive style made piety accessible and attractive in spite of the severity of its demands. *The Treatise of the Love of God*, 1612, completed the purpose of the *Introduction*, and became the foundation of the religious instruction of a vast number of souls. *The Spiritual Discourses*, posthumously published, like *The Degrees of Prayer*, and *The Spiritual Letters*, link DE SALES with the saints and mystics of all ages.

The chief apologist of the Society of Jesus was ROBERT FRANCES ROMULUS BELLARMINE, 1542-1621, 'the hard headed controversialist' who in 1576 was given the chair of Controversies in the Roman College. His lectures grew into the important work *Disputations concerning Controversies of the Christian Faith against the heretics of these Times.* This was published in three volumes during the years 1586-1589 and forms BELLARMINE'S chief title to fame. It was the first attempt to systematise the various controversies of the age; it exercised very considerable influence on contemporary thought, and still holds its place as the classical textbook on its subject matter. In 1586, also, he 'dissected' the Lutheran *Book of Concord*.

On behalf of the English Catholics who were forbidden to take the oath of allegiance, 1606, KING JAMES wrote in defence of the oath a book entitled *A Threefold Wedge for a Threefold Knot*, to which BELLARMINE replied with his famous *Answer of Matthew Tortus to a Book inscribed A Threefold Wedge* etc., 1608, and carried the controversy a stage further with an *Apology of Bellarmine for his Answer to the book of James King of Great Britain*, 1609.

In 1610 he answered the criticisms of WILLIAM BARCLAY by issuing *The Power of the Highest Pontiff in Temporal Things*. His abilities as a constructive theologian were shown in a work entitled *Advice to Bishop Theanensis*, 1612. Various books of practical and devotional theology witness to his true Christian temper, *e.g. The Ascension of the Mind to God*, 1615, *The Eternal Felicity of the Saints*,

1616, *The Seven Words of Christ*, 1618, and *The Art of Dying Well*, 1620.

A more technical but less influential theologian was PETER CANISIUS, 1521-1597, a native of the Netherlands, who in 1543 published *The Enlightening of Dr. John Tauler.* Several of the great preacher's works appear for the first time in this book which is notable as the first book published by a Jesuit. CANISIUS edited *The Works of Cyril of Alexandria*, 1546, *The Works of Pope Leo I*, 1546, and wrote *The Consolation of the Sick*, 1554. His chief work however is his Triple Catechism, entitled *Summary of the Christian Doctrine . . . . for the use of Christian Children*, 1555, from which he extracted two smaller works for popular use.

He was now entrusted by the Pope with the task of confuting the writers of the *Magdeburg Centuries*, and for this purpose he prepared an exegetical and historical work entitled *Commentaries concerning the Corruption of the Word of God*, 1571. He then wrote *The Incomparable Virgin Mary and Holy Mother of God*, 1577. These two works were united in what has been called "the classic defence of the whole Catholic doctrine about the Blessed Virgin"; it was entitled *Commentaries on the Corruption of the Word*, 1583.

The Society of Jesus found its hymn writer in FRIEDRICH VON SPEE, 1591-1635, "the first important writer of sacred poetry that had appeared in the German Catholic Church since the Reformation." His book entitled *Beware of Evildoers, or a Book concerning the Proceedings against Witches*. 1631, was the means of reducing the prevailing persecution of witches to a minimum.

As a poet SPEE reflects the popular taste for daintiness of language, florid description, and far-fetched comparisons. He had more originality and a richer poetic inspiration than OPITZ. His work shows a sincere pleasure in nature as well

a deep religious spirit. The most important of his volumes
is *The Lusty Nightingale, or Religious-poetical Woodland
pleasures,* 1649.

> Ah! Jesus, Jesus, Hero true
> Why dost Thou pain me sore.
> I am tormented through and through,
> Ah! burden me no more.
> Yet Thou shalt see
> Pain and grief flee
> In a brief moment's space,
> When my eyes gaze
> With glad amaze
> Upon Thy lovely Face."

SPEE lives less in popular song than in the influence he
exercised upon poetry through JOHANN SCHEFFLER, 1624-
1677, the Franciscan, who is best known as ANGELUS SILE-
SIUS.   SCHEFFLER came under the influence of JACOB
BOEHME through friendship with ABRAHAM VON FRANK-
ENBERG who edited the great mystic's writings.   He was
also affected by JOHN TAULER whose works were deeply
pondered by the Jesuits of Breslau.   He passed from the
Lutheran to the Roman communion in 1653 and wrote
some fifty controversial works in connection with his new
faith.   Thirty-nine of these were gathered into a volume
with the title *Ecclesiologia,* 1677.

As early as 1641 SCHEFFLER began publishing his poems,
many of which were collected into *Epigrams and Refrains,*
1657, better known under its later title *The Cherubic Trav-
eller,* 1675.   "In the whole range of literature there is no
book in which pantheism has found a more original poetic
expression than in the childlike sibylline verses" of this book.[5]

In 1657 he published his most important collection of
Hymns, entitled *The Holy Delight of Souls, or Spiritual
Shepherd Songs of Souls enamoured of Jesus, sung by John
Angel Silesius.*   The work was in four volumes containing

---

[5] Kuno Francke, *History of German Literature,* p. 196.

in all one hundred and fifty-five Hymns. A fifth volume was added in 1668, bringing the number of the Hymns up to two hundred and five. Many of these songs had been written during his Lutheran days; they were welcomed by the Lutheran Church, and became special favourites among the Moravians.

His best pieces are "the work of a true poet, almost perfect in style and in beauty of rhythm, concise and profound," as in the Hymn:

> Thee will I love, my Strength, my Tower;
> Thee will I love, my Joy, my Crown;
> Thee will I love with all my power,
> In all Thy works, and Thee alone;
> Thee will I love, till sacred fire
> Fill my whole soul with pure desire.

His last work of poetry was a collection of coarsely realistic pieces on Death, Judgment, Hell, and Heaven, to which he gave the title *Sensible Descriptions of the Four Last Things put into Print to Alarm and Arouse all Mankind*, 1675.

The *Secret Instructions*, forged at Cracow, 1602, contained a damaging caricature of the methods of the Jesuits whose ways were often censured by well wishers of the papacy. JUAN DE MARIANA, 1536-1624, the Spanish historian, himself a Jesuit, and the teacher of BELLARMINE, left among his papers a *Discourse concerning the Errors which Occur in the Form of Government of the Society of Jesus*. This was printed in 1625, and reprinted by order of Charles III when he banished the Jesuits from Spain.

But more damaging attacks were to follow. LOUIS DE MOLINA, 1535-1600, in a famous book entitled *The Agreement of Free Will with the Gifts of Grace, Divine Foreknowledge, Providence, Predestination, and Reprobation*, 1588, tried to reconcile AUGUSTINE'S doctrine of predestination with the teaching of MICHAEL DE BAINS, 1513-1589, which the Roman Church had condemned. The views of

DE BAINS were more thoroughly expounded by CORNELIUS
JANSEN, 1585-1638. His influential work was called
*Augustine, or the Doctrine of St. Augustine concerning the
Sickness, Health, and Medicine of Human Nature.* It was
posthumously published in 1640. "It was a learned attempt to revive the full teaching of the great Latin father,
emphasizing the corruption and weakness of human nature
and the irresistible character of the grace bestowed by God
upon the heart." "Although couched in technical scholastic language, it is an organised attack on the first principles
of scholasticism." Its first thesis is human helplessness:

> Why should it be hard to remember and easy to for-
> get—hard to be industrious and easy to be idle—unless
> some cruel blight had warped our nature through and
> through?"

The second thesis is human sin:

> Naturally the human soul, being rational and the
> image of God, is of such immense capacity that it can
> find neither rest nor satisfaction, save in his infinitude.

The third theme of the book is redeeming grace.

JANSEN'S successor at Port Royal was JUAN DU VER-
GIER DE HAURANNE, 1581-1643, better known to history
as ST. CYRAN. He had indicted the Jesuits for "every sort
and kind of misdemeanour," in a large treatise entitled *Peter
Aurelius*, 1633. His *Spiritual Letters* won the heart of
Mother Angelica Arnauld, and under his leadership the Port
Royalist crusade of anti-Jesuit literature began. A leading
principle of his teaching is expressed in the sentence:

> It is an indignity scarcely to be tolerated that the
> doctrine of faith is recalled to the puerile principles of
> logic or at all to the little measures of the human mind.

Jansenism found one of its best advocates in ANTOINE
ARNAULD, 1612-1694. His *Treatise of Frequent Com-*

munion, 1643, "was an elaborate attack on the priests who
gave absolution easily, without due enquiry into their penitent's character or the sincerity of his repentance." It
aroused so great a storm against its author that for twenty
years he dared not show himself in Paris. He dealt equally
serious blows at Jesuistical methods by two other works,
for which he gathered materials from the authorised publications of the Society. These works were *The Moral Theology of the Jesuits,* the second edition of which is dated
1644, and *The Moral Practice of the Jesuits.* The first
volume of this latter work was issued in 1669, the last volume did not appear until 1694.

But the most popular and powerful of all the anti-Jesuit
writings were the *Provincial Letters* of BLAISE PASCAL,
1623-1662. PASCAL was a prodigy whose knowledge of
science, depth of thought, and excellence of character were
as remarkable as his literary gifts. His two experiences of
religious conviction led him to write a little work *The Conversion of the Sinner.*

> When God deigns to speak to sinners, His first step
> is to raise their soul on to a higher plane whence their
> nature and surroundings appear in a wholly new per-
> spective. They see that perishable things are perishing,
> nay, already perished. Every moment snatches some
> enjoyment from their hand. All they held dearest slips
> away, as they hasten on towards a day when they will
> be stripped for ever of the vain and fleeting treasures
> wherein they put their trust.

The *Provincial Letters* were provoked by a work on Jesuit
casuistry compiled by ANTONIO ESCOBAR, 1589-1669, from
the various directories of the Order. It was entitled *The
Book of Moral Theology,* 1644; it had been preceded by a
Summary of Cases of Conscience, 1627, and was followed

by *The Problems of Morals in the World of Theology*,
1652-1666.

PASCAL wrote to criticise the general principle of ESCO-
BAR'S moral teaching, and the startling success of his first
Letter encouraged him to continue the series. He ranged
over many disputed matters, choosing the most outrageous
passages from the least reputable writers in order to expose
the Jesuit system, "its bones, its muscles and its nerves":

> Talk to the good Fathers, and you will soon dis-
> cover that their lax moral standards are at the root of
> their opinions on grace. You will find that, knowing
> nothing of what Christian virtue means, they divorce
> it from the love of God, which should be its life and
> soul. You will see so many crimes glozed over, so
> much licentiousness excused, that it will not surprise
> you if they maintain the power of every man to lead
> what they fancy is a moral life. Their ideals being
> altogether heathen, the force of Nature amply avails
> to reach them. When we preach the need of efficacious
> grace we set its face towards a different goal. Grace
> is not content to cure one vice by another, or to make
> men practise the outward duties of religion; it aspires
> to virtues beyond the ken of heathen sage or Pharisee.
> Law and reason are sufficient graces for all that they
> require. But to wean our souls from the love of the
> world; to tear it from its dearest delights; to bind us
> wholly, only, and for ever to God can only be the work
> of an All-Powerful Hand (from the *Fifth Provincial
> Letter*).

FATHER DANIEL, 1649-1728, lacking both the brilliance
and the wit of PASCAL, attempted a reply in *The Discourses
of Cleander and Eudoxius concerning the Provincial Letters*.
GEORGE PIROT, 1599-1657, 'the scoffing Jesuit' wrote *An
Apology for the Casuists*, 1657, in which he insisted that

they were wholly right and their critics wrong; but his book brought down a torrent of denunciation. FATHERS ANNAT, NOUET, and BRISACIER issued *An Answer to the Provincial Letters made by some Fathers of the Society in France*, 1659. But the workmanship of the Jansenist writings far surpassed that of any Jesuit work. Some of the Fathers were only learning the literary art. "FATHER ANNAT, the King's confessor, was dry and inconclusive; FATHER PETAU, a profound patristic scholar, was water-logged by his erudition; FATHER PINTHEREAU'S dreary catalogues of Jansenist errors roused no man to enthusiasm . . . ."[6]

In 1713 the papal bull Unigenitus set forth a hundred and one heretical clauses in PASQUIER QUESNEL'S, 1634-1719, book entitled *Moral Reflections*. This condemnation led to the production of *The Body of Doctrine*, and also to *An Explanation* through which a compromise was secured, 1720. The Jesuits however were driven from France, 1764-5, "stoned with the ruins of Port Royal", and in 1775 the Papacy suppressed the Order.

Having collected and published the Letters, 1657, PASCAL proposed to spend the rest of his life in working upon *An Apology for Christianity, against Libertines and Deists*. His unfinished labour was arranged by editorial hands and published with the title *Thoughts on Religion and certain other Subjects*, 1670. The book contains a noble argument for following religion for its own sake. It represents the ideal greatness of man obscured by his actual infirmities, which reason cannot remove. Faith alone can serve the needs of the soul.

> Man is a reed—the feeblest in nature; but he is thinking reed. The universe need not arm for his defeat; a fume, a drop of water will dispatch him. Yet crush him, and he still remains nobler than his de-

---

[6] Viscount St. Cyres, *Pascal*, p. 285.

stroyer, because he knows that he is dying; whereas the universe knows nothing of its victory *(Thoughts 347)*.

Man is neither a beast nor an angel, and the worst of it is that he that tries to be an angel ends as a beast *(Thoughts 358)*.

The preachers of the day had their share in either resisting or promoting the Counter Reformation. JEAN DAILLE, 1594-1670, published a famous *Treatise on the Use of the Holy Fathers*, 1632, in which he subtly and forcibly attacked the controversial use of the Church Fathers as authoritative. "The novelty and piquancy of the subject," together with the simple method and easy style, "made this *Treatise* the first truly popular book of controversy." MOISE AMYRAUT, 1596-1664, wrote a strong book on *Christian Morals*, from the standpoint of reform. JEAN CLAUDE, 1619-1687, a conspicuous Protestant, wrote a *Plaint of the Protestants*, 1686, and a far more popular *Essay on the Composition of a Sermon*, 1688. After the Revocation of the Edict of Nantes, he became the apologist of his distressed Church.

On the Catholic side the French pulpit was adorned by some of its most splendid ornaments. JACQUES BENIGUE BOSSUET, 1627-1704, passed through three stages as a preacher. The first, at Metz, was marked by a certain roughness and stiffness mingled with the impetuous vigorous impatience of youth. The second stage, at Paris, was distinguished by strength, pathos, dignity, even sublimity. The third, at Meaux, was characterised by order, regularity, finish and symmetry, with less effusion and less energy.

In a *Catechism* written by PAUL FERRY, the work of the Reformation was described as a necessity, the results of which made it impossible for men to be saved in the Church of

Rome. BOSSUET felt bound to refute this and wrote *A Refutation of the Catechism of Paul Ferry*, 1655.

> Does not le sieur Ferry know in his conscience that
> we confess Jesus Christ as the sole Saviour and only
> Redeemer of our souls; that we believe Him to have
> more than sufficiently paid our debt to His justly of-
> fended Father; and that, so far from questioning
> whether His Death is all sufficient to our salvation we
> teach that one drop of His Precious Blood, even one
> tear or sigh, would suffice to redeem countless worlds?

BOSSUET settled in Paris in 1659. His genius as a
preacher brought him an immense popularity. His great
series of sermons were preached in the following order: The
Lenten Sermons at the Minimes of the Place Royal, 1660;
the *Lenten Sermons* at the Carmelites of the Faubourg Saint
Jacques, 1661; the *Lenten Sermons* before the Court, 1662;
the *Advent Sermons* before the Court, 1665; the *Advent
Sermons* at St. Thomas of the Louvre, 1668; the *Advent
Sermons* before the Court, 1669.

During his "first period" BOSSUET wrote *On the Bounty
and the Discipline of God,* and some panegyrics, of which
the finest is the *Panegyric of St. Paul,* 1657. In his second
manner he wrote *On Providence,* 1662, *On Death, On Ambition, On Delay of Conversion, On Justice,* 1666, and *The
Feast of All Saints Day,* 1669. During his third "period"
he pronounced his ever memorable *Funeral Orations.*

> We forgive ourselves so easily when fortune for-
> gives us! and it is so easy to believe ourselves skilful
> and enlightened above all other men, when we are the
> most conspicuous and most fortunate among them!
> Reverses are the only instructors who can rebuke us
> profitably, and wrest from us the confession of failure,
> so hard for pride to make. But when misfortune opens

our eyes, we review our errors in bitterness of heart:
we are overwhelmed alike by what we have done and
left undone, and we no longer see how to defend that
presumptuous wisdom which once we believed infallible
(*Oration on Queen Henrietta Maria*, Nov. 16, 1669).

"It would probably be difficult to find in the history of
literature a career so pre-eminently deserving of the name of
glorious as BOSSUET'S." For the education of the Dauphin
he wrote *A Treatise of the Knowledge of God and of One's
Self*, which was published posthumously and "has become
of world-wide fame among philosophers." PERE GRATRY,
in his own great work *The Knowledge of God*, speaks of
it as "a book truly vast in its results and in its depth." For
the same purpose he compiled *A Discourse of Universal History*,
the first serious attempt to describe the course of history
as a whole, and as the product of design. He also prepared
a work entitled *Politics drawn from the Holy Scripture*.

In 1671 he published a brief *Exposition of the Catholic
Doctrine*, and in 1688 he sent forth his immensely influential
controversial *History of the Variations of the Protestant
Churches*. Hallam says of the beginning, "Nothing, perhaps,
in polemical eloquence is so splendid as this chapter.
The eagle of Meaux is there truly seen, lordly of form,
fierce of eye, terrible in his beak and claws."

The History is composed of fifteen books, the first five of
which narrate the story of the rise and progress of the Reformation
in Germany. Book six discusses the sanction which
Luther and Melancthon were supposed to have given to the
adulterous marriage of the Landgrave of Hesse. The ecclesiastical
history of England, 1520-1553, occupies two books,
and then, two books more discuss the French Calvinists and
the aid given them by Queen Elizabeth. Book eleven is devoted
to the Albigenses from the ninth to the twelfth cen-

tury, and the story of the Huguenots is continued in books twelve and thirteen. The dissensions of the Councils of Dort, Charenton, and Geneva occupy the fourteenth book. In the last book BOSSUET describes the marks of the true Church, which, he claims, belong only to Rome.

The criticisms of JURIEN and BASNAGE led to the publication of *A Defence of the History of the Variations,* as also to a "succession of six *Informations* answering different points of attack." BOSSUET wrote again on the subject of Communion in both kinds contending in reply to objections that:

> From the earliest times it has been the custom of the Church to communicate under one or both species, without either being held to be deficient as regards a perfect Communion.

Controversial writing now became the leading interest in the life of BOSSUET. Against a prophetical work of JURIEN he issued *An Exposition of the Apocalypse,* 1689, and against LOUIS DUPIN'S work on the *Fathers and Councils of the Church,* 1691-1692, he issued a *Memoir,* which is in fact an elaborate history and criticism of the Councils of Ephesus and Chalcedon. In 1697 he wrote a *Letter to Pope Innocent XII* against the errors of CARDINAL SFONDRATI as expressed in a work on *Predestination.*

His writings in connection with the Quietist controversy are referred to later as part of the literary history of that movement. That great discussion however did not satisfy his contentious spirit, he prepared a large critical work in 1702 against SIMON'S writings on the criticism of the New Testament, and in 1703 he issued *Reflections concerning the Case of Conscience,* a work that had for its theme the kind of submission due to the papal utterances on Jansenism.

VOLTAIRE'S judgment was justified when he said "BOS-SUET ceased to be accounted the first among the preachers from the moment Bourdaloue appeared." LOUIS BOURDALOUE, 1632-1704, represented the complete perfection of preaching at its best moment. His Sermons achieved an immense success on account of their moral quality, their vivid 'portraits', their apt allusions, and their plain outspokenness. He had no superior in the art of handling a subject oratorically.

His only works are Sermons, some fragments arranged as Thoughts, and some Letters.

An atrocious crime in high life which BOURDALOUE felt could not be ignored led him to preach his "terrible" *Sermon on Impurity*.

> There is no sin which throws a man into a deeper blindness of soul—nor which involves him in more fatal disorders, nor which brings him more under the devil's rule, nor which forms in his heart a worm of conscience more unbearable or more biting; and all that by a power which is peculiar to him. From which I infer that this sin is then a manifest sign of the unhappy state of reprobation.

The third outstanding preacher was JEAN BAPTISTE MAS-SILLON, 1663-1742, a most delightful rhetorician, whose style was so flawless as to be almost counted a demerit. His Sermons are real literature. They are published in two series of *Advent Sermons; Forty-one High Lent Sermons; Ten Minor Lent Sermons; Eight Sermons on the Mysteries; Ten Panegyrics; Six Funeral Orations;* and *Four Sermons on Taking the Veil.*

The effect of the exordium to his *Funeral Sermon for Louis XIV,* from the text Ecclesiastes i.16, is said to have been tremendous.

> God only is great, my brethren; and above all in those last moments when He presides at the death of the kings of the earth. The more their glory and their

power have shone forth, the more in vanishing then
do they render homage to His supreme greatness; God
then appears all that He is, and man is no more at all
that which he believed himself to be.

In England the Counter Reformation connects with the
reign of Queen Mary, 1516-1558.

STEPHEN GARDINER, 1493-1555, a thorough-going
enemy of the reformed doctrine, wrote a work entitled
True Obedience, 1535, to vindicate the claim of Henry VIII
to be the spiritual head of the national Church. This very
able attempt to justify the royal, as against the papal supremacy, was however weakened by a now lost retraction entitled
Palinodia. REGINALD POLE, 1500-1558, began a similar
work at Henry's command, but it resolved itself into a
trenchant attack upon the king's policy and was issued under
the title *For the Unity of the Church*, 1536. Under the
régime of Mary REGINALD POLE became Papal Legate and
wrote *The Legatine Constitutions*, 1555, on which he based
his story of *The Reformation in England*, 1556.

All other English leaders of the Church were surpassed in
influence by WILLIAM LAUD, 1573-1645, the living and
learned embodiment of ecclesiastical reaction. Only seven of
his *Sermons* remain. These were all preached by Royal command and are of genuine historic interest.

LAUD'S godson, WILLIAM CHILLINGWORTH, 1602-
1644, was a Romanist in his youth, but was converted by
study 'from a doubting papist into a confirmed Protestant.'
His main work *The Religion of the Protestants a Safe Way
to Salvation; or, An Answer to a Book entitled, "Mercy
and Truth, or Charity Maintained by Catholics,"* 1637,
exercised an enormous and long continued influence. CHIL-
LINGWORTH maintained that the Bible is the final authority
for faith; that no Church is infallible; and that the Apostles'

Creed is a sufficient statement of belief. His book was long regarded as the bulwark of the reformed faith.

> . . . . as, on the one side, I do not understand by your religion the doctrine of . . any . . private man among you; nor the doctrine . . . of any . . particular company among you, but that wherein you all agree, or profess to agree, 'the doctrine of the Council of Trent;' so accordingly on the other side, by the 'religion of protestants,' I do not understand the doctrine of Luther, or Calvin, or Melanchthon; . . . but that wherein they all agree, and which they all subscribe with a greater harmony, as a perfect rule of their faith and actions; that is, the Bible. The Bible, I say, the Bible only, is the religion of protestants. Whatsoever else they believe beside it, and the plain, irrefragable, indubitable consequences of it, well may they hold it as a matter of opinion; but as a matter of faith and religion, neither can they with coherence to their own grounds believe it themselvs, nor require the belief of it of others, without most high and most schismatical presumption.

This great book was part of a mixed controversy. In 1630, one WILSON, a Jesuit, under the assumed name of 'KNOTT,' wrote *Charity Mistaken*, to defend the Romanist view that Protestants are excluded from salvation. CHRISTOPHER POTTER, 1591-1646, replied in a work called *Want of Charity Justly Charged*, 1633, to which 'KNOTT' replied in *Mercy and Truth, or, Charity Maintained by Catholics*, 1634. To this work he added a pamphlet called *Directions to be Observed by N. N. if He Means to Proceed in Answering the Book entitled Mercy and Truth, or, Charity Maintained by Catholics*. N. N. was CHILLINGWORTH who was

known to be preparing to intervene in the discussion.[8]
CHILLINGWORTH then took 'KNOTT'S' book and replied
to "every assertion in every paragraph and to every insinua-
tion in every assertion." This elaborate and detailed reply
is *The Religion of Protestants*. It is meticulously detailed
as an argument, but its style has "a naked severity and
nervous simplicity, occasionally dashed by a vein of eloquence," and the whole book is marked by an earnest love
of truth.

CHRISTOPHER DAVENPORT, 1598-1680, who became a
Catholic during his residence on the Continent, and in 1617
became a Franciscan, stood out, on his return to England,
among the ecclesiastical figures of the day as FRANCISCUS
A SANCTA CLARA. With the hope of reuniting Christendom
he wrote an important treatise entitled *God, Nature and
Grace, or a Tractate on Predestination, Merit, and Forgiveness of Sins, or of Justification, and then of the Invocation
of the Saints*, 1634. To this main work SANCTA CLARA
subsequently added *A Paraphrastic Exposition of the rest of
the Articles of the Anglican Confession*. This attempt to
align the teaching of the Thirty-nine Articles with the doctrines of Rome is more ingenious than convincing, but it
has historic interest as an early foreshadowing of the efforts
of JOHN HENRY NEWMAN.[9]

Controversy however was only one of the interests of
English Christian literature during this period. The claims
of practical religion were remembered, and the life of the
spirit made itself known.

FRANCIS QUARLES, 1592-1644, modelled an extraordin-
arily popular collection of *Divine Emblems*, 1635, on a
work by HERMAN HUGO, 1588-1629, entitled *Pia Desideria*.
The best of QUARLES' work was original, full of fashion-

---

[8] Cp. John Tulloch, *Rational Theology in the XVII Century*, Vol. I.,
pp. 282-292.
[9] Wilfrid Ward, *The Oxford Movement*, pp. 44-45.

able conceits and extravagances of language and wit. "His poems include *A Feast for Wormes set forth in a Poeme of the History of Jonah,* 1620; *Hadassa: History of Queene Ester,* 1621; *Job Militant,* 1624; *Sion's Elegies,* 1625; *Historie of Samson,* 1631; and *Hieroglyphikes of the Life of Man,* 1638."

> So faire is man, that Death (a parting blast)
> Blasts his fair flower, and makes him earth at last;
> So strong is man, that with a gasping breath
> He totters and bequeathes his strength to Death;

RICHARD FLECKNOE, 1600-1678, who, according to Dryden,

> In prose and verse was owned without dispute
> Throughout the realms of nonsense absolute.

represented the devotional spirit of Romanism in his *Hierothalamium, or the Heavenly Nuptials of our Blessed Saviour with a Pious Soul,* 1626. *The Affections of a Pious Soul unto our Saviour Christ,* 1640, is the only other poem of a religious character that is remembered among his works.

In JOHN DONNE, 1573-1631, "the mediaeval and the modern consciousness clashed. He was a storm-point where the force of the old world and the intelligence of the new strove for mastery." Born of Catholic parents he became an Anglican on attaining manhood, and ultimately, in 1614, after a much varied career, entered holy orders and died as Dean of St. Paul's Cathedral. Most of his lyrical poetry was written during his visit to Europe, 1595-1597, but was not printed until 1633. After his ordination he wrote little poetry; "his trenchant thought, his brilliant fancy, his profound insight, and his command of the English tongue finding outlet in his sermons."

The longest of his extant poems is *The Progress of the Soul, or Metempsychosis,* 1601, a fanciful discussion of the transmigration of a soul. He assisted in the controversy with

Romanists by writing *The Pseudo-Martyr,* 1610, and a satirical and caustic pamphlet against the Jesuits entitled *Ignatius, his Conclave,* 1611.

His *Divine Poems* belong to this period; they include *An Anatomy of the World,* 1611; *The Tears of Tears,* 1613; and two cycles of religious sonnets entitled *The Crown,* and *The Holy Sonnets.* DONNE is a philosophical mystic.

> But we know our selves least; Mere outward shews
>   Our mindes so store,
> That our soules, no more than our eyes disclose
> But forme and colour. Onely he who knowes
>   Himselfe, knowes more. (Ode: *Of our Sense of Sinne.*)

His *Devotions* were published in 1624. *LXXX Sermons* in 1640, *Fifty Sermons* in 1649, *Essays in Divinity* in 1651, *Paradoxes, Problems, and Essays* in 1652, and *Six and Twenty Sermons* in 1661. The second of his 'Prebend Sermons', 1625, has been described as "one of the most magnificent pieces of religious writing in English literature . ."

> . . as in the face of Death, when he layes hold upon me, and in the face of the Devill when he attempts me, I shall see the face of God (for everything shall be a glasse, to reflect God upon me); so in the agonies of Death, in the anguish of that dissolution, in the sorrows of that valediction, in the irreversiblenesse of that transmigration, I shall have a joy which shall no more evaporate than my soule shall evaporate, a joy that shall passe up and put on a more glorious garment above, and be joy superinvested in glory. Amen.

It was GEORGE HERBERT, 1593-1633, the "first in English poetry who spoke face to face with God", who represented the point of rest between Puritan severity and Cavalier gaiety. His work entitled *The Temple: Sacred Poems and Private Ejaculations,* printed soon after his death, is a collection of more than a hundred and fifty short poems suggested by the Church and its services. In this universally known book GEORGE HERBERT gave expression to the fullness of the Anglican devotion; above all he made it a faithful reflection of his own holy character. "As a manual of devotion it is as though a seraph covered his face with his wings in rapturous adoration; as a poem it is full of that subtle perception of analogies to be found only in works of genius . . ." The very crown and flower of all the poems is that on Man:

> More servants wait on man
> Than he'll take notice of: in every path
> He treads down that which doth befriend him
> When sickness makes him pale and wan.
> Oh, mighty love! man is one world and hath
> Another to attend him.

His wise and excellent work on Pastoral Theology entitled *A Priest of the Temple, or the Country Parson,* 1653, is less well known, although a wiser or a better book for its purpose could hardly be written. A collection of proverbs, the *Jacula Prudentium,* exhibits the pithy thought which characterises so many of the poems.

> The Country Parson is full of all knowledge. They say it is an ill mason that refuseth any stone; and there is no knowledge but in a skilful hand serves either positively as it is, or else to illustrate some other knowledge . . . But the chief and top of his knowledge consists of the Book of books, the store-house and magazine of life and comfort—the Holy Scriptures. There he sucks and lives (*A Priest of the Temple. The Parson's Knowledge*).

SIR THOMAS BROWNE, 1605-1682, spoke for the broad-minded laity in his masterly *Religio Medici* (Religion of a Doctor), written in 1635, but not published until 1643. It is a confession of faith combined with a minute account of opinions upon many subjects, and it made its author famous as one of the great writers of the English tongue.

> Now for my life, it is a miracle of thirty years, which to relate were not a history, but a piece of poetry, and would sound to common ears like a fable. For the world, I count it not an inn but an hospital, and a place not to live but to die in. The world that I regard is myself; it is the microcosm of my own frame that I can cast my eye on; for the other, I use it but like my globe, and turn it round sometimes for my recreation. . . . . Nature tells me I am the image of God, as well as Scripture. He that understands not thus much, hath not his introduction or first lesson, and hath yet to begin the alphabet of man.

The "Evening Hymn," suggested by BISHOP KEN'S lines, appeared in the *Religio Medici* in connection with some thoughts on sleep, which

> . . is that death which we may be literally said to die daily . . In fine so like death I dare not trust it without my prayers and an half adieu unto the world, and take my farewell in a colloquy with God:

> > The night is come, like to the day
> > Depart not Thou, great God, away.
> > Let not my sins, black as the night,
> > Eclipse the lustre of Thy light.

BROWNE expressed the wistfulness of a quiet confidence in life beyond death in his *Hydriotaphia; Urn Burial, or a Discourse of the Sepulchral Urns lately found in Norfolk,* 1658. In this work "his reflections on death, oblivion, and immortality are, for solemnity and grandeur, unsurpassed in English literature, and are set forth in language of rich and gorgeous eloquence."

THOMAS FULLER, 1608-1661, was a type of the irrepressible humourist. Having written the tedious poem entitled *David's Hainous Sinne*, 1631, he abandoned poetry for history, and then finally turned to works of practical divinity. Among other books he published *The Holy and the Prophane State*, 1642; *Good Thoughts in Bad Times*, 1645; *Better Thoughts in Worse Times*, 1660, and *The Cause and Cure of a Wounded Conscience*, 1647. His *Church History of Britain*, 1656, has been described as a rhapsody containing three hundred and fifty errors. His chief work, by which FULLER will ever be remembered, is *The History of the Worthies of England*, a magnificent miscellany of character sketches and memoranda. This was published posthumously in 1661, and has been the delight of many readers because of its wealth of notes on places, notabilities, and antiquities.

The mediating theology as well as the devout practical religion of the time was perhaps most fully represented by JEREMY TAYLOR, 1613-1667, whose many adventures and imprisonments as a Royalist ended in a quiet Welsh retreat where most of his writing was done.

TAYLOR has been called "the Shakespeare of English prose." "In exuberance of poetic fancy, vast learning, and untiring industry he stands almost unrivalled in the annals of Anglican Churchmen." He began as an author by writing the controversial work entitled *The Sacred Order of Episcopacy*, 1642, but soon passed to the literature of devotion, and issued *The Psalter of David*, 1644. Then followed *A Discourse Concerning Prayer*, 1646; *An Apology for Authorized and Set Forms of Liturgy against the Presence of the Spirit*, 1649; and the excellent little manual of devotion, *The Golden Grove*, 1655.

His first long and independent work was the *Liberty of Prophesying, Showing the Unreasonableness of Prescribing to other Men's Faith, and the Iniquity of Persecuting Differing Opinions*, 1646. This is "the first distinct and avowed defence of toleration which had been ventured on in England, perhaps in Christendom."

> . . any man may be better trusted for himself, than any man can be for another; for in this case his own interest is most concerned, and ability is not so necessary as honesty, which certainly every man will best preserve in his own case, and to himself—and if he does not, it's he that must smart for it; and it is not required of us not to be in error, but that we endeavour to avoid it.

It aroused opposition. HENRY HAMMOND, 1605-1660, argued against it in a *Letter of Resolution of Six Queries of Present Use to the Church of England, 1653*; and SAMUEL RUTHERFORD attacked it in his savage libel entitled *A Free Disputation against Pretended Liberty of Conscience,* 1648.

TAYLOR gave to England "the earliest modern treatise of popular piety" when he wrote his original *Life of Christ, or the Great Exemplar, 1649. The Rule and Exercises of Holy Living, 1650,* is the best known of all his writings, although it is not the finest expression of his genius. That expression is given in the sequel, entitled *The Rules and Exercises of Holy Dying, 1651,* a work of brilliant freshness adorned with many passages of sustained brightness and written in a fullness of style of extraordinary merit.

> But so have I seen a rose newly springing from the clefts of its hood, and at first it was fair as the morning, and full with the dew of heaven as a lamb's fleece; but when a ruder blast had forced open its virgin modesty, and dismantled its too youthful and unripe retirements, it began to put on darkness, and to decline to softness and the symptoms of a sickly age; it bowed the head, and broke its stalk; and at night,

having lost some of its leaves and all its beauty, it fell into the portion of weeds and out-worn faces. The same is the portion of every man and every woman; the heritage of worms and serpents, rottenness and cold dishonour, ...

Many sermons and doctrinal writings followed until, in 1659, came that "most elephantine of all theological works," the *Ductor Dubitantium, or the Rule of Conscience in all her General Measures*. This was intended to serve as a definitive manual of Anglican casuistry, but it is unreadable and is now as forgotten as a stranded hulk.

CHAPTER XXXIII
POST-REFORMATION MYSTICISM

The great age of mysticism had passed before the Reformation turned the mind of the Church to the definition of doctrine and to the cleansing of the body ecclesiastical. During the days of division and change a few choice spirits kept alive the essential elements of mystical thought. Such were Paracelsus, 1493-1541; Andreas Osiander, 1498-1522; and Caspar Schwenkfeld, 1490-1561, who was the first true mystic among the Protestants. Sebastian Franck, 1500-1545, passed on the tradition to Valentine Weigel, 1533-1588, from whom JACOB BOEHME, 1575-1624, received the mystic flame.

BOEHME, of whom ANGELUS SILESIUS said, "God's Heart is Jacob Boehme's Element", may be called the last of the great European mystics, or the first of the modern mystics and the father of modern philosophy. "He would teach us that there is nothing nearer to each one of us than heaven, paradise and hell, and that we may, if we will, be now in heaven . . ."

His mysticism consists of a threefold system of thought. As a philosophy it is a pursuit of the Divine Wisdom, of which BOEHME wrote in *The Aurora*, or *Morning Glow*, 1612. As an explanation of the world, an 'astrology' as the philosopher calls it, his mysticism is unfolded in *The Three Principles of the Divine Essence*, 1619, in *The Threefold Life of Man*, 1620; *The Humanity of Christ*, 1620; and in *The Signature of all Things*, 1621. As a system of theology, or exposition of the life of God in the life of

man, BOEHME'S views are described in *The Gracious Choice,
a Book of Predestination and Election of God*, 1623; in
The Great Mystery, 1623; and in *The Two Testaments of
Christ*, 1624.

> The whole outward visible world with all its being
> is a signature, or figure of the inward spiritual world;
> whatever is internally, and however its operation is, so
> likewise it has its character externally; like as the spirit
> of each creature sets forth and manifests the internal
> form of its birth by its body, so does the Eternal Being
> also.
>
> . . if my will is a nothing, then he (*i.e.* God) is in
> me what he pleases, and then I know not myself any
> more, but him; and if he will that I shall be some-
> thing, then let him effect it; but if he wills it not,
> then I am dead in him, and he lives in me as he
> pleases, and so then if I be a nothing, then I am at
> the end, in the essence out of which my father Adam
> was created; for out of nothing God has created all
> things (*Signature of all Things*, chap. ix.1, 61).

BOEHME wrote other books, some controversial, some expository, some devotional, but all subsidiary to the mystic's
purpose of discovering in man "what was before nature
and creature." He saw the visible world as a manifestation
of the inner spiritual world, a copy of eternity wherewith
eternity has made itself visible.

The spiritual quiescence upon which BOEHME insisted
became a leading principle in the teaching of JOHANN ARNDT,
1555-1621, whose book entitled *The True Christianity*,
1605, exercised far-reaching influence, and still holds its
place as a classic of German Christianity. Impressed by its
message and moulded by its spirit PHILIP JACOB SPENER,
1635-1705, became the founder of Pietism, a semi-mystical
movement in the Lutheran Church, which brought a mes-

sage of love and godliness that fell like rain from heaven upon a country blighted by the drought of dogmatic dissensions. SPENER founded a College for Piety in 1670, and five years later issued his *Pia Desideria, or Earnest Desires for a Reform of the True Evangelical Church.* This work was critical of the laxity of the age to which it offered a programme of reforms whereby holiness would be cultivated; it was instrumental in starting a new effort towards the attainment of the Christian ideal. SPENER laid special emphasis upon the study of the Scriptures, the universal priesthood of all believers, Christian charity and service, the avoidance of religious controversy, the need of piety as well as of learning in candidates for the ministry, and the necessity of preaching with simplicity and directness.

Since our entire Christianity consists in the inner or new man, and its soul is faith, and the effects of faith are the fruits of life, I regard it as of the greatest importance that sermons should be wholly directed to this end. On the one hand they should exhibit God's rich benefits, as they affect the inner man, in such a way that faith is advanced and the inner man forwarded in it. On the other hand they should not merely incite to external acts of virtue and restrain from external acts of vice, as the moral philosophy of the heathen does, but should lay the foundation in the heart.

SPENER'S pupil and successor in the leadership of the movement, AUGUST HERMANN FRANCKE, 1663-1727, tried to take theology back to the teaching of Scripture. To accomplish this he wrote *The Guide to the Reading of the Sacred Scriptures,* 1693, *Studies in Interpretation,* 1717, and *A Commentary on the Aim of the Books of the Old and New Testaments,* 1724.

PAUL GERHARDT, 1607-1676, was the poet of Pietism.

He was "next to Luther . . . . the most gifted and popular hymn writer of the Lutheran Church," his writing was as attractive, simple and pleasing as his thinking. He surpassed LUTHER in poetic fertility. "His one hundred and twenty-three hymns are among the noblest pearls in the treasury of sacred poetry. More than thirty of them are still in use . . . ."

He was carried by a living faith and an evangelical joyfulness of mind above the narrowness of formal orthodoxy. He makes us forget that "he was an uncompromising Lutheran zealot, an irreconcilable foe of Calvinistic heresies." He rejoiced in the government and the grace of God, but more than all else the death and resurrection of Christ moved him to praise. He adapted part of the hymn of BERNARD OF CLAIRVAUX into his wonderful apostrophe:

> O Sacred Head, now wounded,

but very many of his hymns breathe the same passionate vows of fidelity to his Saviour.

> Jesus, Thy boundless love to me
> No thought can reach, no tongue declare;
> O knit my thankful heart to Thee,
> And reign without a rival there:
> Thine wholly, Thine alone I am;
> Lord, with Thy love my heart inflame.

Under the influence of the scholarly JOHN ALBERT BENGEL, 1687-1752, Pietism underwent a change, for he carried into it the interests of Biblical criticism. His edition of the *New Testament in Greek* was based on his fresh criticism of ancient MSS. It was followed in 1742 by the celebrated *Gnomon*, or *Index to the New Testament* which has proved a mine of priceless gems of exposition. The *Gnomon* gave a vital stimulus to the study of the New Testament; as more matter for thought is often contained in a line than can be found in whole pages of less gifted expositors.

The pietistic mysticism which dominated the religious thought of Germany was altogether foreign to the Christianity of Spain. LOUIS OF GRENADA, 1504-1588, is usually counted among the mystics, but his work is characterised by didactic and practical aims rather than by those which distinguish the true mystic. His *Guide for Sinners* became a great converting agent. His best known book is the *Guide for Preachers*, which with his *Tractate on Prayer and Meditation* was placed on the Index. Even after revision and reprinting, these works left him under the suspicion of being guilty of 'illuminism.' But the public gave welcome to his writings in which "the sweetness of his nature so flows over in his words that didacticism becomes persuasive even when he argues against our strongest prepossessions . . . ."

> There be some that would know for this end only, that they might know—and it is foolish curiosity. There be some that would know, that they might be known—and it is foolish vanity; and there be some that would know that they might sell their knowledge for money or for honours—and it is filthy lucre. There be also some that desire to know, that they might edify—and it is charity. And there are some that would know, that they may be edified—and it is wisdom. All these ends may move the desire, and, in choice of these, a man is often deceived, when he considereth not which ought especially to move; and this error is very dangerous.

Mysticism found a distinguished exponent in the apostle of Andalusia, JUAN DE AVILA, 1502-1569, who maintained "that only those visions which minister to our spiritual necessities, and make us *more humble*, are genuine." His

Spiritual Writings are "redolent of religious unction combined with the wisest practical spirit, the most sagacious counsel, and the rarest loving kindness . . . . though he considered letters a vanity, his own practice shows him to be a master in the accommodation of the lowliest, most familiar language to the loftiest subject."[1]

JUAN DE VALDES, d. 1541, represents mysticism among the Protestants of Spain. He must be accounted "at least among the very first masters of Castilian prose." His *One Hundred and Twelve Sacred Considerations* is a careful presentation of the mysticism of German thinkers, and, at the same time, it is a searching study of the springs of motives —of the innermost recesses of the human heart.

The most correct of all Spanish writers without exception was LUIS PONCE DE LEON, 1527-1591. He was sentenced to imprisonment for having made a translation of the Song of Solomon, but he improved his seclusion by writing "his celebrated treatise, the greatest of Spanish mystic books," entitled *The Names of Christ*. The work is in the form of a dialogue, in the course of which the author expounds the symbolic value of the titles given to Christ, such as The Mount, The Shepherd, The Arm of God, The Prince of Peace, The Bridegroom, etc. It was published in 1583.

His fine qualities as a writer are also shown in his *Exposition of the Book of Job,* and in the work entitled *The Perfect Wife,* a singularly brilliant paraphrase of Proverbs xxxi.

He was no less great in verse than in prose. "With ST. JOHN OF THE CROSS he heads the list of Spain's lyrico-mystical poets."[2] He however set little or no value upon his verses which were published by QUEVEDO in 1631 with the hope of counteracting the growing influence of *culture*.

---

[1] J. Fitzmaurice-Kelly, *Spanish Literature,* p. 161.
[2] *Ibid.* p. 182.

When to the heavenly dome my thoughts take flight
With shimmering stars bedecked, ablaze with light,
Then sink my eyes down to the ground,
In slumber wrapped, oblivion bound,
Enveloped in the gloom of darkest night. . . .

O dwelling fit for angels! sacred fane!
The hallowed shrine where youth and beauty reign!
Why in this dungeon, plunged in night,
The soul that's born for Heaven's delight
Should cruel Fate withhold from its domain?

All these representatives of the spirit of mysticism were surpassed in genius and in fame by THERESA OF CREPEDA AND AHUMADA, 1515-1582, the reformer of the Carmelites. "Santa Teresa is not only a glorious saint and a splendid figure in the annals of religious thought: she ranks as a miracle of genius, as, perhaps, the greatest woman who ever handled pen, the single one of all her sex who stands beside the world's most perfect masters."[3] Her books, which were all published posthumously in 1587, give a complete and vivid account of the psychological experiences of the mystic; they are strictly orthodox in doctrine and emphasise the necessity of good works and of self mortifying discipline. The three most important are *The Spiritual Castle*, *The Interior Castle*, or *The Mansions*, and *The Way of Perfection*.

Her masterpiece is *The Interior Castle* in which she unites the passion of the loftiest mysticism with the finest practical sense. Like many others she speaks much of 'spiritual espousals' and 'spiritual marriage.'

That which God here communicates to the soul . . is so great a secret and so sublime a grace, and what she feels is so excessive a delight, that I know nothing with which to compare it, except that Our Lord is pleased at that moment to manifest to her the glory which is in Heaven.

[3] *Ibid.*, p. 193.

Her *Autobiography*, "that many-sided, shrewdly wise book," is to be counted among the classics of mysticism. In it she relates the story of her spiritual conversion and growth with a completeness of self revelation that leaves nothing hidden.

> . . . a saintly nobleman . . . a married layman, who had spent nearly forty years in prayer, seems to me to have been, by the pains he took, the beginning of salvation to my soul.

> In the beginning I did not know that God is present in all things . . . Unlearned men used to tell me that He was present only by His grace. I could not believe that . . . A most learned Dominican told me He was present Himself . . . this was a great comfort to me.

> Once when I was holding in my hand the cross of my rosary, He took it from me with His own hand. He returned it; but it was then four large stones incomparably more precious than diamonds: the five wounds were delineated on them with the most admirable art. He said to me that for the future that cross would appear so to me always, and so it did. The precious stones were seen, however, only by myself.

In a book entitled *Foundations,* THERESA told the story of her work as the founder of many nunneries. This record also ranks among the great documents of Christian devotion. Her general manner of teaching when untouched by the inspiration of her mystic nuptials is illustrated in the following passage:

> There are four ways in which the watering (of a garden) may be done. There is water which is drawn wearily by hand from the well. There is water drawn

by the ox-wheel, more abundantly and with greater labour. There is water which is brought in from the river, which will saturate the whole ground; and, last and best, there is rain from heaven.

Four sorts of prayer correspond to these. The first is a weary effort with small returns; the well may run dry: the gardener then must weep. The second is internal prayer and meditation upon God; the trees will then shew leaves and flower buds. The third is love of God. The virtues then become vigorous. We converse with God, face to face . . . The fourth kind cannot be described in words. Then there is no more toil . . . . The soul enjoys undoubting certitude; the faculties work without effort and without consciousness . . . .

THERESA was a poet whose "artless songs, with their resplendent gleams of ecstasy and passion" have been thrust into the background by her more impressive prose writings.

> Not for Thy promised Paradise, O Lord,
> I tread the steep way of Thy holy hill
> Nor for Hell's terrors, and its doom abhorred,
> I guard my soul from act or thought of ill;
>
> But 'tis Thyself—to see Thy members pure
> Outstretched in pain upon the bitter tree;
> It is the thought of all Thou didst endure,
> Thine agony and death—and all for me!
>
> Thy love it is, Thy love, which moves me so
> That if there were no Hell of darkness drear
> And if there were no shining heaven above me,
> Yea, though I lost the hope wherewith I glow,
> And though I feared not that which most I fear,
> Even as I love Thee now, I still should love Thee.

THERESA'S disciple, JUAN DE YPEZ Y ALVAREZ, 1542-1591, better known as JOHN OF THE CROSS, was 'a massively virile contemplative' who gave almost unrestrained expression to the emotional element in mysticism. "There are moments when his prose style is of extreme clearness and force, but in many cases he soars to heights where the sense reels in the attempt to follow him."

In *The Ascent of Mount Carmel* he traced the steps of the austere self-discipline which he considered to be necessary for the attainment of the contemplative life.

> The letter killeth, the spirit quickeneth; we must therefore reject the literal sense, and abide in the obscurity of faith.

> He that will abide on the letter of the divine locutions or on the intelligible form of vision, will of necessity fall into delusion; for he does not yield to the Spirit in detachment from sense.

> One act of the will, wrought in charity, is more precious in the eyes of God, than that which all the visions and revelations of heaven might effect.

The Song of the Obscure Night of the Soul may have been inspired by its author's sufferings in prison, but it sounds an essential note of his mystical philosophy. He called the journey of the soul towards union with the Divine an Obscure Night, for three reasons. In the first place because the journey begins with the discipline of denying one's self all pleasure in the things of this world; then, because the soul must travel by the obscure way of faith; and finally, because God, Who is the goal of desire, is incomprehensible.

> In an obscure night,
> With anxious love inflamed,
> O happy lot!
> Forth unobserved I went
> My house being now at rest......
>
> O guiding night!
> O night more lovely than the dawn!
> O night that hast united
> The lover with his beloved
> And charged her with his love.

The Living Flame of Love, and *The Spiritual Canticle*
are also among his works, none of which were published
during his lifetime. They became known to the world at
large in 1618. JOHN OF THE CROSS realised his own limitations, for he wrote in *The Spiritual Canticle:*

> It would be foolishness to think that the language of
> love and the mystical intelligence can be at all explained
> in words of any kind. . . . It is better to leave the out-
> pourings of love in their fulness, that every one may
> apply them according to the measure of his spirit and
> power, than to pare them down to one particular sense
> which is not suited to the taste of every one.

> One of the greatest favours, bestowed transiently on
> the soul in this life, is to enable it to see so distinctly
> and to feel so profoundly, that it cannot comprehend
> Him at all. These souls are herein, in some degree,
> like the Saints in Heaven, where they who know Him
> most perfectly perceive most clearly that He is infinitely
> incomprehensible; for those who have the less clear
> vision do not perceive so distinctly as the others how
> greatly He transcends their vision (*Spiritual Canticle,*
> vii. 10).

Although PEDRO MALON DE CHAIDE OF CASCANTE,
1530-1590, professed a distrust of secular literature, he
nevertheless followed the most learned models when writing
his *Conversion of the Magdalene.* The severity of his teaching combined with the rich sumptuousness of his style have
"ensured him permanent popularity." In his poetical paraphrase of the *Song of Solomon* he imitated the fervour,
without copying the sensuous imagery, of JOHN OF THE
CROSS. JOHN OF THE ANGELS, fl. 1595, is a better representative of pure mysticism. His work entitled *The
Triumph of the Love of God* is "a profound psychological

study," in which spiritual insight is matched with a fine style notable for its beauty of language.

In England the ideals and aspirations of mysticism had an excellent exponent in RICHARD CRASHAW, 1612-1649. He is the most mystical of English poets; his work is characterised by "power and wealth of invention, dazzling intricacy of meaning, choice and subtle speech." He is one of the 'erotic' mystics of which there are very few in English literature; he describes his love for God with an ardour that has never been surpassed. The greater part of his volume entitled *Steps to the Temple: Sacred Poems, with other Delights of the Muses*, 1646, consists of "religious poetry, in which the poet addresses the Saviour, the Virgin Mary, and Mary Magdalene, with all the passionate earnestness and fevour of a lover."

> Here, where our Lord once laid His head
> Now the grave lies buried.
>   (*Upon the Sepulchre of our Lord.*)

> Come, lovely Name! Life of our hope!
> Lo, we hold our hearts wide ope!
> Unlock Thy cabinet of Day,
> Dearest Sweet, and come away.
>   . . . . . .
> Sweet Name! in Thy each syllable
> A thousand blest Arabias dwell;
> A thousand hills of frankincense;
> Mountains of myrrh and beds of spices,
> And ten thousand paradises,
> The soul that tastes Thee takes from thence.
> (*Hymn to the Name above every Name, the Name of Jesus.*)

Another of the so-called metaphysical poets, HENRY VAUGHAN, 1621-1695, commonly styled 'The Silurist,' wrote much that is tedious and obscure in his poems and meditations entitled *Silex Scintillans, or Sacred Poems and Private Ejaculations*, 1650, but the imperfections are redeemed by much that is fine.

Mornings are mysteries; the first world's youth,
Man's resurrection, and the future's bud,
Shroud in their births; the crown of life, light, truth,
Is styled their 'starre,' the 'stone,' and 'hidden food.'
Three blessings wait upon them, two of which
Should move; they make us holy, happy, rich.

The Flowers of Solitude, 1652, and *The Mount of Olives,* of the same year are devotional prose pieces. *The Retreate* and *Beyond the Veil* "are universally counted amongst the purest and most exquisite reflective pieces of the age in which VAUGHAN lived."

Happy those early days, when I
Shined in my angell-infancy!
Before I understood this place
Appointed for my second race,
Or taught my soul to fancy ought
But a white, celestiall thought;
                    (*The Retreate.*)

Dear beauteous Death! the jewel of the just,
        Shining no where but in the dark;
What mysteries do lie beyond thy dust,
        Could man outlook that mark!

He that hath found some fledg'd bird's nest may know
        At first sight if the bird be flown;
But what fair well or grove he sings in now,
        That is to him unknown.
                    (*The Veil.*)

Pietism in England owed much of its development to the influence of the little book mentioned by JOHN BUNYAN as one of the two belonging to his wife. This was *The Practice of Pietie,* 1613, by LEWIS BAYLY, d. 1631, Bishop of Bangor. The vigour of its style and the devout spirit it reveals are marred by occasional coarseness of expression; it was however a thoroughly representative book of devotion in its day.

Mysticism could not escape criticism. The Dominicans ignored it; the Jesuits formally denied its doctrine, even though some of the outstanding mystical writers of the seventeenth century were members of the Society of Jesus. The very possibility of the prayer of silence and of spiritual sleep was denied by THEOPHILE RAYNAUD, 1583-1663, in his book entitled *So-called Spirituality,* 1665. He was a prolific writer who left his works unpublished; ninety-two of them were published after his death by his confrère FR. JOHN BERTET.

Anti-mystical criticism was elaborated in detail by FRANCISCO SUAREZ, in a work entitled *The Virtue of Religion,* and by GIOVANNI BONA, 1609-1674, in his book *The Way of Approach to God,* 1657.

Mysticism passed into Quietism. This was a development of that spiritual 'passivity' which had been advocated by many ardent mystics who cherished an ideal of absolute surrender to God. The conception of God as the active agent in the soul's bliss and perfection was separated from the ideals of self-discipline and service by JUAN FALCONI, 1596-1638, the author of *The Alphabet and Letters.* This fine work contains "with unsurpassed directness and clearness, the central doctrine of Quietism: an exhortation to the production of one single lively act of Faith, which will then continue uninterruptedly through the whole earthly life into eternity . . ."[4]

His view influenced MIGUEL DE MOLINOS, 1640-1697, whose mystical treatise of great interest entitled *The Spiritual Guide,* 1675, became the text-book of the Quietists. In this work MOLINOS laid emphasis upon the 'negative way' of the neo-Platonists in order to encourage the cultivation of an 'empty' consciousness. A series of *Brief Tracts* appeared from his pen in 1681, with the approval of five reputable theologians. These works became so generally popular that the Inquisition forbade criticism of them.

---

[4] F. von Hugel, *The Mystical Element in Religion,* 2d ed., Vol. II., p. 144.

If thou receivest an injury from any man remember
that there are two things in it, viz., the sin of him who
does it, and the suffering which is inflicted on thyself.
The sin is against the will of God, and it greatly dis-
pleases Him though He permits it. But the suffering,
which thou art called to endure, is not in opposition
to His will. But on the contrary, He wills it for thy
good. Wherefore, thou oughtest to receive it as from
His hand (*The Spiritual Guide*).

The doctrines of MOLINOS were spread throughout France
by FRANCOIS MALAVAL, 1627-1719, who wrote *The Practice of the True Life: Mystic Theology*, 1670. But it was
owing to JEANNE MARIE DE LA MOTHE GUYON, 1648-
1717, that Quietism acquired its notoriety and became the
subject of a long and bitter controversy. MADAME DE
GUYON was converted to a religious life in 1668, and in
1672 under the direction of Genivieve Granger she signed
a marriage contract with Jesus Christ.

I henceforth take Jesus Christ to be mine. I promise
to receive Him as a husband to me. And I give myself
to Him, unworthy though I am, to be His spouse. I
ask of Him, in this marriage of spirit with spirit, that
I may be of the same mind with Him—meek, pure,
nothing in myself, and united in God's will. And
pledged as I am to be His, I accept, as part of my marriage portion, the temptation and sorrows, the crosses
and the contempt which fell to Him.
                    Jeanne M. B. De La Mothe Guyon.
Sealed with her ring.

In 1680 she began a correspondence with FRANCIS LA
COMBE, d. 1714, who had published a small treatise entitled
A Short Letter of Instruction, and a more ambitious work
An Analysis of Mental Prayer. This latter work was con-

demned as heretical in 1688; its author was imprisoned until a few months before his death.

During a stay at Grenoble in 1685 MADAME DE GUYON began a series of practical and devotional Commentaries on the Bible. These were ultimately published in 20 volumes with the title *The Holy Bible, or the Old and New Testament with Explanations and Reflections Regarding the Interior Life*, 1790. It was at Grenoble also that she wrote her famous and widely welcomed work *The Short and Easy Method of Prayer*, written, as the authoress says in her preface:

> . . . for a few individuals, who were desirous to love God with their whole heart . . .

> An unprejudiced reader may find, hidden under the most common expressions, a secret unction, which will excite him to seek after that Sovereign Good, whom all should wish to enjoy.

The principle of her Method will be seen in the following passage:

> . . when the senses are all recollected, and withdrawn from the circumference to the centre, and the soul is sweetly and silently employed on the truths we have read, not in reasoning, but in feeding thereon, and in animating the will by affection, rather than fatiguing the understanding by study; when, I say, the affections are in this state . . . . . we must allow them sweetly to repose, and peacefully to drink in that of which they have tasted: . . . . this method is, indeed, highly necessary; and will advance the soul farther in a short time, than any other in a course of years (chap. ii.).

During the same year she also wrote *The Spiritual Torrents*, which she speaks of as "an entire treatise on the principle of Faith, considered in its inward and sanctifying action." Her plan was to illustrate the progress of the soul by a reference to "streams or torrents, flowing from mountain tops . . . . . and mingling at last in the ocean."

MADAME DE GUYON met FENELON in 1688; later on she submitted her writings to him, and in 1689 wrote him a long letter in which she described how a completely dedicated soul attains inward crucifixion. This Letter is usually printed as a separate treatise entitled *A Concise View of the Soul's Return to God and of its Reunion with Him.* FENELON replied to this letter in 1689; but strong opposition was offered to Quietist teaching by PETER NICOLE, 1625-1695, the friend and literary associate of ARNAULD of Port Royal. His book was issued as *A Refutation of the Principle Errors of the Quietists,* 1694. MADAME DE GUYON replied to his criticisms in a work entitled *A Concise Apology for the Short and Easy Method of Prayer.* This book is very rich in valuable teaching and is an important contribution to the controversy; it was moreover a prelude to a more serviceable apology entitled *Justifications of the Doctrine of Madame De La Mothe-Guyon, Plainly explained, Proved and Authorised by the Holy Fathers, Greek, Latin, and Authors Canonical or Approved: written by herself,* 1694. This large and valuable work was designed to show that Quietism is in perfect accord with patristic teaching; the book contains a multitude of citations regarding the interior life.

Nothing however availed to resist the opposition against her and her doctrines. She was arrested and imprisoned at Vincennes in 1695, and after a brief release was again put under restraint—this time in the Bastille—where she remained from 1690 to 1702. She was then banished from Paris to the city of Blois for life.

The other prose writings of MADAME DE GUYON comprise *Christian and Spiritual Discourses on Divers Subjects Regarding the Interior Life,* taken for the most part from *the Scriptures; The Soul's Love for God;* together with many *Christian and Spiritual Letters. The Life of Madame de Guyon written by herself,* 1791, belongs to the class of great religious autobiographies. Of her state of privation and desolation which began in 1674 and continued for some six years, she writes:

> I seemed to myself cast down as it were from a throne of enjoyment like Nebuchadnezzar, to live among beasts—a very trying and deplorable state, when regarded independently of its relations, and yet exceedingly profitable to me in the end, in consequence of the use which Divine Wisdom made of it:
>
> I being in the Bastille said to Thee O my God! If Thou art pleased to render me a spectacle to men and angels Thy holy will be done! All that I ask is, that Thou wilt be with me and save those who love Thee.

The *Poems and Spiritual Songs* of MADAME DE GUYON are well known in the English translations made by WILLIAM COWPER.[5]

> Peace hath unveil'd her smiling face,
> And woos thy soul to her embrace;
> Enjoyed with ease, if thou refrain
> From earthly Love, else sought in vain;
> She dwells with all who Truth prefer,
> But seeks not them who seek not Her.
>
> Yield to the Lord, with simple heart,
> All that thou hast, and all thou art;
> Renounce all strength but strength divine,
> And peace shall be for ever thine:
> Behold the path which I have trod,
> My path, 'till I go home to God.
>   (*The Entire Surrender.*)

The elastic and exquisite FRANCOIS DE SALIGNAC DE LE MOTHE FENELON, 1651-1715, became the most notable

[5] *Poetical Works,* Oxford ed. (1913), pp. 478-520.

product of French Quietism. Although partly won over to the teaching of MADAME DE GUYON he was lacking in the temper that makes for utter self-committal. He has been described as "the Jesuits friend without ever becoming their slave and opposed to the Port Royalists without ever being their enemy."

FENELON became the favourite pupil of BOSSUET and at his suggestion wrote *A Treatise on the Existence of God,* part one, 1712, part two, 1718, to correct some metaphysical errors of Malebranche. His *Dialogues on Eloquence,* 1712, sustained a plea for naturalness and simplicity in preaching. Perhaps the most influential of all his writings was *A Treatise on the Education of Girls,* 1687, the first systematic treatise on the whole question of female training. As an educationalist he also wrote *The Adventures of Telemachus,* 1699, "a political novel with a purpose."

During the year 1695 BOSSUET gave much earnest thought to Quietism and wrote a learned *Treatise on the States of Prayer,* in which he dealt with MADAME DE GUYON'S book and criticised her teaching as "seeking sublimity and perfection in things which do not exist, or at all events do not exist in this life." An episcopal Commission drew up thirty-four articles concerning Quietism and the states of prayer, which FENELON signed, and after the Commission disbanded BOSSUET began one of the ablest of his works *Instructions on the States of Prayer.* He submitted the MS. to FENELON in 1696, but FENELON withheld his approval because of its harsh references to the opinions and character of MADAME DE GUYON. He was not satisfied with expressing disapproval, but issued *An Interpretation of the Maxims of the Saints on the Inner Life,* 1697, "in which he restated MADAME GUYON'S fundamental convictions in a more cautious and sober way."

The holy soul delights in acts of contemplation; to think of God and of God only. But the contemplative state, existing without any interruption, is hardly consistent with the condition of things in the present life. It may be permitted to exist, however, and ought not to be resisted in its approach . . .

This is the doctrine of many experimental and theological writers—of St. Clement of Alexandria, of St. Gregory Nazianzen, St. Augustine, Pope St. Gregory, St. Thomas, Bernard, Cassian, and others (Art. 22).

We find in some devout writers on inward experience, the phrase Spiritual Nuptials. It is a favourite method with some of these writers to represent the union of the soul with God by the figure of the bride and bridegroom.

We are not to suppose that such expressions mean anything more, in reality, than that intimate union which exists between God and the soul, when the soul is in the state of pure love (Art. 41).

About a month after the publication of this work, BOSSUET'S book, entitled *Instructions on the States of Prayer*, appeared. FENELON'S *Maxims* created intense excitement, it was submitted to Rome for judgment, and while it was still under consideration he prepared a Latin translation of it as well as of his remarkably rich *Pastoral Instruction*, and of his reply to *The Declaration* of BOSSUET.

BOSSUET was now thoroughly roused, and issued *The Traditionary History of the New Mystics*, 1696, in which he examined the opinions of CLEMENT of Alexandria and some passages of the writings of pseudo-DIONYSIUS. He then published, in 1697, the first of a series of *Memoirs of the Bishop of Meaux, addressed to the Archbishop of Cambray, on the Maxims of the Saints.* These *Memoirs* included *The Doctrinal Summary, The Declaration, The New Question,*

and *The Little Questions.* FENELON maintained his side
of the controversy with brilliance and power. His wonderfully clear and sober *First Reply to the Difficulties of the
Bishop of Chartres,* like his admirably penetrating *Letter
concerning Passive Prayer,* and his *Letter concerning Charity,*
served to increase the influence of moderate Quietism.

BOSSUET, surprised at the strength and skill of his opponent, made a still more vigorous effort and wrote *A History
of Quietism, particularly that of Madame Guyon, Containing
her Life, Prophecies, and Visions,* 1698, a work in which he
combined narrative with argument; he drew upon private
and confidential papers and letters weaving them into the
substance of his work with a skill that evoked universal admiration.

FENELON'S supporters were greatly disturbed by this fine
work, but he prepared *An Answer to the History of Quietism,* one of the noblest effusions "of the indignation of in-
sulted virtue and genius" ever written.

> He who reads my heart knows that I hold neither
> to any person nor any book; that I am bound only to
> Him and to His Church; that I ask continually with
> many a sigh before His Presence for restored peace, and
> an end to these days of scandal; I ask Him to restore
> His shepherds to their flocks, to gather them together
> in His fold, and to grant to M de Meaux as many
> blessings as he has showered crosses on me.

Stung by the effect of this work BOSSUET issued *Remarks
upon the Reply to the History,* to which FENELON made
answer in a pamphlet which strengthened the impression
he had already created. He was finally, at BOSSUET'S in-
stigation, banished from Versailles never to return.

An anonymous *History of the Origin, the Progress, and
the Condemnation of Quietism in France,* is generally as-

cribed to MONSIEUR PHELIPEAUX, an intimate friend of BOSSUET.

The controversy ended in the suppression of the movement which counted among its minor prophets ANTOINETTE BOURIGNON, 1616-1680, of Flanders. She was a Quietist "even more thorough-going, certainly more violent and less lovable" than MADAME DE GUYON.

When I am recollected in my solitude in a forgetfulness of all things, then my spirit communicates with Another Spirit and they entertain one another as two friends who converse about serious things.

Better known is NICHOLAS HERMAN of Lorraine, 1610-1691, Brother Lawrance, who made a popular appeal on behalf of the devotional spirit of Quietism. His much appreciated book, entitled *The Practice of the Presence of God*, is a winsome work in which religious simplicity is united with a rare practical sagacity. His less popular *Book of Maxims* is intended to serve as a guide to those who are seeking the Divine Presence.

The mystical temper shows itself in many forms, especially in forms of fervent devotion. A popular treatise entitled *The Heart of Christ in Heaven towards Sinners on Earth*, 1643, written by the English Congregationalist THOMAS GOODWIN, 1600-1680, became a powerful influence in the mind of MARGARET MARY ALACOQUE of Paray-le-Monial, 1647-1690. To her visions is due the realistic form in which the present devotion to the Sacred Heart of Jesus has attained its wide popularity.

ALFONSO MARIA DI LIGUORI, 1696-1787, "the most influential Roman theologian since the days of the Counter Reformation," was the author of a large devotional book *The Glories of Mary*, 1750, which has become universally famous. LIGUORI wrote it to counteract what he regarded as a veiled attack upon the simple acts of devotion to Mary which formed an important part of the Neapolitans' worship in his day.

In this work he exalts Mary to the highest honours, and in order to accomplish this he quotes a multitude of legends and many sayings as from the Fathers with an inaccuracy that has become proverbial.

LIGUORI exercised an even stronger influence in another direction. In 1648 he published his views on morals in a *Commentary* on a text-book entitled *Medulla*, written by HERMANN BUSENBAUM. This *Commentary*, when rewritten, became the celebrated treatise entitled *Moral Theology*, 1753, which was much enlarged in 1755, and in its Latin version was renamed *The Apostolic Man*. "The gist of his system (known as equiprobabilism) is that the more indulgent opinion may always be followed, whenever the authorities in its favour are as good, or nearly as good, as those on the other side."

> A doubtful law does not bind. But when two opposite opinions are equally or nearly equally probable, you have a strict doubt as to the existence of the law. Therefore the law, being only doubtfully promulgated, has no binding force. Therefore it is true that you can follow an equally probable opinion in favour of liberty.

The literature of 'Platonic mysticism' was much enriched by the Cambridge Platonists, a group of thinkers who exercised far reaching influences on English religious thought. They represented the greater thoughts of their age on the questions that had been raised by various sects which were equally disliked by Puritans and Prelatists. *A Testimony of the Ministers in the Province of Essex*, 1647, described these sectaries as "Anti-Scripturists, Familists, Antinomians, Anti-Trinitarians, Arians, Anabaptists." *A Testimony Subscribed by the Ministers within the Province of London*

against the Errors, Heresies, and Blasphemies of these Times,
1648, called them "the very dregs and spawn of old accursed
heresies which had been already condemned, dead, buried
and rotten in their graves, long ago."

The Cambridge Platonists lifted the discussion to the high
levels of refined thought. They made "the first elaborate
attempt to wed Christianity and philosophy" from the Protestant side.

BENJAMIN WHICHCOTE, 1609-1683, was the earliest of
the group, and "in a true sense he may be said to have
founded the new school of philosophical theology."[6]   In
Four Letters to his former tutor Tuckney he dealt with the
main points of his contention against orthodox Puritanism.

"Two years after his death appeared a small volume of
eight sheets under the title *God-borne Opinions: or, some
Select Notions of that Learned and Reverend Divine, Dr. B.
Whichcote. Faithfully Collected by a Pupil and Particular
Friend of His.* The volume consists of notes on a few texts
of Scripture and a series of what the editor calls 'Apostolical
Apothegms' . . . . Then in 1697 there was published *A
Treatise of Devotion, with Morning and Evening Prayer
for all the Days of the Week* . . . . In the following year
his *Select Sermons* were printed in two parts."[7]

> There is no inconsistency between the grace of God
> and the calling upon men carefully to use, improve, and
> employ the principles of God's creation . . . . Indeed,
> this is a very profitable work to call upon men to an-
> swer the principles of their creation, to fulfil natural
> light, to answer natural conscience, to be throughout
> rational in what they do; for these things have a divine
> foundation. *The spirit of man is the candle of the*

---

[6] John Tulloch, *Rational Theology in the XVII Century*, Vol. II.,
p. 45.

[7] *Ibid.,* p. 94.

Lord, lighted by God, and lighting man to God (Sermon on the Exercise and Progress of a Christian).

Among the *Aphorisms* are the following:

Those that differ upon reason may come together by reason.

Nothing is desperate in the condition of good men, they will not live and die in any dangerous error.

The state of religion lies in a good mind, and a good life; all else is about religion; and men must not put the instrumental part of religion for the state of religion.

WHICHCOTE'S ancient and most learned friend RALPH CUDWORTH, 1617-1688, is the most celebrated and the most systematic and formal writer of the group. In 1642 he published *A Discourse concerning the True Nature of the Lord's Supper.* It contains an introduction and six chapters in which the author expounds with a wealth of quotation his idea of the Sacrament as a feast upon sacrifice. It is

not the offering of something up to God upon an altar, but the eating of something which comes from God's altar, and it is set upon our tables.

Another publication of the same time is entitled *The Union of Christ and the Church; in a Shadow,* in which he teaches that the marriage relation is a true, and not an accidental, likeness of the relation between Christ and His Church. In 1644, in two *Theses* for his divinity degree he discussed in Latin verse, *The Nature of Good and Evil,* and *The Existence of Incorporeal Substances.* CUDWORTH'S great work is *The True Intellectual System of the Universe: the first part, wherein all the reason and philosophy of atheism is confuted and its impossibility demonstrated,* 1678. This enormous effort to prove that the existence of God, moral distinctions, and human freedom are grounded in the nature of things was never finished. *A Treatise concerning Eternal and Immutable Morality*, 1731, and *A Treatise on Free Will*, published long afterwards, 1837, were parts of the unfinished project.

The *True Intellectual System* was the outcome of CUDWORTH'S meditations on the questions raised by Hobbes in his *Leviathan*, 1651. The massive style of its thoughts is wholly unrelieved by any literary grace but "taken as a whole, it is a marvellous magazine of thought and learning and remains one of the most undoubted monuments of the philosophical and theological genius of the seventeenth century."

Against various forms of fatalism which misrepresent the true order of the universe he sets forth his own philosophy:

> These three things are the fundamentals or essentials of true religion—namely, that all things do not float without a head and governor, but there is an omnipotent understanding Being presiding over all; that God hath an essential goodness and justice; and that the difference of good and evil moral, honest and dishonest, are not by mere will and law only, but by nature. . . . . (These three) taken altogether, make up the wholeness and entireness of that which is here called 'The True Intellectual System of the Universe,' in such a sense as Atheism may be called a false system thereof.

The typical mystic of the school was HENRY MORE, 1614-1687, who could never swallow the severe Calvinistic doctrines. "He was a voluminous author. His writings fill several folio volumes; they are in verse as well as prose; they were much read and admired in their day; but they are now wellnigh forgotten."[8] His states of mind before

---

[8] *Ibid.*, p. 303.

and after he found light and peace are reflected in two epigrams:

> Know I:
> Nor whence nor who I am, poor wretch!
> Nor yet—oh, madness!—whither I must goe:....
> Lies, night-dreams, empty toys, fear, fatal love,
> This is my life: I nothing else do see.
>
> I come from heaven; am an eternal ray
> Of God; O joy! and back to God shall go....
> Faith, wisdom, love, fix'd joy, free winged might,
> This is true life: all else death and decay.

In 1640 he embodied his religious thoughts in a poem
called *Psychozoia, or the Life of the Soul;* this was published in 1642 along with *Psychathanasia; or, the second
part of the Song of the Soul.* Four other poems on similar
subjects, with some lesser pieces, were gathered with these earlier works into a volume of *Philosophical Poems,* 1647,
which is now forgotten.

His first prose publication was the *Antidote against Atheism,* 1652; the next year he issued *Cabbalistical Conjec-
tures, or Attempt to Interpret the Three First Chapters of
Genesis in a Threefold Manner—Literal, Philosophical and
Mystical, or Divinely Moral.* *Triumphant Enthusiasm* was
published in 1656, *The Immortality of the Soul,* in 1659,
and *An Explanation of the Grand Mystery of Godliness,* in
1660. A companion, but contrasted, work was his *Enquiry
into the Mystery of Iniquity,* 1664, in which he discussed
first the papacy and next the subject of anti-Christ. His
better known *Handbook of Ethics, or Manual of Morals,*
1666, was succeeded by the only one of his works which
"can be said to have retained any literary popularity, or to
be commendable to the modern reader," the *Divine Dia-
logus,* 1668. He published a *Prophetical Exposition of the
Seven Epistles to the Seven Churches of Asia,* 1669, *A Criticism of the Teutonic Philosophy,* 1670, against the teaching
of JACOB BOEHME, and *A Handbook of Metaphysics,* 1671.

"The *Divine Dialogues* are certainly, on the whole, the most interesting and readable of all More's works . . . . the style is here and there fresh and powerful . . . . (they condense) his general views in philosophy and religion."[9]

> When I had arrived to riper years of reason, and was imbued with some slender rudiments of philosophy, I was not then content to think of God in the gross only, but began to consider His nature more distinctly, accurately, and to contemplate and compare His attributes; . . . . I did confidently conclude that infinite power, wisdom, and goodness, were the chiefest and most comprehensive attributes of the divine nature, and that the sovereign of these was His goodness, the summity and power, as I may so speak, of the divinity . . .

JOHN SMITH, 1618-1652, was the greatest of WHICHCOTE'S pupils and the true Platonist of the group; in some respects the most remarkable, the richest and most beautiful mind, and certainly by far the best writer of them all except NATHANIEL CULVERWELL. Such of his papers as were "homogenical and related to the same discourse" were issued after his death as ten *Select Discourses*, 1660. Of all the products of the Cambridge Platonists these *Discourses* are perhaps the highest; their choice literary style, their refined and high thought have kept them alive. "Profound glimpses of spiritual truth everywhere open to the reader as he advances, charmed with the rich unfoldings of an exuberant intelligence, rejoicing in the amplitude of its powers and the sweep and glory of its flight."

> He that is most practical in divine things hath the purest and sincerest knowledge of them, and not he that is most dogmatical. Divinity, indeed, is a true efflux from the eternal light, which, like the sunbeams,

9 *Ibid.*, p. 344.

does not only enlighten, but heat and enliven, and therefore our Saviour hath in His beatitudes connected purity of heart with the beatifical vision" *(Discourse 1)*.

True religion never finds itself out of the infinite sphere of the Divinity; and wherever it finds beauty, harmony, goodness, love, ingenuity, wisdom, holiness, justice, and the like, it is ready to say, here and there is God *(Discourse 9)*.

JOHN NORRIS, 1657-1711, in a work entitled *Reason and Revelation or the Grounds and Measures of Devotion,* 1689, coined the phrase "seeing all things in God" in which the characteristic note of the school was expressed. His most popular book was *Miscellanies,* 1687, but his *Root of Liberty,* 1685, and *Christian Blessedness,* 1690 were also useful in helping to form Latitudinarian opinion. In *The Theory of the Ideal or Intelligible World,* part one, 1701, part two, 1704, he handed on the torch of idealism until it was caught by the vigorous hands of Berkeley.

The other members of the group were less important. RICHARD CUMBERLAND, 1632-1718, secured an important place in the history of British philosophy by writing the first treatise against Hobbes. This was his *Philosophical Disquisition of the Laws of Nature,* 1672. JOHN GLANVILLE, 1636-1680, defended the paradoxical view that scepticism helps faith. NATHANIEL CULVERWELL, d. 1651, author of *A Discourse of the Light of Nature,* 1652; THEOPHILUS GALE, 1628-1678; and JOHN PORDAGE, 1607-1681, were also of the company of the Cambridge Platonists.

PART VII

THE MODERN PERIOD
(1600-1800)

CHAPTER XXXIV

THE ENLIGHTENMENT

A growing deference to the claims of reason as against the demands of authority characterised the Post-Reformation period. The turning-point in this transition, so far as theology was concerned, may be dated 1637 when RENE DESCARTES, 1596-1650, published his *Discourse on Method*.

JOHN LOCKE, 1632-1704, attacked the philosophy which DESCARTES had propounded in the *Method*, and issued his equally influential *Essay concerning the Human Understanding*, 1690; and BARUCH DE SPINOZA, 1632-1677, transformed the new teaching into pantheism. The famous *Theological and Political Tract*, 1670, in which SPINOZA expressed his views is described in the subtitle as "Certain attempts to show that perfect liberty to philosophise is not only compatible with devout piety and with the peace of the State; but, moreover, to take away that liberty is to destroy the public peace and also all real piety itself."

This work was important not only for philosophy but also for biblical interpretation. After discussing prophecy, the prophets, the Divine purpose with the Hebrews, the Divine Law, the reason why ceremonies were appointed in olden days, and miracles, SPINOZA deals with the exposition of the Scriptures in chapter seven. He thus defines the true rule of interpretation:

> Nothing must be imputed to the Scriptures save what is quite clearly derived therefrom.

LOCKE carried his rational principles into the realms of

religion by writing *The Reasonableness of Christianity,*
1695, in which he discussed the uncertainties attaching to
the meaning of 'justifying faith.' His aim was to show that
"the one and only gospel-article of faith is . . . . that Jesus
is the Messiah, the promised Saviour." This faith, followed
by repentance for sins and an honest effort to obey the commandments of Christ, is all that is required to make any one
a Christian.

His contention had been anticipated by ARTHUR BURY,
1624-1714, in *The Naked Gospel, to Free the Gospel from
Late Additions and Corruptions,* 1650. These efforts to go
back to the primitive simplicity of the Faith were seriously
attacked, and LOCKE thought it well to defend his statement
by writing a second book which he entitled *A Vindication
of the Reasonableness of Christianity,* 1695.

The road to the Deistic controversy in England was thus
opened; it was soon overcrowded with writers and thinkers
who were eager to reach the goal of pure rationalism. Lord
Herbert of Cherbury, 1583-1648, Charles Blount, 1654-
1693, Matthew Tindal, 1657-1733, William Wollaston,
1659-1724, Thomas Woolston, 1669-1733, Junius Janus,
John Toland 1670-1722, the Earl of Shaftesbury, 1671-
1713, Viscount Bolingbroke, 1678-1751, Anthony Collins, 1676-1729, Thomas Morgan, d. 1743, Thomas
Chubb, 1679-1747, Peter Annet, 1693-1769, and Henry
Dodwell the younger, d. 1784, all wrote with varying cogency and wisdom on the Deistic side. But great as was their
influence upon their own age the question of Edmund Burke
in his *Reflections on the Revolution in France,* 1790, becomes
more appropriate with each succeeding decade: "Who born
within the last forty years, has read one word of Collins and
Toland and Tindal and Chubb and Morgan and that whole
race who called themselves Free-thinkers?"

The deistic temper however showed its influence on the
literature of practical religion, as in the case of *The Whole*

Duty of Man, 1659. "Its author's name was never known, but it sprang at once into a semi-official position. It was chained in churches for the people to read. It was made the basis of instruction in the Charity schools. It was accepted as the recognised statement of sound and sober Church teaching."[1] The book represents the desire to reduce Christianity to its most prosaic elements. The religious man must deal with spiritual things:

> by the same rules of common reason, whereby he proceeds in his worldly business.

During this period much of the Christian literature of England took the form of controversial defences of the supernatural, in which the writers, while granting to reason its full place and rights, sought to save the fundamentals of the Faith from being dissipated into the dictates of self-interest, or the simple rules of common sense. "All forms of literature were drawn into the strife—essays, sermons, the philosophical treatise, the political pamphlet."

Besides their conflict with the common enemy, Deism, Christian writers in England were also involved in disputes among themselves concerning the Trinitarian, the Bangorian, and the Subscription controversies, each of which called forth its own literature.

The first specific attack on Deism was made by EDWARD STILLINGFLEET, 1635-1699, in *A Letter to a Deist,* 1677. He was an all-round controversialist who contended with the Catholics, the Socinians, and the representatives of the philosophy of LOCKE, as well as with the Deists. But in spite of this his chief work was his *Irenicum, a Weapon Salve for the Church's Wound . . . . etc.,* 1659, by which he tried to heal the breach between the Anglican and the Presbyterian communions in England. In this broad-minded

---

[1] G. R. Balleine, *History of the Evangelical Party in the Church of England,* p. 74.

work he described Christianity as a religion of peace and tolerance and asked:

> What possible reason can be assigned or given why such things should not be sufficient for communion with a Church which are sufficient for eternal salvation? And certainly those things are sufficient for that which are laid down as the necessary duties of Christianity by our Lord and Saviour in His Word. What ground can there be why Christians should not stand upon the same terms now which they did in the time of Christ and His apostles?

His lengthened preface to a treatise on *The Unreasonableness of Separation,* 1680, shows that he maintained this generous temper to a large extent, although he says, in that preface, that the *Irenicum* was "a book written twenty years since with great tenderness towards Dissenters before the laws were established." In a work entitled *Sacred Origins,* 1662, and again in a later book *A Defence of the Christian Doctrine of the Trinity,* 1697, he attempted to give a rational account of the Christian faith.

JOHN PEARSON, 1612-1686, made a solid and splendid contribution to the task of steadying belief when he wrote his learned *Exposition of the Creed,* 1659, excellent in arrangement, weighty in argument, and notable in style, its "very dross being gold."

> The day dies into a night, and is buried in silence and in darkness; in the next morning it appeareth again and reviveth, opening the grave of darkness, rising from the dead of night: this is diurnal resurrection. As the day dies into night, so doth the summer into winter: the sap is said to descend into the ground; the earth is covered with snow, or crusted with frost, and becomes a general sepulchre; when the spring ap-

peareth, all begin to rise; the plants and flowers peep out of their graves, revive and grow, and flourish: this is the annual resurrection.

In answer to the criticisms of JEAN DAILLE he issued a *Vindication of the Epistles of St. Ignatius,* 1672, defending their authenticity, and in 1682 he wrote another work of pure scholarship, the *Annals of Cyprian.* His *Two Dissertations on the Succession and Times of the First Bishops of Rome* were published posthumously, 1688.

The writer whom Dryden acknowledged as his model of style, JOHN TILLOTSON, 1630-1694, sought to refute the rationalists in his Sermons, which are characterised by great clearness of thought. He published *The Wisdom of being Religious,* 1663, and in 1666 he issued a controversial pamphlet entitled *The Rule of Faith,* in reply to *A Sure Footing in Christianity* by JOHN SARGENT.

> Truth is always consistent with itself, and needs nothing to help it out; it is always near at hand, and sits upon our lips, and is ready to drop out before we are aware: whereas a lie is troublesome, and sets a man's invention upon the rack, and one trick needs a great many more to make it good. It is like building upon a false foundation which continually stands in need of props to shore it up, and proves at last more chargeable than to have raised a substantial building at first upon a true and solid foundation; . . . . the crafty man . . . . is the last man that finds himself to be found out; and whilst he takes it for granted that he makes fools of others, he renders himself ridiculous (from Tillotson's last Sermon).

RICHARD CUMBERLAND, 1632-1718, accepted the utilitarian standard of the greatest good of the highest number as the law of morals, and applied his principles in an answer to Hobbes, entitled *A Philosophical Disquisition of the*

Laws of Nature, 1672. This is a learned but wordy treatise, the work of an acute thinker but a poor writer who was
the first to discuss natural law without using arguments
drawn from revelation. Hallam says that it "may be justly
considered as the herald, especially in England, of a new
ethical philosophy, of which the main characteristics were,
first, that it stood complete in itself without the aid of revelation; secondly, that it appealed to no authority of earlier
writers whatever, though it sometimes used them in illustration; thirdly, that it availed itself of observation and experience, alleging them generally, but abstaining from particular instances of either, and making, above all, no display
of erudition; and, fourthly, that it entered very little upon
casuistry, leaving the application of principles to the reader."[2]

CUMBERLAND summed up his theory of ethics in the sentence:

> No action can be morally good which does not in
> its own nature contribute somewhat to the happiness
> of men.

The "only writer of this period who lifted the argument
to a higher level, with some glimmer of historical perspec-
tive" was WILLIAM SHERLOCK, 1641-1707, a moderate,
rational, anti-enthusiastic theologian of whom Macaulay
says "perhaps no simple presbyter of the Church of England
has ever possessed a greater authority over his brethren than
belonged to Sherlock at the time of the Revolution." His
Vindication of the Doctrine of the Trinity, 1691, led him
into a controversy with South who charged him with being
a tritheist. In *A Discourse on Future Judgment,* 1692, as
also in a book entitled, *Divine Providence,* 1694, he handled
the argument from Nature in favour of the immortality of
the soul and the future state with conspicuous ability and
persuasive force.

---

[2] *Literature of Europe,* Vol. IV., p. 165.

The appeal to Nature was made with the greatest cogency by JOHN RAY, 1627-1705, whose famous treatise entitled *The Wisdom of God Manifested in the Works of Creation*, 1691, began the systematic and popular study of natural theology.

THOMAS SHERLOCK, 1678-1761, the son of William, published against Anthony Collin's deistic *Grounds of the Christian Religion*, a volume of Sermons, entitled *The Use and Interest of Prophecy in the Several Ages of the World*, 1725; and in reply to Thomas Woolston's *Discourses on the Miracles*, he wrote a volume entitled *The Tryal of the Witnesses of the Resurrection of Jesus*, 1729, which soon ran through fourteen editions. This characteristic specimen of the popular type of answer to the deistical views employs an elaborate parody of legal forms in order to give reality to the argument.

> The judge and the rest of the company were for bringing on the cause a week sooner; but the counsel for Woolston took the matter up, and said, Consider, sir, the gentleman is not to argue out of Littleton, Plowden, or Coke, authors to him well known; but he must have his authorities from Matthew, Mark, Luke, and John; and a fortnight is time little enough of all conscience to gain a familiarity with a new acquaintance; and turning to the gentleman, he said, I will call on you before the fortnight is out, to see how reverend an appearance you make behind Hammond on the New Testament, a Concordance on one hand and a folio Bible with references on the other.

No book of this period reached so high a reputation as *A Short and Easy Method with Deists, wherein the Certainty of the Christian Religion is Demonstrated by Infallible Proof from Four Rules*, 1697, written by CHARLES LESLIE, 1650-1722. He had previously written *A Short*

Method with the Jews, 1689, and these titles may have suggested to DANIEL DEFOE the name under which he published his anonymous satire in connection with another controversy, viz., *The Shortest Way with Dissenters*, 1702.

LESLIE sought to define the distinctive marks of the miracles of Scripture,—the characteristics that make them believable. His Four Rules were as follows: the facts to be judged must be capable of sensible proof; they must be public; they must be attested by enduring monuments; and these monuments must date from the age of the facts to which they bear witness. The purpose of the work was better than the performance, despite the verdict of Samuel Johnson who said "Leslie was a reasoner and a reasoner who was not to be reasoned against."

Other works from his pen were *The Socinian Controversy Discussed*, 1697; *The True Notion of the Catholic Church*, 1703; and *The Case Stated between the Church of Rome and the Church of England*, 1713.

Notwithstanding his suspected heterodoxy SAMUEL CLARKE, 1675-1729, was a vigorous opponent of Deism. Having issued *Three Essays on Baptism, Confirmation, and Repentance*, 1699, and *Some Reflections on that Part of a Book called Amyntor, or a Defence of Milton's Life, which Relates to the Writings of the Primitive Fathers and the Canon of the New Testament*, 1699, he delivered his famous Boyle Lectures. The first series was published in 1704, under the title *The Being and Attributes of God;* the second series bore the name *A Discourse on the Evidences of Natural and Revealed Religion*, 1705. The two series were afterwards united as *A Discourse concerning the Being and Attributes of God, the Obligations of Natural Religion, and the Truth and Certainty of the Christian Revelation in Opposition to Hobbes, Spinoza, the Author of the Oracles of Reason, and other Deniers of Natural and Revealed Religion.*

There was plainly a necessity of some particular revelation to discover in what manner, and with what kind
of external service, God might acceptably be worshipped. There was a necessity of some particular
revelation, to discover what expiation God would accept for sin, by which the authority, honour, and dignity of His laws might be effectually vindicated. There
was a necessity of some particular revelation, to give men
full assurance of the truth of those great motives of
religion, the rewards and punishments of a future
state, which, notwithstanding the strongest arguments
of reason, men could not yet forbear doubting of. In
fine, there was a necessity of some particular divine
revelation, to make the whole doctrine of religion clear
and obvious to all capacities, to add weight and authority to the plainest precepts, and to furnish men with
extraordinary assistances to enable them to overcome
the corruptions of their nature (Proposition vii. 1).

In a thesis for the degree of Doctor of Divinity CLARKE
argued: "that no dogma of the Christian faith given in
the Sacred Scriptures is discordant with right reason, and
that without freedom of human action no religion is possible."

His famous work entitled *The Scripture Doctrine of the
Trinity*, 1712, consists of a collection of New Testament
passages in which the doctrine is suggested, an exposition of
the doctrine, and a consideration of the passages in the Anglican liturgy which refer to it.

The critical spirit of the Enlightenment showed itself in
the satires of JONATHAN SWIFT, 1667-1745, whose misuse
of remarkable powers made his life an utter tragedy. His
Tale of a Tub, 1704, has been called a work of "overpow-
ering and overshadowing greatness." It is a satire on the
warring and jarring divisions of political Christianity; but

its theme melts away into a wide, ironic survey of all the beliefs, principles, creeds, and habits of humanity. In his misanthropic *Argument to Prove that the Abolishing of Christianity may be Attended with Some Inconveniences,* 1708, he so mocked at religious abuses as to make it doubtful whether his criticisms were in jest or in earnest:

> If Christianity were once abolished, how could the freethinkers, the strong reasoners, and the men of profound learning be able to find another subject so calculated in all points whereon to display their abilities . . . . We are daily complaining of the great decline of wit among us, and would we take away the greatest, perhaps the only topic we have left? Who would ever have suspected Asgill for a wit, or Toland for a philosopher, if the inexhaustible stock of Christianity had not been at hand to provide them with materials? What other subject through all art or nature could have produced Tindal for a profound author, or furnished him with readers?

The defence of Christianity brought many authors into the field. FRANCIS ATTERBURY, 1662-1732, one of the zealous divines whom Collins proposed to deport as missionaries to foreign lands, wrote a famous *Representation of the State of Religion,* 1711.

His literary ability was shown in the *Examination of Bentley's Dissertations on the Epistles of Phalaris,* 1698, which he wrote, although it was published as the work of Charles Boyle. Macaulay says, "It really deserves the praise, whatever that praise may be worth, of being the best book ever written by any man on the wrong side of a question of which he was profoundly ignorant." His Sermons are characterised by a style "not unworthy of the friend and critic of the most brilliant writers of the day . . . . and here and there . . . . the pathos has not entirely evaporated."

HUMPHREY PRIDEAUX, 1648-1724, who was long remembered for a solid work of reference entitled *The Old and New Testaments connected in the History of the Jews and Neighbouring Nations,* 1715-1717, tried to discredit the Deists equally with the Moslems in a polemical *Life of Mahomet,* 1697. He appended to this *Life* a *Letter to the Deists,* in which he thus defined the gist of the controversy:

> whether the Christian religion be a truth really given us by divine revelation from God our Creator; or else a mere human invention, contrived by the first propagators of it to impose a cheat upon mankind."

The deistic controversy was really brought to an end by CONYERS MIDDLETON, 1683-1750. He challenged the Deists' assumption of a breach of continuity between sacred and profane history. His *Letter from Rome Shewing an Exact Conformity between Popery and Paganism,* 1729, was a Protestant attack upon Catholicism. It was his *Introductory Discourse,* 1747, and *A Free Inquiry into the Miraculous Powers Claimed for the Post-Apostolic Church,* 1748, that overshadowed the deistic argument against miracles, and created the impression that he himself was an unbeliever. He denied the credibility of all miracles later than the age of the apostles.

With Hume's *Essay on Miracles* this work forms "the starting point for the discussion which exercised the next half century."

Strict orthodoxy had a champion in NATHANIEL LARDNER, 1684-1768, whose elaborate and laborious work *The Credibility of the Gospel History,* two volumes, 1727, twelve volumes, 1755, served the cause of apologetical theology for many years. His *Jewish and Heathen Testimonies to the Truth of Christianity,* 1764-1767, added much to the controversial resources of the Church.

"The best and clearest" of the replies made to Deism was by JOHN CONYBEARE, 1692-1755, in a work entitled *A Defense of Revealed Religion against the Exceptions of a Late Writer in his Book Intituled Christianity as Old as Creation, etc., 1732.* It contains an effective argument against the idea that religion is always and everywhere the same, but it adds nothing to the general nature of the answers to Deism —that natural religion needs to be supplemented by revelation.

JOHN LELAND, 1691-1766, also replied to Tindal in his *Defence of Christianity, 1733.* He answered Morgan's *Moral Philosopher* by his work on *The Divine Authority of the Old and New Testaments Asserted, 1738.* His two volumes written in the form of Letters under the title *Remarks on a Late Pamphlet entitled Christianity not founded on Argument, 1741,* criticised Dodwell's book of that name. In 1753 he issued his *Reflections on the Late Lord Bolingbroke's Letters on the Study and Use of History.*

LELAND'S chief and most valuable work however was his historical and critical *View of the Principal Deistical Writers that have appeared in England, 1754-1756.* This still remains as an indispensable contemporary guide for all students of the great controversy.

The writings of these apologists of the supernatural were only heralds of one of the masterpieces of Christian literature. JOSEPH BUTLER, 1692-1752, won a substantial victory in argument, and checked, and in a measure diverted, the deistic attack by his famous *Analogy of Religion, Natural and revealed, to the Constitution and Course of Nature, 1736.*

This crushing philosophical retort was divided into two parts; in the first part BUTLER showed that the deists' views of the course and constitution of nature fully justify faith in the future life, in divine government by means of rewards and punishments, and in a future probation; in the second part he showed that the essential elements of revealed religion are suggested in nature. The style of the work is heavy and the effort to crowd much thought into narrow room tends to make the writing rather involved, but few books have been more directly serviceable to the Church. *The Analogy* became a classic of theology. It obtained a success greater, perhaps, than any modern book of its kind. Its argument that all the objections raised against religion apply with equal cogency to the constitution of Nature, was unanswerable by the Deists of BUTLER's day.

> The analogy here proposed to be considered is of pretty large extent, and consists of several parts; in some more, in others less exact. In some few instances perhaps it may amount to a real practical proof; in others not so. Yet in these it is a confirmation of what is proved otherwise. It will undeniably show, what too many want to have shown them, that the system of Religion, both natural and revealed, considered only as a system, and prior to the proof of it, is not a subject of ridicule, unless that of Nature be so too. And it will afford an answer to almost all objections against the system both of natural and revealed Religion . . . .

BUTLER's antagonism to the moral teaching of Hobbes appears in the *Fifteen Sermons*, and in the *Dissertation on Virtue* appended to the *Analogy*. Of these the most important are the *Sermons upon the Love of God*, (Matt. xxii.37) to which the *Sermons upon Human Nature*, (Romans xii.4, 5) were a preface, and the *Sermons upon Compassion, Resentment*, and *Forgiveness*, a supplement.

> Our resignation to the will of God may be said to be perfect, when our will is lost and resolved up into

his; when we rest in his will as our end, as being itself most just, and right, and good. And where is the
impossibility of such an affection to what is just, and
right, and good, such a loyalty of heart to the Governor of the universe, as shall prevail over all sinister
indirect desires of our own? Neither is this at bottom
anything more than faith, and honesty, and fairness
of mind; in a more enlarged sense indeed, than those
words are commonly used *(Upon the Love of God)*.

The sum of the whole is plainly this. The nature
of man considered in his single capacity, and with respect only to the present world, is adapted and leads
him to attain the greatest happiness he can for himself
in the present world. The nature of man, considered
in his public or social capacity, leads him to a right behaviour in society to that course of life which we call
virtue *(Upon Human Nature)*.

The ground of controversy was shifted after David
Hume, 1711-1776, instituted a new type of attack upon
religious opinion.

The attention of the apologists was focussed upon evidences of the miraculous by Hume's celebrated *Essay on Miracles*, 1748, in which he claimed that no event could be sustained by such proof as would give it the evidential value of
a miracle. Other provocative works were *An Essay on Providence and a Future State*, 1748, and *Dialogues concerning
Natural Religion*, written in 1751 published in 1778, a
work in which the disputants are a supernaturalist, a deist,
and a sceptic. *The Natural History of Religion*, 1757, was
a powerful contribution to the deistic controversy; in it
Hume scouted the idea that a perfect and universal form of
natural religion had ever existed.

The first reply to Hume from the ranks of orthodoxy
was made by WILLIAM ADAMS, 1706-1789, in *An Essay*

on *Mr. Hume's Essay on Miracles,* 1752. This was a temperate and able statement of the ordinary and obvious argument that the divine power is an adequate cause for miracles, which are therefore sufficiently well proved.

GEORGE CAMPBELL, 1719-1796, made answer in *A Dissertation on Miracles,* 1763, in which he claimed that trustworthy testimony can prove the truth of miracles, and that the Christian miracles are adequately attested. This work "was and still is a valuable contribution to theological literature." It won a letter from Hume in reply to its contentions. CAMPBELL'S greater work was a *New Translation of the Gospels,* 1778, with valuable critical notes.

JOHN DOUGLAS, 1721-1807, replied to Hume in a *Criterion by which the True Miracles contained in the New Testament may be distinguished from those of Pagans and Papists,* 1752. This work took the form of a Letter to an unnamed correspondent, believed to be Adam Smith. It attempted to prove that so-called ecclesiastical miracles lack the sufficiency of evidence which warrants faith in the Gospel records of the miracles of Jesus. The historical part is curious and well written; it attacks the evidence for the miracles attributed to Loyola, Xavier, and the Jansenists.

The most conspicuous defender of the positions attacked by Hume was WILLIAM PALEY, 1743-1805, a typical apologist of his day, a clear and ready reasoner whose admirable lucidity and shrewd sense are wholly praiseworthy.[3] He was the moralist of utility as BUTLER was of conscience. He won fame by *The Principles of Moral and Political Philosophy,* 1785, which became the text-book on ethics in the University of Cambridge. He then wrote his more original and more celebrated *Horae Paulinae, or, the Truth of the Scripture History of St. Paul evinced by a Comparison of the Epistles which bear his Name with the Acts of*

---

[3] Cp. Sir Leslie Stephen, *English Thought in the Eighteenth Century,* 3d ed. (1902), Vol. I., p. 405-409.

the Apostles and with one another, 1790.   His only less famous *View of the Evidences of Christianity,* was written in 1794.

> The question is, whether falsehood was ever attested by evidence like this. Falsehoods, we know, have found their way into reports, into tradition, into books; but is an example to be met with of a man voluntarily undertaking a life of want and pain, of incessant fatigue, of continual peril; submitting to the loss of his home and country, to stripes and stoning, to tedious imprisonment, and the constant expectation of a violent death, for the sake of carrying about a story of what was false, and what, if false, he must have known to be so?   *(Horae Paulinae)*.
> . . . . they who acted and suffered in the cause, acted and suffered for the miracles; for there was no anterior persuasion to induce them, no prior reverence or partiality to take hold of.   Jesus had not one follower when he set up his claim.   His miracles gave birth to a sect *(View of the Evidences of Christianity)*.

PALEY'S *Natural Theology, or, Evidences of the Existence and Attributes of God collected from the Appearances of Nature,* 1802, is now forgotten although in some respects it is a remarkable book, and gives the best expression of the theology of the previous period.   It is a marvel of skillful exposition written in an excellent literary style.

> It is a happy world after all.   The air, the earth, the water, teem with delighted existence.   In a spring noon or a summer evening, on whichever side I turn my eyes, myriads of happy beings crowd upon my view. 'The insect youth are on the wing.' . . . . Suppose, then, what I have no doubt of, each individual of this number to be in a state of positive enjoyment; what a

sum, collectively, of gratification and pleasure have we
here before our view.

Of a totally different type was WILLIAM WARBURTON,
1698-1770, 'proud, pragmatical, and insolent,' a lawyer to
the backbone. He described his life as "a warfare upon
earth; that is to say with bigots and libertines . . . ." He
overwhelmed his purposes by the immensity and triviality
of his now worthless treatise entitled *The Divine Legation
of Moses, demonstrated on the Principles of a Religious
Deist from the Omission of the Doctrine of the Future State
of Rewards and Punishments in the Jewish Dispensation,*
1737-1741. His argument for the truth of the Mosaic religion rests on three propositions, viz., that the doctrine of
a future state of rewards and punishments is necessary to the
well-being of society; that the utility of this doctrine has
been admitted by all mankind; that this doctrine is not to
be found in the Mosaic dispensation. The argument wan-
ders through all knowledge. Samuel Johnson declared that
WARBURTON was "perhaps the last man who has written
with a mind full of reading and reflection."

"In 1776 appeared a very significant book by SOAME
JENYNS, 1704-1787, entitled *A View of the Internal Evidences of the Christian Religion,* in which prophecy and miracle were minimised, and Christianity was proved from
character alone." JENYNS regarded forgiveness, charity,
repentance, faith, and humility as the characteristic virtues
of Christianity, the work of which was to better mankind
and:

> to select the most meritorious of them to be succes-
> sively transplanted into the kingdom of heaven.
>
> To prove, therefore, the truth of the Christian relig-
> ion, we should begin by showing the internal marks
> of divinity which are stamped upon it: because on
> this the credibility of the prophecies and miracles in a

great measure depends: for if we have once reason to be convinced that this religion is derived from a supernatural origin, prophecies and miracles will become so far from being incredible, that it will be highly probable that a supernatural revelation should be foretold and enforced by supernatural means.

What Deism had attempted to do in England, the *philosophes* of France tried to achieve in their country. The anonymous work entitled *The Three Verities against the Atheists, Idolators, Jews, Mahommedans, and Schismatics,* 1593, an elaborate vindication of the Christian and Catholic religion, was the work of one suspected of infidelity. PIERRE BAYLE, 1647-1706, ranged himself against religion in his *Historical Dictionary,* 1695-1697. BERNARD LE BOVIER, of Fontenelle, 1675-1757, handled religious themes with reckless freedom in a famous allegory entitled *Rome and Geneva,* 1686, and in *The History of Oracles,* 1686. FRANCOIS MARIE AROUT DE VOLTAIRE, 1694-1778, devoted his versatile genius to this task of discrediting the religious condition of France; and so also did the Encyclopedists—Diderot, D'Alembert, etc.

The Christian reaction to their attacks produced no permanently great works of apologetic literature, although that reaction was both passionate and determined.

LOUIS GABRIEL AMBROISE, VICOMTE DE BONALD, 1754-1840, the theorist of authority and the metaphysician of the religious revival, wrote a highly conservative work entitled *The Theory of Political and Religious Authority,* 1796, in which he elaborated the view that society is neither the work of nature nor of man but is of God. Starting from the theory that language is of divine origin, he claimed that the first language contained the essence of all truth. Thence he proceeded to argue for the existence of God, for the divine inspiration and infallible authority of the Bible, and for the infallibility of the Roman Church.

JOSEPH MARIE COMTE DE MAISTRE, 1753-1821, who was an ecclesiastically-minded layman, insisted upon the absolute authority of the Papacy over the Anglican and Greek Churches as well as over the Church of Rome. His book entitled *The Pope*, 1817, in which he discussed this view created an immense sensation. He reviewed the religious condition of the age in *The Gallican Church*, 1821. In a much more popular work *The Soirees of St. Petersburg, or Conversations on the Temporal Government of Providence*, which was left unfinished at his death, DE MAISTRE elaborated his basic principle—the necessity of maintaining order in society and religion.

VOLTAIRE, the poet, the philosopher, and above all the critic, "poured forth a constant stream of fiery and witty invectives against the abuses of Church and State. All theological creeds and political shibboleths encountered his scathing sarcasms." His own claim was that he "combatted atheists."

In a poem entitled *The Law of Nature*, 1756, he outlined his theory that the sentiments of right and wrong are implanted in man by his Maker. This poem was published as *The Religion of Nature*, and as such fell under the ban, and was burned with the usual indignities by the public executioner. In it VOLTAIRE had sung:

> The God who made me did not make me in vain.
> He placed the seal of his divinity on the brow of every
> mortal. I cannot but know what has been ordained
> by my master. He has given me his law since he has
> given me existence. A morality, uniform in all places,
> speaks in the name of that God to ages without end.
> . . . . Of this everlasting worship Nature is the
> apostle . . . . From one end of the world to the

other it speaks, it exclaims: 'Adore a God, be just and cherish thy fatherland!'

In 1762 VOLTAIRE for the first time directly assailed the documents on which Judaism and Christianity are based, by sending forth the JUBILEE SERMONS "in which the seminal facts in the narratives of the Old and New Testaments were dealt with contemptuously, as absurd, often ridiculous, and sometimes pernicious, fictions." He repeated his exposition of the limitations of human knowledge in *A Profession of a Theist's Faith*, 1768, and continued his crusade against orthodoxy in *The Bible Fully Explained*, 1776, and in *The History of the Establishment of Christianity*, 1776. His religious position is stated in his *Examination of the Works of Lord Bolingbroke*, 1761:

> Every man of sense, every good man, ought to hold the Christian sect in horror. The great name of theist, which is not sufficiently revered, is the only name one ought to take. The only gospel one ought to read is the great book of nature, written by the hand of God, and sealed with his seal. The only religion that ought to be professed is the religion of worshipping God and being a good man. It is as impossible that this pure and eternal religion should produce evil, as it is that Christian fanaticism should not produce it.

France was unequal to the task of finding a competent theologian who could produce a first class apologetic for the faith which the criticisms of VOLTAIRE tended to dissolve and to replace with theism.

In Germany the rationalistic movement from 1740-1836 owed much to the English Deists, something to the Pietists, and not a little to the French critics of the supernatural.

The first definite trace of the Enlightenment appeared when HERMANN SAMUEL REIMARUS, 1694-1768, published *A Treatise on the Principal Truths of Natural Religion,* 1755, and left among his MSS. *An Apology for the Rational Worshippers of God.* In the latter work the historic evidences of Christianity were minutely discussed, and the religion was represented as having sprung from deliberate fraud. The main attack was directed against the doctrine of the Resurrection of Jesus. "Reimarus adduced in his discussion of the subject ten "irreconcilable contradictions" in the Gospel narratives of that event, and argued that narratives so inconsistent with each other were unworthy of credence." He had not purposed to publish the MS. but to let it "remain in secret for the use of understanding friends . . . . until the times had grown more enlightened."

GOTTHOLD EPHRAIM LESSING, 1729-1781, the illustrious dramatist and critic, was refused permission by the theological censorship in Berlin to publish parts of this Apology in 1771. Two years later he printed one piece, *On Toleration of the Deists,* in the *Wolfenbüttel Contributions.* In 1777 five other Fragments were issued in the same magazine. These were *On the Denunciation of Reason in the Pulpits; The Impossibility of a Revelation which all Men can believe on Grounds of Reason; The Passage of the Israelites through the Red Sea; That the Books of the Old Testament were not written to reveal a Religion;* and *On the Accounts of the Resurrection.* A final fragment, *On the Aims of Jesus and His Disciples,* was published separately in 1778.[4]

All these were then edited by LESSING as *Anonymous Wolfenbüttel Fragments,* 1784, and they acquired immense popularity. In 1787 other Fragments saw the light, and others again in 1850-1852.

LESSING expected that these publications would arouse controversy; the first attack upon them was made by DIRECTOR SCHUMANN of Hanover in a treatise entitled *On the*

---

[4] Cp. T. W. Rolleston, *Life of Lessing,* pp. 162-165.

Evidence of the Proofs of the Christian Religion, 1777, in which he insisted that the miracles recorded of Jesus together with His fulfilment of prophecy were "proofs of the Spirit and the Power." To his arguments LESSING made answer in *The Proof of the Spirit and the Power*, 1777, in which he contended that neither historical fulfilments of prophecy nor miracles could become "the very criterion of all truth" even though the best documentary evidences supported them.

An anonymous treatise entitled *A Defence of the Account of the Resurrection*, 1777, sought to refute in detail the objections offered by the Fragments to the evangelical records of the Resurrection of Jesus. LESSING replied to this work by writing *A Rejoinder*, 1778, "that most characteristic and most powerful of all his utterances," in the course of which he dealt with the offered explanations one by one, with the object of showing that "on any natural system of interpretation they were entirely inadequate."

> Not the truth of which any one is, or supposes himself to be, possessed, but the upright endeavour he has made to arrive at truth, makes the worth of a man. For not by possession, but by the investigation, of truth are his powers expanded, wherein alone his ever growing perfection consists. Possession makes us easy, indolent, proud,— If God held all truth shut in His right hand, and in His left hand nothing but the ever-restless instinct for truth, though with the condition of for ever and ever erring, and should say to me "Choose!" I should bow humbly to His left hand, and say, "Father, give! pure truth is for Thee alone!

The controversy waxed fast and furious. More than thirty separate works beside pamphlets and newspaper articles were launched against LESSING and the Fragments during the years 1778 and 1779.

JOHANN MELCHOIR GOEZE, 1717-1786, zealously took up the work of refuting LESSING; he gathered together a number of articles written against the Fragments and issued them with the title *Lessing's Direct and Indirect Attacks upon the Christian Religion and Scriptures, 1778.* This book made a personal attack upon the motives of LESSING as well as upon the positions maintained in the Fragments. GOEZE added to it a pamphlet entitled *Lessing's Weaknesses.*

In answer to these and similar strictures LESSING published once a week for eleven weeks a series of papers entitled *Anti-Goeze, 1778,* and "so marvellous was his use of all the resources of controversy that Goeze was at last fairly argued, or awed, into silence." The civil authorities forbade any further discussion although LESSING challenged "the most scrupulous theologian to point out a sentence in his writings which could lay him open to the charge of holding unorthodox views." He issued from Berlin a *Necessary Answer to a Very Unnecessary Question of Pastor Goeze, 1778,* in which he replied to the enquiry as to what he understood by Christianity and what religion did he profess, by pointing to the creeds of the Church as the authoritative standards of Christian doctrine. In a work entitled *Axioms, 1778,* he said:

> The letter is not the spirit, and the Bible is not religion. Consequently criticisms of the letter and of the Bible are not necessarily criticisms of the spirit and of religion. There was religion before there was a Bible. Christianity existed before the evangelists and the apostles wrote. The Christian religion is not true because the evangelists and apostles taught it; but the evangelists and apostles taught it because it is true.

The last of his replies to GOEZE was a book printed in Hamburg entitled *A First Sequel, 1778,* exposing the misinterpretation of a crucial passage in IRENAEUS concerning the place of the New Testament in the early Church. GOEZE thereupon retired from the fray covered with confusion. These Anti-Goeze polemics are among the few controversial writings of the world's literature which are creative rather than destructive.

LESSING formulated his religious views systematically in the inspiring little treatise *The Education of the Human Race,* 1780. In this work he gave expression to the view that religion is a progressive revelation of truth; it educates the race in the knowledge of God—Providence is the teacher, mankind is the pupil, the various systems of revelation are the text-book.

The first fifty-three paragraphs of the book were issued among the *Objections* to REIMARUS; with the fifty-fourth paragraph the theory is applied to Christianity, and the closing paragraphs apply it to the individual. In its complete form it was issued in 1780.

> It will come, the time of consummation, when man, however firmly his mind is convinced of an ever better future, will yet have no need to borrow motives for his conduct from that future. For he will do what is right because it is right, and not because arbitrary rewards are attached to it, which were merely intended to attract and strengthen his wandering attention so that he might recognise its inward and better rewards.

Although JOHANN SALOMO SEMLER, 1725-1791, published *A Reply to the Anonymous Fragments,* 1779, his attitude towards historical criticism won for him the title of the father of German rationalism, and to him may be traced the beginnings of that critical movement which was destined to transform the whole religious outlook. His "life typifies the entire critical process of the eighteenth century."

SEMLER'S literary output was very large; as many as a hundred and seventy-one works relating to Scripture, Church

History, Doctrine, and Practical Theology bear his name. His interest in the history of the Church was shown by the publication of three volumes of *Selected Chapters of Ecclesiastical History, 1767-1769*. His critical work began with the issue of his *Apparatus for the Free Interpretation of the New Testament, 1767*, which he followed up by writing a similar *Apparatus* for the Old Testament, 1773. "He was the first to reject with sufficient proof the equal value of the Old and the New Testaments, the uniform authority of all parts of the Bible, the divine authority of the traditional canon of Scripture, the inspiration and supposed correctness of the text of the Old and New Testaments, and, generally, the identification of revelation with Scripture."[5]

In an important *Treatise on the Free Investigation of the Canon*, issued in parts during 1771-1775, SEMLER overthrew the traditional view of the formation of the Canon, and proved that centuries had passed before the limits now recognised were definitely fixed. *An Introduction to Christian Doctrine freely expounded, 1774*, and *An Introduction to Baumgarten's Dogmatic, 1774*, show him as one of the first to open up the historical study of Christian doctrine. He "uttered the magic word which emancipated theology from the fetters of tradition." *An Experiment of a Freer Method of Teaching, 1777*, was a pioneer work in which the practical value of the historical method was explained.

SEMLER laid great stress upon the idea of 'accommodation' in teaching and argued that many of the stories of miracles, as well as some forms of the teaching of Jesus, were of the nature of concessions to the popular mind; this he claimed is the meaning of "He spake the Word to them as they were able to bear it."

SEMLER'S influence was continued and extended by the more able and prolific genius of JOHANN GOTTFRIED VON

[5] *Encyclopaedia Britannica*, 11th ed., Vol. XXIV., p. 630.

HERDER, 1744-1803, whose writings gave him the leadership of the 'Sturm und Drang' movement.

HERDER'S grasp of the idea of historical evolution enabled him to originate that genetic or historical method of literary study which now holds the field, and to infuse "into the lifeless learning of his day the glowing heat of a poetic soul." He laid the foundation of the comparative study of religion and mythology.

> Poetry, philosophy, history, are in my opinion, the three lights which illuminate the peoples, the sects, and the generations—a holy triangle.

An early fragment on *The Origin and Propagation of the first idea of Religion* was written in accordance with Hume's theory that religion was originally based on fear; a view that HERDER abandoned later on. He contributed to the study of primitive legends a work entitled *The Archaeology of the Hebrews* in which he expounded the theory that local legends become poetic myths, a theory which led him to regard the early stories of Genesis as divinely inspired poems. He explained his views in *The Oldest Document of the Human Race*, 1774, and as if to shew the uncertainty of immature theories he published *Interpretations of the New Testament from a newly opened Eastern Source*, the source being the Zend Avesta.

His *Songs of Love*, 1778, and *Maran Atha*, 1779 are among the best exegetical works in his theological writings. From the vagaries of poetic mysticism he recovered himself by the help of the axiom, "Christianity is the ideal religion and religion is ideal humanity." He insisted upon the need of studying the documents of Christianity, and wrote *Notes on the New Testament, The Christian Writings,* and *Letters on the Study of Theology*, 1780. In the last named work he maintained that:

The Bible must be read in a human manner, for it is a book written by men for men. The best reading of this divine book is human. The more humanly we read the Word of God, the nearer we come to the design of its Author, who created man in His image, and acts humanly in all the deeds and mercies, wherein He manifests Himself as our God.

The Spirit of Hebrew Poetry, 1782-1783, was the most significant and influential of all his theological writings. In it he searched into the primitive ideas of Deity, Creation, Providence, etc., contradicted Hume's theory that religion is the product of fear, and explained that it arises as an elucidation of the universe and becomes the vehicle of the ethical feelings of humanity.

. . . . it is the essential and distinctive character of man, and that which places him above all classes of beings merely animal, that he is susceptible of religion. The propensity to worship one or more superior beings is known to have been present among men in all nations and periods of the world, and why must this be derived only from anxiety and fear?

The movement towards critical study in all matters theological was strengthened by the efforts of JOHN AUGUSTUS ERNESTI, 1707-1781, who carried into biblical study the grammatical principles that he had already applied to the classics.

During the years 1760-1769 he issued ten volumes of *The New Theological Library*. In conjunction with SIEGMUND JACOB BAUMGARTEN, 1706-1757, he endeavoured to disengage "the current dogmatic theology from its many scholastic and mystical excrescences and so paved the way for a revaluation in theology." With this end in view he issued a second series of ten volumes, *The Latest Theological Library*, 1771-1775.

His *Method of Interpreting the New Testament*, 1775, exemplified his leading principle:

> the verbal sense of Scripture must be determined in the same way in which we ascertain that of other books.

He rejected the idea that a difference exists between the literal sense and the sense of the letter, as he also resisted the claim that the words of the Bible must be made to mean as much as they can.

> There is no other sense than the grammatical, and what the grammar yields.

JOHN DAVID MICHAELIS, 1716-1791, the successor of A. H. FRANCKE as Professor of Hebrew at Halle, freely handled the Old Testament records in *The Fundamental Exposition of the Mosaic Law*, 1770-1771.

The tendency towards naturalism which characterised the Enlightenment was carried to great lengths by HEINRICH EBERHARD GOTTLOB PAULUS, 1761-1851, who brought great Oriental learning to the study of Scripture; his leading principle is expressed in the canon: "that in the Gospels we must look for nothing but actual facts, not for poetry or legends, and that these facts were natural and not supernatural events, and that they had acquired the appearance of supernatural occurrences, or miracles, partly through the errors of commentators, partly through the erroneous apprehension and judgment of the narrators."[6]

His *Philological Key to the Psalms*, 1791, and *Philological Key to Isaiah*, 1793, were the precursors of a laborious *Philological Critical and Historical Commentary on the New Testament*, 1800-1804.

It was, however, by his *Life of Jesus as the Basis of a*

---

[6] Otto Pfleiderer, *The Development of Theology in Germany*, p. 211.

Purely Historical Account of Early Christianity, 1828, that
he carried the rationalistic method to extreme conclusions.
The work is divided into two parts, in the first of which
the Gospels are expounded section by section; the second
part contains a Synopsis with explanatory notes. In the
Preface PAULUS says:

> It is my chief desire that my views regarding the
> miracle stories should not be taken as by any means the
> principal thing. How empty would devotion or re-
> ligion be if one's spiritual well-being depended on
> whether one believed in miracles or no!
>
> The truly miraculous thing about Jesus is Himself,
> the purity and serene holiness of His character, which
> is, notwithstanding, genuinely human, and adapted to
> the imitation and emulation of mankind.

He applied his guiding principle to the Synoptic narratives in an *Exegetical Handbook to the First Three Evangelists,* 1830-1833. "His pet aversion was Schelling" whose
lectures on the *Philosophy of Revelation,* 1841, 1842, he
published with criticisms under the title, *The Philosophy of
Revelation at length revealed and set forth for General Examination, by Dr. H. E. G. Paulus,* 1842. For this dastardly
act SCHELLING dragged PAULUS into court, but was finally
obliged to resign his professorship.

A reaction in favour of 'rational supernaturalism' was
begun by KARL GOTTLIEB BRETSCHNEIDER, 1776-1848.
His theological views were represented in a work entitled *A
Systematic Development of all Earlier Ideas in Dogmatics according to the Symbolic Creeds of the Evangelical, Lutheran,
and Reformed Churches,* 1805. In *The Probability that the
Gospels and Epistles of the Apostle John are Natural and
Original presented to the Judgment of the Learned,* 1820, he
attacked the theory that the Fourth Gospel contains the earliest and most authentic account of the life of Jesus. The

essay consists of a collection of doubts that had been expressed at the close of the eighteenth century as to the authorship of John.   Notwithstanding his critical views, he repudiated the charge of rationalism to which his *Apology for
the Newer Theology of Evangelical Germany,* 1826, exposed
him.

JOHANN GOTTFRIED EICHORN, 1752-1827, "the founder
of modern Old Testament criticism" held and fortified the
ground so far won by legitimate historical methods. His
Introduction to the Old Testament, 1780-1783, is a landmark in biblical study, for it gives the first comprehensive
treatment of the Old Testament as literature. In 1804 in
An Introduction to the New Testament, he laid down the
rule which SEMLER, LESSING and HERDER had observed:
The New Testament writings are to be read as human books
and tested in human ways.

As a solution of the problem of the verbal agreements between the Synoptics he suggested that their common source
was an early Aramaic Gospel, of which many versions and
translations were in use. His *Commentary on the Apocalypse
of John* was issued in 1791, and a work entitled *The Hebrew
Prophets* in 1816-1819.

The controversy with rationalism was carried on by many
whose interest in religion was entirely practical. It did not
degenerate into a battle of biblical critics. The larger issues
were kept in view by men like the Swiss mathematician,
LEONHARD EULER, 1707-1783, who published *A Defence
of the Divine Revelation against Free Thinkers,* 1747. Such
another was CHRISTIAN FURCHTEGOTT GELLERT, 1715-
1769, whose writings were intended to serve the practical
needs of Christian people. He became widely known as a
religious poet with a clear and accurate style.

His *Fables and Stories,* first series, 1746, second series,
1748, marked an epoch in popular verse making. They
"still rank among the classics of German literature" on ac-

count of their charm of style and their spirit and humour. In 1757 GELLERT published a collection of fifty-four hymns entitled *Spiritual Odes and Songs*. Like his Fables these also left very definite impressions on popular Christian literature. They are characterised by sound sense, by ethical motives, and by a distinct didactic purpose. The "Hymn for Easter" is an excellent example of his work:

> Jesus lives! thy terrors now
> Can O death no more appal us.
> Jesus lives! by this we know
> Thou O grave, canst not enthral us.
>   Alleulia.

MATTHIAS CLAUDIUS, 1740-1815, editor of the *Wandsbeck Messenger*, was an unassuming and homely representative of the German peasant in literature. While much of his poetry was distinctively Christian in spirit, and many of his pieces rank as popular sacred songs, he wrote no hymns designed for use in Church worship. He is everywhere known by his harvest song:

> We plough the fields, and scatter
> The good seed on the land,
> But it is fed and watered
> By God's almighty hand.

This was written as a "Peasant's Song" in a sketch entitled *Paul Erdmann's Feast*.

The fame of JOHANN KASPAR LAVATER, 1741-1801, is most commonly associated with his studies in physiognomy. But he was a preacher of considerable ability and a poet of no mean skill. As a mystic his interest lay rather in the spiritual elements of Christianity than in its historical setting, but he was a thorough-going opponent of rationalism His writings were widely popular during his life time although now they are wholly forgotten. *The Prospect of Eternity*, 1768, was a work of introspective piety. Other pieces of practical religious writing were *The Private Diary of an Observer of Himself*, 1772, and *Pontius Pilate, or, The Man in All Fashions*, 1782.

As a would-be poet he issued a collection of *Christian Songs*, 1776, and two dreary and uninspired religious epics, *Jesus the Messiah*, 1780, and *Joseph of Arimathea*, 1794.

The model for these epic efforts had been furnished by FRIEDRICH GOTTLIEB KLOPSTOCK, 1724-1803, "the first inspired poet of modern Germany." His work gave him a place among the classics of his country and exercised a strong and lasting influence upon his successors.

He issued a collection of *Sacred Songs*, 1758, in which he included versions of earlier hymns; but in the second collection, 1769, only his own work was given. *The Death of Adam*, 1757, and *Solomon*, 1764, were not altogether successful treatments of biblical stories.

In 1771 he published a number of Odes, some of which rank as the "finest modern examples for perfection of form, lyric grace, majesty, and purity of rhythm. In these he appears at his best." The collection was enlarged in 1794, and again enlarged in 1804.

KLOPSTOCK'S most famous work is his *Messiah*, of which the first instalment was published in 1748. This epic owed its inspiration to MILTON'S *Paradise Lost*. It drew its material from the Gospels, Acts, and Apocalypse, of the New Testament, but it added many details from later Christian myth and legend. It was the work of a true poet and a sincere Christian, and on its publication it aroused an enthusiasm almost unprecedented in German literary history. The 'Oath of Christ' may be taken as a representative passage:

> Lo! here am I my Father. I will endure the Almighty's wrath,
> And with profound obedience Thy judgment bear.
> Thou art eternal. The anger of the Godhead knows no end—
> Forever none. No mortal soul has e'er perceived the Godhead's
>   wrath,—
> Eternal slaying through eternal death—none yet.
> God in Himself alone is able God to reconcile.

Lift Thyself up, Judge of the world. Lo! Here am I.
Slay me. Take my eternal sacrifice to reconcile Thee.
Yet am I free. Yet do I entreat Thee. So may heaven open wide
With myriads of Seraphim and lead me back exultant,—
Back to Thy peerless throne in endless triumph Father.
But I shall bear more than the Seraphim can know,
More than the brooding Cherubim in contemplation deep, may
    see.
I shall endure death's uttermost of woe. I, the Eternal, suffer!
Again he spake and said: I lift my head to heaven,
My hand into the clouds, and swear to Thee by mine own self—
I, who am God as Thou, I will redeem mankind.
So Jesus spake and raised himself,
His mien was lofty, tranquil, earnest, and compassionate,
As he stood thus face to face with God.

CHAPTER XXXV

ROMANTICISM

The philosophy of EMMANUEL KANT, 1724-1804, mediated a change from the rationalism of the Enlightenment to the more spiritual thinking of the Romantic revival. KANT was a rationalist and he gave classical expression to German naturalistic rationalism in his work entitled *Religion within the Bounds of Reason only*, 1793. He had prepared the way for this work by his mightily influential *Critique of Pure Reason*, 1781, revised in 1787. But, as Heine said, he was "the executioner of Deism"; for in his *Critique of Practical Reason*, 1788, he taught that the will has a practical supremacy and is able to exercise its freedom.

JOHANN GOTTLIEB FICHTE, 1762-1814, seized upon KANT'S teaching of the inherent moral worth of man and made it fundamental to his own philosophy. *An Essay towards a Critique of all Revelation*, 1792, prepared the way for the solution of many problems untouched by KANT. In *The Destiny of Man*, 1800, he defined the absolute ego, on which he had built his philosophy, as the infinite moral will of the universe. In *The Way to a Blessed Life*, 1806, he discussed the union of the finite self-conscious life with the infinite ego, or God.

FRIEDRICH WILHELM JOSEPH VON SCHELLING, 1775-1854, "grasped FICHTE'S amended form of the critical philosophy" with readiness. He became the philosophical leader of the new Romantic school in German literature. AUGUST WILHELM SCHLEGEL, 1767-1845, was the literary prophet of that school; and with his brother KARL WILHELM FRIED-

RICH, 1772-1829, conducted *The Athenaeum,* its literary organ.

SCHLEGEL traced the poetical form of the Romantic movement to Goethe's *Wilhelm Meister;* its political characteristics he attributed to the French Revolution, 1789; and its philosophy to FICHTE'S doctrine of knowledge. The movement itself he regarded as the expression of that inner freedom and rationality which constituted the essence of the practical philosophy of KANT.[1]

The spirit of the Romantic revival passed into Christian literature in the works of FRIEDRICH DANIEL ERNST SCHLEIERMACHER, 1768-1834, the founder of modern theology. Having exchanged his early Pietism for the rationalism of SEMLER, he surrendered that for the romanticism of FRIEDRICH SCHLEGEL whose confidence he won by an early essay.

In 1799 he published his epoch-making work, *Concerning Religion; Discourses addressed to the Educated among its Despisers,* which contained an elaboration of his first main principle that spiritual experience is the true basis of theology. "The rhetorical form is a fiction. The addresses were never delivered. . . . . They are a cry of pain on the part of one who sees that assailed which is sacred to him, of triumph as he feels himself able to repel the assault, of brooding persuasiveness lest any should fail to be won for the truth."[2]

The Discourses first justify their purpose, and then in turn discuss the Essence of Religion, Religious Culture, the Social Principle in Religion, and Religions.

So far as your feeling expresses the life and being common to you and the universe, it constitutes your piety; your sensations, and the effects upon you of all the life surrounding you, are all elements, and the sole

---

[1] Cp. *Ency. Religion and Ethics,* Vol. IV., p. 360.
[2] Edward Caldwell Moore, *History of Christian Thought since Kant* (1918), p. 76.

elements, of religion; there is no feeling which is not religious, save such as indicates an unhealthy condition of life (*Discourse* 2).

Ruin and salvation, enmity and mediation, these are the two inseparably connected fundamental relations underlying this habit of feeling, and determining the shape of the entire religious content and form of Christianity (*Discourse* 5).

How a Jewish Rabbi of philanthropic mind and somewhat Socratic morals, with a few miracles, or at least what others took for such, and the ability to utter some clever gnomes and parables—how One who was this and nothing more, and who, were He only this, were not fit to stand before Moses or Mohammed, could have caused such an effect as a new religion and Church—to be able to conceive how this were possible one must first take leave of his senses!

In this work and in his *Monologues*, 1800, SCHLEIERMACHER embodied his best thoughts and his finest feelings. The Monologues deal with Contemplation, Examination, The World, Prospect, Youth and Old Age. Their main thesis is summed up in the sentence:

I live in the consciousness of my whole nature. To become ever more what I am is my sole aim; every act of my life is a special phase of this one aim. Let time bring, as it may, material and opportunity for the moulding and manifesting of my inner self I shun nothing; all is the same to me (*Monologue* 4).

By his *Brief Plan of Theological Studies*, 1811, he attempted to do for theology what the Discourses had done for religion. He set up an ideal of theological science, dominated by the view that there is an organic connection between all parts of the subject. The Plan was a pioneer work in the department of Theological Encyclopaedia.

His monumental work, *The Christian Faith shewn in its Agreement with the Principles of the Evangelical Church,* 1821, marks an epoch in the history of the interpretation of Christianity. It has been called the most influential treatise in theology since the Institutes of CALVIN; by means of it SCHLEIERMACHER became the "reformer of the German Protestant theology." In it he defined religion as "the feeling of absolute dependence," a feeling that is a basal fact of man's constitution; he then examined the Christian consciousness and found that the specifically Christian feeling is the feeling of redemption. As the champion of experimental religion SCHLEIERMACHER transformed the whole method and scope of theological dogmatics, and focussed attention upon the idea of salvation as the vital element in Christianity.

In 1819 he began a series of lectures on the Life of Jesus. He was "the first theologian who had ever lectured upon this subject." The course was given in 1832 for the last time, but the lectures were not published until 1864. This *Life of Jesus* is now only valuable as a guide to the thought of its author, and as a point in the historical development of the theology of Germany. "Schleiermacher is not in search of the historical Jesus, but of the Jesus Christ of his own system of theology; that is to say, of the historic figure which seems to him appropriate to the self consciousness of the Redeemer as he represents it."[3]

> I have already said that it is inherently impossible that such a predilection (*sc.* for the Book of Daniel) would have been manifested by Christ, because the Book of Daniel does not belong to the prophetic writings properly so called, but to the third division of the Old Testament literature.

---

[3] Albert Schweitzer, *The Quest of the Historical Jesus* (1922), p. 62.

His contribution to the criticism of the narratives of the Life of Jesus is epitomised in the sentence:

> The first three Gospels are compilations formed out
> of various narratives which had arisen independently;
> their discourses are composite structures, and their pres-
> entation of the history is such that one can form no
> idea of the grouping of events.

The mediating theology of SCHLEIERMACHER, and especially his lectures on the Life of Jesus as delivered in 1832, roused the mind of DAVID FRIEDRICH STRAUSS, 1808-1874, whose *Life of Jesus*, 1835, opened a new era in the study of Christian origins. This work was intended to form a prologue to a history of the ideas of primitive Christianity; a plan which STRAUSS subsequently carried out under the title *Christian Theology in its Historical Development and in its Antagonism to Modern Scientific Knowledge*, 1840.

The *Life of Jesus* was in three parts; i. a history of earlier work in criticism and interpretation; ii. a critical examination of the career of Jesus—his birth and childhood, his public ministry, his passion and death; iii. a philosophical interpretation of the value of the life for religion. The book rendered STRAUSS "famous in a moment." "Considered as a literary work, STRAUSS'S first *Life of Jesus* is one of the most perfect things in the whole range of learned literature. In over fourteen hundred pages he has not a superfluous phrase . . . his style is simple and picturesque, sometimes ironical, but always dignified and distinguished."[4]

The standpoint of this remarkable work is that:

> Orthodox and rationalists alike proceed from the
> false assumption that we have always in the Gospels
> testimony, sometimes even that of eye-witnesses, to

---

[4] *Ibid.*, p. 78.

fact . . . We have to realise, that the narrators testify sometimes, not to outward facts, but to ideas, often
most poetical and beautiful ideas, constructions which
even eye-witnesses had unconsciously put upon facts,
imaginations concerning them, reflections upon them,
reflections and imaginings such as were natural to the
time and at the author's level of culture. What we
have here is not falsehood, not misrepresentation of the
truth. It is plastic, naive, and, at the same time, often
most profound apprehension of truth, within the area
of religious feeling and poetic insight. It results in narrative, legendary, mythical in nature, illustrative often
of spiritual truth in a manner more perfect than any
hard, prosaic statement could achieve (Preface).

The work aroused a storm of almost unparalleled fury.
STRAUSS answered his many critics in *Polemics for the Defence of my Writing on the Life of Jesus and for the Char-
acterisation of Contemporary Theology*, 1837. But in 1838
a third edition of the *Life* appeared bearing marks of drastic
revision which the author explained as the results of the
criticisms of DE WETTE and NEANDER. He was now doubtful of his former doubts regarding the genuineness and credibility of the Fourth Gospel, and "the historic personality
of Jesus again began to take on intelligible outlines for him."
Under the impression of this new outlook he wrote the
monologues entitled *The Transient and Permanent Elements
in Christianity*, 1839, reissued the following year as *Leaves
of Peace*. But he withdrew all his concessions in *The Christian Theology*, 1840; the conception of which is perhaps
even greater than that of the *Life of Jesus*. In it he endeavoured to relate the Christian theology to the ideas of
the ancient world, and to trace the way whereby the two
systems of thought had been harmonised by rationalism and
speculation.

His apologue entitled *Julian the Apostate, or the Romanticist on the Throne of the Caesars,* 1847, was a brilliant satire upon Frederic William IV. He almost repeated the first tremendous sensation of his literary career when he issued *The Life of Jesus adapted for the German People,* 1864. He hoped that he had "written a book as thoroughly well adapted for Germans as Renan's is for Frenchmen." But thought had been modified and STRAUSS himself had changed. He no longer treated Jesus as the mythical creation of religious feeling or philosophy, but as a unique historical figure—the chief creative source of the Christian religion. In answer to further criticisms he wrote *The Half and the Whole,* 1865, and handled SCHLEIERMACHER'S *Life of Christ,* 1864, very severely in a Preface to *The Christ of Faith and the Christ of History,* 1865. *The Life of Jesus for the German People* is in two parts. In the first part STRAUSS constructs a portrait from the data of the Gospels which he considers to be historical; in the second part he traces the "Origin and Growth of the Mythical History of Jesus." The book really presents a spiritualised portrait of the Christ of the first three *Gospels; e.g.* of the answer of Jesus to the question of John the Baptist STRAUSS says:

> Is it possible, Jesus means, that you fail to find in Me the miracles which you expect from the Messiah? And yet I daily open the eyes of the spiritually blind and the ears of the spiritually deaf, make the lame walk erect and vigorous, and even give new life to those who are spiritually dead. Any one who understands how much greater these spiritual miracles are, will not be offended at the absence of bodily miracles; only such an one can receive, and is worthy of the salvation that I am bringing to mankind.

The last of his theological writings however is a frank surrender to the materialistic philosophy. *The Old Faith and the New*, 1872, was almost as provocative as his first work, although it was "a dead book with no force and no greatness in it." STRAUSS hoped to show that a new faith must be fashioned by the aid of science and art.

> My conviction, therefore, is, if we would not evade difficulties or put forced constructions upon them, if we would have our yea yea, and our nay nay—in short, if we would speak as honest, upright men, we must acknowledge we are no longer Christians.

Among the outstanding followers of SCHLEIERMACHER was JOHANN AUGUST NEANDER, 1789-1850, who turned to the original investigation of Christian history in order that he might give a higher and a more effective form to the principles of his master. In this enterprise he wielded a tireless pen. His first important book was *The Emperor Julian and his Times*, 1812, which was succeeded by *St. Bernard and his Times*, 1813, in which the contest between the priesthood and the monarchy was vividly described. *A Genetic View of the Principal Gnostic Systems*, 1815, revealed NEANDER'S interest in the philosophical side of Christian history. *St Chrysostom and the Church Peculiar to the East in those Times*, 1822, elucidated a difficult passage in the story of the Church's life; and in 1824, *Antignosticus, a Review of the Writings and Life of Tertullian*, traced the chief traits of a method of Christian ethics which is to be found in the works of the great Carthaginian.

The first volume of the chief work of NEANDER'S life was issued in 1825 as part of a complete *History of the Christian Religion and Church*. This vast undertaking was never finished, but as it stands it is still one of the great Church histories and of real service to the student. In his Preface NEANDER said:

To exhibit the history of the Church of Christ, as
a living witness of the divine power of Christianity;
as a school of Christian experience; a voice, sounding
through the ages, of instruction, of doctrine, and of re-
proof, for all who are disposed to listen; this, from the
earliest period, has been the leading aim of my life and
studies (Preface).

Looking back on the period of eighteen centuries,
we have to survey a process of development in which
we ourselves are still involved; a process which moving
steadily onwards, not always indeed in a straight line,
but through various windings, is yet in the end
furthered by whatever attempts to arrest its advance
(Introduction).

Then came a separate treatise *The History of the Planting and Training of the Christian Church by the Apostles,*
1832, the chief distinction of which consists partly in the
author's spiritual point of view, partly in the mass of literary information used for its composition, and partly in the
Christian temper of the critical discussions.

NEANDER'S *Life of Christ in its Historical Character and
its Spiritual Development,* 1837, was written as a reply to
STRAUSS'S work. It was as brilliant as the book that provoked it; it became equally famous, and it served as a model
for numberless other efforts to tell the inimitable story. It
"had one pre-eminent quality—it was an honest effort,
marked by sympathetic insight into the character portrayed,
to get face to face with the facts."

Even though we can form no clear idea of the exact
way in which the exaltation of Christ from the earth
took place—and indeed there is much that is obscure
in regard to the earthly life of Christ after His resurrection—yet, in its place in the organic unity of the

Christian faith, it is as certain as the resurrection, which apart from it cannot be recognised in its true significance.

Other works from his tireless pen were *A History of Christian Dogma*, 1857; *Catholicism and Protestantism*, 1863; and *An Introduction to the History of the Christian Ethic*, 1864.

Among other important adherents of the school which looked to SCHLEIERMACHER for inspiration and direction was KARL EMMANUEL NITZSCH, 1787-1868. His earlier writings were special studies on such themes as *The Use and Abuse of the Apocryphal Gospels; The Testament of the Twelve Patriarchs;* and *The Theologoumenon concerning the Holy Spirit as the Mother of Jesus,* 1816. His later books dealt with the *Book of Wisdom; Biblical Theology; An Introduction to the New Testament; Ecclesiastical Law;* and *A History of Missions.*

NITZSCH'S most important work was his *System of Christian Doctrine,* 1829, in which "his point of departure is the declaration of the independence of religion which has its seat in sentiment, over against philosophic thought."

JULIUS MUELLER, 1801-1878, a follower of both NEANDER and SCHLEIERMACHER left a permanent mark upon theological thought by his impressive work entitled *The Christian Doctrine of Sin,* 1839. He defined sin as selfishness, but he supported his theory with a "curious speculation . . . according to which finite selves have . . . timelessly and primordially torn themselves loose from God and made self the principle of life." His apologetic work *The Relation of Dogmatic Theology to the Anti-Religious Tendencies of the Present Time,* 1843, was a defence of the supernatural against the current philosophical objections to miracle.

KARL ULLMANN, 1796-1865, "is, with NEANDER and

NITZSCH, the most eminent representative of the school of SCHLEIERMACHER." His *Gregory of Nazianzen*, 1825, is not inferior in value to the greater works of NEANDER. In 1828 he founded, and for years afterward continued to edit, the famous *Studies and Reviews* magazine in which loyal support was given to the 'mediation' theology. The first article, entitled "The Non-Sinfulness of Jesus," created a tremendous sensation. It was republished separately as *The Sinlessness of Jesus*, 1829: it is an almost classical apologetic; and has been welcomed with widespread approbation as a most substantial addition to the understanding of the character of Jesus. His important historical work, *The Reformers before the Reformation*, 1841, still retains its value as a text-book for the student of the period. It contains the life story and a record of the writings of JOHN WESSEL, JOHN OF GOCH, JOHN OF WESEL, the Brothers of the Common Life, and the mystics of the banks of the Rhine. He wrote *The Essence of Christianity*, 1845, in order to emphasise the distinction between religion and the dogmatic symbols of the Church.

In FRIEDRICH AUGUST GOTTREU THOLUCK, 1799-1877, the seekers after a theology that should conciliate all parties had an able and conspicuous representative whose book entitled *The True Consecration of Doubts*, 1823, reissued as *The Doctrine of Sin and of Reconciliation*, 1870, made him "the modern Pietistic apologist of evangelical Christianity." In his work entitled *The Credibility of the Gospel History, with an Incidental Criticism of Strauss's Life of Jesus*, 1837, he offered a "historical argument for the credibility of the miracle stories of the Gospels." F. C. BAUR later on called this "a master-piece of scientific charlatanry and pettifogging." THOLUCK states his idea of miracles thus:

> Even if we admit the scientific position that no act can have proceeded from Christ which transcends the laws of nature, there is still room for the mediating

view of Christ's miracle-working activity. This leads us to think of mysterious powers of nature as operating in the history of Christ—powers such as we have some partial knowledge of, as, for example those magnetic powers which have survived down to our own time, like ghosts lingering on after the coming of day.

In spite of BAUR'S criticism, the book touched the weakest point in the work of STRAUSS who wrote in his third edition of the *Life of Jesus:*

> From the lofty vantage ground of Tholuck's many-sided knowledge I have sometimes, in spite of a slight tendency to vertigo, gained a juster point of view from which to look at one matter or another.

THOLUCK wrote Commentaries on Romans, John, Hebrews, and The Sermon on the Mount. His *Hours of Christian Devotion,* 1839, was written to displace a rationalistic work of the same title issued by J. D. H. ZSCHOKKE.

> O blessed Jesus, so close is the fellowship into which Thou hast entered with man, that to Thyself, from us on whom they lay, Thou hast transferred all the penalties of transgression, and instead hast given to us Thyself with all Thy purity and holiness to be possessed as our own. . . . .
>
> I have part in the anguished sweat of Gethsemane, and in the sacred blood that was shed on Golgotha. I have part in the cry, 'I Thirst;' and in the appeal, 'My God, my God, why hast Thou forsaken me?' Mine is Thy descent into hell, and mine Thine ascension into heaven.

In France the Romantic movement in Christian literature was brilliantly inaugurated by RENE VICOMTE DE CHATEAUBRIAND, 1768-1848. He presented an entirely fresh apology for religion in his celebrated book entitled *The Genius of Christianity, or the Beauties of the Christian Religion,* 1802, concerning which he said in a later *Defence:*

> The author did not write his apology merely for the scholars, for Christians, for the priests, for the doctors; he wrote it especially for the men of letters and for the world.

The most conspicuous feature of this master-piece of literary art is its insistence upon the unrivalled themes which Christianity offers to art and poetry. It is divided into four parts, viz., Dogmas and Doctrines, The Poetry of Christianity, Fine Arts and Literature, and Cultus; each Part being subdivided; thus Part II contains in its five books, a general view of the Christian epics; reviews of poetry in its relation to human characters; to human passions; to supernatural beings; and a chapter on the Bible and Homer.

As a serious argument to counteract the influence of VOLTAIRE, or as a satisfactory description of the part played by Christianity in civilisation the work was inefficient, but its enchanting style, the warmth of its emotion, and the energy of its imagination made it a powerful agent for the restoration of religious sentiment to its rightful place in Christian life.

> It was necessary to prove that . . the Christian religion, of all the religions that ever existed, is the most humane, the most favourable to liberty, and to the arts and sciences. . . . . It was necessary to prove that nothing is more divine than its morality, nothing more lovely and more sublime than its tenets, its doctrine, and its worship; that it encourages genius, corrects the taste, develops the virtuous passions, imparts energy to the ideas, presents noble images to the writer, and perfect models to the artist; that there is no disgrace in

being believers with Newton and Bossuet, with Pascal
and Racine . . .

CHATEAUBRIAND'S next work was entitled *The Martyrs,
or the Triumph of the Christian Religion,* 1809—a prose
epic written to emphasise the differences between paganism
and Christianity, and especially to prove that Christianity is
a vastly superior source of poetic inspiration. It influenced
the growth of historic feeling by its art of 'individualising'
historic epochs, and of giving them character and colour; it
revived the Christian centuries in pictures which gave expression to the power and beneficence of the Faith.

In HUGUES FELICITE ROBERT DE LAMENNAIS, 1782-
1854, one of the apostles of the religious revival, the clerical
power found a liberal champion. His first literary essay was
The Spiritual Guide, 1807, a fine translation of *The Mirror
for Monks* written in Latin by LOUIS DE BLOIS. LAMEN-
NAIS added a Preface "which in pure spirituality of thought
and expression equals, if it does not surpass, the original
tract; Lamennais himself never afterwards surpassed it."

He next issued a plea for a revival of religion, a plea that
sounded the war-cry of his genius, *Reflections upon the State
of the Church in France during the 18th century and upon
the Actual Situation,* 1808. It was a fierce arraignment of the
authority exercised by the civil power over the Church. It
inspired the important Ultramontane movement which became the means of winning for religion the balance of power
in politics and literature, of creating a great Catholic literature, and of securing an influential place in European thought
for the Catholic Church.

*The Tradition of the Church concerning the Institution
of Bishops,* 1814, written in collaboration with his brother
Jean, condemned the practice of creating bishops without
papal sanction. His greatest achievement, *An Essay on Indifference in the Matter of Religion,* 1817, affected Europe like

a charm. Sainte Beauve said of it: "Its effect upon the world was that of a sudden explosion, the author was bombarded into celebrity by it." It represented an effort to establish spiritual infallibility upon a sound philosophical foundation; by its eloquence, enthusiasm, and theory of history it "kindled such a flame in the young clergy of France and gave such an impulse to their faith and zeal as renewed and moulded a whole generation." The Essay ran into four volumes, 1818-1824, and was followed by a second work on the same theme, entitled *Religion considered in its Relations to the Civil and Political Order,* 1825-6.

Two years later a change passed over the fabric of his vision. LAMENNAIS surrendered his earlier royalist views and expressed his new faith in *The Progress of the Revolution and of the War against the Church,* 1828. With the aid of MONTALEMBERT and LACORDAIRE he then founded *The Future,* 1830, a magazine devoted to the cause of liberty, "which bore for its motto and had for its platform "God and Liberty." It was soon suppressed by the powers it was intended to oppose. The breach of LAMENNAIS with the Church was signalised by his publication of *The Words of a Believer,* 1834. The Archbishop of Paris spoke of it as a book that could wake the dead; Pope Gregory XII condemned it as a "book small in size but great in perversity—false, calumnious, reckless, impious, scandalous and erroneous."

> When you see a man conducted to prison or to execution, do not hasten to say, That is a wicked man who has committed a crime against men. For perhaps he is a good man, who wished to serve men, and is being punished for it by their oppressors . . . .
> Eighteen centuries ago, in a city of the East, the pontiffs and king of the day nailed upon a cross, after having scourged him with rods, a rebel, a blasphemer, as they called him.

The day of his death there was a great terror in hell, and a great joy in heaven. For the blood of the Just had saved the world.

Oh, if you knew what it was to love! You say that you love, and many of your brothers lack bread to sustain life; clothing to cover their naked limbs; a roof to shelter them; a handful of straw to sleep upon; while you have abundance of everything . . . .
You say that you love your brothers; and what would you do if you hated them?

His last words on religious themes were uttered in *The Affairs of Rome, or the Ills of the Church and of Society,* 1837. Thenceforward he posed as an apostle of democracy.

One convert gained by the *Essay on Indifference* was JEAN BAPTISTE HENRI LACORDAIRE, 1802-1861. He had helped in the publication of *The Future,* but left it for the pulpit of Notre Dame, 1830, from which he led the reaction against VOLTAIRE'S scepticism with brilliant and ardent eloquence, clearness of thought, and fullness of resource.

His views concerning the religious reclamation of France were unfolded in *A Memorial for Re-establishing the Order of Preaching Friars in France,* 1838. His devotion to the ideals of St. Dominic was further shown by an exquisitely written *Life of St. Dominic,* 1840. This was one of his two best works, the other being *Letters to a Young Man concerning the Christian Life,* 1857.

As a preacher he introduced a new form of pulpit ministration called *Conferences* in which he made a complete reform; "new subjects, new objects, new methods" were adopted. The themes of these Conferences were Jesus Christ, 1869; God, 1870; God and Man, 1872; and Life, 1875. His treatment of these subjects was given in such fresh and even 'romantic' forms, and with such boldness and brilliance as to revive the flagging vitality of religion.

Another contributor to *The Future* was CHARLES FORBES
RENE DE MONTALEMBERT, 1810-1870, who quietly
withdrew to more substantial literary work when the magazine was suppressed. He wrote *The Life of St. Elizabeth of
Hungary*, 1836, as a manifesto on behalf of a deeper interest
in the lives of the saints. His unabated enthusiasm for this
subject led him to prepare a large biographical history entitled *The Monks of the West*, 1860. This is a splendid
creation of historical zeal designed to dispel the lukewarm-
ness and unbelief to which the author ascribed the enfeebled
grip of the Church upon France. The greater part of the
work is consecrated to the history of the Anglo-Saxon and
Celtic monks.

The bridge between classicism and romanticism in English religious literature was built by *The Spectator*, the
original English periodical. RICHARD STEELE, 1672-1729, a
good-hearted, lovable Irishman, had written *The Christian
Hero*, 1701, to strengthen himself against temptation, before
he joined *The Spectator* which JOSEPH ADDISON, 1672-
1719, had founded. ADDISON was a master in the art of
gentle living; he was sincerely religious and was gifted with
a remarkably clear and graceful style. *The Spectator* dealt
repeatedly with religious subjects. The Being of God, Immortality, The Mischief of Atheism, The Truth of Christianity, were discussed in its pages. The Vision of Mirza
is a masterpiece of allegory as a picture of the uncertainty of
life.

The Christian memory still cherishes some of the hymns
that appeared in *The Spectator, e.g.* "When all Thy mercies
O my God," and "The spacious firmament on high."
ALEXANDER POPE, 1688-1744, contributed to its pages
*The Messiah: a Sacred Eclogue composed of Several Passages
of Isaiah the Prophet.*

As the good shepherd tends his fleecy care,
Seeks freshest pasture, and the purest air,
Explores the lost, the wandering sheep directs,
By day o'ersees them, and by night protects,
The tender lambs he raises in his arms,
Feeds from his hand, and in his bosom warms;
Thus shall mankind his guardian care engage,
The promised Father of the future age.

ISAAC WATTS, 1674-1748, the Father of English psalmody, whose hymns "created a new era in religious poetry" by their simplicity and fervour, was also a contributor to *The Spectator*. His prolific muse however needed wider room than its narrow limits afforded. He wrote more than five hundred hymns, besides turning the Psalms into metre. His industrious facility gave to English hymnology some of its most treasured possessions in the pages of his various books: *Horae Lyricae*, 1705; *Hymns and Spiritual Songs*, 1707; *Divine and Moral Songs for Children*, 1715; *The Psalms of David imitated*, 1719; *and Reliquiae Juveniles*, 1734.

"As long as pure, nervous English, unaffected fervour, strong simplicity, and liquid yet manly sweetness are admitted to be the characteristics of a good hymn, works such as WATTS' must command universal admiration." "Jesus shall reign where'er the sun" is the first great missionary hymn. "When I survey the wondrous Cross" is the most majestic hymn in English speech. "O God our help in ages past" keeps its place as one of the finest songs of the Christian Church.

The prose writings of WATTS have perished as completely as has the type of piety they were intended to serve. Sir Leslie Stephen says of the Sermons: "They appeal strongly to the inner witness of the Spirit . . . Unlike most of his contemporaries he addresses the heart rather than the intellect; and in his hands Christianity is not emasculated Deism, but a declaration to man of the means by which God is pleased to work a supernatural change in human nature."[5]

WATTS defended his choice of subjects by writing in the Preface of the *Horae Lyricae*:

> . . the naked themes of Christianity have something brighter and bolder in them, something more surprising and celestial than all the adventures of gods and heroes, all the dazzling images of false lustre that form and garnish a heathen song: here the very argument would give wonderful aids to the muse, and the heavenly theme would so relieve a dull hour and a languishing genius, that when the muse nods, the sense would burn and sparkle upon the reader, and keep him feelingly awake.

PHILIP DODDRIDGE, 1702-1751, must be associated with ISAAC WATTS as a zealous servant of the religious revival. His pamphlet entitled *The Means of Reviving the Dissenting Interest*, 1730, like the volumes of Sermons that succeeded it, was eclipsed in popularity and influence by the famous manual of devotion *The Rise and Progress of Religion in the Soul*, 1745, "one of the few works of practical religion which have been accepted by all denominations of Evangelical Christians as next to the Bible the best aid to the devout life." Second in popularity among his writings was the book entitled *Some Remarkable Passages in the Life of Colonel Gardiner*, 1747. This was the story of the conversion of a libertine to a life of strict piety: it still ranks among classical first-hand authorities for the psychological study of religious experience.

DODDRIDGE left permanent impress upon the hymn books of England, few of which are without some of his songs. Perhaps the noblest of these is the everywhere acceptable prayer:

---

[5] *English Thought in the Eighteenth Century*, Vol. II., p. 386.

O God of Bethel, by Whose hand
    Thy people still are fed;
Who through this weary pilgrimage
    Hast all our fathers led:

Our vows, our prayers, we now present
    Before Thy throne of grace;
God of our fathers, be the God
    Of their succeeding race.

The simplicity of WATTS and DODDRIDGE paled before the complex genius of WILLIAM LAW, 1686-1761, a great writer of English, a controversialist of consummate ability, a devout and notable mystic. LAW entered the lists of literature by writing *Three Letters to the Bishop of Bangor* (Bishop Hoadly). 1717. These "are probably the most forcible piece of writing in the Bangorian controversy." They were written to support the High Church position. LAW next attacked Mandeville's *Fable of the Bees* in an argumentative work of considerable power entitled *Remarks upon a Book entitled The Fable of the Bees, or Private Vices Public Benefits*, 1723.

> You tell us 'that the moral virtues are the political offspring, which flattery begot upon pride.' You therefore, who are an advocate for moral vices, should by the rule of contraries be supposed to be acted by humility; but that being (as I think) not of the number of the passions, you have no claim to be guided by it. The prevailing passions which you say have the sole government of man in their turns, are pride, shame, fear, lust, and anger; you have appropriated the moral virtues to pride, so that your own conduct must be ascribed either to fear, shame, anger, or lust, or else to a beautiful union and concurrence of them all.

The Case of Reason, 1732, contained his reply to TINDAL'S work *Christianity as Old as Creation*. In *Letters to a*

Lady inclined to enter the Church of Rome, 1731-1732, he vindicated the character and the rites of the Church of England.

His controversial defence of High Churchmanship and of the Christian faith was overshadowed by his more justly famous works for the furtherance of practical piety. The first of these was a *Treatise of Christian Perfection*, 1726, in which he assails the various devices for setting aside the injunction "Go sell all that thou hast and give to the poor;" an injunction which he regarded as of general and literal application.

> Our bodies and all bodily pleasures are at one dash struck out of the account of happiness.
>
> When we are at the top of all human attainments we are at the bottom of all human misery, and have made no further advance towards true happiness than those whom we see in the want of all these excellences. Whether a man die before he had writ poems, compiled histories, or raised an estate, signifies no more than whether he died an hundred or a thousand years ago.

His greatest and most memorable work in this connection is *A Serious Call to a Devout and Holy Life adapted to the State and Condition of all Orders of Christians*, 1728. It contains an appeal "so lucid in its language and so convincing in its persuasions that the reader feels shut up to the conclusion that only the devotional life is worth living." A more earnest, vigorous, and convincing call to religion has rarely been written.

> The short of the matter is this, either reason and religion prescribe rules and ends to all the ordinary actions of life or they do not; if they do, then it is necessary to govern all our actions by those rules, as it is necessary to worship God.

To the leisured classes he said:

> You are not laborer or tradesman, you are neither merchant nor sailor; consider yourself, therefore, as placed in a state in some degrees like that of the good angels, who are sent into the world as ministering spirits, for the general good of mankind, to assist, protect and minister for them who shall be heirs of salvation.

A third and an even more interesting phase of LAW'S literary life originated in his study of JACOB BOEHME; he turned to mysticism and issued *A Demonstration of the Gross and Fundamental Errors of a late Book called A Plain Account etc. of the Lord's Supper,* 1737. Then came the more constructive treatise entitled *The Grounds and Reasons of the Christian Regeneration,* 1739.

> God is love, yea, all love; and is so all love that nothing but love can come from him: and the Christian religion is nothing but an open full manifestation of his universal love towards all mankind.

One of the two most important of his mystical works is *An Appeal to All that Doubt and Disbelieve the Truths of Revelation,* 1740; it "is a clear and fine exposition of his attitude with regard more especially to the nature of man, the unity of all nature, and the quality of fire or desire." In the same year he published his *Earnest and Serious Answer to Dr. Trapp's Sermon on being Righteous Overmuch.* LAW imitated the great mystics when he wrote *The Spirit of Prayer,* 1749.

> . . the God who is revealed to us by the heart is an entirely different being to the God who is built up by external demonstration. . . . We recognise him by a sensibility of our nature which reveals the spiritual world as the senses reveal the visible world . . . .

The Way of Divine Knowledge, 1752, continues the scond part of *The Spirit of Prayer; The Spirit of Love,* 1752, is of the nature of an Appendix.

LAW was associated with a notable group of men known as Non-jurors, who scrupled to take the oath of allegiance to King William III and King George I. In their own words they "held a State point", viz., that William's title to the kingship was unsound, and "a Church point", viz., that even a legitimate sovereign could not deprive bishops of their rights without the sanction of the Church authorities.

Among the four hundred non-juring clergy were some men of note in the literary history of Christian England. THOMAS KEN, 1637-1711, published *A Manual of Prayers For the Use of the Scholars of Winchester College,* 1674, in which he refers to his famous Morning and Evening Hymns —"Awake my soul and with the Sun," and "All praise to Thee my God this night."

JOHN KETTLEWELL, 1653-1695, was the author of a popular *Exposition of the Apostles' Creed,* and of a work entitled *The Practical Believer,* 1687, and other useful works of devotion. HENRY DODWELL, 1641-1711, was a man of immense learning which he consecrated to the service of interpreting the government of the Church. WILLIAM SANCROFT, 1616-1693, wrote *The Ordained Thief,* 1651, *Modern Politics,* 1652, and many other works.

The case and characters of the Non-jurors were described and mocked by COLLEY CIBBER in his play entitled "The Non-juror," 1718.

The action of the American colonists, who secured episcopal ordination from the Scottish Church for a short lived succession of bishops founded by the non-juring Ralph Taylor in 1722, led to a long paper warfare in which various writers and many voluminous pamphlets were engaged.

The *Prayer Book* of 1662 was at first satisfactory to most men of this party, but the growing demand for some changes led JEREMY COLLIER, 1650-1726, the author of *Reasons for Restoring Some Prayers*, 1717, to unite with THOMAS BRETT, 1667-1743, in the work of producing *A Service Book*, 1718, based on the *Prayer Book* of 1549. This work divided the Non-jurors into two parties—Usagers and Non-usagers. Their differences of opinion involved them in discussions concerning the mixed chalice, prayers for the faithful departed, prayers for the descent of the Holy Ghost, and other points.

JEREMY COLLIER is best remembered for his *Short View of the English Stage*, 1698, in which he condemned the profanity, irreverence, and pleasing representation of successful wickedness that ran riot in the London theatres. In spite of the published replies by Dryden, Congreve, Vanburgh and others, COLLIER maintained his case, and eventually succeeded in abolishing the baser elements from the play-houses. He was favourably known by an elaborate *Ecclesiastical History of Great Britain from the First Planting of Christianity to the End of the Reign of Charles II*, 1708-1711.

The religio-political views of BENJAMIN HOADLY, 1676-1761, started the acrimonious Bangorian controversy. GEORGE HICKS, 1642-1715, the Non-juror, left at his death a work entitled *The Constitution of the Christian Church, and the Nature and Consequences of Schism*, which was published in 1716. HOADLY seized the opportunity and issued an able reply, *A Preservative against the Principles and Practices of Non-jurors*, 1716, in which he assailed the inconsistency of Protestant sacerdotalism. He urged that a Church that ascribes the highest spiritual authority to fallible mortals must come into conflict with the State. The State, therefore, should resist it. His Sermon, preached before George I and afterwards printed with the title *The Nature of Christ's Kingdom*, 1717, was supposed to be an attack upon the established endowments and privileges, as well as upon the government and discipline, of the Anglican Church.

If therefore, the church of Christ be the kingdom
of Christ, it is essential to it that Christ himself be the
sole lawgiver and sole judge of his subjects, in all points
relating to the favour or displeasure of Almighty God;
and that all his subjects, in what station soever they
may be, are equally subjects to him; and that no one
of them, any more than another, hath authority either
to make new laws for Christ's subjects, or to impose
a sense upon the old ones, which is the same thing; or
to judge, censure, or punish the servants of another
master, in matters relating purely to conscience or salvation.

WILLIAM LAW answered these contentions and the controversy raged furiously during 1717-1718. More than
fifty divines joined in the fray. During one month, July,
1717, there appeared seventy-four pamphlets of argumentative writing.

The true character of Christian romanticism in England
was exhibited in the Evangelical Revival of which the
brothers JOHN and CHARLES WESLEY were the leaders, and
George Whitefield was the orator.

JOHN WESLEY, baptised John Benjamin, 1703-1791,
figures in the history of Christian literature as a remarkable
inspiring force. He owed his religious conversion to Christian literature, for it was during a religious meeting while
some one was reading LUTHER'S Preface to the Epistle to
the Romans, that for the first time he "really grasped the
central doctrine of the Reformation theology."

Although the funeral formula of 'Dust to Dust' has long
ago been pronounced over the greater part of the writings
of JOHN WESLEY, his works were of very real value to the
cause to which he gave his life. He was a prolific author.
Besides many Extracts and Abridgments and many Tracts
he left a goodly array of more or less substantial books.

"He first appeared in print in 1733 with *A Collection of Prayers for Every Day in the Week.*" His first *Hymn Book* was issued in America, 1737. In 1739 came *Hymns and Sacred Poems, by John and Charles Wesley,* and another Hymn Book was issued in 1740. In 1741 appeared *An Extract from the Life of M. de Renty,* whom Wesley regarded as a true saint. His first controversial work, with which he says he began to tread "an untried path with fear and trembling—fear not of my adversary, but of myself—" was entitled *The Principles of a Methodist, in Answer to the Rev. Josiah Tucker,* 1742. One of the most telling of all his writings, *An Earnest Appeal to Men of Reason and Religion,* was begun in 1743. "That very remarkable volume," *Hymns on the Lord's Supper . . . . with Dr. Brevint's Preface concerning the Christian Sacrament and Sacrifice,* saw the light in 1745, as did also the first part of *The Farther Appeal,* a work which was even more telling than its predecessor, *The Earnest Appeal.* Parts two and three were published during the following year. In a curious work entitled *Primitive Physic,* 1747, the great evangelist put into print the medical advice which he had been accustomed to give freely to his people. He gave a *Plain Account of the People called Methodists,* 1749, in a letter to Vincent Perronet. "In 1755 appeared the most important work he ever produced—his *Explanatory Notes on the New Testament.*" The notes are short, but his own remarks are very pungent and pithy, and his selections, mainly from MATTHEW HENRY'S *Commentary* and BENGEL'S *Gnomon,* are good. The Notes together with the Sermons of WESLEY constitute the doctrinal standard of the people called Methodist. The fifty-three Sermons to which this peculiar honour is given were published in four volumes during the years 1746-1760.

It (the new birth) is that great change which God works in the soul when he brings it into life; when he raises it from the death of sin to the life of righteousness. It is the change wrought in the whole soul by the almighty Spirit of God, when it is 'created anew in Christ Jesus, when it is renewed after the image of God, in righteousness and true holiness;' when the love of the world is changed into the love of God, pride into humility; passion into meekness; hatred, envy, malice, into a sincere, tender, disinterested love for all mankind. In a word, it is that change whereby the earthly, sensual, devilish mind is turned into the 'mind which was in Christ Jesus'. This is the nature of the new birth; 'So is every one that is born of the Spirit' (from a *Discourse* entitled *The New Birth*).

If then we take this word in the strictest sense, a man of a catholic spirit is one, who, ... gives his hand to all whose hearts are right with his heart; one who knows how to value, and praise God for, all the advantages he enjoys, with regard to the knowledge of the things of God, the true Scriptural manner of worshipping him, and above all, his union with a congregation fearing God and working righteousness, one who . . . . at the same time loves—as brethren in the Lord, as members of Christ and children of God, as joint partakers now of the present kingdom of God, and fellow-heirs of his eternal kingdom—all of whatever opinion, or worship, or congregation, who believe in the Lord Jesus Christ; who love God and man; who rejoicing to please and fearing to offend God, are careful to abstain from evil, and zealous of good works (from a *Discourse* entitled *Catholic Spirit*).

In addition to these literary enterprises JOHN WESLEY prepared the *Christian Library,* a collection of fifty volumes abridged, edited, and annotated for the use of his people. This collection was completed in 1755.[6]

The evangelist's *Journal* is as remarkable as was the life of which it keeps the amazing record. As one of the supreme works of autobiography it is assured of literary immortality.

CHARLES WESLEY, 1707-1788, was the hymn writer of the movement; his contributions to hymnology amount to sixty-five hundred pieces, among which are some of the best in the language. "No movement has been more happy in its singers than the Methodist revival," and CHARLES WESLEY holds an assured place as "the great hymn writer of all ages."

"Nor was he alone in his work. TOPLADY'S 'Rock of Ages'; CENNICK'S 'Children of the Heavenly King'; PERRONET'S 'All hail the power of Jesus' name'; OLIVER'S 'The God of Abram praise'; SHIRLEY'S 'Sweet the moments rich in blessing' and WILLIAMS' 'Guide Me, O Thou Great Jehovah'; show how rich the revival was in hymn writers."[7]

CHARLES WESLEY stood high above them all, both on account of the mass of his work and on account of its quality. Many of his hymns are of the highest degree of excellence. Some have attained the distinction of classics; among these are such universal favourites as: "Jesu, Lover of my soul"; "Oh, for a heart to praise my God"; "Christ the Lord is risen to-day"; "O for a thousand tongues to sing my great Redeemer's praise"; "Rejoice the Lord is King"; and, "Soldiers of Christ arise."

JOHN WESLEY might well ask as he did in his Preface to the *Wesleyan Hymn Book*, 1780:

---

[6] J. H. Overton, *John Wesley*, new ed. (1905), chap. xi., pp. 169-178.

[7] G. R. Balleine, *History of the Evangelical Party*, p. 36.

In what other publication have you so distinct and full an account of Scriptural Christianity; such a declaration of the heights and depths of religion, speculative and practical; so strong cautions against the most plausible errors, particularly those now most prevalent; and so clear directions for making your calling and election sure; for perfecting holiness in the fear of God?

In 1738 JOHN WESLEY had visited COUNT NICHOLAS LUDWIG VON ZINZENDORF, 1700-1760, who was the leader of the whole community of the United Brethren. At Herrnhut an organised evangelical settlement was engaged in printing books, tracts, catechisms, hymn books, and cheap Bibles. ZINZENDORF contributed a valuable Diary and some Sermons to Christian literature; but his best works were his Hymns of which he wrote more than two thousand. Some of these are of rare beauty. Their key-note "was a deep and earnest personal devotion to and fellowship with the crucified Saviour."

· The evangelical spirit passed over into the Anglican Church where it operated with telling effect upon many leaders. The name Methodist gradually became restricted to those who left the Church of England, those who remained within her communion came to be known as 'Evangelicals.'

After a remarkable religious experience, which began by his discovery of a copy of THOMAS A KEMPIS, JOHN NEWTON, 1725-1807, became a curate at Olney. Here with his neighbour WILLIAM COWPER, 1731-1800, he produced *The Olney Hymns*, 1779, "to promote the faith and comfort of sincere Christians." The book is darkened by a sense of exile from the Divine favour, but it contains such bright songs as "Jesus where'er Thy people meet," "God moves in a mysterious way," and "Glorious things of Thee are spoken."

COWPER contributed among other pieces the well known hymns: "Hark my soul it is the Lord," "O for a closer walk with God," "There is a fountain filled with blood," "Sometimes a light surprises." In all, sixty-seven of the hymns were written by COWPER. NEWTON gave an account of his life in *An Authentic Narrative of some Interesting and Remarkable Particulars in the Life of John Newton*, 1764. He published a volume of Sermons, 1767, and a series of letters on religion entitled *Omicron*, 1774. A second series of letters entitled *Cardiphonia*, 1781, is perhaps the best known of all his prose writings. It did much to promote the cause of evangelicalism. He said, "It is the Lord's will that I should do most by my letters." Of his slave trading days he wrote:

> I was then favoured with an uncommon degree of dependence upon the providence of God, which supported me; but this confidence must have failed in a moment, and I should have been overwhelmed with distress and terror if I had known, or even suspected, that I was acting wrongly. I felt greatly the disagreeableness of the business . . . . but I considered it as the line of life which God in His providence had allotted me, and as a cross which I ought to bear with patience and thankfulness till He should be pleased to deliver me from it.

COWPER who was essentially a Christian poet was also "the most popular poet of his generation." His first volume of *Poems*, 1782, contained "Table Talk," "The Progress of Error," "Truth," "Hope," "Charity," etc. His second volume entitled *The Task: A Poem in Six Books*, 1785, was immediately successful, and indeed "marks an epoch in literary history."

All flesh is grass, and all its glory fades
Like the fair flow'r dishevell'd in the wind;
Riches have wings, and grandeur is a dream:
The man we celebrate must find a tomb,
And we that worship him ignoble graves.
Nothing is proof against the gen'ral curse
Of vanity, that seizes all below.
The only amaranthine flow'r on earth
Is virtue; th' only lasting treasure, truth.
(Bk. III., lines 261-269.)

The Evangelical movement within the Anglican Church was promoted from three important centres—Cambridge, Clapham, and London. In Cambridge the finest representative of the cause was CHARLES SIMEON, 1759-1836. As an undergraduate he discovered that the rules of his College required his attendance at the Communion. Not knowing what to do he read BISHOP WILSON'S book on *The Lord's Supper,* and learned from it the meaning of the Atonement. This discovery gave him his work in life; thereafter his one ambition was to teach the doctrine to all his fellows. His chief work is his *Horae Homileticae,* 1819-1820, a devotional Commentary in eleven volumes; in the preface of it he wrote:

> Scripture is broader and more comprehensive than some very dogmatical theologians are inclined to allow, and as wheels in a complicated machine may move in opposite directions and yet subserve one common end, so many truths apparently opposite equally subserve the purposes of God in the accomplishment of man's salvation.

The chief intellectual power of the party in Cambridge was ISAAC MILNER, 1750-1820, who edited and completed *The History of the Church of Christ,* 1810, which his brother JOSEPH MILNER, 1744-1797, had issued in parts during the years 1794-1797. This is one of the greatest books that the movement produced. It was designed as a record of the good which Christianity had accomplished, and to describe the real followers of Christ irrespective of their denominational allegiance.

Among "the Clapham sect," as Sidney Smith nicknamed them, the outstanding figure was WILLIAM WILBERFORCE, 1759-1833, the light-hearted Member of Parliament for Yorkshire. He stated the case for evangelicalism in *A Practical View of the Prevailing Religious System of Professed Christians in the Higher and Middle Classes in this Country, Contrasted with Real Christianity, 1797.* The grace, frankness and humour of this work won for it an instant popularity. "It was a challenge to those who accepted the creed but declined to live the life."

> I apprehend the essential practical characteristic of true Christians to be this; that relying on the promises to repenting sinners of acceptance through the Redeemer, they have renounced and abjured all other masters, and have cordially and unreservedly devoted themselves to God. . . . . But this is not all—It is now their determined purpose to yield themselves without reserve to the reasonable service of their rightful Sovereign. . . . .
>
> Thus it is the prerogative of Christianity "to bring into captivity *every thought* to the obedience of Christ." They who really feel its power, are resolved "to live no longer to themselves, but to Him that died for them": . . . . they deliberately purpose that, so far as they may be able, the grand governing maxim of their lives shall be *"to do all to the glory of God."*
>
> Behold here the seminal principle, which contains within it, as in an embryo state, the rudiments of all true virtue; which, striking deep its roots, though feeble perhaps and lowly in its beginnings, yet silently progressive, and almost insensibly maturing, will

shortly, even in the bleak and churlish temperature of this world, lift up its head and spread abroad its branches, bearing abundant fruits . . . . (chap. iv., sect. 1).

JOHN VENN, 1759-1813, carried into the movement the spirit of his father HENRY VENN, 1725-1797, who had written *The Compleat Duty of Man*, 1763, as a substitute for the earlier anonymous *Whole Duty of Man*, 1659. VENN put in the place of the principle "Duty first" which the older book had maintained, the evangelical principle, Christ the beginning and the end of all. He based his formal statement of the creed of his party upon the view:

There dwells in the heart of every man till changed by grace, an aversion to the very author of his being.

London counted among its prominent evangelicals THOMAS HARTWELL HORNE, 1780-1862, the author of more than forty books. The first of these was *A Brief View of the Necessity and Truth of the Christian Revelation*, 1800. The most important and influential was the popular *Introduction to the Critical Study of the Holy Scriptures*, 1818, which "took its place in literature as one of the principal class books for the study of the Scriptures in all English speaking protestant colleges and Universities." He also issued *Deism Refuted; or Plain Reasons for being a Christian*, 1819, and in the following year *The Scripture Doctrine of the Trinity briefly Stated and Defended* . . . , 1820.

JOHN JAMES BLUNT, 1794-1855, was the curate of REGINALD HEBER, 1783-1826, the notorious hymn writer, and succeeded him at Hodnet. His service to the evangelical cause was rendered chiefly through his defence of the veracity of Scripture upon which the evangelical preachers relied for their authority in teaching. His literary labours began with *A Sketch of the Reformation in England, 1832.* In 1827 he began a long series of Sermons and Lectures which at length were gathered into one of the works which made his name famous. *The Veracity of the Gospels and Acts of the Apostles Argued from the Undesigned Coincidences to be found in them when Compared (i) with each other, and (ii) with Josephus,* was published in 1828. Two years later a similar work dealing with the five books of Moses saw the light; the Hulsean Lectures of 1831 dealt in like manner with the historical books of the Old Testament, and the Lectures of 1832 were entitled *Principles for the Proper Understanding of the Mosaic Writings Stated and Applied.* All these various works were then rearranged and re-edited under the title *Undesigned Coincidences in the Writings of the Old and New Testaments, an Argument for their Veracity,* 1847.

Before the conclusion of this important work BLUNT undertook a series of works on the Fathers of the Church and on its history. He published an *Introduction to a course of Lectures on the Early Fathers,* 1840, and in 1843, *A Second Part of an Introduction on the Early Fathers.* His more widely known and still useful book, *On the Right Use of the Early Fathers,* was posthumously published in 1857.

More influential than either of these upon the spirit of the London Evangelicals was THOMAS SCOTT, 1747-1821, who succeeded JOHN NEWTON in 1781 as curate of Olney. His spiritual autobiography entitled *The Force of Truth,* 1779, made a profound impression on the mind of J. H. NEWMAN as it did on many others. In it SCOTT told of his religious adventures as he had been driven from one Unitarian position to another until he found rest in the full evangelical faith. "A more impressive piece of spiritual autobiography has rarely been written . . . . it details the process by which a mind of singular earnestness . . . .

made its way from a bald rationalistic unitarianism to the highest type of Calvinistic fervour."

His even more widely known *Commentary* was begun in weekly numbers in 1788, and after many publishing vicissitudes which involved Scott in debt and anxiety was finished with the 174th number in 1792. This has been called "the greatest theological performance of our age and country." It was a work of infinite labour for Scott held the theory that the meaning of Scripture can only be learned from Scripture itself.

> Every passage of Scripture has its literal and distinct meaning, which it is the first duty of a commentator to explain, and speaking generally the *spiritual meaning* is no other than this *real meaning* with its fair legitimate application to ourselves (Preface).

Evangelicalism made substantial progress in French-speaking Switzerland, where the Bible classes of the Scotchman ROBERT HALDANE, 1764-1842, cradled the movement. At Geneva, 1816 and at Montauban, 1817, he brought his personal influence to bear upon many theological students. In this way he aided the Awakening that gave French Protestant preaching its second great period, 1820-1850.

HALDANE'S first religious writing was a work entitled *The Evidences and Authority of Divine Revelation*, 1816. He also expounded his views in a French *Commentary on the Epistle to the Romans*, 1819. He returned to Scotland the same year and plunged into the controversy which raged over the question of including the Apocryphal books in copies of the Bible distributed by the British and Foreign Bible Society in certain European countries. He "is said to have composed fifteen pamphlets, so great was his anxiety to suppress 'that dreadful abomination of the Apocrypha.' "[8]

His treatise *On the Inspiration of Scripture,* 1828, and a second *Exposition of the Epistle to the Romans,* 1835, attained great popularity and were frequently reprinted.

Among those inspired by the evangelical fervour of ROBERT HALDANE was HENRY ABRAHAM CAESAR MALAN, 1787-1864, who became the leader of the so-called Awakening.

The National Church at Geneva was practically Unitarian, but, under the influence of HALDANE, MALAN came to a belief in the Divinity of Christ and in the free gift of salvation. His Sermon of Jan. 19, 1817, was described as a republication of the Gospel.

He was probably the greatest of French hymn writers. The modern movement for cultivating hymn singing in the French Reformed Church is due to him, and to it he contributed about one thousand hymns in which he analysed the Christian experience, and gave intimate descriptions of the Christian emotions. His first volume entitled *Christian Songs for Family Devotions,* was issued in 1823. In 1824 he sent out translations of fifty Psalms under the title *Hymns of Sion,* and he kept this title for all the many subsequent editions and enlargements of his Hymn Books.

Against the Unitarians he published a polemical treatise called *Jesus Christ is the Eternal Revelation of God in the Flesh,* 1831. He wrote many tracts and pamphlets on the questions in dispute between the National and Evangelical Churches and the Church of Rome. One of the more notable of these was *Never Could I Enter into the Roman Church,* 1837. Among his truly evangelical tractates are *Eighty Days of a Missionary,* 1842, *The True Friend of the Children,* 1843, *Are you Happy, fully Happy?* and *Sincere Confessions of Certain Friends,* 1851.

---

[8] Cf. Henry F. Henderson, *The Religious Controversies of Scotland,* pp. 95-110.

During a visit to Scotland MALAN aroused the poetic instinct in CHARLOTTE ELLIOTT, 1789-1871, and through his teaching she was moved to write her famous hymn:

> Just as I am without one plea
> But that Thy blood was shed for me
> And that Thou bidd'st me come to Thee
> O Lamb of God I come.

CHARLOTTE ELLIOTT composed about one hundred and fifty hymns after this. Her work appeared in various Hymn Books as well as in *Hours of Sorrow Cheered and Comforted*, 1836, *Hymns for a Week*, 1839, and *Thoughts in Verse on Sacred Subjects*, 1869.

JEAN HENRI MERLE D'AUBIGNE, 1794-1872, was early caught by the tide of the Awakening which he did much to augment by his numerous writings. He possessed both zeal and learning and his religious earnestness was expressed with great charm of literary style. As early as 1828, he entered into the controversy between Rome and the Reformed Churches by writing *Christianity and Protestantism, are They Two Different Things?* 1828. His historical works began with a *Discourse on the Study of the History of Christianity*, 1832, which he followed with *The Voice of the Church One through all its Successive Forms*, 1834.

The literary devotion of his life was given to historical works connected with the Reformation of the sixteenth century. A book called *Geneva and Oxford*, 1842 foreshadowed this, and the work entitled *Lutheranism and the Reformation*, 1844, was an early expression of it. The full fervour of his devotion was aroused by the preparations which were on foot to celebrate the tercentenary of the Reformation in Germany, and he wrote his universally famous *History of the Reformation in the sixteenth century*, 1835-1853. He made a study of English conditions in *The Protector, or the Commonwealth of England in the days of Cromwell*, 1848, and he described the struggle for religious liberty in Scotland, from JOHN KNOX to the founding of the Free Church in 1843, in a work entitled *Three Centuries of Struggle in Scotland*, 1850.

His second great work was *A History of the Reformation in Europe in the Time of Calvin*, 1862-1877, the last three volumes of which were issued after his death. This second part of the great story was less successful than its predecessor; but in all his work D'Aubigne used the original sources from which he enriched the narrative with many details. He brought to the task a vigorous imagination and a sincere sympathy for the Protestant cause, he was an apologist as well as a historian.

Not content with employing prose, Hutten had recourse to verse also. He published his *Outcry on the Lutheran Conflagration* in which, appealing to Jesus Christ, he beseeches him to consume with the brightness of his countenance all who dared to deny his authority. Above all, he set about writing in German. . . . . His German *rhymes* unveiled to the people the long and disgraceful catalogue of the sins of the Roman court. But Hutten did not wish to confine himself to mere words; he was eager to interfere in the struggle with the sword . . . .

Many persons wielded weapons against the papacy, that had but little connexion with the holiness of a christian life. Emser had replied to Luther's book (*To the Goat of Leipsic*) by another whose title was *To the Bull of Wittemberg*. The name was not ill chosen. But at Magdeburg Emser's work was suspended to the common gibbet with the inscription: 'The book is worthy of the place,' and a scourge was hung at its side, to indicate the punishment the author merited.

The theological aspect of the movement was finely represented in the writings of ALEXANDER RODOLPHE VINET, 1797-1847. He was interested in literature before he turned to religion and his patriotic song "The Awakening of the Vaudois" had given him popularity before he was seventeen years old. Clerical intolerance aroused him to set forth the "kernel of all his theories on religious liberty" in a pamphlet entitled *Respect for Opinions*. In 1826 he gained a prize of two thousand francs for *A Memoir in favour of Liberty of Worship*.

VINET'S leading principle, that conscience creates a direct relationship between man and God as his moral sovereign, and therefore involves the complete freedom of religious belief, gave a fresh impulse to Protestant theology in England as well as in France. His *Sermons on various Religious Subjects*, 1831, are classic in form but evangelical in their fervour. In his *New Discourses on various Religious Subjects*, 1841, he expressed his antagonism to the unmoral and purely intellectual tendencies of the theology of the Awakening. The character of his religious views appears at its best in his almost classic *Essay on the Profession of Religious Convictions and on the Separation of the Church and the State*, 1842.

His popular books such as *Vital Christianity*, 1846, *Evangelical Studies*, 1847, *New Evangelical Studies*, 1851, acquired an international fame, whilst his *Pastoral Theology*, 1850, and his *Studies on Blaise Pascal*, 1848, still rank among the best books on their themes.

In France the Evangelical movement was revived and fostered by ADOLPHE LOUIS FREDERIC THEODORE MONOD, 1802-1856, whose literary works are few and consist mainly of Sermons and poems. He was the foremost Protestant preacher of nineteenth century France, "his merciless logic, his intense earnestness, his almost exclusive selection of the weightiest questions of salvation for his themes" gave him an immense pulpit influence. In 1844 he issued a volume of *Sermons*, the first of which, entitled "The Unbelief of the Unbelieving," is regarded as one of the finest apologetics of modern days.

The Work of Paul, His Christianity or His Tears, His Conversion, His Weakness, and His Example for us, 1851, contains his theory of practical Christianity:

> The Word of God is as living and powerful now as then, but our sinful example in life is the cause of the little success of preaching. The *life* of the ancient Christians was the world conquering power of their witness. Restore that life in the Church of Christ, and she will be able to perform wonders as of old.

Perhaps the most popular of all his works was *The Farewell Words of Adolphe Monod, to his Friends and the Church*, 1856, which was composed of notes made by those who listened to the addresses that he gave from his sick bed to his intimate friends.

One of his best known poems is:

THE HAPPINESS OF THE CHRISTIAN

How shall I not, O God who hast delivered me,
    Fill both the earth and heaven above with Thy high praise,
    And make them witness all my gratitude to Thee
While everywhere my song of happiness I raise.

Happy am I to hear Thee, as Thy mighty word
    Which said 'Let there be light' and light began its sway,
    Whispers to me the truth and comfort of the Lord
And tells my heart, 'Here is salvation's only way.'

Happy am I to call Thee, and with Thee to speak
    While from my dust I worship Thee and pay my vows
    With freedom, as a loving son his sire may seek,
With fear, as when a sinner in Thy presence bows. . . . . .

Happy always! The mighty God my Father is;
    Christ is my Brother; and the Holy Ghost no less
    My Counsellor. Hell is removed, and earthly bliss
Unites with heaven and God in three-fold happiness.

CHAPTER XXXVI

THE MODERN AGE

The history of Christian literature during the nineteenth century is the history of the development of tendencies created by the Enlightenment and by Romanticism. The history becomes crowded with minor issues; books are indefinitely multiplied in number and variety; it is easy to lose all sense of connection between the masses of material that lie to hand.

This chapter will attempt to sketch the outline of the story as it relates to four important issues, viz., The Collapse of Calvinism; The Growth of Liberalism; The Oxford Movement; and The Development of New Testament Criticism.

The collapse of Calvinism can be followed most easily in the Christian literature of America, where the rapid growth of humanitarian sentiment became a most forceful influence in the disintegration of the old creed. The first outstanding[1] protagonist of the change was WILLIAM ELLERY CHANNING, 1780-1842, an eminent Unitarian, who won a literary reputation by his discussions of the characters and works of JOHN MILTON, Napoleon Bonaparte, and FRANCOIS FENELON.

A minor controversy on the Unitarian position began during 1815, and CHANNING had taken part in it by writing a pamphlet entitled *The System of Exclusion and Denunciation in Religion Considered.* The question was

[1] Cf. F. H. Foster. *A Genetic History of the New England Theology,* chap. x., pp. 273-281.

494

brought into the very forefront of interest by an ordination Sermon which he preached in 1819, and which he defended in a pamphlet *Objections to Unitarian Christianity Considered*, 1819. The necessity for this defence was created by the *Letters* which had been written against the Sermon by MOSES STUART, 1780-1850. CHANNING'S position is made clear in such passages as this:

> We do, then, with all earnestness, though without reproaching our brethren, protest against the irrational and unscriptural doctrine of the Trinity. 'To us' as to the Apostle and the primitive Christians, 'there is one God, even the Father'. With Jesus, we worship the Father, as the only living and true God. We are astonished that any man can read the New Testament and avoid the conviction that the Father alone is God.

Seven years later he returned to the subject in a Sermon upon *Unitarian Christianity Most Favorable to Piety*, 1826.

> Unitarianism is a system most favorable to piety, because it presents to the mind one, and only one, Infinite Person, to whom supreme homage is to be paid. It does not weaken the energy of religious sentiment by dividing it among various objects. It collects and concentrates the soul on one Father of unbounded, undivided, unrivalled glory.

His fundamental objection to Calvinism was that it contradicts the reasonableness of the divine love; this objection was clearly stated in the Sermon, but he had already expressed it in an earlier work entitled *The Moral Argument against Calvinism*, 1820. This work was a review of a book compiled from the writings of ROBERT FELLOWES, 1771-1847, entitled *A General View of the Doctrines of*

Christianity, 1809. CHANNING gave the compilation his hearty commendation.

> The work under review is professedly popular in its style and mode of discussion. . . . It expresses strongly and without circumlocution the abhorrence with which every mind, uncorrupted by false theology, must look on Calvinism. . . . Calvinism, we are persuaded, is giving place to better views. It has passed its meridian, and is sinking to rise no more. It has to contend with foes more formidable than theologians; with foes from whom it cannot shield itself in mystery and metaphysical subtilties—we mean with the progress of the human mind, and with the progress of the spirit of the gospel. Society is going forward in intelligence and charity, and of course is leaving the theology of the sixteenth century behind it. We hail this revolution of opinion as a most auspicious event to the Christian cause.

CHANNING gave unquestionable proof that humanitarian motives governed his theology when he turned with ardour to the social implications of Christianity. He wrote *Slavery*, 1835, in order to show that man cannot be justly held and used as property; that man has sacred rights, the gifts of God and inseparable from human nature, of which slavery is an infraction—to unfold the evils of slavery, and to discuss means of removing it.

His *Thoughts on the Evils of a Spirit of Conquest and Slavery*, 1837, also served to show that the foundation of his thought was a high estimate of human nature; together with his other works it justified the judgment of the Chevalier Bunsen that CHANNING was "the prophet in the United States for the presence of God in mankind."

The Unitarian argument was maintained by ANDREWS NORTON, 1786-1852, in his *Statement of Reasons for Not*

Believing the Doctrines of Trinitarians respecting the Nature of God and the Person of Christ, 1819, in which he contended that Trinitarianism is incredible. LEONARD WOODS, 1774-1854, took up the task which MOSES STUART began but left unfinished. His *Letters to Unitarians,* 1820, contained expositions of the theology commonly held by those who accepted the doctrinal teaching of the Church. He was answered by HENRY WARE, 1764-1845, who, in *Letters to Trinitarians and Calvinists,* 1820, insisted that the vital question at issue was the question of the natural character of man, who is:

> an accountable being, a proper subject to be treated according as he shall make a right or wrong choice, being equally capable of either, and as free to the one as to the other.

A more conspicuous advocate of liberal Christianity came to the front in JAMES FREEMAN CLARKE, 1810-1888, some of whose writings won an international reputation. His books entitled *The Peculiar Doctrine of Christianity,* 1844, and *The History of the Doctrine of the Atonement,* 1845, showed the point of his departure from the common creed of Christianity which he discussed in *Orthodoxy,* 1866. He gave positive expression to his own religious philosophy in *Self Culture,* 1872, *Common Sense in Religion,* 1873, and *Every-Day Religion,* 1886. "Few Americans have done more to broaden the discussions of literature, ethics, and religious thought" than he did by such works as *Ten Great Religions,* 1871-1883, *Memorial and Biographical Sketches,* 1878, and *Events and Epochs in Religious History,* 1881.

The poet of the liberal movement in America was JOHN GREENLEAF WHITTIER, 1807-1892, the Quaker poet of freedom and faith. His apprenticeship to verse was served with various journals, but his earlier work like the *Apos-*

trophe to Lloyd Garrison, and *Legends of New England*, 1831, was lacking in the inspiration that came later. The emancipation question stirred him deeply with the result that his *Poems written during the Progress of the Abolition Question in the United States*, 1837, revealed the true quality of his genius.

> We wage no war,—we lift no arm,—we fling no torch within
> The fire-damps of the quaking mine beneath your soil of sin;
> We leave ye with your bond men, to wrestle, while ye can,
> With the strong upward tendencies and godlike soul of man!
>
> But for us and for our children, the vow which we have given
> For freedom and humanity is reg:stered in Heaven;
> *No slave-hunt in our borders,—no pirate on our strand!*
> *No fetters in the Bay State,—no slave upon our land!*

The numerous later books which came from his pen, *Lays of my Home and other Poems*, 1843, *Songs of Freedom*, 1846, *Songs of Labour*, 1850, *The Tent on the Beach*, 1867, etc., reveal him as "the most representative of New England's poets, affectionately reminiscent of her lore of superstition and romance, and, most significantly, the poet of religious sympathy and hope and trust. Though he wrote few hymns, many have been detached from his poems and sung in churches of all Protestant denominations, to the great enhancement of his fame." Thus from *My Psalm* has come the familiar fragment:

> All as God wills, who wisely heeds
>   To give or to withold,
> And knoweth more of all my needs
>   Than all my prayers have told!......
>
> And so the shadows fall apart,
>   And so the west-winds play;
> And all the windows of my heart
>   I open to the day.

The poem entitled *Our Master* which appeared in *The Panorama and other Poems*, 1856, has been broken up

into several most popular hymns such as "Immortal love
for ever full, for ever flowing free," "We may not climb the
heavenly steeps," and "O Lord and Master of us all."

As "the national bard of justice, humanity, and reform,"
Whittier wielded a very considerable influence among plain
and pious folk.

The finest poem America has yet given to the world is
Thanatopsis, 1817, the work of WILLIAM CULLEN BRY-
ANT, 1794-1878. With this work "American poetry may
be said to have commenced"; it is conceived in a large and
grand spirit. Because it dwells on the majesty of death it
has been described as the culmination of the poetry of the
churchyard school, of which HERVEY'S *Meditations among
the Tombs*, 1745, had been for years the outstanding English example.

> So live that when thy summons comes to join
> The innumerable caravan that moves
> To that mysterious realm, where each shall take
> His chamber in the silent halls of death,
> Thou go not, like the quarry-slave at night,
> Scourged to his dungeon; but, sustained and soothed
> By an unfaltering trust, approach thy, grave
> Like one who wraps the drapery of his couch
> About him, and lies down to pleasant dreams.

The disintegration of Calvinism in America was actively
assisted by the writings of HORACE BUSHNELL, 1802-
1876, whereby "he changed the point of view, and thus not
only changed everything, but pointed the way to unity in
theological thought." His first important contribution to
this work was a book entitled *Christian Nurture*, 1847,
"one of the great works of American theology."

He had already written upon *The Spiritual Economy of
Revivals of Religion*, 1838, but in *Christian Nurture* he
traversed the whole theory of religion involved in the popular revivalism of the JONATHAN EDWARDS type. The
central thesis of the book was:

That the child is to grow up a Christian and never know himself to be otherwise.

This thesis had appeared in a paper entitled *Growth not Conquest the True Method of Christian Progress,* written by BUSHNELL in 1844, which he incorporated in the book. In it he anticipated much that has now become commonplace concerning heredity, environment, and development.

> Our very theory of religion is that men are to grow up in evil and be dragged into the church of God by conquest. The world is to lie in halves and the kingdom of God is to stretch itself side by side with the kingdom of darkness, making sallies into it and taking captive those who are sufficiently hardened and bronzed in guiltiness to be converted.

During 1848 BUSHNELL published his addresses to the divinity schools of Harvard, Yale, and Andover. These addresses dealt with *The Atonement, The Divinity of Christ,* and *Dogma and Spirit.* In *The Atonement,* he claimed that all theories which represent Christ as suffering a legal penalty in our stead

> are capable, one and all of them, of no light in which they do not offend some right sentiment of our moral being.

In his efforts to reach a vital theology he became convinced that the symbolic use of language and the imperfections of logic were responsible for much that was unreal in the dogmatic teaching of his day. He therefore prefixed to a work entitled *God in Christ,* 1849, his famous *Dissertation on Language,* in which he claimed that words:

> are related to the truth only as form to spirit—earthen vessels in which the truth is borne, yet always offering their mere flattery as being the truth itself.

Criticisms of all kinds were made against these views and theories and BUSHNELL undertook to reply to many of them in *Christ in Theology*, 1851.

His third important deliverance against the older type of dogma was made in a book entitled *Nature and the Supernatural*, 1858, which followed up and completed the teaching of the earlier *Christian Nurture*. He describes the volume in the Preface:

> Here is a wide hypothesis of the world, and the great problem of life and sin and supernatural redemption and Christ and a Christly Providence and a divinely certified history and of superhuman gifts entered into the world and finally of God as related to all, which liquidates these stupendous facts in issue between Christians and unbelievers and gives a rational account of them.

"The superb tenth chapter" of the book has been separately issued with the title *The Character of Jesus Forbidding His Possible Classification with Men*, 1861. In that chapter as in *Christ and His Salvation*, 1864, BUSHNELL shewed his essential fidelity to the historic faith of the Church.

His *Vicarious Sacrifice*, 1866, put the divine relation to the work of Atonement in a truly ethical light, and emphasised the fact that God was actuated by the motive of love. Although BUSHNELL pressed these new thoughts upon his contemporaries he clothed many of them in the old forms and phrases.

> In order to make men penitent, and so to want forgiveness,—that is, to keep the world alive to the eternal integrity, verity, and sanctity of God's law,—that is, to keep us apprised of sin, and deny us any power of rest while we continue under sin, it was needful

that Christ, in his life and sufferings, should consecrate or reconsecrate the desecrated law of God, and give it more exact and imminent authority than it had before.

But in a second volume on the same theme, *Forgiveness and Law,* 1874, he made confession that his theology was still growing:

Having undertaken to find the truth on this great subject at whatever cost I am not willing to be excused from further obligation because the truth appears to be outgrowing my published expositions. There is no reason, personal to myself, why I should be fastened to my own small measures, when larger measures are given me.

An even more popular antagonist of the older Calvinism was HENRY WARD BEECHER, 1813-1887, whose place in the liberal movement may be understood from his declaration:

I think that when I stand in Zion and before God, the highest thing that I shall look back upon will be that blessed morning of May when it pleased God to reveal to my wondering soul the idea that it was His nature to love a man in his sins for the sake of helping him out of them.

Whilst still the most conspicuous preacher in America he acted as editor-in-chief of *The Independent,* 1861-1863. In 1870 he founded and edited *The Christian Union* which later on became *The Outlook,* an undenominational weekly. He was not a theologian, his part was that of "hauling bricks for the new theology," but his repudiation of even an alleviated Calvinism was definite and complete.

Even under that the iron entered my soul. There
were days and weeks in which the pall of death over
the universe could not have made it darker to my eyes
than those in which I thought, 'If you are elected you
will be saved, and if you are not elected you will be
damned, and there is no hope for you.'

Among many miscellaneous works his *Bible Studies*
1878, were notable as giving forecasts of the higher criticism, and his *Evolution and Religion*, 1885, was a popular
exposition of the then new theory. Few, if any, of his
books have kept their place in public favour; they served
their end by promoting the transition of thought.

GEORGE PARK FISHER, 1827-1909, defended that transition in his work entitled *Faith and Rationalism*, 1879,
and indicated the stages of the progress of biblical criticism in
The Nature and Method of Revelation, 1890. THEODORE
THORNTON MUNGER, 1830-1910, gave even more effective support to the cause of theological liberalism by his volume of Sermons entitled *The Freedom of Faith*, 1883, the
introduction to which "stands in some respects unparalleled
as a summary of the new theology in America." The work
of PHILLIPS BROOKS, 1835-1893, registered the victory of
the new over the old. In him the collapse of Calvinism in
America was complete. He described Christianity, as he
realised it, in a work entitled *The Influence of Jesus*, 1879.

A poetic conception of the world we live in, a willing acceptance of mystery, an expectation of progress
by development, an absence of fastidiousness that
comes from a sense of the possibilities of all humanity
and a perpetual enlargement of thought from the arbitrary into the essential—these, then, I think, are the
intellectual characteristics which Christ's disciples gathered from their Master.

An analogous but by no means parallel movement ran its course in England. The poetry of WILLIAM WORDS-WORTH, 1770-1850, like that of SAMUEL TAYLOR COLE-RIDGE, 1772-1834, promised at first to carry the romantic movement to its perfect fulfilment, but he soon fell back upon the customary lines of the Anglican traditions. His *Lines, Composed a Few Miles above Tintern Abbey,* . . . . 1798, were the record of his early mystical emotions. The *Ecclesiastical Sketches,* 1822, reflect his acceptance of the traditional teaching of his Church. COLERIDGE passed very quickly from poetry to philosophy and gave a new impulse and a new direction to the almost effete theology of England.

COLERIDGE exercised his diffused but quickening influence through the medium of a very few of his numerous writings. The first and most important of these was *Aids to Reflection,* 1825, "a commentary in the form of aphorisms and selected passages from the writings of Archbishop Leighton." It was an effort to harmonise faith and reason, a kind of manual of liberal orthodoxy. COLERIDGE assumed as the foundation of his teaching the existence of a moral will:

> If there be ought spiritual in man the will must be such. If there be a will, there must be a spirituality in man.

He found that Christianity rests on three ultimate facts:

> the reality of the law of conscience; the existence of a responsible will as the subject of that law; and lastly the existence of God.

From these assumptions COLERIDGE derived his views of Christianity which he interpreted as a living expression of the spiritual consciousness. "England heard with as much surprise as if the doctrine was new, that the Christian faith, the Athanasian Creed, of which they had come to wish that the Church was well rid, was "the perfection of human intelligence"; that

> the compatibility of a document with the conclusions of self-evident reason and with the laws of conscience is a condition *a priori* of any evidence adequate to the proof of its having been revealed by God," . . . . "there are mysteries in Christianity, but these mysteries are reason in its highest form of self-affirmation (*Aids to Reflection,* Preface).[2]

COLERIDGE, without doubt, was the chief agent in reviving in England the idea of the Church as something "distinct from an estate of the realm or a department of the State on the one hand, and a mere voluntary association on the other." Even in the *Aids to Reflection* he had written:

> My fixed principle is: that a Christianity without a Church exercising spiritual authority is vanity and delusion.

He elaborated this principle in *The Church and State according to the Idea of Each,* 1830. From a literary point of view this work is most unsatisfactory; it is rambling and involved but it presents

> the *Idea* of a national church as the only safe criterion by which we can judge of existing things.

But the Church that COLERIDGE had in view was a sort of third estate of the realm in which the learned of all denominations could foster and spread abroad intellectual and religious knowledge of every kind. It would be a custodian of the nation's civilisation.

---

[2] Mark Pattison, *Essays and Reviews,* "Tendencies of Religious Thought in England, 1688-1750."

The Confessions of an Inquiring Spirit, which he held
back during his lifetime, was published in 1840. This was
an earnest effort to solve some of the vexed problems associated with the Scriptures.

> In the Bible there is more that finds me than I have
> experienced in all other books put together; the words
> of the Bible find me at greater depths of my being;
> and whatever finds me brings with it irresistible evi-
> dence of its having proceeded from the Holy Spirit.

He frankly rejected the theory of verbal inspiration which
he declared turns:

> This breathing organism, this glorious *panharmon-
> icon* . . . . into a colossal Memnon's head, a hollow
> passage for a voice, a voice that mocks the voices of
> many men, and speaks in their names, and yet is but
> one voice, and the same;—and no man uttered it, and
> never in a human heart was it conceived . . . . the
> Doctrine evacuates of all sense and efficacy the sure and
> constant tradition, that all the several books bound
> up together in our precious family Bibles were com-
> posed in different and widely distant ages, under the
> greatest diversity of circumstances, and degrees of light
> and information, and yet that the composers, whether
> as uttering or as recording what was uttered and what
> was done, were all actuated by a pure and holy
> Spirit. . . .

The influence of COLERIDGE was potent in many minds.
JULIUS CHARLES HARE, 1795-1855, was, perhaps, his only
whole-hearted disciple. In his devotional book *The Mission of the Comforter,* 1846, he acknowledged his indebtedness and his allegiance.

Of all recent English writers, the one whose sanction I have chiefly desired is the great religious philosopher to whom the mind of our generation in England owes more than to any other man, and whose it was to spiritualise not only our philosophy but our theology, to raise them both above the empiricism into which they had fallen, and to set them free from the technical trammels of logical systems.

In conjunction with his brother AUGUSTUS WILLIAM, 1792-1834, HARE published a book which became immensely popular, under the title *Guesses at Truth*, 1827. It was a collection of thoughts, suggestions and short essays which carried the characteristic notes of a dangerously liberal theology. HARE was an able controversialist as his *Contest with Rome*, 1851, and his *Vindication of Luther*, 1854, showed.

The tradition of COLERIDGE passed into what is commonly called the "Broad Church" movement, of which JOHN FREDERICK DENISON MAURICE, 1805-1872, was an exponent. His diffuse but essentially dogmatic system of theological opinions centred in the doctrine of "universal redemption", *i.e.*, that the work of Christ is for all. Much that he wrote was tentative, awkward, and inappropriate, but his aim was definite.

The sense of our substantial union as men with Christ, and of His union with the Father, sometimes comes to me with over-powering conviction, not of delight such as a Santa Theresa or Fenelon may have felt, but of its stern, hard, scientific reality, which makes me long that I had the fervour and earnestness in making my belief known, which I admire and ought not to envy in other men."

The long list of his contributions to Christian literature began with *The Kingdom of Christ,* 1838, in the second edition of which he acknowledged his debt to COLERIDGE and "his deep and solemn obligations" to the *Aids to Reflection.* In 1842 he published *The Kingdom of God* to endorse the Quaker doctrine of the inner light. His most popular book was a survey of the ethnic faiths, entitled *The Religions of the World,* 1847, in which he gave voice to his view that Catholicity consists in drawing together the positive aspects of truth and neglecting what is merely negative.

His *Theological Essays,* 1853, written to confute Unitarianism, showed wherein he diverged from popular religious belief and involved him in the controversy that at length cost him his professorship.

> I cannot dissemble my belief, that if we are resting on any formulas—supposing they are the best formulas that were ever handed down from one generation to another—or on the divinest book that was ever written by God for the teaching of mankind, and not on the Living God Himself, our foundation will be found sandy, and will crumble under our feet.

In a work entitled *What is Revelation,* 1859, he subjected *The Limits of Religious Thought* published by HENRY LONGUEVILLE MANSEL, 1820-1871, in 1858, to severe criticism from the Christian standpoint and in reply to MANSEL'S *Examination of Rev. F. D. M.'s Strictures,* he wrote *A Sequel to the Enquiry What is Revelation,* 1860. "The great waste of energy" with which his writings were done "was probably never better illustrated than in his answers to Dr. Mansel, full of noble truth and passion as they were. The Dean did not catch his drift at all, and even the theologians of the day hardly caught his drift; it was only those who had got the key to his mind from the study of many previous writings who really understood what he meant."[3]

No man was ever less of a purely historical critic, his *Lectures on the Prophets and Kings of the Old Testament*, 1853, *The Patriarchs and Lawgivers of the Old Testament*, 1855, and his expositions of the Johannine Books of the New Testament were reinterpretations of what is eternally true religion. "It never occurred to him that either physical science or historical criticism, whatever might come of either, could possibly break down either the truth or the importance of revelation."

> All historical criticism is good, it seems to me, just so far as it tests facts, in love and reverence for facts and for what facts contain; all is bad and immoral which introduces the notion that it signifies little whether they turn out to be facts or no, or the notion that their reality as facts depends on certain accidents in the narration of them.

MAURICE became the moving spirit of an effort to achieve a Christian Socialism, an effort which numbered CHARLES KINGSLEY, 1819-1875, among its warmest advocates. KINGSLEY declared that he owed more to MAURICE'S *Kingdom of Christ* than to any book he had ever read, but to all that he learned from his "Master in Theology" he added a belief in symbolism that he had gained from Thomas Carlyle's *Sartor Resartus*, and a very deep repugnance from the evangelical teaching concerning heaven and hell.

His first published volume contained *The Saint's Tragedy*, 1848, a poetical drama describing the renunciation of Elizabeth of Hungary which KINGSLEY wrote as a protest against the Roman Catholic ideal of sainthood. His own ideal is revealed in the lines:

---

[3] R. H. Hutton.

Could we but crush that ever-craving lust
For bliss, which kills all bliss, and lose our life,
Our barren unit life, to find again
A thousand lives in those for whom we die.
So were we men and women, and should hold
Our rightful rank in God's great universe,
Wherein, in heaven and earth, by will or nature,
Nought lives for self—

(Act. IV. Scene iii.)

"As a preacher he was vivid, eager and earnest, equally plain-spoken and uncompromising when preaching to a fashionable congregation or to his own village poor. One of the very best of his writings is a sermon called *The Message of the Church to Working Men;* and the best of his published discourses are the *Twenty-five Village Sermons,*"[4] 1849.

KINGSLEY made his novels the vehicles of some of his most pronounced views. *Alton Locke,* and *Yeast,* both published in 1849, revealed his social ideals. *Hypatia,* 1853, gave a picture of early Christianity in conflict with Alexandrian philosophy, and was written to show that new foes had old faces. His volume of history, *Alexandria and her Schools,* 1854, displayed the background against which the novel of the previous year had been drawn. *Westward Ho,* 1855, was a passionately anti-Catholic story of adventure in the Spanish main.

A liberal movement that was independent of COLERIDGE was heralded as early as 1811 when ROBERT FELLOWES, 1771-1847, issued his *Religion without Cant,* in which he crossed swords with dissent and other forms, which he considered misrepresentations, of Christianity. His later work *The Religion of the Universe,* 1836, represented religion as a theistic scientific culture. The real father and master mind of the early "Oriel" or "Noetic" school, as it came to be called, was EDWARD COPLESTON, 1776-1849, the head of

---

[4] *Encyclopedia Britannica,* Vol. XV., p. 818.

Oriel College, Oxford.   His strong sympathies with liberalism in Church and State inspired his influence with vigour
and vitality.

Among the men who gathered about him was RICHARD
WHATELY, 1787-1863, who became known to Christian
literary history as the author of a clever caricature of sceptical criticism.   This was his *Historic Doubts relative to
Napoleon Bonaparte,* 1819.   By the application of sceptical
methods to the history of Napoleon he evaporated the person and achievements of the little Corsican into fiction and
thus reduced to an absurdity Hume's doctrine that no testimony is sufficient to prove a miracle.   It was "perhaps the
cleverest and most famous piece of ironical argumentation
produced in England during the first quarter of the century."

His Bampton Lectures entitled *On the Use and Abuse of
Party Feeling in Religion* were published in 1822.   In due
succession there followed a series of Essays designed to show
how little the traditional dogmatism of the Church could
bear the light of reason and of historical knowledge.
WHATELY was "the subverter of prejudice and commonplace."   The first of the series was entitled *Essays on Some
Peculiarities of the Christian Religion,* 1825.   In 1828 came
a second series *On Some of the Difficulties in the Writings
of St. Paul,* in which he dealt with such subjects as Election, Perseverance, Assurance and Imputation.   "Election"
is used always in a general sense of the body of the Church:

> the Apostles address these converts universally as the
> 'elect' or 'chosen' of God, this must be understood of
> their being chosen out of the whole mass of the Gen-
> tiles to certain peculiar privileges.

> The Almighty, of his own arbitrary choice, causes
> some to be born to wealth or rank, others to poverty
> or obscurity, some in a heathen and others in a Chris-

tian country; the advantages and privileges are various, and so far as we can see arbitrarily dispensed. But the final rewards or punishments depend, as we are plainly taught, on the use or abuse of those advantages.

The third series was On the Errors of Romanism traced to their Origin in Human Nature, 1830.

His Thoughts on the Sabbath, 1832, contained an unanswerable statement of his views. A handbook of Christian Evidences, 1837 became so widely used that it was translated into more than a dozen languages during his lifetime. His Essays on some of the Dangers to the Christian Faith, 1839 and The Kingdom of Christ, 1841 were less generally known than his editions of PALEY and a work on Logic in which he is seen at his best.

The member of this school whose writings created most excitement was RENN DICKSON HAMPDEN, 1793-1868. He gave evidence of his departure from the systematic consistency of "logical theology" in an Essay on the Philosophical Evidence of Christianity; or the Credibility obtained to a Scriptural Revelation from its Coincidence with the Facts of Nature, 1827. In his notorious Bampton Lectures entitled The Scholastic Philosophy considered in its Relation to Christian Theology, 1832, he attempted to show that systematic theology was a product of Scholasticism. "It has very little foundation in Scripture and no response in the religious consciousness," and is "the principal obstacle to the union and peace of the Church."

The combination and analyses of words which the logical theology has produced have given occasion to the passions of men to arm themselves in behalf of the phantoms thus called into being.

Whilst theologians of the schools have thought they were establishing religious truths by elaborate argumentation, they have been only multiplying and rearranging theological language.

The book aroused a controversy of the utmost bitterness. *An Elucidation of Dr. Hampden's Theological Statements*, 1836, which rumour attributed to J. H. NEWMAN, was characterised by THOMAS ARNOLD as containing a series of deliberate falsehoods. EDWARD PUSEY and SAMUEL WILBERFORCE claimed that the lectures evaporated the doctrine of the Trinity into a mere series of scholastic propositions.

Calumny whispered that the actual author of the book was JOSEPH BLANCO WHITE, 1775-1841, who had been tutor in HAMPDEN'S family during 1832-1835. WHITE had written *Internal Evidences against Catholicism*, 1825, and *Second Travels of an Irish Gentleman in Search of a Religion*, 1833, but is now only remembered by what COLERIDGE extravagantly acclaimed as "the finest and most grandly conceived sonnet in our language."

> Mysterious Night! when our first parent knew
>   Thee from report divine, and heard thy name,
>   Did he not tremble for this goodly frame,
> This glorious canopy of light and blue?
> But through a curtain of translucent dew,
>   Bathed in the rays of the great setting flame,
>   Hesperus with the host of heaven came:
> And lo! Creation broadened to man's view!
> Who could have guessed such darkness lay concealed
>   Within thy beams, O Sun? or who divined,
> When bud and flower and insect lay revealed,
>   Thou to such countless worlds hadst made us blind?
> Why should we then shun Death with anxious strife?
> If Light conceals so much, wherefore not Life?

The year 1860 was a landmark in the history of Christian literature in England, for it saw the publication of *Essays and Reviews* a collection of papers written to show the actual state of religious thought. It was both a manifesto and a challenge, and although the Essays, with one exception, were not signally brilliant, they marked a turning point in the history of opinion by establishing the right of free enquiry into matters of faith. The volume was sent forth as:

> an attempt to illustrate the advantage derivable to the cause of religious and moral truth from a free handling, in a becoming spirit, of subjects peculiarly liable to suffer by the repetition of conventional language, and from traditional methods of treatment (To the Reader).

FREDERICK TEMPLE, 1821-1902, wrote on "The Education of the World."

> We may, then, rightly speak of a childhood, a youth, and a manhood of the world . . . . In childhood we are subject to positive rules, which we cannot understand, but are bound implicitly to obey. In youth, we are subject to the influence of example; . . . . In manhood, we are comparatively free from external restraints; and, if we are to learn, must be our own instructors. First come Rules, then Examples, then Principles. First comes the Law, then the Son of Man, then the Gift of the Spirit.

ROWLAND WILLIAMS, 1817-1870, wrote on "Bunsen's Researches"; BENJAMIN JOWETT, 1817-1895, inserted a long remembered paper on "The Interpretation of Scripture."

> The book itself remains, as at the first, unchanged amid the changing interpretations of it. The office of the interpreter is, not to add another, but to recover the original one; the meaning, that is, of the words as they first struck on the ears or flashed before the eyes of those who heard and read them . . . . The history of Christendom is nothing to him; but only

the scene at Galilee or Jerusalem . . . . All the after-thoughts of theology are nothing to him: they are not the true lights which guide him in difficult places. . . . . His object is to read Scripture, like any other book, with a real interest, and not merely a conventional one.

MARK PATTISON, 1813-1884, was responsible for the important paper on "Tendencies of Religious Thought in England 1688-1750," which set an example for a fresh series of studies of Christian history. The chief promoter and planner of the book, HENRY BRISTOW WILSON, 1802-1888, wrote on "The National Church."

> Jesus Christ has not revealed his religion as a theology of the intellect, nor as an historical faith; and it is a stifling of the true Christian life, both in the individual and in the Church, to require of many men a unanimity in speculative doctrine, which is unattainable, and a uniformity of historical belief which can never exist. The true Christian life is the consciousness of bearing a part in a great moral order, of which the highest agency upon earth has been committed to the Church.

BADEN POWELL, 1796-1860, contributed a paper on "The Study of the Evidences of Christianity." The only lay member of the group was CHARLES WYCLIFFE GOODWIN, 1817-1878, whose essay "On the Mosaic Cosmogony" was a plea for the interpretation of the creation stories of Genesis as poems.

JOHN ROBERT SEELEY, 1834-1895, broke fresh ground in the study of the life of Jesus when he wrote *Ecce Homo, a Survey of the Life and Work of Jesus Christ,* 1866. "It deliberately excluded consideration of the supernatural and insisted on Christ's human work as the founder of a Church of humanity." "It was not directly critical, but, upon the basis of the narratives of the four Gospels, drew a picture of the moral personality of Jesus with great delicacy of feeling and a profound perception of his peculiar greatness and originality." The secret of His ministry was found to lie in His insight and "enthusiasm for humanity."

A later work entitled *Natural Religion*, 1882, was put forth by SEELEY as an eirenicon to unite all believers in virtue and the worth of life in a religion which would be free from supernaturalism but would include every form of truth, goodness, and beauty. "Nowhere perhaps could we find a more signal example of the characteristic excellences of the English prose of the (time), of its mingled subtlety and trenchancy, of its flashes of impassioned feeling seen through an atmosphere of steady self-control."[5]

> Nature presents itself to us as a goddess of unweariable vigor and unclouded happiness but without any trouble or any compunction in her eye, without a conscience or a heart. But God as the word is used by ancient prophets and modern poets . . . . conveys all this beauty and greatness and glory and conveys besides whatever more awful forces stir within the human heart, whatever binds men in families and orders them in states.

MATTHEW ARNOLD, 1822-1888, like J. R. SEELEY, was of the class of scholarly laymen who wished to liberate religion from dependence upon either critics or clerics. He unfolded his undogmatic liberalism in *St. Paul and Protestantism*, 1870, which contains a fine exposition of St. Paul's teaching.

> The three essential terms of Pauline theology, are not as popular theology makes them: *calling, justification, sanctification;* but are rather these: *dying*

---

[5] F. W. H. Myers, *Essays*, Modern viii., Eversley Series, p. 306.

with Christ, resurrection from the dead, growing unto Christ.

In *Literature and Dogma*, 1873, ARNOLD distinguished between the religion of conduct—conduct being three-fourths of life—and the religion of the creeds. *God and the Bible*, 1875, offered a survey of the Old Testament faith in which ARNOLD found that God is "the stream of tendency that makes for righteousness." His *Last Essays on Church and Religion*, 1877, were further examples of that "sweetness and light" which he sought to diffuse throughout the English Church. ARNOLD however was ill fitted for applying the results of Biblical criticism, "he arrived at results which no disinterested critic, regarding the Bible merely as literature, could accept as approximating to the actual meanings of the writers."

The work which liberal thinkers were trying to do in England was being attempted in Scotland by THOMAS ERSKINE of Linlathen, 1788-1870, whose main aim next to the promotion of pure religion was "to insist on the ultimate universal salvation of mankind, and to argue that the conscience and not miracle, was the chief evidence for a divine revelation." In 1820 he published *Remarks on the Internal Evidences for the Truth of Revealed Religion*, to prove that Christian faith finds its "surest evidence in the inner life of the soul." The book marked if it did not create a crisis in the theological thought of Scotland.

The reasonableness of a religion seems to me to consist in there being a direct and natural connection between a believing of the doctrines which it inculcates, and a being formed by these to the character which it recommends. If the belief of the doctrines has no tendency to train a disciple in a more exact and more willing discharge of its moral obligations, there is evidently a very strong probability against the truth of that religion.

In a work entitled *The Unconditional Freeness of the Gospel*, 1828, he describes the essential character of Christianity as consisting in the revelation of Divine love.

> The pardon of the gospel is in effect a declaration on the part of God to every individual sinner in the whole world that His holy compassion embraces him, and the blood of Jesus Christ has atoned for his sins.

The Brazen Serpent, or Life Coming through Death, 1831, is the most theological of his writings. *The Doctrine of Election, and its Connection with the General Theory of Christianity*, 1837, contained the exposition of his fundamental principle:

> Restoration to a condition of salvation cannot . . . be effected otherwise than by the restoration of the love of God to its place as the paramount principle in the heart, resulting in the due subordination of self and the creatures under it. Any remedy which falls below this restoration falls below man's need. No pardon which leaves this undone is of any value to him.

"There can be no question, that for the finer orthodoxy of the heart, for supreme and untainted loyalty to Christ, for singular sweetness and charm of disposition, no Church in Scotland has produced the equal" of JOHN MCLEOD CAMPBELL, 1800-1872. He applied the principles of ERSKINE to the study of the central theme of Christianity in his immensely influential work entitled *The Nature of the Atonement*, 1856, one of the greatest books on the subject.

The aim of CAMPBELL was to find a moral basis for the Atonement, and thus to overthrow the long current legal and substitutionary theories. He had written a volume entitled *The Bread of Life,* 1851, in answer to the teaching of the Church of Rome concerning the Lord's Supper, and in 1852 he issued a series of expositions of passages of Scripture with the title *Fragments of Truth.* His last theological work was *Thoughts on Revelation,* 1862, written to oppose the teaching of *Essays and Reviews,* and in which he developed his views on religious assurance. The style of this work showed marked improvement over that of his earlier writings, it is "as clear as sunshine."

CAMPBELL'S influence tended to disintegrate the older Calvinistic theology of Scotland and encouraged the harmonising of the critical and the constructive elements in the religious thought of the age.

The invasion of Italy by the spirit of Romanticism was signalised by the work of ALESSANDRO FRANCESCO TOMASSO ANTONIO MANZONI, 1785-1873. He abandoned the scepticism of the followers of Voltaire for a fervent Catholicism which coloured all his later life. His first religious work consisted of a series of sacred lyrics, *Sacred Hymns,* 1815. He then wrote a treatise on Catholic morality.

His most famous work *The Betrothed Lover,* 1825, which has been translated into almost every European language, does not fall within the limits of this Outline. It is by his Hymns that he holds a place in the history of Christian literature. These were begun as early as 1812; they were mostly concerned with the festivals of the Church and perhaps suggested KEBLE'S Christian Year. From one point of view "he founds the Neo-Catholic school, and personifies the revival of the religious spirit in its most gentle and edifying form."[6]

A neo-Catholic revival was heralded in England by JOHN KEBLE, 1792-1836, whose volume of sacred poems *The Christian Year,* 1827, expressed the quieter mood of the

[6] Richard Garnett, *Italian Literature,* p. 342.

romantic spirit. These poems were the result of KEBLE'S discovery of a religious symbolism and a divine message in Nature; but they were written to arouse reverence and affection for the order, the history, and the spiritual heroes of the Anglican Church.

> Thus everywhere we find our suffering God,
>   And where He trod
> May set our steps: the cross on Calvary
>   Uplifted high
> Beams on the martyr host, a beacon light
>   In open fight.

KEBLE'S *Sermon on National Apostasy*, preached July 14, 1833, may be regarded as the definite point of departure of the Oxford Movement. This movement had an immense influence on Christian literature through the writings of JOHN HENRY NEWMAN, 1801-1890, a subtle and lucid thinker, a profoundly religious spirit, and a supreme master of literary style.

In conjunction with RICHARD HURRELL FROUDE, 1803-1836, he issued *Lyra Apostolica*, 1836, a collection of poems' by six writers reprinted from the *British Magazine*. In these religious poems the note of battle against liberalism was unmistakeable. The famous lines "Lead, Kindly light, amid the encircling gloom," appear in the book; but the purpose of it is shewn in:

LIBERALISM

> Ye cannot halve the Gospel of God's grace;
>   Men of presumptuous heart! I know you well.
>   Ye are of those who plan that we should dwell,
> Each in his tranquil home and holy place;
> Seeing the Word refines all natures rude,
> And tames the stirrings of the multitude......
> But, as for zeal and quick-eyed sanctity,
> And the dread depths of grace, ye passed them by.
> And so ye halve the truth; for ye in heart,
>   At best, are doubters whether it be true,
>   The theme discarding, as unmeet for you,
> Statesmen or sages......

At his suggestion the famous series of *Tracts for the Times* was begun to sound the alarm of "stress and danger and appeal as a man might give notice of a fire." Of the ninety Tracts that were issued, NEWMAN wrote twenty-nine; the others were the work of FROUDE, PUSEY, BOWDEN, PALMER, PERCIVAL, WILLIAMS, and behind these "was the figure of that wonderful old scholar, theologian, and tory, MARTIN JOSEPH ROUTH, 1755-1854, the author of *Reliquiae Sacrae,* 1814-1848. The series was suddenly brought to an end when NEWMAN in *Tract* No. XC, 1841, tried to prove that the Thirty-Nine Articles though "the product of an un-Catholic age," were "patient of a Catholic interpretation." This aroused "an immense commotion" and the Tracts were abandoned.

Their influence however had been enormous and it was much strengthened by NEWMAN'S *Parochial and Plain Sermons,* 1837-1843, and by his work on *The Prophetical Office of the Church* 1838, in which he said:

> It still remains to be tried whether what is called Anglicanism, the religion of Andrewes, Laud, Hammond, Butler, and Wilson, is capable of being professed, acted on, and maintained on a large sphere of action, and through a sufficient period, or whether it be a mere modification of Romanism, or of popular Protestantism, according as we view it.

NEWMAN'S conversion to the Roman Catholic communion, 1845, wrecked the organised Oxford Movement, but it did not hinder his literary labours. His first work as a Catholic was *An Essay on the Development of Christian Doctrine,* 1845, in which he argued that the doctrines of the Church have been evolved with

> efforts, hesitation, suspense, interruption, swayings to the right hand and to the left.

Two pieces of fiction came from his pen in 1847, *Callista,* a story of the third century, and *Loss and Gain,* the record of a man's conversion to Rome. It was however by his wonderful *Apologia pro vita sua,* 1864, that he gained and held the mind of the general public. This most beautiful of all autobiographies was written to contradict charges of insincerity and duplicity which CHARLES KINGSLEY had brought against him in a pamphlet entitled *What, then, does Dr. Newman mean? A Reply to a Pamphlet Lately Published by Dr. Newman,* 1864. The *Apologia* overwhelmed the aspersions by its passionate sincerity and by its splendour as a work of art. It ranks among the few Confessions in which genius discloses its soul. "The *Apologia* carried the country by storm. It became a classic of the language, and it had to be re-edited that its form, as well as its substance, might befit its permanent character. Its form had to be no longer that appropriate to a controversy of the hour in which rapier thrusts and colloquialisms were suitable weapons, but that of an earnest autobiography which could stand side by side with those of St. Augustine and Rousseau. Its very title was changed to 'History of my Religious Opinions'."[7]

In *The Dream of Gerontius,* 1865, NEWMAN made his one sustained flight into the realm of poetry. It recounts the emotions of one at the point of death who sees himself borne to the judgment seat and thence committed to the purifying influence of Purgatory.

> O Lord, how wonderful in depth and height,
>   But most in man, how wonderful Thou art!
> With what a love, what soft persuasive might
>   Victorious o'er the stubborn fleshly heart,
> Thy tale complete of saints Thou dost provide,
>   To fill the thrones which angels lost through pride!

His *Essay in Aid of a Grammar of Assent,* 1870, sought

---

[7] Newman's *Apologia* . . . . Oxford ed. (1913), Intro. pp. vii-viii.

to define the mental sense by which choice of truth is made
and to trace it in its various relationships and activities.

> By religion I mean the knowledge of God, of His
> Will, and of our duties towards Him; and there are
> three main channels which Nature furnishes for our
> acquiring this knowledge, viz., our own minds, the
> voice of mankind, and the course of the world, that is,
> of human life and human affairs . . . . . And the
> most authoritative of these three means of knowledge,
> as being specially our own, is our own mind.

NEWMAN was a prolific author and a most industrious
editor; he not only enriched Christian literature by adding
to it some of its most notable Sermons and many serviceable
discussions of theology and history but he projected and
wrote for a fine edition of the Church Fathers and a series of
credulous *Lives of the Saints.*

The scholar of the Oxford Movement was EDWARD
BOUVERIE PUSEY, 1800-1882, who alone of the Tractarians
was familiar with the German language. In controversy
real learning "was his sledge-hammer and battle mace." In
reply to an attack upon German rationalism made by HUGH
JAMES ROSE, 1795-1838, in a work entitled *The State of
the Protestant Religion in Germany,* 1825, PUSEY wrote his
interesting, well-informed and still useful *Historical Inquiry
into the Probable Causes of the Rationalistic Character of
German Theology,* 1828. This Inquiry exposed him to denunciation as "a German rationalist who dared to speak of a
new era in theology." Pusey defined rationalism as:

> The assumption that uncontrolled human reason in
> its degraded form is the primary interpreter of God's
> Word, without any regard to those rules or principles
> of interpretation which have guided the judgments of

Christ's Holy Catholic Church in all ages of its history and under every variety of its warfare.

His first big constructive work *Scriptural Views of Holy Baptism*, 1835 contained Nos. 67, 68, and 69 of the *Tracts for the Times*, and gave him the position of the head and centre of the Tractarian movement.

> . . if we use any image, we might better speak of the whole Gospel as an elixir of immortality, whereof some ingredients may be more powerful than the rest, but the efficacy of the whole depends upon the attemperment of the several portions; and we, who formed neither our own souls, nor this cure for them, dare not speak slightingly of the necessity of any portion.

His neo-Catholic position appears in his work entitled *The Church of England Leaves her Children Free to whom to open their Griefs*, 1850, and in *The Doctrine of the Real Presence as contained in the Fathers*, 1855. He gained an immense influence over the piety of his admirers by means of his personal Letters. As an expositor he is still remembered by his *Commentary on The Minor Prophets*, 1877. A little volume of *Private Prayers*, 1883, increased his reputation for saintliness.

The literary influence of the Oxford Movement was deep and far reaching. It encouraged a directness and severity of speech, it taught men to depend upon history, and it turned its sympathisers back to ancient liturgies, and hymns and traditions of the Church. Its spirit was a moulding force in the minds of men like Richard William Church, 1815-1890, Richard Chenevix Trench, 1807-1886, William Stubbs, 1825-1901, Henry Parry Liddon, 1829-1890, John Mason Neale 1818-1866, and John Bowling Mozeley, 1813-1878.

The extreme criticism of the Christian origins to which the work of STRAUSS had given expression called for a fresh study of the character of the New Testament and thus turned the attention of FERDINAND CHRISTIAN BAUR, 1792-1860, to the labour that created an epoch in Biblical criticism. BAUR had been the teacher of STRAUSS at Tubingen, but until the advent of the *Life of Christ* his interests had been philosophical rather than critical.

In 1824 he published *Symbolism and Mythology, or the Nature Religion of Antiquity.* In 1832 JOHANN ADAM MOEHLER, 1796-1838, the most eminent representative of Roman Catholic theological science, issued his important work entitled *Symbolic, or a Representation of the Dogmatic Antithesis of the Catholics and Protestants according to their Published Confessions.* This was a manifesto of the liberal school of Catholicism and as such was not acceptable in official quarters; Protestants also complained that it was scarcely just to the positive aspects of the Reformation. BAUR wrote in answer to it *The Antithesis of Catholics and Protestants,* 1833, a work of remarkable breadth and power, superior in everything but style to the book against which it was written.

Under the influence of the philosophy of Hegel, BAUR gave his attention to the study of history and wrote *The Religious System of the Manichaeans,* 1831; *The Beginning of Ebionitism,* 1831; and *Apollonius of Tyana and Christ, or the Relation of Pythagoreanism and Christianity,* 1832. These were preparatory to more definitely Christian studies.

His famous working theory for the criticism of early Church history first appears in *The Christ Party in the Corinthian Community,* 1831. "The oppostion between ebionitism or Petrinism and Paulinism is the key destined to open all the closed doors to the critical intelligence; it is the great discovery that allowed BAUR to pronounce in a

regal way upon all the controversial questions concerning
the apostolic century."

In *The So-called Pastoral Epistles*, 1835, BAUR sought
to prove that these Letters were written to oppose the growth
of Gnosticism; they therefore could not have been the
work of the Apostle Paul. During the same year he wrote
the most suggestive of all his books on the history of religious thought: this was *The Christian Gnosis*, 1835, in
which he declared:

> All that Christ is as God-man He is only in faith
> and through faith; what lies behind faith as historical
> reality is veiled in mystery.
>
> For faith, therefore, the appearance of the God-man,
> an incarnation of God, His birth in the flesh, may be
> an historical fact; but to speculative thought the incar-
> nation of God is no single event which once happened,
> but an eternal determination of the essence of God, by
> virtue of which God only in so far becomes man in
> time (in every individual man) as He is man from
> eternity. The finitude and humiliation and passion
> which Christ as God-man endured God at every mo-
> ment suffers as man . . . . Christ as man, as God-
> man, is man in His universality; not a single individ-
> ual, but a universal individual.

BAUR next turned his attention to dogmatic theology,
and issued *The Christian Doctrine of Redemption*, 1838,
and *The Christian Doctrine of the Trinity and of the Incarnation of God in Christ*, 1841-1843. At length he embodied the results of years of study in *Paul the Apostle of
Jesus Christ, his Life and Work, his Letters and Doctrine*,
1845, a work in which he applied with thoroughness the
characteristic theory of Tubingen, viz., that keen rivalry
existed between the early Christian parties of Peter and Paul,
and that these conflicts directed, even if they did not distort,

the writings of the New Testament. The theory claimed that the Pauline Epistles exhibit the Church as first rent by division, then as passing through a period of conciliation which is reflected in the *Synoptic Gospels,* and finally as reaching a compromise of which the *Fourth Gospel* is the product. BAUR worked out his theory with consummate skill. His book made an epoch in New Testament criticism. "This was the first time that a true historical method had been applied to the New Testament literature as a whole."

His *Critical Examination of the Canonical Gospels,* 1847, maintained the theory that *Mark* is based on *Matthew* and *Luke,* while the *Fourth Gospel* which is irreconcilable with the Synoptics, is unhistorical.

BAUR then gave his attention to the history of doctrine and issued *A Text Book of the History of Christian Dogma,* 1847, but ere long went back to the investigation of history proper and wrote *Epochs of Church Historical Writing,* 1852, *Christianity and the Christian Church of the First Three Centuries,* which was not issued until after his death, and *The Christian Church from the Beginning of the Fourth to the End of the Sixth Century,* 1859. Finally came the great *Church History,* 1853-1863, in which BAUR himself, his son FERDINAND, and his son-in-law EDUARD ZELLER all had a share. This was "the first thorough and satisfactory attempt to explain the rise of Christianity and the Church on strictly historical lines."

Our first task, then, in a history of Christianity or of the Christian Church, must be to place ourselves at the point where Christianity enters into the stream of the world's history, and to gain a general idea of its relation to the other elements of the history of the time. With this end we have first of all to ask, whether there is anything in Christianity which we may recognize as, on the one hand, belonging to the essence of that religion, and, on the other, expressive of the general character of the age in which it appeared? If any such points of contact can be distinctly recognised, a ray of light will at once be shed on the historical origin of Christianity . . . .

But what is Christianity itself? What common unity underlies these different aspects, and combines them into a whole? We answer in a word, its spirituality. We find Christianity to be far more free than any other religion from everything merely external, sensuous, or material. It lays its foundations more deeply in the inmost essence of man's nature and in the principles of the moral consciousness. It knows, as it says of itself, no worship of God but the worship in spirit and in truth. When we inquire what constitutes the absolute character of Christianity, we must point to its spirituality (*The Church History*, trans. ed. by Allan Menzies. Vol. I., pp. 2, 9).

ALBERT SCHWEGLER, 1819-1857, made his entrance into the world of Christian literature with *A History of Montanism, or the Christian Church of the 2nd century,* 1841; a really remarkable work. He exhibited the results of the Tubingen theory, with characteristic vigour and clearness in a book entitled *The Post-Apostolic Age in the Critical Moment of its Development,* 1845. This was a violent, arbitrary, but picturesque presentation of the extreme tendencies of BAUR'S criticism. It reduced Christianity to ebionitism and it exaggerated the supposed division between the Petrine and the Pauline elements.

EDUARD ZELLER, 1814-1908, contributed a notable work entitled *The Apostolic History Critically Examined,* 1854, "it regards the Acts as an "offer of peace" made by a Paulinist to the Judaisers with a view to the union of the two parties." It possesses "the merit of having by its incisive criticism brought out the problem of early Christian history into the full light of day." ZELLER also wrote *A History of the Christian Church*, 1898.

The Tubingen school, which numbered among its adherents many most able scholars, gradually receded from the critical positions occupied by its leader; but in spite of the modification of its original claims its work still continues to influence the course and character of biblical study.

ALBRECHT BENJAMIN RITSCHL, 1822-1889, represents the break-up of the school. As an enthusiastic disciple of BAUR, he wrote *The Gospel of Marcion and the Canonical Gospel of Luke*, 1846; but his opinions changed as he showed in the most important work that came from his hands—*The Origin of the Old Catholic Church*, 1851. In its second edition, 1857, this book reveals "an entire emancipation from BAUR'S method," and it displays a total antagonism to his fundamental principle. RITSCHL maintained the essential unity of the attitude of the disciples to Christ. He asserted that Jewish Christianity had little to do with the growth of Old Catholicism, upon which Gentile Christianity exercised a dominating influence.

RITSCHL is best known by his three volumes on the doctrine of salvation. The first volume was *A Critical History of the Christian Doctrine of Justification and Reconciliation*, 1870. In a second volume he gathered together and examined the biblical material on which the doctrine is based. The third volume entitled *The Christian Doctrine of Justification and Reconciliation*, 1874, contained a constructive statement.

> Christianity is the monotheistic, completely spiritual, and ethical religion, which, on the basis of the life of its Founder as redeeming and as establishing the Kingdom of God, consists in the freedom of the chil-

dren of God, includes the impulse to conduct from the motive of love, the intention of which is the moral organisation of mankind, and in the filial relation to God as well as in the Kingdom of God lays the foundation of blessedness.

RITSCHL showed his interest in personal and practical religion by publishing a work *On Christian Perfection*, 1874, in which he describes perfection as life in the Kingdom of God,

together with humility and the moral activity proper to one's vocation.

In a summary statement of his theological opinions entitled *Instruction in the Christian Religion*, 1875, he developed his view of the Kingdom of God as the objective of the love of God.

The Kingdom of God is the highest good assured by God to the community founded by His revelation in Christ; yet it is regarded as the highest good, only inasmuch as at the same time it is reckoned as the moral ideal, for the realisation of which the members of the community bind themselves to one another by a definite mode of reciprocal action.

His *History of Pietism*, 1880-1886, is a valuable authority although he was not sympathetic to the movement; he was critical of its reactionary influence but he saw its historical value in the development of Christianity.

The teaching of RITSCHL, especially his doctrine of value-judgments brought him many followers among whom were some of the foremost modern theologians, *e.g.* Wilhelm Herrmann, 1846- , Adolph Harnack, 1851- , Emil Schurer, 1844-1910, Bernhard Stade, 1848-1906, Julius Kaftan, 1848- , and Hans Hinrich Wendt, 1853- .

In France the result of the whole process of German criticism was gathered up in the work of ERNEST RENAN, 1823-1892. He won attention in the literary world by his series of monographs of which the first was *Averroes and Averroism,* 1852. His *General History of Semitic Languages,* 1857, *Studies of Religious History,* 1848-1857, and *An Essay on the Origin of Language,* 1858, were notable for their erudition and above all for their infinite grace of style. They "helped to extend to a sensible degree the domain of literature by including in it, thanks to the power of style, the results achieved by learning, philosophy, and exegesis."[8]

It was, however, by his *Life of Jesus,* 1863, that RENAN arrested the attention of the religious world. In it he gave the most advanced claims of criticism stripped of all pedantry and set forth with the skill to make men "see blue skies, seas of waving corn, distant mountains, gleaming lilies, in a landscape with the Lake of Gennesareth for its centre, and to hear with him in the whispering of the reeds the eternal melody of the Sermon on the Mount." The Life will never be quite forgotten, nor is it ever likely to be surpassed. Its few lapses from good taste like its sceptical implications are forgettable among the impressions of concrete reality that it leaves upon its readers.

A penetrating word, a look falling upon a simple conscience, which only wanted awakening gave him an ardent disciple. Sometimes Jesus employed an innocent artifice, which Joan of Arc also used; he affected to know something intimate respecting him whom he wished to gain, or he would perhaps recall to him some circumstance dear to his heart. It was thus that he attracted Nathanael, Peter, and the Samaritan woman.

---

[8] F. Brunetière, *Manual of French Literature,* p. 518.

The *Life of Jesus* was intended to be a purely historical work—the first of a series entitled *The Origins of the Christian Church*—which the author hoped to make "the most important book of the century." The volumes were issued in due course: *The Apostles*, 1866, *St. Paul*, 1869, *Anti-Christ*, 1876, *The Gospels*, 1877, *The Christian Church*, 1878, and *Marcus Aurelius*, 1880. As RENAN proceeded with this undertaking he approached more and more closely to total religious scepticism, but he maintained his vividness of vision, mastery of material, flexible and genial style and his power dramatically to interpret the minds and purposes of men.

> It was the state of Paul's mind, it was his remorse on his approach to the city where he was to commit the most signal of his misdeeds, which were the true causes of his conversion . . . . That a delirious fever, resulting from a sun-stroke or an attack of ophthalmia, had suddenly seized him; that a flash of lightning blinded him for a time; that a peal of thunder had produced a cerebral commotion, temporarily deprived him of sight—it matters little . . . .

RENAN'S work like that of STRAUSS evoked innumerable replies. Writers of every school of Christian thought put forth criticisms or endorsations, and the publication of Lives of Christ became a characteristic feature of the second half of the century. It will be enough to mention EDMOND DEHAULT DE PRESSENSÈ, 1824-1891, as a conspicuous representative of liberal orthodox opinion. He had studied under VINET, THOLUCK, and NEANDER, and he brought to his task the piety and the historical methods of his masters. His *History of the First Three Centuries of the Christian Church*, 1856-1877, was followed by *The Church and the French Revolution*, 1864. The most permanently successful of his writings however was the widely known work entitled *Jesus Christ, His Times, His Life, and His Work,* 1865, in which PRESSENSÈ sought to offset the romantic Life by Renan by a searchingly accurate historical description of the Great Career.

ALFRED EDERSHEIM, 1829-1889, turned his deep knowledge of late Jewish and Rabbinic ideas to excellent use in *The Life and Times of Jesus the Messiah,* 1883. He disclaimed the intention of writing a Life on the ground that the materials for it do not exist. The work was to be a study of the life of Jesus the Messiah, and next a view of that life and its teaching in all their surroundings. It is an elaborate plea for the orthodox judgment of Jesus and His work.

EDERSHEIM did his work in England where THOMAS ARNOLD, 1795-1842 had opened the way to liberal criticism by his translation of Niebuhr's historical researches into early Roman history. The first decisive inroad of German criticism into English thought appears in *A History of the Jews,* 1829, written by HENRY HART MILMAN, 1791-1868, who claimed to make use of "all the marvellous discoveries of science and all the hardly less marvellous if less certain conclusions of historical, ethnologica', linguistic criticism." His next work was a less disturbing and less satisfactory *History of Christianity to the Abolition of Paganism,* 1840. Then he published his outstanding *History of Latin Christianity to the Pontificate of Nicholas V,* 1854-1856. This is a complete epic and philosophy of mediæval Christianity, written with brilliance both of style and imagination.

On a dreary winter morning, with the ground deep in snow, the King, the heir of a long line of emperors, was permitted to enter within the two outer of the three walls which girded the castle of Canossa. He had laid aside every mark of royalty or of distinguished station; he was clad only in the thin white linen dress of the penitent, and there, fasting, he awaited in humble patience the pleasure of the Pope. But the gates did not unclose. A second day he stood, cold, hungry, and mocked by vain hope. And yet a third day dragged on from morning to evening over the unsheltered head of the discrowned King . . . . To female entreaties and influence Gregory at length yielded an ungracious permission for the King to approach his presence.

ARTHUR PENRHYN STANLEY, 1815-1881, also wrote on the assumption that the theory of development held the field in theology. His one theological work is a *Commentary on the Epistles of St. Paul to the Corinthians*, 1854. It was by his record of the geography and customs of the Holy Land in a work entitled *Sinai and Palestine in connection with their History*, 1855, that he gained popular fame. His *Lectures on the History of the Eastern Church*, 1861, form a vivid introduction to some of the great passages in the story of early Christianity. The work is especially memorable for its description of the Council of Nicaea and its sketch of ATHANASIUS. The *Lectures on the History of the Jewish Church*, 1863, 1865, 1876, gave STANLEY a place among the leading liberal thinkers of the English Church.

The peculiar type of STANLEY'S historical instinct is found in "his delight in striking anecdote, in unlooked for parallels, in the picturesqueness of the past; he deals with thought and emotion in their dramatic manifestation on the great theatres of the world."

Important work of a thoroughly constructive type was done by three outstanding Cambridge scholars, FOSS BROOKE WESTCOTT, 1825-1901; JOSEPH BARBER LIGHTFOOT, 1828-1889; and FENTON JOHN ANTHONY HORT, 1828-

1892. The strength of this modern Cambridge school lay in its criticism of the New Testament. The famous Westcott and Hort edition of the text of the New Testament, 1881, was the product of thirty years labour. LIGHTFOOT'S Commentaries attained the position of exegetical and grammatical classics. WESTCOTT'S were only less honoured, and the studies of HORT in early Christianity are universally accepted as standard works.

Liberal criticism had a brilliant representative in England in EDWIN HATCH, 1835-1889. His work entitled *The Organisation of the Early Christian Churches*, 1881, set the much discussed questions of episcopacy and apostolic succession in a fresh historical light. The brilliant and still unsurpassed lectures on *The Influence of Greek Ideas and Usages upon the Christian Church*, 1888, constitute "a study in historical development, an analysis of some of the formal factors that conditioned" the growth of Christianity.

I have ventured as a pioneer into comparatively unexplored ground: I feel that I shall no doubt be found to have made the mistakes of a pioneer; but I feel also the certainty of a pioneer . . . . For though you may believe that I am but a dreamer of dreams, I seem to see, though it be on the far horizon—the horizon beyond the fields which either we or our children will tread—a Christianity which is not new but old, which is not old but new, a Christianity in which the moral and spiritual elements will again hold their place, in which men will be bound together by the bond of mutual service, which is the bond of the sons of God, a Christianity which will actually realize the brotherhood of men, the ideal of its first communities.

INDEX